New Series on
Home Mortgage Yields
Since 1951

NATIONAL BUREAU OF ECONOMIC RESEARCH
Number 92, General Series

New Series on Home Mortgage Yields Since 1951

BY

JACK M. GUTTENTAG
University of Pennsylvania
AND

MORRIS BECK
Rutgers University

1970

NATIONAL BUREAU OF ECONOMIC RESEARCH
NEW YORK

DISTRIBUTED BY
COLUMBIA UNIVERSITY PRESS
NEW YORK AND LONDON

Relation of the Directors to the Work and Publications
of the National Bureau of Economic Research

1. The object of the National Bureau of Economic Research is to ascertain and to present to the public important economic facts and their interpretation in a scientific and impartial manner. The Board of Directors is charged with the responsibility of ensuring that the work of the National Bureau is carried on in strict conformity with this object.

2. The President of the National Bureau shall submit to the Board of Directors, or to its Executive Committee, for their formal adoption all specific proposals for research to be instituted.

3. No research report shall be published until the President shall have submitted to each member of the Board the manuscript proposed for publication, and such information as will, in his opinion and in the opinion of the author, serve to determine the suitability of the report for publication in accordance with the principles of the National Bureau. Each manuscript shall contain a summary drawing attention to the nature and treatment of the problem studied, the character of the data and their utilization in the report, and the main conclusions reached.

4. For each manuscript so submitted, a special committee of the Board shall be appointed by majority agreement of the President and Vice Presidents (or by the Executive Committee in case of inability to decide on the part of the President and Vice Presidents), consisting of three directors selected as nearly as may be one from each general division of the Board. The names of the special manuscript committee shall be stated to each Director when the manuscript is submitted to him. It shall be the duty of each member of the special manuscript committee to read the manuscript. If each member of the manuscript committee signifies his approval within thirty days of the transmittal of the manuscript, the report may be published. If at the end of that period any member of the manuscript committee withholds his approval, the President shall then notify each member of the Board, requesting approval or disapproval of publication, and thirty days additional shall be granted for this purpose. The manuscript shall then not be published unless at least a majority of the entire Board who shall have voted on the proposal within the time fixed for the receipt of votes shall have approved.

5. No manuscript may be published, though approved by each member of the special manuscript committee, until forty-five days have elapsed from the transmittal of the report in manuscript form. The interval is allowed for the receipt of any memorandum of dissent or reservation, together with a brief statement of his reasons, that any member may wish to express; and such memorandum of dissent or reservation shall be published with the manuscript if he so desires. Publication does not, however, imply that each member of the Board has read the manuscript, or that either members of the Board in general or the special committee have passed on its validity in every detail.

6. Publications of the National Bureau issued for informational purposes concerning the work of the Bureau and its staff, or issued to inform the public of activities of Bureau staff, and volumes issued as a result of various conferences involving the National Bureau shall contain a specific disclaimer noting that such publication has not passed through the normal review procedures required in this resolution. The Executive Committee of the Board is charged with review of all such publications from time to time to ensure that they do not take on the character of formal research reports of the National Bureau, requiring formal Board approval.

7. Unless otherwise determined by the Board or exempted by the terms of paragraph 6, a copy of this resolution shall be printed in each National Bureau publication.

(Resolution adopted October 25, 1926, and revised February 6, 1933, February 24, 1941, and April 20, 1968)

This report is one of a series emerging from an investigation of interest rates made possible by a grant to the National Bureau from the Life Insurance Association of America. The Association is not, however, responsible for any of the statements made or views expressed.

Advisory Committee on the Interest Rates Study

In the planning and review of its studies of interest rates, the National Bureau has benefited from the advice and guidance of this committee. The committee's concurrence with the views expressed in this report, however, is not to be assumed. The members of the committee are:

* W. A. Clarke was a member of the Committee until his death on February 8, 1965.

Table of Contents

Acknowledgments

PART I

APPENDIXES

INDEX

Tables

Charts

Figures

Acknowledgments

A large number of people have contributed to this study at various stages. A committee consisting of William H. Brown, Jr., Gerhard Bry, William A. Clarke, Joseph W. Conard, George T. Conklin, Jr., Saul Klaman, Jacob Mincer, Geoffrey H. Moore, and James J. O'Leary helped plan the general design of the study. Joseph Conard and James J. O'Leary provided particularly valuable counsel and assistance in the early stages. Among the many university students who helped compile and process data at the participating companies, Herbert Grossman, Jacob DeRooy and William Stellenwerf were particularly helpful. Invaluable technical assistance on many phases was freely given by many mortgage loan specialists at life insurance companies. Fred Avril, J. J. Carney, Lawrence Cortelyou, Thomas J. Maconkey, and Peter Samuelsen saved us from grievous error on numerous occasions. The IBM Corporation was particularly generous in giving us computer time. Most of the programming was done by Juanita Johnson with the assistance of Martha Jones, while Gerhard Bry and Charlotte Boschan counseled us on special programming problems. Extensive clerical operations with the final data were supervised with great skill and dedication by Irene Sampson. H. Irving Forman drew the charts. The manuscript was skillfully edited by Gnomi Schrift Gouldin, who also saw it through production. A committee consisting of Phillip Cagan, Avery Cohan, Robert Moore Fisher, Manuel Gottlieb, and Richard Selden read an early version and made valuable suggestions for revision. Finally, we would like to thank Harold G. Halcrow, Wallace J. Campbell and Willis J. Winn of the NBER Board of Directors reading committee.

JACK M. GUTTENTAG
MORRIS BECK

PART ONE

1
Purpose, Scope, and Findings

This paper is part of the broader NBER study of interest rates. Because existing statistical data on mortgage yields were inadequate for refined analytical use, new data had to be compiled on this important segment of the capital market. This task was, of course, only a step toward the ultimate goal of explaining the pattern and behavior of yields.

Need for Data

Residential mortgages are the single most important capital market instrument. At the same time, they are the most poorly documented in the area of yields and other terms on which transactions are made. There is no mystery to this. The residential mortgage market is "messy." It embraces millions of small individual transactions disbursed yearly throughout the country. Although there is a national mortgage market—which is indeed a basic premise of this study—it is superimposed on a congeries of local markets, subject to local influences and peculiarities. Each transaction, furthermore, has many dimensions, of which interest rate or yield is only one. Obtaining reliable data on the terms of residential mortgage transactions is thus a statistical problem of costly proportions and imposing technical difficulties.

A scarcity of data on residential mortgage terms has been a source of misgiving among lenders, who need reliable data for a rational allocation of funds; among scholars with an interest in understanding the mechanics of this market and its relationship to other markets; and among policymakers with responsibility for influencing the aggregate supply of mortgage credit.

Inadequate time series data has been a particular problem to policymakers. Thus, the residential construction sector has grown increasingly important in monetary policy deliberations because of its acknowledged short-run sensitivity to changing credit conditions.[1] Postwar experience suggests that this sector may be the single most important channel through which a countercyclical monetary policy has made its influence felt. Yet, the monetary authorities have not had reliable data showing the extent to which credit conditions in the residential mortgage market had changed.

The New Data and Other Series

Time series analysis requires monthly data covering a reasonably long span of time and having a broad geographical basis. Given this objective and our limited resources, we turned to large life insurance companies. These companies acquire residential mortgages on a nationwide basis, their records are generally in good order and reasonably accessible, and (most important) the size of their operations makes it possible to draw a relatively large number of observations from a small number of institutions. No other approach to the task of acquiring historical series having the desired analytical characteristics was even remotely feasible.

These new data contain important attributes heretofore unavailable in a single series. First, the date of record is the date when the loan was committed or authorized by lenders, rather than the date on which funds were disbursed; thus, the long and erratic lag characteristic of series recorded on a disbursement basis is largely eliminated.

Second, the data cover all three types of residential mortgages (FHA, VA, and conventional); also, separate series are available on mortgages acquired through correspondents as opposed to those originated directly by the life insurance company.[2]

Third, the data include loan-value ratios and maturities, as well as

[1] See Jack M. Guttentag, "The Federal Reserve and the Mortgage Market: Some Perspectives of the 'Crisis' of 1966," in *A Study of Mortgage Credit*, Senate Committee on Banking and Currency, Washington, D.C., May 22, 1967, pp. 392–406; also "The Short Cycle in Residential Construction: 1946–59," *American Economic Review*, June 1961; and Warren L. Smith, "The Impact of Monetary Policy on Residential Construction, 1948–58," in *A Study of Mortgage Credit*, Committee on Banking and Currency, Washington, D.C., 1958.

[2] Coverage, however, is limited to first-mortgage loans by life insurance companies on one- to four-family properties; not covered are such segments of the mortgage market as junior financing, all loans on multifamily and other income-producing properties, and home mortgage loans by lenders other than life insurance companies. A separate National Bureau study by Royal Shipp will cover loans on income-producing properties.

fees and charges collected and paid by the lender over and above the contract rate. The contract rate adjusted to take account of net fees and charges received by the lender is referred to as "effective yield" or simply "yield."[3]

Fourth, the data have a broad geographic base, since the lenders covered by the series operate in the national market. Series covering the national mortgage market are particularly useful for times series analysis, since this is the most sensitive component of the residential market. The lenders in the national market have a wide range of investment options, and shift at the margin from one investment to another. Changes in the national market thus register tendencies operative in local markets, to a degree depending on the extent to which a local market is segmented from outside influences. Cross-section yield variability in the national market is relatively small, moreover, and the series tend to be relatively homogeneous. While homogeneity is useful in time series analysis, it is, of course, a shortcoming in cross-section analysis.

The sources and main characteristics of the new series compared with other series are summarized in Table 1-1.[4] Most widely used is the FHA secondary market series, which is current and extends as far back as 1948. This series has always been suspect because it is based on opinions by FHA insuring-office directors rather than actual records of loans authorized or disbursed. A minor contribution of our study is to test the FHA series against the new data (Chapter 9). The FHA also has an opinion-based series on conventional contract rates beginning in 1957. An additional serious drawback to this series is that it does not specify the type of lender covered (on conventional loans, rates vary considerably by type of lender).

A second mortgage series, covering all three types of loans, has been compiled by the Federal Reserve Bank of Chicago. It covers the period 1958–63, but only during 1960–63 is it on an authorization basis, and coverage is limited to the Chicago metropolitan area.[5] This

---

[3] The qualifier "gross" or "net" is used to indicate that mortgage servicing costs, expressed as a per cent per annum, are included or netted from the yield.

[4] We omit from this discussion the annual mortgage rate series covering all types of real estate, that are used and described by Leo Grebler, David M. Blank, and Louis Winnick, *Capital Formation in Residential Real Estate: Trends and Prospects,* Princeton University Press for NBER, 1956, Appendix O.

[5] These data are relatively rich, however, in collateral information on terms and characteristics and are, therefore, valuable for examining the cross-section structure of yields and terms. For some preliminary results of such examination, see Jack M. Guttentag, *Mortgage Interest Rates: Trends and Structure,* 1964 Proceedings, Conference on Savings and Residential Financing, pp. 124–146.

series was superceded by the Federal Home Loan Bank Board (FHLBB) series.

The FHLBB series covers only conventional loans and extends back only to December 1962, but it is kept current and is on an authorization basis. This series overlaps the National Bureau's conventional loan series by one year. Although the two differ in a number of ways, as explained later, the similarities are close enough to warrant splicing. The FHLBB series thus provides valuable historical continuity on conventional loans. The FHLBB series also covers four major institutional lender groups in addition to life insurance companies, which provides

TABLE 1-1

Summary of Principal Features of Various Statistical Series on
Residential Mortgage Rates and Terms

	National Bureau	Federal Home Loan Bank Board	Federal Reserve Bank of Chicago
Type of loan	FHA, conventional, some VA	Conventional	FHA, conventional, some VA
Time period	1951-63	Dec. 1962-current	April 1958-July 1963
Monthly (M) or quarterly (Q)	M	M	M
Geographical coverage	National	National	Chicago Metropolitan area
Authorization (A), closings (C), or secondary market (SM) basis	A	A	C through April 1960, A thereafter
Source of data	Lenders' historical records on individual loans	Current reports by lenders on new loans approved	

revealing insights into the advantages and limitations of series covering life insurance companies alone.

Saul Klaman compiled series on conventional mortgage rates covering the period 1947–56, drawn from aggregate accounting data provided by a few large life insurance companies. These data are on a disbursement rather than an authorization basis and measure contract rate rather than yield.

Since 1953, the Federal National Mortgage Association (FNMA) has compiled price data on FHA and VA mortgages. The data are generally not made public but they were provided to Klaman and our-

Federal Housing Administration

FHA Series	Conventional Series	Saul Klaman	Federal National Mortgage Assn.
FHA	Conventional	Conventional	FHA, VA
1949-current	1957-current	1947-56	Feb. 1953
M	Q to 1962, M thereafter	Q	M (beginning Nov. 1953)
National	National	National	National
SM	?	C	SM
Opinions of directors of FHA insuring offices on current sales		Lenders' historical records on company-wide rates	Reports by mortgage companies on current sales

(continued)

TABLE 1-1 (concluded)

	National Bureau	Federal Home Loan Bank Board	Federal Reserve Bank of Chicago
Lender coverage	Few large life insurance companies	Samples of savings and loan assns., life insurance companies, commercial banks, mutual savings banks, and mortgage companies	Samples of savings and loan assns., commercial banks, and mortgage companies
Detail available			
Contract rate	X	X	X
Fees and charges	X	X	X
Maturity	X	X	X
Loan-value ratio	X	X	X
Service fee	X	–	–
Purpose of loan	–	X	X
Income of borrower	–	–	X
Loan volume	X	–	
Geographical breakdowns available	9 regions 8 states	18 metropolitan areas	Chicago SMA only

Source: *Federal Home Loan Bank Board*: Data are contained in monthly press releases of the Board. Summary figures are also published in the *Federal Reserve Bulletin* and the *Survey of Current Business*. The Board kindly provided us with a tape record of individual loans covering the period December 1962-July 1965. The cross-section tabulations referred to in this book covering the period of rate stability, May-December 1963, were calculated by us from the basic data on individual loans contained on the tape.

Federal Reserve Bank of Chicago: Data are contained in monthly press releases of that Bank. The series is described in the June 1960 and May 1960 issues of *Business Conditions*, a monthly publication of the bank.

Federal Housing Administration: The basic price data through 1960 are shown in the August 1961 issue of *Construction Review*, a monthly publication of the Department of Commerce. Subsequent quotations are contained in monthly press releases of the FHA. A series based on FHA secondary market quotations during 1948-56 was used by one of

Federal Housing Administration

FHA Series	Conventional Series	Saul Klaman	Federal National Mortgage Assn.
Lenders reporting to insuring office directors		Few large life insurance companies	Life insurance companies and mutual savings banks buying from reporting mortgage companies
X	X	X	X
X	–	–	X
–	–	–	–
–	–	–	–
–	–	–	–
–	–	–	–
–	–	–	–
–	–	–	–

6 regions

the authors in his Ph.D. dissertation (Jack M. Guttentag, *Some Studies of the Post World War II Residential Construction and Mortgage Markets,* Columbia University, 1958); it was later extended to 1957, and published by Leo Grebler in, *Housing Issues in Economic Stabilization Policy,* Occasional Paper 72, New York, NBER, 1960; subsequent extensions were published intermittently in the *Bond Buyer* (no source given). The secondary market series used in this paper and shown in Appendix Table 9-4 has been recalculated to make it as comparable as possible to the new NBER series.

Saul Klaman: Data are contained in his *Postwar Residential Mortgage Market,* NBER, 1961, Chapter 4 and Appendix Tables A-4, A-5, and A-7.

Federal National Mortgage Association: Available on direct request from that agency.

selves. These series are based on sales reported to FNMA by mortgage companies, mainly by life insurance companies and mutual savings banks. An interesting and useful feature of these data is that, following a change in maximum contract rate, FNMA continues for a time to compile data on prices of "old" mortgages carrying the old contract rate.

None of the above series has all the attributes of the NBER series described earlier. The other series do provide a valuable supplement to the NBER series, however, and several of them are used in this book.

Data-collecting and Data-using

This book is divided into two parts. Part I describes the new series and presents some analysis of their behavior. Part II is concerned with technical problems connected with the collection, interpretation, and usefulness of mortgage yield data. Thus, the two parts of the book correspond broadly to a functional distinction between creating new data and using it.

Combining data-collecting and data-using in one study has important advantages and disadvantages. The main disadvantage is that it inverts the usual order of scientific inquiry whereby one begins with a question and looks for the data to answer it. If one begins with new data and looks for significant questions to put to the data, there is a tendency for the inquiry to lose focus. Superficiality is an added danger since the new data may provide an increment of insight into a problem without nearly exhausting it, yet any reasonably adequate and self-contained treatment of the question may require going well beyond the new body of data. Still, any attempt to exhaust the question may shift the entire nature of the study in a direction which may not warrant the investment.

How well have we avoided the twin dangers of triviality and resource misallocation? The reader will have to decide this for himself. In Chapters 3 and 4, we tried to pose questions which could take advantage of the new data and the materials already at hand, but clearly none of the questions has been exhausted. Others employing the more congenial scientific procedure of defining the question first are invited to finish the task.

The advantage of combining the data-collecting and data-using functions is that you get better data that way. Few data-users have not experienced the frustration of finding that a data-collector with no sensitivity to the ultimate purposes of the data has left out the one most important piece of information, or has defined a crucial concept in an ambiguous way. The reader will see evidence in Part II that analytical problems related to the ultimate purposes of mortgage yield data arose at numerous points in the data-collection operation. The data-collector who anticipates being a data-user clearly is in a much better position to make sensible decisions on such issues. Doubtless we didn't make all the right decisions for every purpose, since we couldn't anticipate every purpose, but we are confident that the decisions are substantially better than if we had confined ourselves to data-collecting.

Summary of Major Findings

1. Life insurance companies, far more than other mortgage-lenders, acquire mortgages outside of the community in which they are domiciled and, to a considerable extent, outside of the region. In 1960, more than half of the loans on single-family homes held by life insurance companies were on properties in a different region, and the companies accounted for more than half of the total of such "foreign-held" loans. Mortgages which potentially might be acquired by distant lenders are in the national market. Such mortgages must be generated in sufficient volume, in a given area, to justify the administrative machinery (branch offices or correspondent relationships) needed to acquire and service mortgages at a distance. For this reason, mortgages in the national market are more likely to be secured by newly built homes in tract developments than by existing structures, and are more likely to originate within metropolitan areas than outside. Mortgages in the national market also tend to have relatively low risk, since distant lenders cannot make the detailed investigation and exercise the close surveillance required on risky loans. As a result, mortgages in the national market are more likely to be federally underwritten than conventional, and if conventional mortgages, are likely to have such characteristics as relatively high borrower income. They also carry relatively low yields. Data from census and other sources indicate that life insurance company loans have these general characteristics.

2. The life insurance companies covered by our new series were chosen because of their convenience and accessibility. Although they accounted for an appreciable share of the total mortgage lending by

life insurance companies—generally one-third to two-fifths—there is no basis for an a priori claim that the series are representative of life insurance companies on the whole. Nevertheless, there is evidence that in fact the series are representative. Yield dispersion of mortgages entering the national market, due to differences in loan and property characteristics, is small. Scope for individual lender yield variability, reflecting differences in lender policies, is correspondingly narrow. Transactions by any one quantitatively important participant in the market thus do not deviate very far from those of other such participants. Loans acquired by life insurance companies, however, are *not* representative of the residential market as a whole, for reasons already indicated. Loans entering the national market are not a cross section of residential loans.

3. There are no systematic biases in our yield series, either over the cycle or over the entire 1951–63 period, arising from cyclical changes or trends in loan and property characteristics for which we have data. This is indicated by analysis of cyclical changes and trends in loan and property characteristics, combined with cross-section regressions relating yield to characteristics. Systematic changes in yield determinants on which we do not have data, such as borrower characteristics, conceivably could bias the series, but the bias would be small as the unexplained cross-section variability is small. Over the cycle, our series probably were not significantly affected by changes in lenders' subjective appraisals of the risk associated with loans of given characteristics. Over the entire 1951–63 period, however, the risk premium on conventional loans probably declined as a result of continuously favorable repayment experience. This is suggested by a narrowing in the yield differential between conventional and FHA loans.

4. The new data show that for the period prior to 1961, conventional mortgage yields had a narrower cyclical amplitude than high-grade bond yields. The new data thus confirm the findings of earlier investigators, but do not support the various hypotheses advanced in earlier studies to explain this phenomenon. The relatively narrow cyclical amplitude of mortgage yields is not due to failure to allow for cyclical changes in fees and charges, at least on loans by life insurance companies. Nor does the evidence suggest that cyclical yield variability is dampened by variability in loan-value ratios and maturities, in borrower characteristics affecting risk, or in the composition of loan aggregates by region or by individual lender. The hypothesis that relatively high origination costs dampen mortgage-yield variability also does not withstand close scrutiny. Cyclical changes in risk premiums

could play a role in dampening mortgage-yield amplitude relative to that of bonds, but most of the available evidence suggests otherwise.

The hypothesis suggested here is that the narrow cyclical amplitude of mortgage yields relative to bond yields reflects differences in market organization. Yields tend to be less volatile in negotiated markets where borrower and lender are in direct contact, than in dealer-type markets. Negotiated markets often involve a continuing relationship between borrower and lender which blunts the tendency to maximize a short-run market position. Lenders in negotiated markets may have heavy nontransferable overhead costs, which tend to have a similar effect. In addition, the smaller amplitude of mortgage yields is affected by a lag in transmitting changes in bond yields to the mortgage market. This factor also underlies the tendency for mortgage yields to lag bond yields at cylical turning points.

5. Differences in market organization also seem to underlie the greater cyclical sensitivity of direct mortgage loan series than of correspondent loan series. Life insurance company acquisitions from correspondents are market transactions, but the parties generally have a continuous relationship which exercises a moderating influence on yield changes. This influence may take a number of forms, including a tendency for the life insurance company to avoid frequent changes in buying rates that may be disruptive to correspondents who extend their own commitments before obtaining a life insurance company commitment. Similarly, the FHA secondary market series is more sensitive than the FHA (life insurance company) commitment series. The organization of the FHA secondary market appears to be somewhere between a negotiated market and a dealer market.

6. The new mortgage-commitment data confirm that mortgage yields tend to lag bond yields at cyclical turning points. This is not explained by the hypothesis that small changes in mortgage market conditions register first in such dimensions of mortgage loans as loan-value ratios, maturities, or fees and charges. The evidence indicates that these characteristics may be even less sensitive than the contract rate. The hypothesis suggested to explain the lag in mortgage yields is that the demand for mortgage credit at given terms is relatively stable and that short-run developments affecting general yield levels ordinarily originate in the bond markets. The transmission of bond-yield changes to the mortgage market is dependent entirely on the activities of primary lenders (there is no dealer arbitrage). Since these lenders respond only to what they consider pervasive movements in bond yields, which

must prove out over time, the transmission process takes time and mortgage yields lag. The transmission lag may account in part for the smaller cyclical amplitude of mortgage yields than of bond yields, since the lag prevents the full range of bond-yield changes from being transmitted to the mortgage market.

7. The sharp swing in mortgage yields during 1961–66 represents a sharp break with past patterns. During the long stretch of easy money extending from 1961 to 1965, mortgage yields continued to decline long past the lower turning point of bond yields. Then, as tight money emerged in 1966, mortgage yields rose with unprecedented rapidity. In contrast to the prior three cycles, the amplitude of conventional mortgage yields (measured in basis points) was comparable to that of bonds in both phases of the 1961–66 cycle.

Structural changes affecting the commercial banking system may have been largely responsible for this. During 1961–66, commercial banks underwent a marked shift in policy toward time deposits. With their secondary reserves of government securities largely depleted, time deposits became a valuable source of funds over which commercial banks could exercise some degree of control. The relative importance of time deposits in bank liability structure, which had been growing steadily for some time, accelerated markedly. The higher deposit costs and reduced liquidity requirements associated with time deposits encouraged a portfolio shift into mortgages that have relatively high yields. This shift put added downward pressure on mortgage yields during the easy-money period of 1961–65.

When tight money emerged in 1966, banks did not withdraw wholesale from the mortgage market as they had in earlier periods of restraint, probably because by then many banks considered mortgages a permanent part of their portfolios. The banks were under the same pressures to meet business loan demands as in earlier periods of restraint, although without a buffer of government securities to liquidate. As a result, they competed for time deposits with unprecedented aggressiveness and considerable success, in good part at the expense of savings institutions which invest most of their funds in mortgages. The withdrawal of funds from savings institutions in 1966 impinged directly on the mortgage market and resulted in an unprecedented rise in mortgage yields.

8. There is some indication that the yield advantage of conventional over FHA mortgages declined secularly over the period 1949–66. Presumably this reflected favorable repayment experience over the

period, which would have reduced ex ante risk premiums on conventional loans.

The conventional-FHA yield differential does not show any systematic cyclical pattern. During two periods of extreme credit stringency, however, in late 1959–60 and in 1966, FHAs came to yield appreciably more than conventionals. This appears to be a real market phenomenon rather than a statistical accident; it shows up in data covering individual lenders and in data for individual states, regardless of whether usury ceilings are low, high, or nonexistent. One explanation is that those mortgage-lenders who prefer FHAs to conventionals are sensitive to yield differentials between mortgages and bonds, and shift out of mortgages when capital markets become very tight. Mortgage-lenders who prefer conventionals are willing to absorb the overhang of FHAs only at premium rates.

9. At various times, FHA mortgages have carried a higher contract rate than VAs, and this has affected their relative yield. Prior to mid-1952, FHAs and VAs carried premiums. Under these conditions, the higher contract rate FHAs carried higher yields. This probably resulted from the aversion of conservative lenders to the uncertainty associated with realized yield when mortgages sell above par. (The yield realized on a mortgage that is not priced at par depends not only on the contract rate and the size of the premium or discount but also on the life of the mortgage, which is not known in advance. Most mortgages are prepaid in full well before maturity.) When mortgages carry premiums, yield is an increasing function of mortgage life and may be very low, even zero or negative, if the mortgage is paid off soon after origination. An overestimate of mortgage life can thus have a seriously adverse effect on realized yield. If the market is dominated by conservative lenders concerned with the "worst that can happen," the premium paid on a high-contract-rate mortgage will not be large enough to equalize yield with a low-contract-rate mortgage when yields are calculated on the basis of any reasonable estimate of expected life.

During 1957–61, FHA contract rates were again higher than VAs, but in this period both carried discounts. When mortgages carry discounts, yield is a decreasing function of life and the lowest possible yield, which is realized if the mortgage runs to maturity, is not much lower than the yield based on expected life. Hence, yield uncertainty associated with uncertainty regarding mortgage life probably does not have much influence on the relative yields of mortgages carrying different contract rates.

Discounts, however, raise public relations problems, particularly with regard to larger lenders in the public eye (such as, the life insurance companies covered by our interest rate study). These lenders, sensitive to public censure, took smaller discounts on VAs than those necessary to equalize the yield with higher contract rate FHAs, but they sharply reduced their VA volume. Hence, for these lenders, FHAs yielded more than VAs. Data provided by FNMA reveal, however, that in the "free" market, where discounts on VAs rose to the level needed to clear the market, VAs yielded more than FHAs. It is ironic that the public pressures on large institutions to limit discounts on VA mortgages, by causing them to sharply reduce their VA volume, had the effect of increasing pressure on VA discounts in the free market.

There are indications, however, that during 1958–59 life insurance company attitudes toward discounting changed in the sense that they accepted the discounts required to bring VA yields into an appropriate relationship to FHA yields. By 1961, the mortgage market had evidently learned to live with discounts.

10. Cyclical changes in loan-value ratios and maturities on life insurance company loans during 1951–63 are broadly consistent with the hypothesis that these characteristics will move in a way to reinforce the effect of yields; that is, they will decline when yields rise and vice versa. The evidence also reveals, however, that this pattern can be suppressed or disrupted by a number of influences. Thus, on conventional mortgages, the expected cyclical changes were constrained by the relatively low legal ceilings on loan-value ratios and the thrust of secular liberalization on maturities; on FHA mortgages, the expected pattern was disrupted by frequent changes in legal ceilings on both loan-value ratios and maturities. Only on VA mortgages did the expected pattern reveal itself, and during part of the period life insurance companies were virtually out of this market. The most important channel through which the expected pattern manifested itself was changes in the mix of the three types of mortgages. The companies tended to shift into conventional and out of FHA and VA mortgages when interest rates rose, which tended to reduce the weighted average loan-value ratio and maturity on all home mortgages.

2

The New Series

The main features of the new National Bureau time series will be summarized in this chapter. Much of the material here receives more detailed consideration in Part II.

Historical versus Current Series

Compiling historical time series on mortgage terms is vastly different than compiling current series. Many lenders are willing to provide current information as the burden is a small one; consequently, coverage may be wide. The investigator need only collect and process the information provided by the lenders. Once the universe has been defined, furthermore, it is often possible to obtain a current reporting sample that comes close to being representative.[1]

In compiling historical series, in contrast, only a relatively small number of lenders can be covered because the burden of collection is thrust largely on the investigator. As a general rule, lenders who are cooperative in opening up their books expect the investigator to do most of his work at their premises. Any attempt to draw a representative sample would require resources much larger than those available for the present study. A large proportion of lending institutions, furthermore, cannot provide historical records over any extended period, and those that can are hardly representative.[2]

Thus, we were limited in our approach to the problem. We decided to concentrate on a small number of large lenders who could provide a substantial number of observations per institution, who maintained historical records in good order, and whose operations were nationwide

---

[1] Some imperfections in the sample are inevitable. These arise from the unwillingness of some lenders chosen for the sample to participate and from changes in the structure of the universe. As an important example of the last factor, commercial banks account for a highly variable share of the total residential market.

[2] The practice of maintaining historical records is related to such lender characteristics as size. These characteristics are in turn related to the type of submarket in which the lenders participate.

rather than local. Large life insurance companies met these requirements. This procedure, of course, raised important questions regarding the segment of the market from which our observations come, and the relation of this segment to the remainder of the market. These questions are considered later in this chapter.

General Procedure in Compiling the New Series

The time series contained in this paper are based on samples of loans authorized on one- to four-family homes (hereafter referred to as "residential" loans), drawn from the internal records of large life insurance companies. As a preliminary step, we obtained complete coverage of loans authorized by six companies during February 1960, and by five companies during June 1953. These censuses, each of which involved about 7,100 separate loans, were used in designing the sample and in preparing the tabulation program. (As noted below, cross-section analysis of these data indicated that a tabulation program consisting of simple averages of loan characteristics was preferable to a more complex regression program. Some results of the analysis of our cross-section data are discussed in Appendix B.) When the time series data ultimately became available, we compared the average value of loan characteristics in June 1953 and February 1960 with the values drawn from the two censuses as one of several checks on the reliability of the sample (see Chapter 9).

The sample, which is discussed in detail in Appendix A, covered four of the initial six companies because two companies could not provide data over the entire period. Our sample target was set to provide about 330 loans of each type (FHA, VA, and conventional) per month. Using a standard error of .04 per cent as a rough criterion of statistical reliability, this sample was broadly consistent with the goal of providing monthly FHA and conventional series on a three- or four-region basis, and quarterly FHA and conventional series on a seven- or nine-region basis. The sampling quota could not be met on VA loans during several years when the life insurance companies had very low VA volume. For this reason, as well as the below-market yields of VA loans authorized during such periods of low volume (see below), the VA series turned out to be generally less useful than the FHA and conventional series.

The data are drawn from the finance committee records of the participating companies. As a more or less standardized procedure, common to all life insurance companies, a record of each individual residential loan is submitted to the finance committee of the company. At the four companies in our sample, the committee meets every week or twice a month. On larger commercial, industrial, or multifamily residential loans, the committee is the authorizing agent of the company. On residential loans, however, lending officers in most cases have authority to commit the company, so that submission of loans to the committee is merely a matter of record. For a large company that authorizes several thousand loans in a month, the finance committee minutes or memoranda for each month would make a sizeable book.

The information available from finance committee records on each residential loan generally includes loan amount, property value, maturity, contract rate, fees paid and received by lender, method of loan acquisition (whether originated directly or acquired through correspondents), service fee on loans obtained from correspondents, and location of property. Data are not available on borrower characteristics or purpose of the loan.

The tabulation program (discussed in Appendix A) involved calculation of monthly and quarterly averages and standard deviations of the following loan characteristics:

1. Loan amount.
2. Value of property.
3. Loan-to-value ratio.
4. Maturity.
5. Contract rate.
6. Net discount. This is fees received less fees paid, expressed as a per cent of the loan amount.
7. Gross effective yield. This is contract rate adjusted for net fees received (or paid).
8. Net effective yield on correspondent loans. This is the effective yield net of the correspondent's service fee.

These characteristics were tabulated separately for each type of loan, further subdivided as a correspondent or direct loan with breakdowns by state and region.

Reliability of the Series

Two checks on the accuracy with which the sample series represented the experience of the participating companies are discussed in detail in

Chapter 6. One check was to compare the sample data for June 1953 and February 1960 with results of the complete censuses taken in these two months. A second check was provided by a set of monthly yield series compiled by one of the participating companies for its own use which cover *all* authorized loans (rather than a sample). The comparisons support the validity of the sampling procedure employed. Differences between census and sample values were distributed about as sampling theory would predict on the assumption of randomness.

Representativeness of the Series

The four life insurance companies included in the sample were chosen because of their convenience and accessibility. Although they accounted for an appreciable share of total mortgage lending of life insurance companies—generally one-third to two-fifths—there is no basis for an a priori claim that the series are representative of life insurance companies generally.

Nevertheless, there is evidence that the series are in fact representative. Yield differences between individual lenders in our series are small. During a thirteen-month period, furthermore, the NBER conventional loan series overlaps the new FHLBB series which covers a much larger group of companies. Despite differences in the sample, in loan coverage, and in certain definitions, the average loan characteristics in the two series are remarkably similar. In general, yield differences between the two series are smaller than the erratic month-to-month changes within both series.

The reason that the NBER series is broadly representative of life insurance companies is that the companies represented, as well as the industry in general, operate for the most part in the national market. As we shall see in Chapter 5, yield dispersion of mortgages entering the national market, due to differences in loan and property characteristics is small. Scope for individual yield variability, reflecting differences in lender policies, is correspondingly narrow. Transactions by any quantitatively important participant in the market do not deviate very far from those of other such participants.

Loans acquired by life insurance companies, however, are *not* representative of the residential market as a whole. As shown in Table 2-1, life insurance company conventional loans carry lower fees, have longer maturities, are secured by more expensive properties, and are

TABLE 2-1

Characteristics of Conventional First-Mortgage Loans in Eighteen Major Metropolitan
Areas Approved by Major Lender Groups, May-December 1963

Lender Group	Contract Interest Rate (per cent)	Fees and Charges (per cent of loan)	Loan-Value Ratio (per cent)	Value of Property (dollars)	Term (years)	Loan Amount (dollars)	Loans on Previously Occupied Homes (per cent of total)
Savings and loan association	6.00	1.03	75.8	21,527	23.2	16,270	66
Commercial banks	5.57	.34	61.6	27,265	18.1	16,609	75
Mortgage companies	5.56	.59	68.5	28,561	24.3	19,229	36
Mutual savings banks	5.46	.20	67.0	22,595	22.6	15,098	67
Life insurance companies	5.50	.18	66.9	31,029	25.4	20,602	31

Source: Federal Home Loan Bank Board.

less likely to be for the purpose of purchasing previously occupied homes than loans authorized by other major lender groups.[3]

Homogeneity of the Series over Time

One fundamental requirement in the construction of any yield series is to maintain an underlying security with reasonably stable yield-determining terms and characteristics. If the nature of the instrument changes over time, it becomes necessary to disentangle the effect of this change upon yield from the effect of changing market conditions.

For example, assume that under any given market conditions the yield on individual conventional loans is given by $Y = C + kT$, where C is a constant and T is a composite measure of ex ante quality, reflecting the maturity, loan-value ratio, borrower credit standing, and the like. For most analytical purposes, a yield series should reflect changes in C, which would arise from shifts in general market conditions, and in k, which would arise from changes in lenders' evaluations of the quality of mortgages having a given bundle of characteristics. The series should *not* reflect changes in T which constitute changes in the underlying instrument.

On series covering outstanding securities that are constantly traded, there is little difficulty in holding T constant over time because the observations always refer to the same instruments. Changes in the yield-determining characteristics of outstanding securities would typically take place very gradually; the period to maturity gradually shortens, for example, or the property securing the loan depreciates. In the case of the well-known outstanding corporate bond averages, this problem is handled with relative ease by making an occasional change in the composition of the bonds in any given classification.

In the case of series covering new issues, the problem cannot be handled as easily because individual instruments entering the series must be completely different from one month to the next. Mortgage yields necessarily cover new issues. Unlike bonds, it is not possible to construct mortgage yield series on the basis of transactions in a few outstanding issues. Whereas a given bond issue is divided up into many individual bonds, which are widely held and for which regular market quotations exist, the individual mortgage is small and indivisible; few

---

[3] Differences in the characteristics of federally underwritten loans acquired by major lender groups probably are less pronounced.

mortgages, furthermore, are exchanged in the market more than once.

An obvious method of dealing with this problem is to set up cross-classifications covering the most important yield-determining characteristics on which data are available. A more efficient method is the regression procedure used by Avery Cohan in his study of directly placed bonds.[4] In this procedure, fixed values of a large number of yield-determining characteristics are plugged into a series of regression equations, each equation relating yield to bond characteristics during a given period (usually a quarter). Changes in yield from period to period thus reflect changes in the constant term of the equation and in the coefficients of the bond characteristics, but the average values of the characteristics themselves are held constant.

In general, a regression-type adjustment is *needed* when the underlying yield data have a substantial degree of cross-section variability and the mix of important, yield-determining characteristics is unstable. (If the mix changes systematically over the cycle, or if there are underlying trends, the series will have cyclical or secular bias. Erratic instability in the mix of characteristics would create erratic series, but they would have no systematic bias.) An adjustment is *feasible* only if sufficient collateral data are available to explain a good part of the cross-section variability. The mortgage loan series collected for this study did not meet these criteria.

1. Cross-section yield variability on life insurance company mortgage loans is relatively small. On a quarterly basis, the standard deviation of our conventional yield series ranged generally from .10 to .30 per cent during the period 1951–63. On FHA and VA loans, it tended more toward the lower end of that range. This may be compared with the standard deviation of Avery Cohan's sample of directly placed bonds during 1951–61, which ranged generally from .30 to .60 per cent on industrials, and from .20 to .50 per cent on public utilities. As we show in Chapter 5, yield variance on conventional mortgage loans is smaller for life insurance companies than for other major mortgage lender groups. The variance of life insurance company loans is not so small, however, as to invalidate a regression-type adjustment if there were systematic changes in important yield determinants on which we have data.

2. Over the cycle, those measurable loan and property characteristics that change systematically are not important yield determinants. As

[4] Avery B. Cohan, *Yields on Corporate Debt Directly Placed,* New York, NBER, 1967.

noted in Chapter 3, loan-value ratios and maturities on life insurance company loans do vary systematically over the cycle. Our cross-section regressions show, however, that the yield implication of this variability is negligible. This will become evident below when we consider the yield implication of *secular* changes in loan characteristics, which were larger than the cyclical changes but did not appreciably affect yields.

On the other hand, those characteristics that do have a significant effect on yield do not change systematically over the cycle. The principal source of explained yield variability in our data is the location of property and identification of the individual lender. To test whether shifts in the geographical and lender mix affected cyclical yield variability, we recalculated conventional yields for each turning-point quarter on the assumption that loan distribution among thirty-six separate strata—four lenders and nine regions—was the same as in the previous turning-point quarter. The results, shown in Table 2-2, indicate that cyclical changes in lender and geographical mix had a negligible effect on over-all cyclical yield variability.

Thus, our data contain no cyclical biases that are removable by a regression-type adjustment.

There remains the possibility of cyclical bias associated with systematic cyclical changes in unknown yield determinants, such as bor-

TABLE 2-2

Cyclical Changes in Conventional Mortgage Yields
With Actual and Fixed Weights, 1951 – 63

Cyclical Rise (R) or Decline (D)	Actual Weights	Fixed Weights	Yield Change Attributable to Changes in Weights
I 1951 to I 1954 (R)	.49[a]	.48[a]	+.01
I 1954 to IV 1954 (D)	-.15	-.14	-.01
IV 1954 to I 1958 (R)	.97	.94	+.03
I 1958 to IV 1958 (D)	-.23	-.19	-.04
IV 1958 to III 1960 (R)	.65	.65	0
III 1960 to IV 1963 (D)	-.59	-.60	+.01

Note: Weights refer to the relative importance of 36 lender-region groups.
[a]Contract rate.
Source: NBER series.

TABLE 2-3

Effect on Conventional Yield of Changes in Loan Characteristics
Between 1951 and 1963, Using June 1953 Regression Weights

	Change in Characteristic[a]	Change in Yield (basis points)
Maturity (months)	+93	-2.1
Loan value (percentage points)	+7.7	1.2
Property value (dollars)	+10,000	-3.2
Individual lender mix (4 lenders)		+2.6
Geographical region mix (9 regions)		.0
Total		-1.5

[a]Uses average 1951 and 1963 values except for geographical region which refers to first quarter of 1951 and last quarter of 1963.
Source: NBER series.

rower characteristics. The quantitative importance of such bias would be very small, however, simply because the unexplained variability in absolute terms is so small.[5]

3. The problem of homogeneity over the entire 1951–63 period appears similar to that of systematic cyclical change. Although there were pronounced trends in maturity and property value, yield corrections based on coefficients for these variables derived from cross-section regressions would not have affected the level of the series in any appreciable way. As an example, the average maturity on conventional loans rose from about 217 months in 1951 to 310 months in 1963. Applying the coefficients drawn from the June 1953 regression,[6] this would have reduced yield by .02 percentage points. As shown in Table 2-3, the yield changes implied by secular changes in the other characteristics are of the same general order of magnitude and tend to offset each other. There is thus no reason to believe that our series

[5] We are inclined to believe, although this cannot be demonstrated, that this unexplained yield variance is due to a complex of factors associated with small individual loan transactions, where borrower and lender have incomplete information and where rates are subject to some degree of indeterminacy associated with bargaining. Such influences would be essentially random.

[6] Use of the February 1960 coefficients gives very similar results.

contain any appreciable secular bias arising from changes in characteristics, and a regression-type adjustment would not change the series appreciably.

Interestingly, the cyclical behavior and trend of Avery Cohan's yield series on directly placed bonds was not changed in any significant way by his regression adjustment, despite the fact that his data had much greater cross-section variability than ours and that his collateral data were able to explain a much larger proportion of total variability.[7]

A yield series may, of course, be influenced by changes in the weights attached by lenders to any given set of objective characteristics of the instrument, as well as by changes in the characteristics themselves. (In the equation $Y = C + kT$, k may change as well as T.) We do not have measures of k over the cycle, but we do know that cyclical changes in delinquencies and foreclosures on residential mortgages held by life insurance companies have been very small (Chapter 3); on conventional loans, there has been no cyclical pattern at all. It is a reasonable inference that if business cycles are so mild as to have little effect on the repayment experience of mortgages in portfolio, the k applicable to new mortgages will not change very much.

Over the 1951–63 period as a whole, there are indications that the kT on conventional loans declined. This is suggested by a reduction in the yield differential between conventional and FHA mortgages, as discussed in Chapter 4. If secular changes in the characteristics of conventional mortgages did not appreciably affect yields, as was suggested above, presumably the decline in yield differential reflects a secular decline in k. This would be a natural consequence of persistently good repayment experience.

Methods of Loan Acquisition

Life insurance companies acquire mortgage loans in two ways: through direct origination (termed "direct" loans), or through purchase from correspondents who originate and usually service the loan (termed "correspondent" loans). The new series cover both, and data are presented on a combined basis as well as separately.

Chapter 6 discusses the analytical advantages and disadvantages of statistical series on direct and correspondent loans. The connection of direct loans with property transfers creates ambiguity in the definition

[7] Cohan, p. 21.

of fees and charges, since payments to the lender may be associated with the property transfer as well as the credit transaction. In contrast, all recorded payments to or by the lender in correspondent loans are connected with the credit transaction; the property transfer is out of sight. Since all direct loan charges by large life insurance companies are quite small, however, the problem is not of great practical importance.

On the other side of the ledger, correspondent loans involve a servicing transaction as well as a credit transaction, and the terms of one may affect those of the other. Prior to 1959, this problem was largely theoretical as well; a standard service fee of .50 per cent generally prevailed. After 1959, variability arose in service fees between individual companies, and shifts within the company mix affected average gross yields on correspondent loans, although the effect was small and not systematic. This problem can be avoided by measuring the yield net of the service fee. Because data are not available on the servicing costs of direct loans, however, net yields on correspondent loans cannot be made comparable to direct loan yields.

Correspondent and direct loans are not strictly comparable on a gross yield basis, but the elements of noncomparability are small and tend to be offsetting. Thus, service fees paid to correspondents appear to be generally higher than servicing costs of large companies that do their own servicing. On the other hand, net origination costs are borne by the correspondent on correspondent loans and by the company on direct loans. A pragmatic case for combining direct and correspondent loans is based on the view that any residual element of noncomparability is small. This view is supported by the fact that gross yield differences between correspondent and direct loans are no larger than intercompany differences in net yield on correspondent loans alone.

Timing of the Series

For analytical purposes, mortgage yield series should be dated as of the time when binding transaction terms are established. In the case of residential loans by life insurance companies, this usually is the date when an authorized officer of the lending institution approves the application of a correspondent, builder, or ultimate borrower (mortgagor). Such approval represents a commitment to make a loan under specified conditions within some stipulated period (the "commitment period"). The NBER series are dated as of the day of finance committee meetings, termed the "authorization date." With some exceptions to be noted, this date lags the true transaction date by only two or three weeks.

In contrast, the date when funds are disbursed and the loan closed may lag the transaction date by from one to twelve months or even longer. In Chapter 7, we show that time series based on the date of disbursement lag series based on the date of authorization by one to six months.

Cases arise where the transaction date precedes the date of approval of the loan application. On some direct loans, the transaction date may precede by several months the date when the formal loan application is approved. Builders planning a large tract development require some assurance of credit availability before submitting of a formal loan application, and this constitutes a sort of "moral commitment" that the lender respects. The number of such loans in our sample, however, was not large enough to have had any significant effect on the timing of series covering direct loans.

A more complex problem arises when a correspondent commits himself to a builder or mortgagor before obtaining a commitment from the company, and the terms in the correspondent's commitment influence the terms of the transaction between the correspondent and the company. Thus, if market yields rise after the correspondent extends a commitment and before he can obtain a commitment from the company, the company under some circumstances might accept the lower yield in the correspondent's commitment. It is not always clear whether such cases should be classified as a "recording lag," wherein the true transaction date is really the date of the correspondent's commitment rather than the date of the company's commitment, or a "behavioral lag," wherein the company's behavior is constrained by concern for continuity in its operations with correspondents. In any case, Chapter 4 presents evidence that correspondent loan series are somewhat more sluggish than direct loan series.

The Concept of Effective Yield

Mortgage interest rates should be calculated to take account of fees paid and received by the lender (or what amounts to the same thing, the price of the instrument), a concept we have termed "effective yield." On FHA and VA loans especially, the contract rate alone has little significance, since it is almost always the current maximum rate allowable and may stay unchanged for long periods. In the short run, market changes take the form of changes in the price of the instrument. On conventional loans, the contract rate is free to vary, but it has long been felt that the rate itself tends to be sluggish, so that marginal changes in market conditions may be better revealed in an effective yield series. The new NBER series are all on an effective yield basis.

One technical problem involved in constructing yield series, discussed in Chapter 5, is that some assumption must be made regarding prepayment of principal. Most mortgages are paid in full prior to maturity, and this affects the yield; the more so, the more the price deviates from par. For some analytical applications, the prepayment assumption may affect results while for others it will not. (For some purposes it is necessary to distinguish the expected yield, based on the assumed prepayment, from the realized yield, which would be based on the actual prepayment. The series in the paper refer, of course, to expected yields.)

The usual practice in calculating yield is to assume a prepayment period equal to average life in the past based on termination experience. We find that the use of past average life, assuming the extrapolation is correct, provides a biased estimate of yield because of the nonlinear relationship between yield and mortgage life. When discounts or premiums are large, the bias is substantial.

Because termination experience indicates that longer-maturity mortgages have longer lives, some observers vary the prepayment assumption with the face maturity. We have not done this, since there is reason to believe that the relationship between life and face maturity during the period covered by the available data on termination experience was affected by the upward ratcheting of interest rates. We also have found that a single prepayment assumption is easier to work with. A ten-year assumption has been employed in all yield calculations, and we provide the data needed to recalculate yield on other assumptions for anyone wishing to do so.

3

The Behavior of Mortgage Yields and Bond Yields

Prior to 1961, mortgage yields had a more narrow cyclical amplitude than outstanding bond yields, and lagged bond yields at turning points. Chapter 3 attempts to explain why this happened. Also, an hypothesis is developed to explain the change in amplitude pattern during 1961–66, when changes in mortgage yields were unusually sharp.

Cyclical Amplitude

In an earlier study, Klaman noted that conventional mortgage interest rates have a smaller cyclical amplitude than bond yields.[1] The same observation had been made earlier by Grebler, Blank and Winnick.[2] Although Klaman's data were recorded on the disbursement date, which tends to dampen amplitude,[3] the point holds when mortgage yields are recorded on an authorization basis as well. As shown in Table 3-1, the change in conventional mortgage yields (measured in basis points) in each of six cyclical phases between 1949 and 1960 was smaller than the change in yields on United States government bonds, outstanding corporate bonds (both Aaa and Baa), and outstanding state and local bonds (both Aaa and Baa).[4] (In the most recent cycle, conventional mortgage-yield amplitude was comparable to that of bonds, but special factors were at work that will be discussed later.) Cyclical changes expressed in terms of percentage changes in yields

NOTE: An earlier, and shorter, version of this chapter and the one that follows appears as Jack M. Guttentag, "The Behavior of Residential Mortgages since 1951," in Jack M. Guttentag and Phillip Cagan (eds.), *Essays on Interest Rates, Volume I,* New York, NBER, 1969.

[1] Saul Klaman, *The Postwar Residential Mortgage Market,* NBER, 1961, pp. 75–78.

[2] Grebler, Blank and Winnick, *Capital Formation in Residential Real Estate: Trends and Prospects,* p. 223.

[3] When mortgage rates are recorded on the disbursement date, the recorded peak and trough values are actually averages of rates authorized during a number of months preceding the turning-point month.

[4] Newly issued bonds, not shown here, display even greater cyclical amplitude than outstanding bonds. See page 44.

TABLE 3-1

Changes in Yields During Specific Cycles, Selected Series
(basis points)

| Period of Rise (R) or Decline (D) | Life Insurance Co. Mortgages – Authorization Basis | | FHA Secondary Market (3) | U.S. Gov't. Long-Term (4) | Corporate | | State and Local | |
	Conventional (1)	FHA (2)			Aaa (5)	Baa (6)	Aaa (7)	Baa (8)
1949-51 D	-12[a]	-18[a]	-28	-26	-27	-37	-63	-97
1951-53 R	56	62	85	94	83	72	134	168
1954 D	-19	-11	-33	-66	-53	-43	-74	-73
1954-58 R	101	104	110	126	125	164	153	155
1958 D	-31	-16	-31	-61	-55	-56	-74	-78
1958-60 R	72	81	94	125	104	81	80	72
Average, 3 cycles	49	49	64	83	75	76	96	107
1960-65 D	-60	na	-85	-64	-42	-56	-60	-101
1965-66 R	105	na	156	106	130	140	104	106
Average, 1 cycle	83	na	121	85	86	98	82	104

Notes to Table 3-1

Note: Dates refer to years containing turning points in conventional mortgage series. Turning points in bond yields are based on series unadjusted for seasonal variation, and differ in some cases from those shown in Phillip Cagan, *Changes in the Cyclical Behavior of Interest Rates,* Occasional Paper 100, New York, NBER, 1966. Cyclical changes are measured between the peaks and troughs of each series. Averages are calculated without regard to sign.

[a]Data cover one company.
na=data not available

Source: Cols. 1 and 2, National Bureau of Economic Research compilations and Federal Home Loan Bank Board; col. 3, FHA; col. 4, Federal Reserve Board; cols. 5,6, 7 and 8, Moody's.

---

would show even more marked differences in amplitude because of the higher absolute level of mortgage yields.[5]

Several possible explanations have been offered for the relatively narrow cyclical amplitude of mortgage interest rates. First, the data used by earlier investigators did not take into account fees and charges received or paid by lenders over the contract rate. Grebler, Blank and Winnick noted that "since the data show contract interest rates rather than yields on mortgages, they fail to reflect changes in premiums and discounts on mortgage loans, at times important in the mortgage market."[6] Furthermore, Avery Cohan points out what can be interpreted as an a priori argument for cyclical sensitivity in fees and charges. "Local institutions would feel less comfortable about raising rates than about raising fees and charges. Everybody knows what the going rate is on mortgages in any given area, but nobody knows anything about fees and charges."[7]

The new authorization series, which take into account fees and charges, do not bear out this supposition. On conventional loans, the inclusion of fees and charges has virtually no effect on cyclical amplitude. This is illustrated in Chart 3-1, which shows gross yield, contract rate, and the difference between them (the difference is on an enlarged scale). It is clear that virtually all cyclical variability in conventional yields stems from variability in contract rate.

Whether fees and charges are cyclically insensitive for lender groups other than life insurance companies is not clear. Federal Home Loan

[5] The cyclical amplitude of mortgage yields may be affected slightly by the prepayment assumption used to calculate yield. See page 154.

[6] Grebler, Blank and Winnick, p. 223.

[7] Quoted from Cohan's comments on an earlier draft of this paper.

CHART 3-1

GROSS YIELD AND CONTRACT RATE ON CONVENTIONAL
LOANS, 1951–63

Bank Board data covering the period of marked increase in rate between September–October 1965 and December 1966–January 1967
suggest that cyclical changes in fees and charges may be significant for
savings and loan associations and perhaps commercial banks and
mortgage companies. During that period, the average effective yield on
new-home loans approved by savings and loan associations rose by
about seventy-eight basis points, with an increase in fees and charges
accounting for about twelve points and increase in contract rate for the
balance. At commercial banks and mortgage companies, the rise in fees
was the equivalent of yield increases of five basis points or less. At life

insurance companies and mutual savings banks fees and charges did not rise significantly. This evidence is hardly conclusive, however, since the data cover only one cyclical phase; furthermore, the Board's definition of fees and charges is not comprehensive.[8]

The popular notion that small changes in market conditions are better revealed in fees and charges on conventional loans than in contract rates seems to derive from the infinite divisibility of fees and charges; in contrast lenders almost invariably write contract rates in multiples of .25 per cent. Indivisibility does not, however, imply inflexibility in an aggregate, i.e., an average contract rate can rise .01 per cent when a small proportion of the mortgages in the aggregate, which previously had barely qualified for a 5.50 per cent rate, are jumped to 5.75 per cent, the others remaining unchanged.

Klaman suggests a second explanation for the relatively narrow cyclical amplitude of conventional mortgage yields.

. . . the element of administrative costs . . . has its own place in the relative stickiness of mortgage rates. In general, the larger such costs are relative to the interest rate the more stable the interest rate is likely to be. The reason is simple: a minimum margin must be maintained between the interest rate and a lender's fixed administrative costs to assure him a reasonable return. . . . On residential loans, administrative costs of acquisition, servicing, and recordkeeping, perhaps 75 basis points compared to 10 on corporate securities, create a relatively stable state in residential mortgage interest rates.[9]

This argument is not convincing. Since mortgage rates at their lowest levels are several times higher than mortgage costs, how could these costs dampen rate variability? Even if there were such a rate-dampening mechanism, one would think that the extent of the rate-dampening effect would depend not on the absolute cost but on its size relative to the average rate level on that instrument. Viewed in this way, it is not at all clear that costs would have more of a dampening effect on mortgages than on bonds. The rate differential between mortgages and bonds (Baa and higher) is almost always greater than the sixty-five basis point cost differential.

A third explanation, also suggested by Klaman, is that adjustments

[8] In the Board's series, fees and charges cover only payments received by lenders, excluding payments made by lenders to third parties, such as "finders fees." In the Bureau series, fees paid are netted from fees received. It is possible that the fees paid by some lenders are cyclically sensitive.

[9] Klaman, p. 78.

in nonrate dimensions of the mortgage loan contract retard or offset rate adjustments.

As we move away from standardized to more differentiated markets and commodities the number of variables, in addition to price, to be negotiated multiplies. The market for residential mortgages is an example of the most differentiated because few markets are characterized by more one-of-a-kind deals. The credit of each borrower must be established, and "credit worthiness" becomes a function of the relative tightness of capital markets. Numerous contract terms other than price are subject to individual negotiation-down-payment requirements, amortization provisions, contract maturities, prepayment penalties and non-interest costs. The nature and location of the particular residential unit securing the mortgage, moreover, are important factors in a mortgage transaction.

All these elements are more sensitive than the mortgage interest rate is to changes in financial market conditions. Down-payment and maturity provisions are particularly responsive. . . .[10]

This argument is illustrated in the upper panel of Figure 3-1. If the aggregate yield series constitutes a weighted average of components A (high-yield) and B (low-yield), and the mix shifts toward B when yields rise and toward A when they fall, cyclical variability in the aggregate will be dampened.

In testing the hypothesis, we examined cyclical variability in the mix of loan characteristics for which data are available. The loan-value ratios and maturities on conventional mortgages by life insurance companies during 1951–63, showed negligible cyclical variability (see Table 3-2). During the 1954 period of declining yields, for example, the average maturity on conventional loans rose by sixteen months and the loan-value ratio by only two-tenths of a percentage point. As noted in Chapter 2, cross-section regression analysis suggests that such increases would not affect yields significantly.

Cyclical changes in borrower characteristics associated with risk could affect cyclical yield variability. This appears to be the case in at least one other negotiated loan market. A larger proportion of commercial bank business loans are to prime borrowers at interest rate peaks than at troughs, and this tends to dampen variability in average business loan rates.[11] There is no evidence, however, of a similar

[10] *Ibid.,* pp. 77 and 78.
[11] Albert M. Wojnilower and Richard E. Speagle, "The Prime Rate," in *Essays in Money and Credit,* Federal Reserve Bank of New York, 1964, pp. 50–51.

FIGURE 3-1

HYPOTHETICAL CYCLICAL CHANGES IN
INTEREST RATES

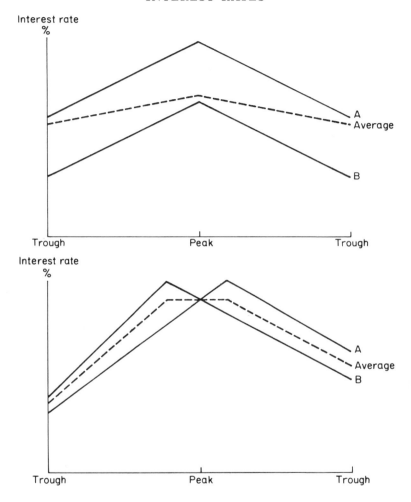

tendency in conventional mortgage loans by life insurance companies. The only measure of borrower risk available from the time series is the average property value underlying the series.[12] Trend-adjusted

[12] On a cross-section basis, property value appears to be a better measure of borrower risk than current income, probably because property value is a better proxy for permanent income. When effective yield on conventional loans is re-

TABLE 3-2

Changes in Maturities and Loan-Value Ratios During Periods of Cyclical
Rise and Decline in Mortgage Yields, 1953 − 63

| | Periods of Rise in Yields | | | | | | |
| | 1951-54 | | 1954-58 | | 1958-60 | | Average Per Month |
	Change	Per Month	Change	Per Month	Change	Per Month	
Changes in Maturity (months)							
Conventional	9.10	.26	18.80	.48	11.60	.55	.42
FHA	42.20	1.32	.40	.01	14.00	.78	.65
VA	-6.70	-.21	-10.00	-.27	4.80	.27	.14
Changes in Loan-Value Ratio (percentage points)							
Conventional	1.00	.03	2.00	.05	3.40	.16	.07
FHA	2.60	.08	4.30	1.20	.60	.03	.09
VA	-3.00	-.09	-4.30	-.12	-.70	-.04	-.09

| | Periods of Decline in Yields | | | | | | |
| | 1954 | | 1958 | | 1960-63 | | Average Per Month |
	Change	Per Month	Change	Per Month	Change	Per Month	
Changes in Maturity (months)							
Conventional	16.10	1.61	11.90	1.49	30.10	.75	1.20
FHA	9.90	.66	22.50	3.75	8.50	.19	.63
VA	48.60	3.20	29.50	4.91	-2.50	-.06	1.15
Changes in Loan-Value Ratio (percentage points)							
Conventional	.20	.02	.30	.04	0.00	0.00	.01
FHA	.60	.04	1.50	.24	1.60	.04	.06
VA	1.90	.13	7.20	1.20	-1.40	-.03	.12

Note: Changes are calculated from three-month averages centered on turning points in conventional yields (for changes in conventional terms) and in FHA yields (for changes in FHA and VA terms). Terminal date for the 1960 − 63 decline is November 1963.

Source: NBER series.

cyclical fluctuations in average property value are in the wrong direction. Values rose considerably faster during three periods of declining yields during 1951–66 than during four periods of rising yields, and therefore tend to *increase* cyclical yield amplitude rather than dampen it.[13]

A potentially more promising application of the shift-in-mix hypothesis is to shifts in lender and geographical mix, since these are the most important source of yield variability on a cross-section basis. Actually, cyclical changes in lender and geographical mix have a neglible effect on over-all cyclical yield variability. This was shown in Chapter 2, Table 2-2.

Following the change-in-mix hypothesis, the FHA mortgage series would be expected to have greater amplitude than conventional series when the two are measured on a comparable basis. Since cross-section yield variability is lower on FHAs than on conventionals and the mix of FHA yield determinants has less cyclical sensitivity (see Table 3-2), changes in mix would dampen yield variability less on FHAs. In fact, however, the amplitude of the FHA authorization series is not significantly different from that of the conventional authorization series (see Table 3-1).

Fourth, the relatively narrow cyclical amplitude of mortgage yields could arise from greater differentiation within the mortgage category which would cause differences in cyclical phasing among the various components of the aggregate. This is illustrated in the lower panel of Figure 3-1. Without any change in mix, the two components of the total may reach a turning point at different times, in which case the amplitude of the average will be smaller than that of either component. The greater the number of component series and the greater the timing differences between them, the stronger will be this dampening tendency. It is likely that conventional mortgage loan series are more heterogeneous than bond series, and thus, in effect, contain more component series with independent cyclical phasing.

This explanation implies, however, that high-grade bond yield series

gressed separately on property value and income, coefficients are negative for both and always larger for value; when value and income are included in the same regression, the latter is much smaller and frequently not significant. On a time series basis, of course, property value is affected by changes in price levels, as well as by changes in the composition of home buyers.

[13] It is unlikely, in any case, that the effect is of quantitative importance. The relationship between property value and yield is smaller for life insurance companies than for other lender groups, reflecting the companies' tendency to maintain relatively conservative standards.

will have a wider cyclical amplitude than lower-grade series, since the former tend to be more homogeneous; similarly, FHA series would be expected to have a wider amplitude than conventional series. Table 3-1 shows that for neither bonds nor mortgages is this the case.

A fifth possible explanation of the relatively narrow amplitude of conventional mortgage yields is based on cyclical changes in risk premiums. It could be argued that the risk premium on mortgages relative to bonds will be smaller at cyclical peaks, which are associated with high levels of business activity, than at troughs. Conventional mortgages in general are riskier than high-grade bonds, and as economic conditions become increasingly favorable, premiums narrow on riskier instruments. To put it differently, the quality of conventional mortgages improves more than that of high-grade bonds during periods of economic expansion.

An indirect test of this hypothesis is as follows: if a decline in risk premiums accounted for the reduction in yield differentials between conventional mortgages and high-grade bonds during business expansions, reductions in yield differential, between high-grade and low-grade bonds and between FHA and conventional mortgages, should have occurred as well. A comparison of yield differentials at business cycle peaks and troughs does not support this hypothesis, as shown in Table 3-3. The changes in the differential between conventional mortgages and high-grade bond yields at reference cycle peaks and troughs is significant at the 1 per cent level, while the other changes are not significant (in two cases they have the wrong sign).[14]

---

[14] Avery Cohan points out that changes in the yield differential are not a perfect proxy for changes in "quality," if quality is defined as the probability that a loan will be repaid. Assume, for example, that the yield differential between a riskless one-year security and a risky security of the same maturity reflects only the probability of loss attached to the latter. At the end of the year, the value of the riskless security will be $1 + G$ where G is the contract rate on that security, while the value of the risky security will be $(1 + r)p$ where r is the contract rate on the risky security and p is the probability that the principal and interest will be paid. The risk premium included in r is, in theory, just large enough to equate the future value of both securities, $1 + G = (1 + r)p$ and $p = \dfrac{1 + G}{1 + r}$. (It can be shown, similarly, that if both securities have a maturity of n years, $p = \left[\dfrac{1 + G}{1 + r}\right]^n$.) This means that if the level of G rises, r must rise even more to maintain a constant p. The risk premium expressed as basis points of yield must get larger even though the probability of loss is constant. The required change in the yield differential, however, is very small. For example, a cyclical rise in G on the order of those shown in Appendix Table 3-1 would require a rise of two to three basis points in the conventional mortgage-Aaa bond-yield differential in order to maintain a constant risk premium.

TABLE 3-3

Comparison of Yield Differentials at Reference Cycle Peaks and Troughs

Yield Differential	Average 3 Peaks	Average 3 Troughs	Troughs Less Peaks
Conv. mtgs. less Aaa corp.	1.53	1.86	.33
Conv. mtgs. less Aaa state and local	2.42	2.86	.44
Aaa corp. less Baa corp.	.71	.83	.12
Aaa state and local less Baa state and local	1.04	1.01	-.03
Conv. mtgs. less FHA mtgs.	.05	-.01	-.06

Source: Appendix Table 3-1.

This test, however, depends heavily on the assumption that lender reevaluations of security risk can be tied to reference-cycle turning points. Another test, crude but perhaps more meaningful in light of our ignorance on this point, is to compare average yield differentials during recession periods with those during expansions. This test is more favorable to the risk-premium hypothesis. As shown in Table 3-4, on corporate and state and local bonds the yield differential between Aaa and Baa issues was higher in each of four recession periods than in the subsequent expansion. This suggests that some cyclical reevaluation of risk may well have occurred on bonds. No similar pattern was evident, however, for the yield differential between conventional and FHA mortgages.

Cyclical changes in mortgage delinquencies may even be more relevant. One would not expect a recession to raise the ex ante risk premium on conventional mortgages unless the repayment experience on mortgages held in portfolio was appreciably affected by the recession. The evidence on delinquencies by and large does not support the risk-premium hypothesis. Major lender groups, including life insurance companies, have found a modest tendency for delinquencies to rise during recent recessions, but this appears to be accounted for entirely by FHA and VA mortgages.[15] A study of monthly time series covering

[15] Some of the evidence on this is shown in James S. Earley, "The Quality of Postwar Credit in the United States," National Bureau of Economic Research, September 1965, mimeograph. A complete compendium of delinquency and

TABLE 3-4

Yield Differential Between Baa and Aaa Bonds and Between
Conventional and FHA Mortgages During Business
Expansions and Recessions
(basis points)

Recession (R) or Expansion (E)		Baa Less Aaa		Conventional Less FHA
		Corporate	State and Local	
Nov. 1948 - Oct. 1949	(R)	75	102	8
Nov. 1949 - June 1953	(E)	57	85	24
July 1953 - Aug. 1954	(R)	62	109	11
Sept. 1954 - June 1957	(E)	50	97	9
July 1957 - April 1958	(R)	98	108	2
May 1958 - April 1960	(E)	75	94	-11
May 1960 - Feb. 1961	(R)	79	96	-11
March 1961 - July 1967	(E)	57	53	-6

Source: Appendix Tables 3-2 and 9-4 plus Moody's.

conventional mortgages does not reveal any cyclical sensitivity during the period since 1953, for which monthly data are available.

In the final hypothesis considered here, the narrow cyclical amplitude of mortgage yields relative to bond yields reflects differences in market organization. For a number of reasons, rates tend to be relatively sluggish in markets where borrowers and lenders negotiate directly —as opposed to impersonal dealer-type markets. First, negotiated markets involve bilateral bargaining which will moderate changes in rates if there is continuity in the relationship between borrower and lender, as in the case of commercial banks and their business-loan customers or of life insurance companies that acquire mortgages through correspondents. A concern for maintaining relationships over the long run blunts the tendency to maximize market position in the short run.

Second, lenders in negotiated markets may have heavy nontransferable overhead costs geared to the specific market, as in the case of

foreclosure series is listed in *Measures of Credit Risk and Experience,* Edgar R. Fiedler, New York, NBER, forthcoming.

life insurance companies that acquire mortgages through their own network of branch offices. Such lenders find it profitable to maintain relative stability in their operations; since each individual lender is in some degree operating in a separate market, this implies rate stability relative to markets that lenders feel free to leave altogether.

Third, lenders in negotiated markets tend to lag in adjusting their offer functions to yield changes in dealer markets (see below). If basic credit demands are less stable in the dealer markets, the full range of rate changes in these markets will not be transmitted to the negotiated market. Because of the transmission lag, peaks and troughs in the dealer market are in effect "lopped off." Here, the explanation of why mortgage yields have smaller cyclical amplitude merges with the explanation given below of why mortgage yields lag bond yields.

Clearly, the market-organization hypothesis goes beyond the immediate focus of this paper and into largely unexplored terrain. It would explain, however, not only the small amplitude of mortgage yields relative to bond yields but also the narrower amplitude of the rates on commercial bank business loans than those on open-market paper of comparable maturity.[16] The amplitude of directly placed bonds also appears to be less than that of marketable new issues.[17] It is also of interest that the FHA secondary market yield series is more volatile than FHA authorization series though less volatile than bond yields (Table 3-1). The market organization underlying the FHA secondary market lies somewhere between that of the markets underlying the life insurance company authorization series and the bond yield series.[18] We will note in Chapter 4, moreover, that direct mort-

---

[16] For evidence of this, see Phillip Cagan, *Changes in the Cyclical Behavior of Interest Rates,* Occasional Paper 100, New York, NBER, 1966, p. 9. An alternative explanation is given by Donald Hodgman, *Commercial Bank Loan and Investment Policy,* Urbana, Ill., 1963, pp. 126–131.

[17] See Cohan, *Yields on Direct Placements,* p. 72. Since directly placed bonds are new issues, it is appropriate to compare them to newly issued marketable bonds. A comparison of Cohan's series on direct placements with mortgages during the period 1951–61 shows that the former have greater amplitude, despite the fact that both are new-issues series and both pertain to negotiated markets. The reason may be that the characteristics of negotiated markets which generate relative yield stability are less powerful in the market for direct placements. Nontransferable overhead costs would not be as large as they are for mortgages, and basic credit demands probably would be as unstable as for marketable bonds.

[18] While there are no dealers in the FHA secondary market, brokers are often used, and buyers and sellers tend to canvass the market for the best available deal.

gage loan series are more sensitive than correspondent loan series, and this is also explained most plausibly by the market-organization hypothesis.

The distinction between dealer and negotiated markets cuts across a distinction between new-issue markets and markets for outstanding instruments. Only in the case of marketable bonds do we have series for both new and outstanding issues, and these show that new-issue series have greater amplitude. This can be explained by differences in market organization within the dealer-market category. Conard and Frankena, in their study of the yield differential between new and outstanding bonds, suggest that "forces determining interest rates operate more directly and immediately on yields in the new issue market and yields in the seasoned market adjust to their equilibrium level only with a lag. . . ."[19] They explain this largely in terms of frictions and imperfections in the dealer market for seasoned securities that are not present in the new-issue market. This suggests that a mortgage yield series covering outstanding issues, if there was one, would show even less amplitude than the existing series, which cover new issues.

Timing at Turning Points

Klaman noted that "changes in mortgage interest rates lagged continually behind changes in bond yields throughout the post-war decade." [20] This lag is reduced by one to six months when transactions are recorded as of the date of loan authorization rather than the date of disbursement. The lag is not eliminated, however, as Table 3-5 indicates. At five turning points during 1954–60, conventional yields lagged behind government bond yields from four to seven months. These might be considered "normal" lags. Lags at the 1949, 1951, and 1965 turning points were considerably longer, but they were affected by special developments that changed the underlying relationship between mortgage and bond yields.[21] The 1965 case will be discussed below.

[19] "The Yield Spread between New and Seasoned Corporate Bonds, 1952–63," in Jack M. Guttentag and Phillip Cagan, *Essays on Interest Rates,* Volume I, New York, NBER, 1969.

[20] Klaman, p. 78.

[21] The changing relationship between mortgage and bond yields during 1949–51 was discussed in Jack Guttentag's "Some Studies of the Post-World War II Residential Construction and Mortgage Markets," unpublished Ph.D. dissertation, Columbia University, 1958, pp. 82–86.

TABLE 3-5

Lag at Turning Points, Conventional Mortgage
Yields Relative to Bond Yields

Turning Point in Conventional Yields	Lag in Conventional Yields (months)			
	U.S. Gov't. Long-Term	Corporate		
		Aaa	Aa New	Baa
P Dec. 1949[a]	14	13		12
T Feb. 1951	14	13		0
P Jan. 1954	7	7	8	4
T Nov. 1954	4	1	8	-2
P Feb. 1958	4	5	4	3
T Oct. 1958	6	4	4	3
P July 1960	6	6	10	5
T Sept. 1965[b]	52	30	32	6
1954-60 average	5	5	7	3

"Normal" brackets the rows from P Jan. 1954 through P July 1960.

[a]Based on data for one company.

[b]Based on FHLBB series on new house purchases.

Source: National Bureau of Economic Research compilations, Federal Reserve Board, Moody's.

Since dating of turning points is unavoidably arbitrary at some junctures, another measure of cyclical sensitivity is employed in Table 3-6. This table uses only one turning point—on long-term government bond yields—and measures yield changes in all the series during periods of specified length (e.g., five, ten and fifteen months) beginning with that date. Relative sensitivity is measured by the rise (decline) during the periods following troughs (peaks) in government bond yields.[22] These comparisons show mortgage yields to be relatively insensitive at every one of the five turning points in the table. As an example, ten months after the April 1958 trough in government bond yields, government bonds were up eighty basis points, high-grade corporates were up fifty to fifty-four basis points, while direct conventional mortgage yields were up one basis point.

[22] These comparisons use series on direct conventional mortgage loans only, since the correspondent loan component may have some residual recording lag. The periods following yield peaks are shorter than those following troughs to avoid extending past the subsequent turning point. The trough following the 1960 peak is not included in this table because the trough dates for the different series are spread over an extraordinarily long period. Turning points in government bond yields are based on seasonally unadjusted series and differ in some cases from those shown in Cagan.

TABLE 3-6

Changes in Yields on Direct Mortgage Loans and on Bonds
Following Turning Points in U.S. Government Bond Yields

Turning Points in Long-Term Government Bond Yields	No. of Months After Turning Point in Bond Yields	Changes in Yield (basis points)			Mortgages (direct authorization)	
		Long-Term Governments (1)	Corporate Aaa (2)	Corporate Aa New (3)	Conventional (4)	FHA (5)
Troughs						
July 1954	+5	+12	+1	+4	-4	+1
	+10	+34	+15	+26	-3	+6
	+15	+40	+21	+27	+8	+18
April 1958	+5	+63	+49	+83	-24	-19
	+10	+80	+54	+50	+1	+3
	+15	+99	+87	+108	0	+8
Peaks						
June 1953	+4	-26	-24	-58	+21	+16
	+8	-51	-45	-75	+21	+13
	+12	-58	-50	-78	+13	+7
Oct. 1957	+3	-49	-50	-119	+8	+8
	+6	-61	-50	-106	+4	+6
	+9	-37	-43	-93	-5	-7
Jan. 1960	+4	-21	-15	-4	+7	+5
	+8	-55	-36	-30	+5	-3

One hypothesis used to explain the lag in conventional mortgage yields is that small changes in market demand and supply register first in changes in loan-value ratios and maturities, and this retards the adjustment of yields. If this is true, terms typically should reach a cyclical turning point before yields. Table 3-7 shows cyclical turning points in loan-value ratios and maturities matching five turning points in yields in the new NBER series (observed separately for each type of loan and for weighted totals covering all loans). Some of these observations are obscured by the effects of changes in legal limits, while in other cases there was no clearly defined turning point in terms. With these exclusions, there are twenty-two usable observations. In eight cases, terms led yields; in five cases, terms lagged; in nine cases, the turning points in terms were within a month of the turning point in yields. If these were independent observations, an eight-nine-five distribution could easily occur by chance and would provide little support for the hypothesis that sensitivity of terms retards yield adjustments.

Since the twenty-two observations are drawn from only five turning points, however, they are not necessarily independent observations. Different characteristics on the same type of mortgage, or the same characteristic on a different type of mortgage, may be subject to similar influences at a given turning point. It is instructive, therefore, to view each of the five turning points in yield as one observation. From this standpoint, the evidence provides no support for the hypothesis at all. At only one of the turning points, the interest rate peak in early 1958, was there a clear tendency for terms to precede yields; seven of the eight "lead" observations come from this turning point.[23] Terms lagged yields at the other four turning points, although the 1953 turning point has only one valid observation.

The new FHLBB series on conventional loans provide additional evidence to test the hypothesis that sensitivity in terms retards adjustments in rates. Although these data as yet cover only two turning points, series are available for five lender groups, separately for new and existing properties, or twenty cases for each loan characteristic. There were eleven identifiable turning points for maturities and the maturities lagged their respective contract rate or had coincident timing

---

[23] As shown in Table 3-5, furthermore, the lag of mortgage yields behind bond yields at this turning point was shorter than usual, whereas it should have been longer according to the sensitivity-of-terms hypothesis used to explain this lag.

TABLE 3-7

Cyclical Turning Points in Loan-Value Ratios and Maturities Corresponding to Turning Points in Yields

	Cyclical Peaks and Troughs in Yield					Number of Cases		
						Terms Lead Yields	Terms Lag Yields	Same Turning Points[a]
	P	T	P	T	P			
Gross Yield								
FHA and VA	Dec. 1953	Feb. 1955	March 1958	Sept. 1958	March 1960			
Conventional	Jan. 1954	Nov. 1954	Feb. 1958	Oct. 1958	July 1960			
All, weighted	Dec. 1953	Oct. 1954	Feb. 1958	Oct. 1958	May 1960			
	Cyclical Troughs and Peaks in Terms[b]							
	T	P	T	P	T			
Conventional								
Maturity	Nov. 1953	Dec. 1954	Aug. 1956	Jan. 1959	March 1961	2	2	1
Loan-value ratio	ntp	ntp	Aug. 1957	Sept. 1959	ntp	1	1	
FHA								
Maturity	June 1953[c]	May 1955	Feb. 1957[c]	Sept. 1958	ntp		1	1
Loan-value ratio	July 1954[c]	June 1955	Jan. 1957[c]	Sept. 1958	ntp		1	1
VA								
Maturity	May 1953[c]	Dec. 1954	Jan. 1957	ntp	ntp	2		
Loan-value ratio	Aug. 1953[c]	Oct. 1954	ntp	ntp	ntp	1		
All, weighted								
Maturity	Aug. 1952[c]	Oct. 1954	Sept. 1957	Dec. 1959	Dec. 1960	1	2	1
Loan-value ratio	Aug. 1952[c]	Oct. 1954	Aug. 1957	Dec. 1959	Dec. 1960	1	2	1

[a]Within one month of corresponding yield series.

[b]Peaks (troughs) in terms corresponding to troughs (peaks) in yields.

[c]Affected by changes in legal limits.

Source: NBER series.

ntp = No well-defined turning point.

TABLE 3-8

Leads and Lags of Loan-Value Ratios, Maturities, and Fees and Charges Relative to
Contract Rate at the 1965 Trough, and the 1966 − 67 peak in Contract Rate
in Ten Conventional Home Loan Series

Characteristic	Number of Identifiable Turning Points in Characteristic	Number of Cases		
		Char. Leads Rate	Char. Lags Rate	Same Turning Point[a]
Maturity	11	0	4	7
Loan-value	12	2	4	6
Fees and charges	9	0	7	2

[a]Within one month of corresponding rate series.
Source: Federal Home Loan Bank Board.

in each case (Table 3-8). Similarly, only two of the twelve identifiable turning points in loan-value ratios led their respective contract rate. Thus, the data do not support the hypothesis that sensitivity in terms retards adjustments in yields at cyclical turning points.

The lag in conventional yields is not explained either by any special sensitivity of fees and charges. The NBER conventional contract-rate series has exactly the same turning points as the gross yield series except at the 1958 peak when the contract rate series leads by one month. The FHLBB series show fees lagging rates at the 1965 trough and 1966–67 peak in most cases (Table 3-8).

Short-term developments affecting general yield levels normally originate in the bond markets, and this may be an important factor underlying the tendency of mortgage yields to lag bond yields. The basic demand for mortgage credit (that is, the demand under given mortgage credit terms) is affected mainly by demographic factors and by "normal" income, changing little in the short run.[24] Demands on the capital markets by the federal government and nonfinancial corporations, in contrast, are subject to sharp cyclical fluctuations.[25]

Bond-yield changes could, of course, be transmitted immediately to the mortgage market; but, in fact, there is a lag. For a number of rea-

[24] See Sherman Maisel, "A Theory of Fluctuations in Residential Construction Starts," *American Economic Review,* June 1963, pp. 374–376.
[25] See Guttentag, "The Short Cycle in Residential Construction," pp. 292–294.

sons, there is virtually no arbitrage between the two markets.[26] Rate adjustments in the mortgage market depend almost entirely on the activities of primary lenders. These lenders appear to be responsive to pervasive but not to short-lived changes in bond yields. As one lender expressed it, "To attempt to follow every wiggle in bond yields would unduly disrupt our market relationships." But a pervasive movement in bond yields usually cannot be distinguished from a reversible one until the passage of time proves it out; the result is that mortgage yields lag. As noted earlier, this lag in conjunction with relatively stable mortgage credit demand may be partly responsible for the narrow cyclical amplitude of mortgage yields.

Longer-run Changes and the 1961–66 Experience

The long-run relationship between conventional mortgage yields and high-grade bond yields is examined in two ways. Chart 3-2 shows the yield differential (mortgages less long-term government bonds) during the period 1948–67.[27] This series is affected by the tendency of mortgage yields to lag bond yields by periods of varying length. Table 3-9 shows differentials at cyclical peaks and troughs only, with the yield on each instrument measured at its respective peak or trough. Thus, at peak 4, the yield on conventional mortgages in July 1960 is compared to the yield on long-term governments in January 1960. These are referred to as "matching differentials."

During the period 1949–60, the monthly series show marked cyclical fluctuations with some indication of widening amplitude, but there is no indication of a trend. Similarly, the matching differentials at the first three troughs and four peaks show no indication of trend.

[26] First, because of differentiation within the mortgage market, yield relationships are not reliable enough to permit effective arbitrage. (Arbitrage transactions must be carried out in individual securities and depend on reasonably reliable yield relationships between the instruments being arbitraged.) Second, the cost of arbitrage transactions involving mortgages is high because the market for outstanding mortgages is rudimentary. Brokers exist who will attempt to sell mortgages on a commission basis, but there are no dealers who will take seasoned mortgages into portfolio. Third, the secondary mortgage market, such as it is, has no direct organizational links to the bond market.

[27] The conventional mortgage yield series used in this chart are based on the new National Bureau series for 1948–63, and the FHLBB series covering loans by life insurance companies on new properties for 1964–67. The entire series is contained in Appendix Table 3-2.

CHART 3-2

CONVENTIONAL MORTGAGE YIELDS AND LONG-TERM GOVERNMENT BOND YIELDS, 1948–67

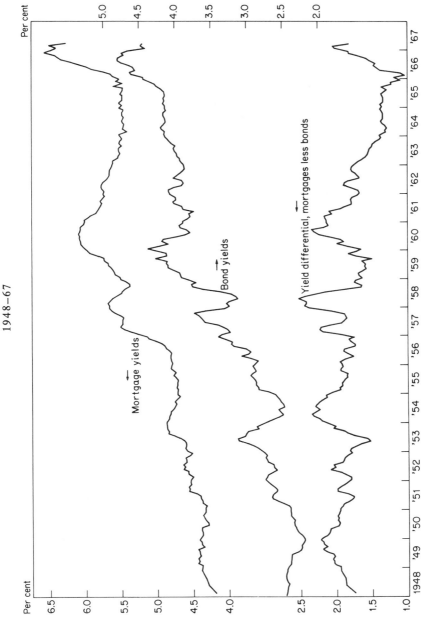

TABLE 3-9

Yield Differentials Between Conventional Mortgages
and Bonds, at Cyclical Peaks and Troughs

	Dates					Yield Differentials				
	(1)	(2)	(3)	(4)	(5)	(1)	(2)	(3)	(4)	(5)
Cyclical Peaks										
Conventional mortgages	Dec. 1949[a]	Jan. 1954	Feb. 1958	July 1960	Nov. 1966					
U.S. gov't. long term	Oct. 1948	June 1953	Oct. 1957	Jan. 1960	Sept. 1966	1.96	1.74	1.96	1.73	1.76
Corporate Aaa	Nov. 1948	June 1953	Sept. 1957	Jan. 1960	Sept. 1966	1.57	1.47	1.57	1.49	1.06
Corporate Aa (new)	–	May 1953	Oct. 1957	Sept. 1959	Dec. 1966	–	.99	.78	.62	.62
Corporate Baa	Dec. 1948	Sept. 1953	Nov. 1957	Feb. 1960	Dec. 1966	.88	.99	.60	.76	.37
Cyclical Troughs										
Conventional mortgages	Feb. 1951	Nov. 1954	Oct. 1958	Sept. 1965						
U.S. gov't. long term	Dec. 1949	July 1954	April 1958	May 1961		2.12	2.21	2.26	1.77	
Corporate Aaa	Jan. 1950	Oct. 1954	June 1958	March 1963		1.74	1.81	1.81	1.31	
Corporate Aa (new)	–	March 1954	June 1958	Jan. 1963		–	1.77	1.57	1.30	
Corporate Baa	Feb. 1951	Jan. 1955	July 1958	March 1965		1.15	1.23	.85	.72	

Note: Yield differentials are measured at peaks and troughs of each series.

[a]Based on data for one company.

Source: Conventional mortgages are the NBER series except at trough (4) and peak (5) which are the FHLBB series for life insurance companies covering purchase of new homes (contract rate); Long-term government bonds are the Federal Reserve series; corporate bond series are from Moody's. Turning points are based on series unadjusted for seasonal variation, and differ in some cases from those in Cagan, *Changes in the Cyclical Behavior of Interest Rates*

During the cyclical decline in yields that began in 1960, however, mortgage yields continued to fall long past the point at which bond yields had begun to drift upward.[28] As a result, the 1960–65 decline in the monthly differential was larger than any earlier cyclical decline (as measured in basis points from peak to trough), and brought the differential some forty-five to forty-eight basis points below the previous lows reached in 1959 and 1953. Similarly, the matching differential at trough 4 was markedly lower than at any of the previous troughs. An observer at the end of 1965 might have speculated, as we in fact did in an early draft of this paper, that perhaps the yield differential had been "permanently" reduced.

The dramatic events of 1966—mortgage yields rose more in one year than they had declined in the previous five—added an additional dimension to this experience. The rise in the yield differential during 1966 was larger than any earlier cyclical rise, and it brought the differential back to high levels, although still below earlier peaks. Thus, it appears less plausible now than at the end of 1965 that a permanent decline in the differential has occurred. What needs explaining is the greater amplitude of the yield differential over the period 1961–66 than in earlier periods, which reflects the increased amplitude of the mortgage yield series during this period.

In order to explain the wide amplitude of mortgage yields during 1961–66 we begin with the following crude "facts." Comparing the 1961–65 period of decline in mortgage yields with the preceding six years, net mortgage acquisitions on one- to four-family properties rose from $65.7 billion to $72.3 billion, or by $6.6 billion. Commercial banks accounted for most of the increase, their acquisitions rising by $5.1 billion. During 1966, when mortgage yields rose precipitously, total net acquisitions dropped $4.6 billion, all of it accounted for by savings institutions. Commercial bank acquisitions held up in 1966, in contrast to earlier periods of monetary restraint when banks tended to desert the mortgage market.

The hypothesis advanced here is that structural changes involving commercial bank policy toward time deposits, and a marked increase in the relative importance of time deposits in bank liability mix, were responsible for the marked variability in mortgage yields during

[28] The dispersion of turning points in various yield series at trough 4 is extremely wide, and several of the series show multiple bottoms. This makes timing comparisons at this turning point hazardous, but the value of matching yield differentials is not significantly affected by the choice of turning point.

1961–66. The shift in bank liability mix encouraged a portfolio shift into mortgages which put downward pressure on mortgage yields during 1961–65. When tight money emerged in 1966, commercial banks bid savings accounts away from savings institutions which channel most of their funds into mortgages, thus placing upward pressure on mortgage yields—stronger pressure than in earlier periods of monetary restraint when banks had raised funds by liquidating government securities.[29]

The marginal value of a dollar of time deposits to commercial banks has grown steadily over the last decade or so. Their government securities portfolios have trended downward ever since World War II. Beginning in the late 1950's and early 1960's, one bank after another found itself in a position where it could no longer rely on government securities liquidation as a means of meeting loan demands in excess of deposit growth. Demand deposit growth, furthermore, had lagged throughout the entire post-World War II period. As a result, time deposits emerged as a valuable source of funds over which banks could exercise some degree of control.

The shift to time deposits was most pronounced after 1961. In that year, New York City banks began to issue large-denomination negotiable certificates of deposit, and they were followed by large banks in other centers. Both large and small banks began to compete vigorously with savings institutions for smaller accounts. Rate differentials between savings accounts at commercial banks and at savings institutions narrowed, rate advertising increased in intensity, and probably elasticity of substitution rose.

Table 3-10 shows three measures of change in bank liability structure during each of three complete cycles in mortgage yields. Each of the three measures shows a marked shift toward time deposits in the 1960–66 cycle relative to the two earlier cycles. The ratio of time deposits to total deposits rose by .68 percentage points per quarter during the 1960–66 cycle, compared to increases of .27 points and .26 points in the two preceding cycles.

As their liability mix shifted toward time deposits, the asset preferences of commercial banks also changed. It is part of received bank

[29] An underlying condition was, of course, the willingness of the Federal Reserve to allow the commercial banks to compete vigorously for time deposits by keeping Regulation Q ceiling rates above constraint levels (until late in 1966 when the System decided that competition for savings had gone so far as to threaten disaster to the residential sector, and they rolled back the ceilings on some types of accounts).

TABLE 3-10

Measures of Change in Bank Liability Structure
During Cycles in Mortgage Interest Rates, 1953 − 66

Mortgage Interest Rate Cycle	$\dfrac{TD_1}{D_1} - \dfrac{TD_0}{D_0}$	$\dfrac{TD_1 - TD_0}{TD_0} - \dfrac{DD_1 - DD_0}{DD_0}$	$\dfrac{TD_1 - TD_0}{D_1 - D_0}$
	(1)	(2)	(3)
Decline IV 1953-I 1955	.25	1.27	.52
Rise II 1955-IV 1957	.28	1.41	.80
Total cycle	.27	1.36	.70
Decline I 1958-III 1958	.67	3.20	.73
Rise IV 1958-I 1960	.06	.26	.46
Total cycle	.26	1.24	.55
Decline II 1960-III 1965	.68	4.39	.81
Rise IV 1965-IV 1966	.41	1.76	.77
Total cycle	.63	3.90	.80

TD = Time deposits.

DD = Demand deposits.

D = Total deposits.

Subscripts zero and one refer to beginning and end of period, respectively. Measures in columns 1 and 2 show differences per quarter.

Source: Board of Governors of the Federal Reserve System, Flow of Funds Accounts.

management philosophy that mortgages can be prudently acquired with funds obtained from time deposits.[30] Cross-section analysis using balance sheet data invariably shows a positive correlation between the relative importance of time deposits on the liability side and mortgages on the asset side.[31] This appears to reflect a combination of cost and liquidity considerations. If deposit costs are high, bankers feel they must invest in higher yielding assets.[32] In addition, time deposits are generally believed to require a smaller liquidity provision than demand deposits, so that asset structure can safely be made less liquid.

[30] See Fred G. Delong, "Liquidity Requirements and Employment of Funds," in Kalman J. Cohen and Frederick S. Hammer (eds.), *Analytical Methods in Banking,* Homewood, Ill., 1966, pp. 38–53.

[31] For 416 individual member banks in the Philadelphia Federal Reserve District on December 31, 1960, the coefficient of correlation between the ratio of time to total deposits and the ratio of mortgages to total assets was .55.

[32] This implies profit-target behavior by banks rather than profit maximization, which many economists find difficult to accept.

TABLE 3-11

Changes in Real Estate Loans and in State and Local Securities of 416 Member Banks, Related to Changes in Deposits, December 1960 to June 1964

Independent Variables	Real Estate Loan Equations			State and Local Government Securities Equations		
	b-Coef.	T	R^2	b-Coef.	T	R^2
Variant 1.						
Per cent change in total deposits	.39	7.1	.39	2.13	1.7	.07
Per cent change in time deposits	.50	22.3		-.57	.2	
Variant 2.						
Per cent change in time deposits	.67	120.8	.39	.19	.1	.07
Per cent change in demand deposits	.22	8.1		1.56	3.3	
Variant 3.						
Per cent change in total deposits	1.22	98.8	.36	.07	.0	.07
Per cent change in demand deposits	-.27	5.4		1.63	1.7	

Note to Table 3-11

Note: The dependent variables are percentage change in real estate loans (in real estate loan equations), and percentage change in state and local government securities (in state and local government securities equations). All equations include, in addition to the independent variables listed, the December 1960 ratio of time deposits to total deposits, size class of bank, and the December 1960 ratio of real estate loans (or state and local securities) to total assets.

To obtain more direct evidence on this relationship, focusing on *changes* in mortgage holdings and *changes* in time deposits during the period under study, we performed the following experiment. Using data on 416 member banks in the Philadelphia Federal Reserve District,[33] we regressed the percentage change in mortgage loans during the period December 1960–June 1964 on various combinations of deposit change. To avoid the effects of relationships between changes and levels in these magnitudes, the initial ratios of mortgages to assets and time deposits to total deposits (both in December 1960) were also included as variables in the regressions. As a form of control, the same procedure was used to explain the percentage change in state and local securities, which banks also acquired in substantial volume during this period. These equations, however, included the initial ratio of state and local securities to assets rather than the ratio of mortgages to assets. Some results are shown in Table 3-11.

In equation (1), the percentage change in mortgages and in state and local securities is regressed on the percentage change in time deposits and the percentage change in total deposits. The regression coefficient for the change in time deposits is positive and statistically significant in the mortgage equation, but not in the state and local equation, suggesting that only mortgage acquisitions were sensitive to the composition of deposit increase.

Equation (2) used the percentage change in time deposits and in demand deposits as separate variables in the regression. In the mortgage equation, the coefficient for time deposits was three times as large as the coefficient for demand deposits, while in the state and local equation, the coefficient for time deposits was not statistically significant.[34]

Since mortgage acquisitions by individual banks were influenced by

[33] The authors are indebted to the Federal Reserve Bank of Philadelphia for these data. Note that real estate loans in these data cover loans on nonresidential as well as residential properties.

[34] Equations were also run in which the dependent variable was the change in real estate loans as a percentage of the initial level of total assets rather than the initial level of real estate loans. The results were very much the same.

changes in their time deposits,[35] it can be inferred that mortgage acquisitions by the banking system as a whole were boosted by the pronounced shift that occurred in bank-deposit mix. This supports the view that the sharp decline in mortgage yields during 1961–65 was due, at least in part, to the marked increase in time relative to demand deposits during the period, and to a related shift in bank portfolio preferences for mortgages.

It might appear at first glance that these structural changes affecting commercial banks would *retard* the rise in mortgage yields during a period of monetary restraint such as emerged in 1966. Presumably, banks would not reduce mortgage acquisitions as sharply as in earlier periods of restraint when they viewed mortgages more as "residual" assets. Indeed, commercial banks maintained a high level of mortgage acquisitions in 1966, as shown in Table 3-12.

This view, however, neglects the effect of intensive bank competition for time deposits on inflows to savings institutions, and their mortgage lending. Although the status of mortgages in bank portfolios has risen, they remain "inferior" to business loans, the demand for which increased very sharply in 1966. The banks' determination to meet these demands, in the face of depleted liquidity positions, caused them to bid a substantial volume of funds away from the savings institutions, which, correspondingly, reduced their mortgage lending.[36] As shown in Table 3-12, the maintenance of bank mortgage lending did not begin to counterbalance the decline in lending by savings institutions losing funds to banks.[37]

[35] There is some reason to believe that the relationship is dominated by small banks. A study of fifty-three large banks by Morrison and Selden did not reveal any positive relationship between changes in real estate holdings and changes in time deposits during 1960–63. See George R. Morrison and Richard T. Selden, *Time Deposit Growth and the Employment of Bank Funds,* Association of Reserve City Bankers, February 1965, Tables A-1 and A-4.

[36] The shift in funds became so large in the summer and fall that the Federal Reserve "took a variety of steps to redress the balance in the flow of funds between business borrowers and the housing industry . . ." (*Federal Reserve Bulletin,* February 1967, p. 189). For a discussion of these measures, see the cited article.

[37] Table 3-12 shows a marked reversal in the pattern of change in savings flows and mortgage lending in the most recent cycle in mortgage yields as compared to two earlier cycles. In the two earlier ones, the net flow of savings and mortgages at savings institutions was almost as large during the period of rising yields as during the preceding period of falling yields, but in the most recent cycle, both flows were markedly lower during the period of rising yields. The pattern for commercial banks changed in the opposite way. In earlier cycles, bank time deposits and mortgage lending fell during tight-money periods while in the recent cycle both flows were maintained.

TABLE 3-12

Changes in Holdings of One- to Four-Family Mortgages and in Time and
Savings Deposits by Commercial Banks and Savings Institutions
During Cycles in Mortgage Interest Rates, 1953-66
(amounts in billion dollars, annual rate)

Mortgage Interest Rate Cycle	Commercial Banks		Savings Institutions		Time Deposits as Per Cent of Total Time and Savings Deposits
	Time and Savings Deposits	Mortgages	Time and Savings Deposits	Mortgages	
Decline IV 1953-I 1955	3.6	1.6	6.7	6.4	35
Rise II 1955-IV 1957	3.1	0.8	7.1	5.7	30
Decline I 1958-III 1958	9.2	1.5	8.8	6.9	51
Rise IV 1958-I 1960	1.4	1.1	8.5	7.7	14
Decline II 1960-III 1965	13.7	2.0	13.2	10.0	51
Rise IV 1965-IV 1966	14.3	2.1	8.4	4.4	63

Note: Savings institutions are mutual savings banks, savings and loan associations and credit unions. Mortgages lead one quarter.

Source: Board of Governors of the Federal Reserve System, Flow of Fund Accounts.

The liquidation of government securities by commercial banks in earlier periods of restraint had, of course, indirectly affected the flow of funds into mortgages by changing yields on alternative investments. This pressure, however, must have been more diffused and less intense than the withdrawal of funds from savings institutions which invest most of their funds in mortgages. Liquidation of government securities in earlier periods probably was absorbed in good part by reductions in "idle balances." In addition, diversified lenders, such as life insurance companies, probably responded more gradually to changes in alternative investment yields than did savings institutions to a reduction in inflows. A good case can be made that the change in bank response to tight money, from an emphasis on reducing investments to an emphasis on increasing time deposits, resulted in transmitting the effects of tight money to the mortgage market more promptly and fully than ever before.

APPENDIX TABLE 3-1

Yields on Bonds and Mortgages at Reference Cycle Peaks and Troughs

	Peaks			
	July 1953	July 1957	May 1960	Average
Conv. mortgages	4.76	5.48	6.09	
FHA mortgages	4.53	5.38	6.28	
Conv. less FHA	.23	.10	-.19	.05
Corporate Baa bonds	3.86	4.73	5.28	
Corporate Aaa bonds	3.28	3.99	4.46	
Baa less Aaa	.58	.74	.82	.71
State and local Baa bonds	3.60	4.29	4.31	
State and local Aaa bonds	2.56	3.17	3.34	
Baa less Aaa	1.04	1.12	.97	1.04
Conv. mortgages less Aaa corporate bonds	1.48	1.49	1.63	1.53
Conv. mortgages less Aaa state and local bonds	2.20	2.31	2.75	2.42

	Troughs			
	Aug. 1954	April 1958	Feb. 1961	Average
Conv. mortgages	4.74	5.63	5.96	
FHA mortgages	4.60	5.61	6.16	
Conv. less FHA	.14	.02	-.20	-.01
Corporate Baa bonds	3.49	4.67	5.07	
Corporate Aaa bonds	2.87	3.60	4.27	
Baa less Aaa	.62	1.07	.80	.83
State and local Baa bonds	2.94	3.78	4.06	
State and local Aaa bonds	1.90	2.70	3.14	
Baa less Aaa	1.04	1.08	.92	1.01
Conv. mortgages less Aaa corporate bonds	1.87	2.03	1.69	1.86
Conv. mortgages less Aaa state and local bonds	2.84	2.93	2.82	2.86

Note: Mortgage yields are from NBER authorization series, with assumed prepayment of ten years. Bond series are from Moody's.

APPENDIX TABLE 3-2

Conventional Mortgage Yields on One- to Four-Family Properties
Authorized by Life Insurance Companies, 1948-67

Year	Jan.	Feb.	March	April	May	June	July	Aug.	Sept.	Oct.	Nov.	Dec.
National Bureau[a]												
1948		4.19			4.28			4.32			4.38	
1949	4.37	4.43	4.42	4.43	4.40	4.42	4.41	4.43	4.34	4.39	4.38	4.41
1950	4.39	4.37	4.37	4.39	4.38	4.29	4.29	4.31	4.34	4.37	4.34	4.34
1951	4.34	4.31	4.36	4.37	4.39	4.40	4.45	4.56	4.55	4.56	4.53	4.54
1952	4.53	4.50	4.56	4.57	4.64	4.61	4.65	4.60	4.60	4.61	4.55	4.51
1953	4.60	4.61	4.60	4.60	4.62	4.68	4.76	4.85	4.84	4.86	4.86	4.87
1954	4.87	4.84	4.83	4.81	4.81	4.77	4.75	4.74	4.76	4.72	4.68	4.72
1955	4.72	4.71	4.73	4.72	4.72	4.71	4.74	4.78	4.74	4.79	4.81	4.80
1956	4.79	4.80	4.81	4.81	4.80	4.82	4.87	4.89	4.93	5.00	5.12	5.14
1957	5.26	5.39	5.47	5.52	5.48	5.49	5.48	5.47	5.52	5.60	5.64	5.67
1958	5.67	5.69	5.66	5.63	5.57	5.50	5.49	5.45	5.38	5.38	5.43	5.51
1959	5.52	5.59	5.60	5.62	5.64	5.67	5.68	5.73	5.74	5.81	5.94	5.97
1960	6.01	6.04	6.06	6.06	6.09	6.08	6.10	6.09	6.07	6.07	6.03	6.01
1961	6.02	5.96	5.94	5.85	5.83	5.81	5.78	5.77	5.79	5.76	5.74	5.75
1962	5.74	5.76	5.78	5.78	5.76	5.71	5.68	5.66	5.66	5.66	5.65	5.64
1963	5.61	5.61	5.55	5.54	5.51	5.53	5.53	5.48	5.52	5.51	5.48	5.50
Federal Home Loan Bank Board[b]												
1962												5.66
1963	5.59	5.59	5.55	5.51	5.57	5.53	5.55	5.51	5.51	5.51	5.49	5.52
1964	5.53	5.42	5.48	5.47	5.46	5.48	5.49	5.47	5.49	5.49	5.47	5.53
1965	5.49	5.53	5.48	5.47	5.50	5.49	5.47	5.47	5.50	5.53	5.55	5.54
1966	5.62	5.63	5.74	5.93	5.96	6.11	6.16	6.32	6.39	6.39	6.55	6.47
1967	6.39	6.49	6.23	6.32	6.22	6.23	6.32	6.28	6.37	6.37	6.32	6.44

[a]Covers four large companies during 1951 – 63, and one company during 1948 – 50. Contract rate adjusted for net fees paid and received, assuming prepayment in ten years.

[b]Covers forty-four companies. Contract rate on loans secured by newly built homes only.

4

The Behavior of Yields and Terms on Conventional, FHA and VA Mortgages

The relationship between different mortgage yield series is examined in this chapter. A comparison of yields on FHA and conventional mortgages illuminates some features of lender preference associated with the characteristics of these loans, especially those concerning risk. A comparison of FHA and VA yields reveals the influence of the contract rates that prevailed at different times on these loans. Comparison of yield series covering direct, correspondent and secondary market transactions reveals the influence of different types of market organization. We also examine the relationship of cyclical changes in mortgage yields to loan-value ratios and maturities on the same type of mortgage.

Relationship Between FHA and Conventional Yields: The Influence of Risk and Lender Preference

Our new data permit an analysis of changes in the relationship between FHA and conventional yields over the cycle, and over the eighteen-year period 1949–66. The dashed line on Chart 4-1, covering 1950–63, shows the differential based on the new National Bureau series. The solid line covering the period 1949–67 is based on the FHA secondary market series and the three linked conventional series used in Chart 3-2.[1] Table 4-1 shows yield differentials calculated at specific cycle peaks and troughs in both series. Since the cyclical amplitude of FHA yields is sensitive to the prepayment assumption, the conventional-FHA yield differential in this table is computed on four different prepayment assumptions.

It would generally be expected that conventionals would carry higher yields than FHAs because the latter are virtually free of default risk. The risk on conventional loans made by life insurance com-

---

[1] Yields in this chart are calculated on a uniform prepayment assumption of ten years. Data on secondary market yields are in Appendix Table 9-4.

CHART 4-1

YIELD DIFFERENTIAL BETWEEN CONVENTIONAL AND FHA LOANS, 1949–67

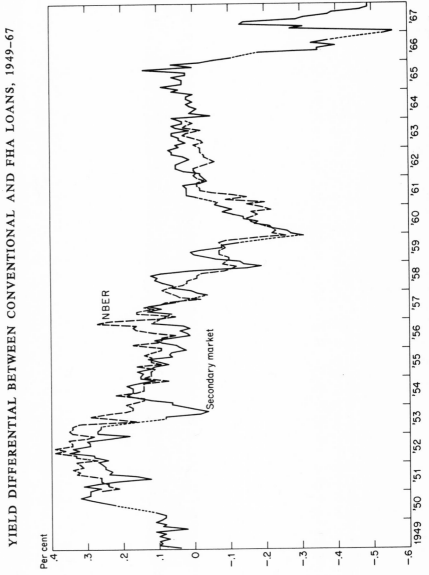

panies, however, is quite small since these loans typically carry down payments of 25 per cent or more. (Largely for this reason conventional loans by life insurance companies typically are in the lower range of yields on conventional loans generally.) For some lenders the modest risk advantage of FHAs is more than counterbalanced by other disadvantages. FHA loans have somewhat higher origination costs because of the need to comply with the insuring agency's reporting and other requirements. Higher delinquency ratios on FHAs raise servicing costs while higher foreclosure ratios are also viewed unfavorably. While financial loss on foreclosed FHAs is quite small, most life insurance companies prefer to avoid foreclosure for public relations and other reasons. In addition, conventional loans may carry prepayment penalties that are attractive to lenders, while borrowers can often be offered faster processing, and the ½ per cent insurance premium is avoided. The evidence indicates that conventionals have usually yielded more, but with some notable exceptions.

There are some suggestions in Chart 4-1 and Table 4-1 of a secular decline in the yield differential over the period 1952–59.[2] Yields declined erratically but persistently over this period. A secular decline might be expected from the favorable repayment experience on conventional mortgages, which would have reduced their risk premiums relative to federally underwritten mortgages.[3]

The yield differential rose during 1950–52, but for very special reasons. With FHA 4.50 per cent mortgages carrying premiums, the maximum contract rate on these mortgages was reduced to 4.25 per cent in April 1950. Since premiums on high-contract-rate mortgages are never large enough to reduce yields to the level of lower-contract-rate mortgages (for reasons discussed in the next section), the reduction in contract rate also reduced FHA yields and raised the yield differential. The rise in yield differential during this period can be discounted, therefore, as essentially reflecting an administrative action by the FHA. This strengthens the case for a secular decline.

The data do not reveal any tendency for the yield differential between FHA and conventional mortgages to change systematically over the cycle. Thus, the average differential at the four peaks and three troughs covered by the authorization data is about the same, as shown on page 68.

---

[2] A small part of the decline in yield differential shown in Chart 4-1 may be due to the fixed prepayment assumption used to calculate yield. See page 154.

[3] An alternative hypothesis is that the liberalization of terms on conventional mortgages during this period kept pace with the increasingly sanguine views of lenders, so that no reduction in risk premiums occurred.

TABLE 4-1

Gross Yields on FHA and Conventional Mortgages
at Specific Cycle Peaks and Troughs

FHA Conventional	Peaks				
	Jan. 1950[a] Dec. 1949[a]	Dec. 1953 Jan. 1954	March 1958 Feb. 1958	March 1960 July 1960	Dec. 1966 Nov. 1966
FHA					
Contract rate	4.50	4.49	5.25	5.75	6.00
Discount (points)	-1.57	1.38	2.47	3.52	6.80
Effective yield – 8 years	4.25	4.73	5.67	6.35	7.17
10 years	4.28	4.70	5.61	6.26	7.01
half maturity	4.28	4.69	5.57	6.17	6.80
maturity	4.33	4.65	5.51	6.10	6.67
Conventional					
Contract rate	4.60	5.02	5.75	6.12	6.55
Discount (points)	-1.27	-.96	-.37	-.13	b
Effective yield – 8 years	4.38	4.85	5.68	6.10	6.55
10 years	4.41	4.87	5.69	6.11	6.55
half maturity	4.40	4.87	5.69	6.11	6.55
maturity	4.44	4.90	5.70	6.11	6.55
Conventional less FHA					
Effective yield – 8 years	.13	.12	.01	-.25	-.62
10 years	.13	.17	.08	-.15	-.46
half maturity	.12	.18	.12	-.06	-.25
maturity	.11	.25	.19	.01	-.12

	Troughs			
	Jan. 1951 Feb. 1951	Feb. 1955 Nov. 1954	Sept. 1958 Oct. 1958	Aug. 1965 Sept. 196⁻
FHA				
Contract rate	4.27	4.50	5.25	5.25
Discount (points)	-1.21	.61	1.45	1.40
Effective yield – 8 years	4.07	4.60	5.51	5.48
10 years	4.10	4.59	5.47	5.45
half maturity	4.11	4.58	5.44	5.41
maturity	4.14	4.56	5.40	5.38
Conventional				
Contract rate	4.48	4.82	5.44	5.50
Discount (points)	-1.20	-.83	-.33	b
Effective yield – 8 years	4.27	4.68	5.39	5.50
10 years	4.29	4.70	5.40	5.50
half maturity	4.28	4.70	5.40	5.50
maturity	4.32	4.74	5.41	5.50
Conventional less FHA				
Effective yield – 8 years	.20	.08	-.12	.02
10 years	.19	.11	-.07	.05
half maturity	.17	.12	-.04	.09
maturity	.18	.18	.01	.12

Note: Data for 1951 – 60 are based on NBER authorization series. Since yields are taken from the *Mortgage Yield Table for Monthly Payment Mortgages* (Boston, 1962) rather than from our own program, the yields at ten years may differ slightly from those shown in Tables C-1 and C-2. Data covering the 1966 peak and 1965 trough are based on the FHA secondary market series and the Federal Home Loan Bank Board conventional loan series (Appendix Tables 3-2 and 9-4).

[a] Data cover one company.

[b] Assumed equal to zero to maintain comparability.

Prepayment	Peak	Trough
8 years	.00%	.05%
10 years	.06	.08
Half maturity	.09	.08
Maturity	.14	.12

However, Chart 4-1 shows that during two periods of extreme credit stringency—in late 1959–60 and in 1966—the yield differential fell sharply to a point where FHAs were yielding appreciably more than conventionals. What could account for this apparent aberration?

The most obvious possibility is a statistical accident arising from lack of statistical comparability between FHA and conventional series. The most convincing evidence against this is that the phenomenon appears in data covering individual lenders, both in 1959 and 1966. It also appears in data covering individual regions and states.

The conventional loans acquired during a period of market tightness are of somewhat higher over-all quality than those acquired in more normal periods, since lenders limit themselves to the best risks. This might cause a *decline* in the yield differential but would not explain why FHAs come to yield more.[4]

A third possibility, suggested by market practitioners, is that usury laws in some states constrained the rise in yields on conventional loans more than on FHA loans. Discounting on FHAs had become an accepted practice by 1959, but on conventionals, charges exceeding customary levels encounter borrower resistance and various kinds of institutional frictions.[5]

If this explanation was correct, we would expect to find rates on conventional mortgages rising more slowly and the margin between FHA and conventional rates increasing most sharply in states with relatively low usury ceilings. In states with high or no ceilings, in contrast, conventional rates should rise enough to maintain a margin over FHAs. Data available on a state basis for the 1959–60 period of market stringency do not support this explanation. Table 4-2

[4] The decline would be small in any case, since life insurance companies change their risk standards on conventional mortgages very little in the short run.

[5] Many lenders are reluctant to charge discounts on conventional mortgages because of adverse public relations arising from complaints by borrowers that they had been forced to pay a usurious charge in disguise. Under the FHA program, only sellers are allowed by law to pay discounts. Even though this requirement is frequently violated by adjusting transactions prices, FHA approval provides the lender with a prima facie valid defense against the charge that the borrower paid the discount.

TABLE 4-2

Yields on FHA and Conventional Home Mortgages in Selected
States, 1958 and 1960

| | First Quarter, 1958 | | | | | | First Quarter, 1960 | | | | | |
| | FHA | | Conventional | | | | FHA | | Conventional | | | |
State	Yield	No. of Loans	Yield	Contract Rate	No. of Loans	Conv. less FHA (yield)	Yield	No. of Loans	Yield	Contract Rate	No. of Loans	Conv. less FHA (yield)
6 Per Cent Usury Law												
New York	5.39	10	5.58	5.64	48	.19	5.75	1	5.87	5.88	44	.12
New Jersey	5.44	61	5.59	5.61	29	.15	6.04	10	5.94	5.94	43	-.10
Pennsylvania	5.44	69	5.48	5.57	43	.04	6.06	24	5.96	5.95	50	-.10
10 Per Cent Usury Law												
California	5.65	55	5.70	5.83	245	.05	6.27	132	6.05	6.15	178	-.22
Florida	5.65	45	5.76	5.78	26	.11	6.29	27	6.07	6.07	37	-.22
Texas	5.69	71	5.82	5.83	71	.13	6.34	72	6.15	6.15	119	-.19

Source: National Bureau of Economic Research series.

shows that in the two-year period ending in the first quarter of 1960, rates on conventional loans did not increase any more in three states with a 10 per cent usury ceiling than in three states with a 6 per cent ceiling. FHA yields came to exceed conventional yields in both groups of states, and, in fact, the margin was wider in states with high usury ceilings.

Many individual lenders must have an institutional preference for conventionals over FHAs at the same rate. Otherwise, barring differences in the timing of transactions or other statistical quirks, conventionals could *never* yield less. Discussions with lenders indicate that some do indeed prefer conventionals. Such lenders may feel that the disadvantages of FHA loans more than offset the value of insurance, particularly on conservative loans where risk is small. As noted earlier, both origination and servicing costs are somewhat higher on FHA loans while some lenders are also influenced by the higher rate of foreclosures on FHAs. Even though the FHA reimburses them, foreclosures involve a public relations cost which they prefer to avoid. In addition borrowers can be offered faster processing on conventional loans and the ½ per cent insurance premium is avoided. Also, lenders place some value on the prepayment restrictions that can be written into conventional loans. Under "normal" market conditions, the impact of lenders with an institutional preference for FHAs more than offsets that of lenders with a preference for conventionals, so that conventionals yield more. Lenders who prefer FHAs, however, tend to maintain more diversified portfolios and are sensitive to rate differentials between mortgages and bonds. Under conditions of extreme market stringency, these lenders tend to shift out of FHA mortgages. The mortgages must then be absorbed largely by lenders who prefer conventionals and will accept FHAs only at premium rates. Unfortunately, there is no way at present to test this hypothesis.

Relationship Between FHA and VA Yields: The Influence of Contract Rate

The relationship between FHA and VA yields is affected by factors bearing on their relative loan quality, and by their contract rates. Klaman noted a tendency for VA yields to be higher (prices to be

TABLE 4-3

Discounts on FHA as Compared to VA Mortgages During
Periods of Equal Maximum Contract Rate

National Bureau Series

Period	Average Contract Rate		Average Discount			FNMA Series Average Discount		
	FHA	VA	FHA	VA	VA less FHA	FHA	VA	VA less FHA
June-Dec. 1953	4.49	4.49	.8	1.5	.7	2.2	2.6	.4
1954	4.49	4.48	.9	1.5	.6	1.1	1.5	.4
1955	4.48	4.48	1.0	1.7	.7	1.2	1.8	.6
Jan.-Nov. 1956	4.48	4.49	1.7	2.2	.5	2.2	2.8	.6
1962	5.26	5.25	3.1	3.4	.3	3.2	3.3	.1
1963	5.25	5.25	1.9	2.0	.1	2.1	2.1	.0
1964						1.8	1.9	.1
1965						1.9	1.9	.0
1966						6.1	6.1	.0

Note: FNMA quotations apply to 4½ per cent mortgages during 1953 − 56, 5¼ per cent mortgages during 1962 − 65, and 5¼ to 6 per cent mortgages during 1966 (current rate used in all cases).

lower) during 1953–56 when their maximum contract rates were the same.[6] He noted that

. . . in general, contract terms—maturities, down payments, and loan-to-value ratios—have been more liberal for VA loans than for FHA loans. Lenders generally have regarded VA property appraisals also as tending to be more liberal than those made by FHA. The fact that the VA guarantee is for 60 per cent of a loan (not to exceed $7,500) and FHA insurance for 100 per cent of a loan may also have influenced investors' judgments about the quality of these mortgages.[7]

Our new data confirm that VA prices were lower (discounts were larger) during the 1953–56 period of contract rate equality (Table 4-3).[8] Such comparisons are not possible during the next five years

[6] Klaman's comparisons were based on secondary market price quotations reported by the Federal National Mortgage Association, described above.

[7] Klaman, *The Postwar Residential Mortgage Market*, pp. 90, 91.

[8] Prices are used in these comparisons because differences in maturities and expected life as between FHA and VA mortgages over the period covered were too small to have any significant effect on yield differences.

because FHA and VA contract rates differed most of the time, but during 1962–66, contract rates were again the same. In this later period, the price differential was negligible. This may reflect the fact that FHA terms became more liberal during the intervening period relative to VA terms. By 1964, average down payments were only a few percentage points lower on FHA than on VA mortgages, and FHA maturities were several years longer. It is possible also that lenders became less concerned with terms during this period.

At various times, FHA mortgages have carried a higher contract rate than VAs, and this has affected their relative yield. In part, this is due to the uncertain yield realized on a mortgage that is not priced at par; the yield depends not only on the contract rate and the size of the premium or discount but also on the life of the mortgage, which is not known in advance. Most mortgages are prepaid in full well before maturity. The more a mortgage deviates from par, the more important is variability in life as a determinant of realized yield.[9] Lender reaction to this uncertainty will affect relative yields.

It is quite possible that lenders will react differently to yield uncertainty when mortgages sell at premiums than when they sell at discounts from par. When mortgages sell at discounts, yield is a decreasing function of life, and the lowest possible yield, which is realized if the mortgage runs to maturity, is not much lower than the yield at some intermediate "expected" life based on past experience or reasonable expectations. The maximum yield in this case approaches infinity as life approaches zero. This is illustrated by the top line in Figure 4-1. When mortgages carry premiums, on the other hand, yield is an increasing function of life, as illustrated by the lower line on Figure 4-1; the lowest possible yield approaches minus infinity as life approaches zero. The maximum yield, which is realized if the mortgage goes to maturity, is not much higher than the expected yield.

The consequence of miscalculating mortgage life is thus quite different when mortgages sell at premiums than when they sell at discounts. When mortgages carry premiums, an error in the wrong direction can be very serious, since yield can be zero or negative. If the market is heavily influenced by conservative lenders, concerned with the "worst that can happen," the premium paid on high-contract-rate mortgages may not be large enough to equalize yield with low-contract-rate mortgages.

[9] See Jack M. Guttentag, "Mortgage Interest Rates: Trends and Structure," p. 128.

FIGURE 4-1

YIELD ON A 5½ PER CENT THIRTY-YEAR MORTGAGE
PRICED AT 95 AND 105

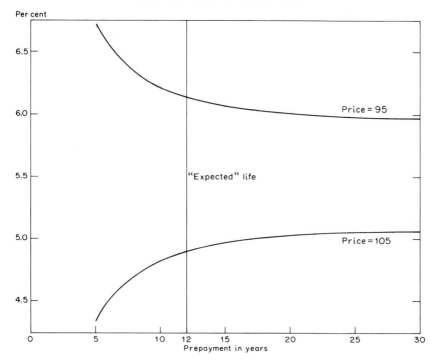

When mortgages carry discounts, in contrast, no serious conse-
quences arise from a mistake in estimating mortgage life. Other factors,
however, including public relations aspects of accepting discounts from
borrowers, may influence the yield.[10]

The evidence examined here can be divided broadly into two phases,
in which, for periods of varying length, the FHA contract rate was

[10] Tax treatment of discounts and premiums does not affect the relative yield of
mortgages carrying different contract rates. For tax purposes, discounts and premiums are considered income rather than capital gains. Typically, the discounts
and premiums of the current year are spread out over a period equal to the estimated life. If the correct estimated life is used to calculate yield and to amortize
discounts and premiums, mortgages with different contract rates carrying the
same before-tax yield will also have the same after-tax yield. If the estimate of
life for tax purposes is, for example, too short, tax payments will be accelerated
but the impact on after-tax yields would be negligible.

higher than the VA rate. These periods are prior to mid-1952, when FHAs and VAs carried premiums, and 1957–61, when they carried discounts.

The Case of Premiums

The data[11] confirm the supposition advanced above that lenders are reluctant to pay a premium on a high-contract-rate mortgage large enough to equalize its yield with a lower-contract-rate mortgage. Prior to April 1950, FHA Section 203 mortgages carried a maximum rate of 4.50 per cent, while the VA rate was 4 per cent. One large life insurance company paid an average premium of 0.8 per cent for VAs during this period and 1.6 per cent for FHAs, producing a yield spread of .37 per cent in favor of the high-rate FHAs (Table 4-4). To put the matter somewhat differently, if prepayment occurred in ten years, which is the assumption used in the yield calculation, FHAs would have required a premium of about 4.0 points to equalize their yield with that on VAs.[12] The FHA rate was only .14 per cent below the conventional rate in this period.

In April 1950, the FHA rate was reduced to 4.25 per cent, and the yield on FHAs immediately fell relative to VAs and conventionals. Chart 4-1 shows a sharp rise in the yield differential of conventionals over FHAs following the rate reduction on FHAs. In the sixteen months ending April 1952, the FHA yield for life insurance companies was .08 per cent lower than in the prior period, while the yields on 4 per cent VAs and on conventionals were higher by .15 per cent and .07 per cent, respectively (see Table 4-4). This shift in the spread can be attributed largely to the decline in the FHA rate. Nevertheless, the 4.25 per cent FHAs continued to yield more than 4 per cent VAs.[13]

It may be asked why, if mortgages carry premiums, the contract rate is not bid down by competition? The rate set by law or regulation on FHAs and VAs is, after all, a maximum rate and not a minimum. Any extended discussion of this would go well beyond the scope of this paper, but clearly the explanation is rooted in the imperfect char-

[11] Publishable data prior to 1951 are limited to one large company. Fragmentary data from other sources, however, confirm the relationship shown in the table.

[12] A shorter prepayment period would tend to reduce the yield disparity. Equal yields, however, imply prepayment in less than two years.

[13] After an adjustment for "quality," the spread would have been wider. It will be recalled that in 1953–56, when contract rates were the same, VAs yielded more.

TABLE 4-4

Premiums and Yields on Mortgages
Authorized By Life Insurance Companies,
January 1949-April 1950 and January 1951-April 1952

	January 1949-April 1950[a]			January 1951-April 1952		
	Contract Rate	Premium	Effective Yield	Contract Rate	Premium	Effective Yield
FHA	4.49	1.6	4.26	4.26	.5	4.18
VA	4.00	.8	3.89	4.00	-.3	4.04
Conventional	4.58	1.3	4.40	4.63	1.1	4.47

[a]Data limited to one company.
Source: National Bureau of Economic Research survey.

acter of the residential mortgage market at the primary (origination) level. Among the relevant factors would be the following.

1. Most mortgage borrowers are ignorant of the market and unwilling or unable to shop.[14]

2. An apparent sanction is provided the maximum rate by the federal agencies; borrowers are encouraged to believe that the Government has set *the* rate, rather than merely the maximum rate.

3. Mortgage lenders tend to view rate-cutting as an "unethical practice." One large lender who did cut rates below the maximum in the period when FHAs carried large premiums was taken severely to task by other lenders.[15] Mortgage lenders tended to view the maximum allowable rate much as personal finance companies view the legal rate ceiling on small loans, namely, as a customary rate that is in the best interest of all lenders to observe.

4. Builders are unwilling to bargain for a lower contract rate; the builder could usually command part of the premium from the high-rate mortgage. This might or might not be reflected in lower house prices.

It would seem from the above analysis that from the standpoint of borrower interest, contract rates on FHA and VA mortgages should never be a high enough for these mortgages to command premiums. As a matter of fact, they have not commanded premiums since 1953.

The Case of Discounts

Beginning in 1957, following the 1953–56 period of contract-rate equality between FHA and VA mortgages, rate differences arose again. For this and later periods, price data on FHAs and VAs are available from FNMA as well as from the new NBER survey. The NBER data cover loans authorized by large life insurance companies, while the former are largely based on over-the-counter sales by mortgage companies, mainly to life insurance companies and mutual savings banks. The two sources show only modest price differences on FHA mortgages, but very substantial differences on VAs. Thus, during February–July 1957, NBER series show VAs carrying a discount of three points, while the FNMA series show VAs carrying a discount

[14] For some evidence on this, see Housing and Home Finance Agency, "Residential Mortgage Financing, Jacksonville, Florida, First Six Months of 1950," *Housing Research Paper No. 23,* Washington, D.C., 5 December 1952, pp. 30–33.

[15] See H. A. Schaaf, "Federal Interest Rate Policy on Insured and Guaranteed Mortgages," unpublished Ph.D. dissertation, University of California, Berkeley, 1955, p. 135.

TABLE 4-5

Discounts on FHA and VA Mortgages as Reported in NBER
and FNMA Series, Selected Periods
(percentage points)

	NBER		FNMA		FNMA less NBER	
	FHA	VA	FHA	VA	FHA	VA
Feb. 1957-July 1957	2.4	3.0	2.9	7.0	.5	4.0
Oct. 1957-March 1958	2.3	3.2	2.6	9.2	.3	6.0
Sept. 1958-June 1959	2.5	4.9	3.1	7.2	.6	2.3
Dec. 1959-Jan. 1960	3.4	5.3	3.8	7.9	.4	2.6
Dec. 1960-Jan. 1961	2.9	4.6	2.4	6.6	-.5	2.0
April 1961-Aug. 1961	2.6	4.5	2.2	4.3	-.4	-.2

Source: National Bureau of Economic Research, Federal National Mortgage Association.

of seven points (Table 4-5). As a result, for the large life insurance companies, the higher-contract-rate FHAs yielded more, while for the lenders covered by the FNMA data, the lower-contract-rate VAs yielded more (Table 4-6). The yield difference was largest during the period October 1957–March 1958, when the contract rate difference between FHAs and VAs was largest (.75 per cent). During this period, FHAs authorized by the life insurance companies yielded .62 per cent *more* than VAs, while on loans sold by mortgage companies FHAs yielded .23 per cent *less* than VAs.

When VA mortgages carried lower contract rates than FHAs, the large life insurance companies reduced their VA volume but took a limited number at relatively small discounts. This action reflected a widespread view, in Congress and elsewhere, that large discounts on VA mortgages were unethical. Klaman noted that "large financial intermediaries, in their widely acknowledged role as public trustees, have been less willing to risk public censure than to ignore the facts of market forces."[16] The result of this policy was, in effect, to create two markets for VA mortgages: a rationed low-discount market by large life insurance companies (and perhaps other lenders with similar compunctions), and a "free" market where discounts rose to the level necessary to clear the market. It is ironical that the public pressures on large institutions to limit discounts on VA mortgages, by causing them

[16] Klaman, p. 89.

TABLE 4-6

Gross Yield on FHA and VA Mortgages as Reported in NBER and FNMA
Series, Selected Periods
(per cent)

Period	Maximum Contract Rate			Gross Yield					
				NBER[a]			FNMA[b]		
	FHA	VA	FHA less VA	FHA	VA	FHA less VA	FHA	VA	FHA less VA
Feb. 1957-July 1957	5.00	4.50	.50	5.33	4.93	.40	5.43	5.52	-.09
Oct. 1957-March 1958	5.25	4.50	.75	5.58	4.96	.62	5.63	5.86	-.23
Sept. 1958-June 1959	5.25	4.75	.50	5.60	5.44	.16	5.69	5.79	-.10
Dec. 1959-Jan. 1960	5.75	5.25	.50	6.19	6.01	.18	6.31	6.40	-.09
Dec. 1960-Jan. 1961	5.75	5.25	.50	6.15	5.91	.24	6.09	6.21	-.12
April 1961-Aug. 1961	5.50	5.25	.25	5.88	5.89	-.01	5.82	5.86	-.04

[a]Yields are calculated from *Mortgage Yield Table for Monthly Payment Mortgages* and may differ slightly from those shown in Table C-2.

[b]Assumes prepayment in ten years and maturity equal to the average on all FHA and VA home loans on new properties during the period indicated.

Source: National Bureau of Economic Research, Federal National Mortgage Association.

to sharply reduce their VA volume, had the effect of increasing pressure on VA discounts in the "free" market.

There are indications that life insurance company attitudes toward discounting underwent a considerable change during 1958–59, in the sense that they began to accept the discounts required to bring VA yields into an appropriate relation to FHA yields. Comparing the October 1957–March 1958 and the September 1958–June 1959 periods, VA discounts rose by 1.7 points in the NBER series and declined by 2.0 points in the FNMA series (Table 4-5). Perhaps even more dramatic was the shift in the FHA-VA yield relationship in the NBER series (Table 4-6). Yields on VA mortgages rose by .48 per cent as VA discounts rose appreciably despite a rise in contract rate (4.50 to 4.75 per cent). Yields on FHA mortgages rose by only .02 per cent, as discounts on FHA mortgages of constant contract rate increased only slightly.

Evidently, by 1961, the market had learned to live with discounts. During April–August 1961, price quotations on VA loans were about the same in the FNMA and NBER series, and differences between FHA and VA yields were small. However, the contract-rate difference between FHAs and VAs was only .25 per cent during this period; it is not clear how the market would have reacted to a .75 per cent difference. Since 1961, contract rates have been the same.

There is, however, additional evidence of a change in lenders' attitudes toward discounting during 1959. The evidence consists of FNMA price quotations, following a change in the FHA or VA maximum contract rate, on old mortgages carrying the old rate. After the contract rate is changed, new commitments are at the new rate, but there will also be some overhang of uncommitted mortgages carrying the old rate for which mortgage companies or other originators must find buyers. FNMA continues to report prices on mortgages carrying the old rate for as long as there is any significant activity in them. During such periods of dual coverage, yield comparisons are possible between old and new mortgages carrying different contract rates (Table 4-7).

These observations reveal a sharp decline during 1959 in the yield on a low-contract-rate mortgage relative to the yield on a high-contract-rate mortgage, indicating a greater willingness to accept discounts as an offset to a lower contract rate. While the yield differentials are sensitive

TABLE 4-7

Prices and Yields on Current and "Old" FHA and VA Home Mortgages, Selected Periods

Period	Mortgage (per cent)	Estimated Average Maturity	Average Price over Period	Average Yield Prepayment in		Yield Differential Prepayment in	
				10 Years	Half Maturity	10 Years	Half Maturity
May 1953-Jan. 1955 (18 observations)[a]	FHA 4¼		96.2	4.80	4.76		
	FHA 4½	23	98.6	4.70	4.68	.10	.08
	VA 4		94.4	4.81	4.70		
	VA 4½	25	98.3	4.74	4.72	.07	-.02
Dec. 1956-June 1957 (7 observations)	FHA 4½		93.4	5.47	5.35		
	FHA 5	25	97.3	5.39	5.34	.08	.01
Aug. 1957-Dec. 1958 (17 observations)	FHA 5		95.5	5.65	5.54		
	FHA 5¼	27	97.7	5.58	5.52	.07	.02
April-Dec. 1958 (9 observations)	VA 4½		92.1	5.64	5.43		
	VA 4¾	28	94.3	5.57	5.41	.07	.02
July-Sept. 1959 (3 observations)	VA 4¾		91.5	5.98	5.73		
	VA 5¼	29	94.8	6.00	5.85	-.02	-.12

Period	Contract rate	Maturity	Price				
Oct. 1959-March 1960 (6 observations)	FHA 5¼		93.0	6.27	6.07		
	FHA 5¾	29	96.2	6.30	6.19	-.03	-.12
Feb.-May 1961 (4 observations)	FHA 5½		97.2	5.90	5.82		
	FHA 5¾	30	98.6	5.95	5.91	-.05	-.09
June 1961-Feb. 1962 (9 observations)	FHA 5¼		96.3	5.78	5.67		
	FHA 5½		97.8	5.81	5.75	-.03	-.08
	FHA 5¾	30	99.4	5.83	5.82	-.05	-.15
March-April 1966 (2 observations)	FHA 5¼		92.6	6.33	6.10		
	FHA 5½	30	94.5	6.30	6.13	.03	-.02
May-June 1966 (2 observations)	FHA 5½		92.6	6.59	6.36		
	FHA 5¾	30	94.6	6.54	6.38	.05	-.02

Note: The high contract rate mortgage indicates the current maximum rate during each period. Maturities are for all FHA or VA loans on new homes during the period indicated.

[a]No observations for July, September or October 1953.

Source: Federal National Mortgage Association.

to the maturity and assumed prepayment, the break in 1959 is clearly evident on any reasonable assumptions.[17]

Relationship Between Direct, Correspondent and Secondary Market Yields: The Influence of Market Organization

In Chapter 3, it was suggested that differences in the cyclical sensitivity of mortgage and bond yields might be explained in terms of differences in the organization of the bond and mortgage markets. Here we consider whether cyclical sensitivity is related to differences in substructures within the mortgage market. We compare direct with correspondent loans and authorization series with secondary market series.

Direct versus Correspondents Loans

Yields on correspondent loans show a tendency to lag yields on direct loans as shown in Table 4-8.

Chart 4-2 shows that the direct loan series also contains two short intracyclical movements (during the second half of 1952 and the first half of 1957) that follow similar movements in government bond yields but which do not appear in the correspondent series. Correspondent lending is thus evidently less sensitive; what is the reason?

As noted in Chapter 6, the transfer of a mortgage between life insurance company and correspondent is a market transaction rather than a transfer between agent and principal. Nevertheless, the parties to the transactions may have a more or less permanent relationship. The mortgages purchased by the company will be serviced by the correspondent, and, also, the parties to the transaction contemplate additional transactions in the future. It is not surprising that this continuing relationship exercises a moderating influence on yield.

1. The life insurance company generally sets a rate at which it will purchase loans from its correspondents. Although this rate is theoretically subject to change without notice, frequent changes may be disruptive to those correspondents who find it necessary to extend their own commitments before obtaining the life insurance company's commitment. As a result, the companies do not change their buying rate

---

[17] The partial reversal in 1966 probably reflects the marked slowdown in mortgage repayments in that year, which could have caused lenders to assume a longer prepayment period.

TABLE 4-8

Lead of Direct Over Correspondent Loans
(number of months)

	FHA	Conventional
Peaks		
1953-54	4	2
1957-58	2	-3
1960	6	2
Troughs		
1953	4	4
1954-55	2	7
1958	-1	1

with every wiggle in the capital markets. By keeping their buying rate more stable than the general market around them, they tend to moderate some of the yield changes on correspondent loans.

2. When the life insurance company raises its buying rate and the correspondent is heavily committed at the old rate the company may

CHART 4-2

GROSS YIELD ON CONVENTIONAL LOANS, 1951–63:
DIRECT VERSUS CORRESPONDENT SERIES

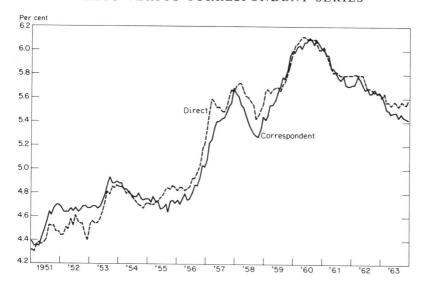

or may not, as an accommodation, extend its own commitment at the same terms as the correspondent's commitment, depending on the nature of the company-correspondent relationship. The company may limit this privilege to certain correspondents, perhaps to "good producers" operating under allotments. (When the buying rate declines between the time a correspondent extends its own commitment and the time it obtains a commitment from the company, the correspondent might pass the higher yield along, but this probably happens less often.) A tendency to "bail out" overextended correspondents also exercises a moderating influence on yield changes.

3. The company may grant a correspondent "precommitment authority," in which the terms in the company's commitment will as a matter of course hark back to the correspondents' commitment (see the discussion in Chapter 6).

A company-by-company analysis suggests that the influence on transactions between company and correspondent of the factors discussed above varies with the size of the company's correspondent loan operation. The larger the volume, the more likely that the company will provide the sole or major outlet for a given correspondent and the greater the pressure on the company to assure continuity in the correspondent's operation. This concern may be reflected in any of the factors discussed above: a relatively stable buying rate, "bail-out" operations following a rate increase, or delegation of precommitment authority, all of which tend to generate sluggish yield series. Precommitment authority is, indeed, a formalized expression of the company's obligation, and it tends to make "bail-out" operations and stable buying rates unnecessary. Thus, it was found that yield series of one company, which adopted the policy of granting correspondents precommitment authority at a point during the period covered by our study, were no more sluggish after this than before. The new policy merely formalized a behavioral pattern that had existed earlier (and which had generated sluggish yield series earlier) on an ad hoc basis.

The moderating influence of the correspondent relationship on rates may be compared with that of the so-called "customer relationship" between a commercial bank and a business customer who is both depositor and borrower.[18] In both cases, transactions are multidimensional, there is a continuing relationship over time, and the relationship

---

[18] See Hodgman, *Commercial Bank Loan and Investment Policy*, Chapters X and XI.

may cause the lender at times to extend credit at rates below what he would expect other customers to pay.

Secondary Market versus Authorization Series

The FHA secondary market series[19] shows a clear tendency to lead the combined authorization and correspondent loan series at turning points (see Table 4-9).[20] The evidence on direct loan series at turning points is not so clear. Although the secondary market series leads at four of the six turning points, it lags at the other two by substantial periods. Nevertheless, by the alternative sensitivity measure (yield changes at specified periods after turning points in long-term governments), the secondary market series ranks first, the direct loan series ranks second, and the correspondent loan series ranks third at four of five turning points (Table 4-10).

The somewhat greater sensitivity of the secondary market series appears not to be due to residual recording lag in the direct loan series (see Chapter 7). Presumably, therefore, it is due to differences in market organization. The secondary market series reflects the activities of lenders who are not as committed as life insurance companies to maintaining continuity in the supply of funds, who have no direct contact with builders or mortgagors, and who cull the market for the best available deal on any given day. For these reasons, it is likely that the secondary market series will be more sensitive both to small shifts in the market equilibrium rate and to factors generating temporary disequilibrium, such as an unforeseen glut that can be moved only at bargain prices.

Changes in Loan-Value Ratios and Maturities

Although there has been a great deal of theorizing about short-run changes in nonrate credit terms, which are associated in the literature

[19] The secondary market series is based on price quotations compiled by the Federal Housing Administration, as noted in Chapter 1. Technical differences between the secondary market series and the authorization series, beyond the differences in market organization at issue here, are discussed in Chapter 9. These differences probably do not affect the relative cyclical behavior of the series.

[20] The early-1951 trough, which is used in Table 4-1 and elsewhere in this study, cannot be employed with confidence here because the turning point in the direct and correspondent loan series may have occurred before January 1951, when the series began. In its stead we use a secondary trough in early 1953.

TABLE 4-9

Turning Points in Effective Yield on FHA Home Mortgages;
Secondary Market and Authorization Series, 1951-63

Peak or Trough	Secondary Market	Authorization			Secondary Market Lead Over Authorization (months)		
		All	Direct	Correspondent	All	Direct	Correspondent
T	April 1953	April 1953	Dec. 1952	April 1953	0	-4	0
P	Oct. 1953	Dec. 1953	Nov. 1953	March 1954	2	1	5
T	March 1955	Feb. 1955	Oct. 1954	Dec. 1954	-1	-5	-3
P	Dec. 1957	March 1958	Feb. 1958	April 1958	3	2	4
T	Aug. 1958	Sept. 1958	Oct. 1958	Sept. 1958	1	2	1
P	Feb. 1960	March 1960	May 1960	Nov. 1960	1	3	9
Average					1	0	3

Changes in Yields on FHA Authorization Series Covering Direct and Correspondent Loans, and on FHA Secondary Market Series Following Turning Points in U.S. Government Bond Yields

Turning Points in Government Bond Yields	Number of Months After Turning Point	Authorization				Secondary Market	
		Correspondent		Direct			
		Yield Change	Sensitivity Rank	Yield Change	Sensitivity Rank	Yield Change	Sensitivity Rank
Troughs							
July 1954	+5	-6		+1		-1	
	+10	-8	(3)	+6	(1)	+3	(2)
	+15	+2		+18		+14	
April 1958	+5	-13		-19		-16	
	+10	+10	(2)	+3	(3)	+11	(1)
	+15	+19		+8		+22	
Peaks							
July 1953[a]	+4	+15		+15		+18	
	+8	+20	(3)	+9	(2)	+3	(1)
	+12	+11		+2		-10	
Nov. 1957[a]	+3	+2		+5		-4	
	+6	-2	(3)	-5	(2)	-22	(1)
	+9	-10		-16		-31	
Jan. 1960	+5	+4		+1		-2	
	+10	+4	(3)	-6	(2)	-15	(1)
	+15	-22		-27		-43	

[a]Because data are not available on secondary market series for June 1953 or October 1957, the month following the turning point in government bond yields was used.

with changes in credit rationing and "availability,"[21] little has been known about the actual behavior of terms over time because of the sparsity of data. Only for VA mortgages had there been monthly series over any extended period, and these loans comprised a progressively diminishing share of the total residential market.[22] Our new data provide insight into the behavior of loan-value ratios and maturities on all three types of mortgages, although for only one major lender group.

1. *Secular Change*. Loan-value ratios have risen and maturities have lengthened on both federally underwritten (particularly FHA) and conventional mortgages throughout the period since World War II. On federally underwritten loans, the main factor underlying the trend has been legislative liberalization of maximum allowable terms. On conventional loans, legal limits have been liberalized for some lenders and favorable repayment experience has encouraged them to use the new authority. Herzog and Earley have extensively documented this change and so it will not be examined in detail here.[23]

During 1951–63 the large life insurance companies in our series lengthened considerably the maturities on all three types of mortgages, and kept pace with the lengthening done by other lenders (see Table 4-11). In contrast, loan-value ratios on conventional loans by life insurance companies did not rise as much as they did on conventional loans by savings and loan associations. (This probably reflects the greater constraint of legal ceilings on life insurance companies; none of the four companies in our survey could go above 75 per cent, whereas after 1958, federally charted savings and loan associations could under certain conditions go as high as 90 per cent.) Loan-value ratios on VA loans by life insurance companies didn't rise much either, but these ratios were very high at the beginning of the period. Only on FHA loans did the rise in loan-value ratios for life insurance companies keep pace with the rise for other lenders.

2. *Cyclical Changes*. Cyclical changes in terms are affected by changes in supply and demand for mortgage credit and by changes in

[21] See Jack Guttentag, "Credit Availability, Interest Rates, and Monetary Policy," *Southern Economic Journal,* January 1960; and Richard F. Muth, "Interest Rates, Contract Terms, and the Allocation of Mortgage Funds," *The Journal of Finance,* March 1962.

[22] A series on VA downpayments is shown in Guttentag, "The Short Cycle in Residential Construction, 1946–59," p. 282; and in Leo Grebler, *Housing Issues in Economic Stabilization Policy,* pp. 118–120.

[23] John P. Herzog and James S. Earley, *Home Mortgage Delinquency and Foreclosure,* New York, NBER, 1970, pages 6–13.

TABLE 4-11

Average Maturities and Loan-Value Ratios in 1951 and 1963,
Life Insurance Companies and All Lenders

	Maturity		Increase		Loan-Value Ratio		Increase	
	1951	1963	Years	Per Cent	1951	1963	Points	Per Cent
FHA								
Life insurance cos.	21.0	29.3	8.3	39.5	81.3	93.6	12.3	15.1
All lenders (new homes)	23.4	31.0	7.6	32.5	82.5	92.7	10.2	12.4
All lenders (existing homes)	21.1	27.9	6.8	32.2	73.6	92.5	18.9	25.7
VA								
Life insurance cos.	24.0	29.5	5.5	23.0	96.4	97.6	1.2	1.2
All lenders (primary, new homes)	24.0	29.3	5.3	22.1	89.6	97.6	8.0	8.9
All lenders (primary, existing homes)	18.2	27.3	9.1	50.0	80.7	95.8	15.1	18.7
Conventional								
Life insurance cos.	18.1	25.9	7.8	43.1	62.4	70.0	7.6	12.2
Savings and loan (new construction)	16.2	23.9	7.7	47.5	65.5	77.0	11.5	17.6
Savings and loan (home purchase)	13.6	20.2	6.6	48.5	63.6	75.6	12.0	18.9

Note: Figures are weighted averages except those applying to savings and loan associations, which are estimated medians. Data on life insurance companies are from the National Bureau of Economic Research survey. Other averages are from John P. Herzog and James S. Earley, *Home Mortgage Delinquency and Foreclosure*, New York, NBER, 1970, Tables 1 and 2.

legal lending limits imposed on institutional lenders, which were quite important in the 1951–63 period. The secular changes already referred to must be accounted for in any interpretation of cyclical changes.

Mainly we will focus on the relationship between changes in terms and changes in yields. Terms are usually believed to change in such a way as to reinforce the effect on demand of changes in rates, i.e., when yields fall, loan-value ratios rise, maturities lengthen, and so on. Two hypotheses have been advanced to support this expectation. One, the "credit-rationing" hypothesis, assumes that shifts in lenders' loan-offer functions involve changes in both rates and terms. When lenders have more money to lend, they will offer lower rates *and* higher loan-value ratios.[24] An alternative hypothesis focuses on changes in borrower mix at different interest rate levels. This hypothesis assumes that loan-offer functions change only with respect to rates. Changes in rates, however, change the composition of demand among borrowers with different preferences for using borrowed funds. Thus, if lenders have more funds to lend and reduce rates, borrowers with high loan-value and long maturity preferences are attracted into the market and average terms become more liberal.[25]

In general, the evidence covering life insurance companies during 1951–63 is consistent with the expectations arising from the two hypotheses.

1. On conventional loans, maturities rose during periods of rising yields as well as during periods of falling yields, but they rose at a much faster rate during periods of declining yields [26] (Chart 4-3 and

[24] See Guttentag, "Credit Availability, . . ."

[25] See Muth. Note that both hypotheses offer the possibility of terms moving to offset rather than reinforce changes in rates under certain conditions (where changes in demand are the principal dynamic factor in the market). Under the Guttentag version of the credit-rationing hypothesis, such an offsetting movement can occur if changes in demand are so large that they cause a pronounced shift in lender's risk functions—that is, in the risk premium associated with loans having given characteristics. Under the Muth hypothesis, an offsetting movement can occur if demand changes result from a shift in the marginal returns schedule of potential borrowers arising from any factor affecting the demand for owner-occupied housing. Guttentag, although not necessarily Muth, views the offsetting case as atypical.

[26] The liberalization of terms on conventional loans during the 1951–54 period of rising yields may have been affected by relaxation of credit controls under Regulation X. As shown on the chart, these relaxations occurred in September 1951, June 1952 (on loan-value ratios only), and September 1952 (when the

CHART 4-3

LOAN-VALUE RATIO AND MATURITY ON
CONVENTIONAL LOANS, 1951–63
(THREE-MONTHS AVERAGE)

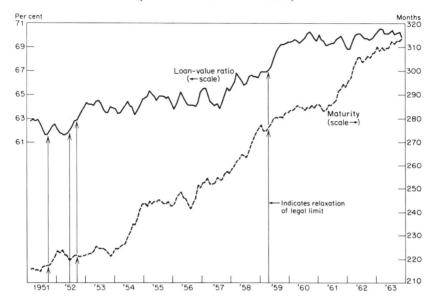

Table 3-2). A pronounced cyclical pattern appears after adjustment for trend, as shown in Chart 4-4. There is hardly any cyclical pattern at all in loan-value ratios, probably because of the dampening influence of low ceilings.[27]

In April 1959, the maximum loan-value ratio on conventional loans was raised from $66\frac{2}{3}$ per cent to 75 per cent, and the maximum maturity was extended from twenty-five to thirty years for two of the companies in our survey. This was a period of rapidly rising yields and increasing tightness in the capital markets. The extension of ma-

regulation was suspended). The effect probably was quite small, however, because most conventional loans made by life insurance companies prior to Regulation X fell within the limits of the regulation.

[27] Loan-value ratios may be subject to bias arising from discrepancies between appraised values and sales prices. If, e.g., lenders are "conservative" in raising appraised values during a period of rising construction and prices, loan-value ratios will rise less than loan-price ratios. It is not clear whether this factor is of any real importance.

CHART 4-4

MATURITY ON CONVENTIONAL LOANS AS PER CENT OF
TREND, 1951–63

(THREE-MONTHS AVERAGE)

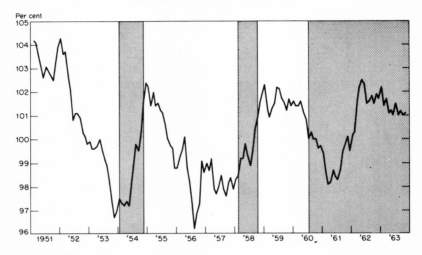

NOTE: Shaded areas are periods of declining yields.

turity had no noticeable effect since the existing twenty-five-year limit
was within the range of maturities generally available in the market at
the time. The loan-value ratio, however, immediately reflected the increase in the limit because the existing 66⅔ limit was well below the
loan ratios available from savings and loan associations.

2. Maturities and loan-value ratios on FHA loans were strongly
affected by the very frequent changes in legal maximum terms that
occurred during the 1951–63 period. As indicated in Chart 4-5, hardly
any cyclical phase does not include some such change. Little can be
said, therefore, about the cyclical behavior of terms on FHA mortgages
in response to market forces alone.

3. In contrast to FHA and conventional loans, terms on VA mortgages show a rough cyclical pattern: liberalization during periods of
declining yields and restriction during periods of rising yields (Chart
4-6). Maximum allowable terms on VA loans were also revised, although not as frequently as on FHA loans, and the VA sample is thin
during certain periods. Nevertheless, allowing for these influences does

CHART 4-5

LOAN-VALUE RATIO AND MATURITY ON FHA LOANS,
1951–63

(THREE-MONTHS AVERAGE)

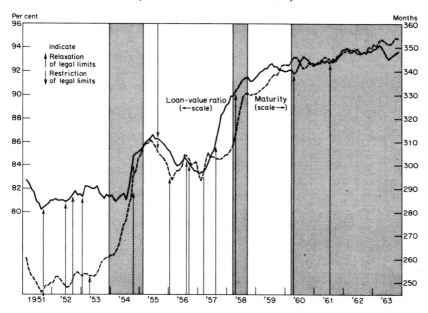

NOTE: Shaded areas are periods of declining yields. In 1957, the relaxation of legal limits applies only to the loan-value ratio; in 1961, it applies to both loan-value ratio and maturity.

not change the conclusion. An important exception, however, is the 1960–63 period of yield decline when loan-value ratios declined and maturities were roughly level.

4. Chart 4-7 shows quite marked cyclical fluctuations in weighted average loan-value ratios and maturities on all mortgages; much of this variability was due to shifts in the mix. Table 4-12 shows actual cyclical changes in average loan-value ratios and maturities on all mortgages, and changes calculated on an assumption of constant composition.[28] The difference in peak-trough changes using actual and

[28] Each peak-trough change is calculated on the assumption that the composition at the trough is the same as at the peak, and each trough-peak change is calculated on the assumption that the composition at the peak is the same as at the trough.

CHART 4-6

LOAN-VALUE RATIO AND MATURITY ON VA LOANS,
1951–63

(THREE-MONTHS AVERAGE)

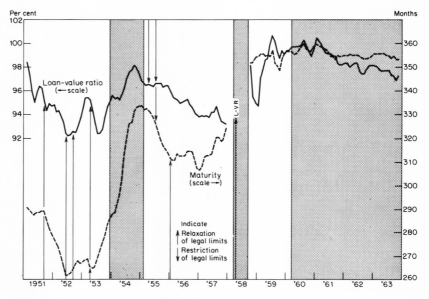

NOTE: Shaded areas are periods of declining yields.

constant weights thus shows the effect of changes in mix during that phase. As an example, the average maturity declined by 9.0 months during the 1951–54 rise in yield, but since the decline would have been only 1.2 months if composition had not changed, the difference, or 7.8, was due to a shift in mix.

Changes in mix were in the direction of tightening credit during each of the three periods of rise in yields, although in the 1958–60 period, the shift was not large enough to offset the easing that occurred separately on each type of mortgage. Shifts in mix were in the direction of easing in the first two periods of yield decline but not in the third (1960–63) period. Thus, shifts in mix usually but not invariably reinforced the effects of changes in yields.

Therefore, the evidence covering life insurance companies is broadly consistent with the hypothesis that over the cycle, terms will move to reinforce the effect of yields, but this pattern can be suppressed or dis-

CHART 4-7

LOAN-VALUE RATIO AND MATURITY ON ALL
RESIDENTIAL LOANS, 1951–63

(THREE-MONTHS AVERAGE)

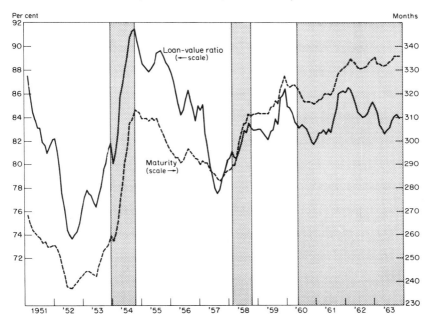

NOTE: Shaded areas are periods of declining yields.

rupted by a number of influences. Thus, the expected cyclical changes
in terms were constrained on conventional mortgages by relatively low
legal ceilings on loan-value ratios, and by the thrust of secular liberalization on maturities; the expected pattern on FHA mortgages was
disrupted by frequent changes in legal ceilings on both loan-value
ratios and maturities. The expected pattern revealed itself on VA mortgages but, during part of the 1961–63 period, the life insurance companies were virtually out of this market. Shifts in the mix of the three
types of mortgages usually changed average terms in the expected direction, sometimes by a substantial amount.

TABLE 4-12

Changes in Maturities and Loan-Value Ratios on All Mortgages During Periods of Cyclical Rise and Decline in Mortgage Yields, 1953-63

Periods of Rise in Yields

	1951-54		1954-58		1958-60		Average Per Month
	Change	Per Month	Change	Per Month	Change	Per Month	
Changes in Maturity (months)							
Actual weights	-9.00	-.28	-24.10	-.60	11.70	.62	-.24
Constant weights	-1.20	-.04	-2.60	-.07	14.70	.77	.12
Changes in Loan-Value Ratio (percentage points)							
Actual weights	-5.70	-.18	-10.30	-.26	0.20	.01	-.17
Constant weights	-1.90	-.03	-3.20	-.08	1.40	.07	-.04

Periods of Decline in Yields

	1954		1958		1960-63		Average Per Month
	Change	Per Month	Change	Per Month	Change	Per Month	
Changes in Maturity (months)							
Actual weights	53.90	5.39	21.60	2.70	13.40	.33	1.48
Constant weights	33.50	3.35	19.20	2.40	15.30	.32	1.13
Changes in Loan-Value Ratio (percentage points)							
Actual weights	9.60	.96	2.00	.25	0.60	.01	.20
Constant weights	2.10	.21	1.10	.14	1.20	.03	.07

Notes to Table 4-12

Notes:　Changes are calculated from three-month averages centered on turning points in weighted total yields. Terminal date for the 1960 – 63 decline is November 1963.

Source:　National Bureau of Economic Research.

Yields on Bonds and Mortgages at Reference Cycle Peaks and Troughs

Peaks

	July 1953	July 1957	May 1960	Average
Mortgages				
Conventional	4.76	5.48	6.09	
FHA	4.53	5.38	6.28	
Conv. less FHA	.23	.10	-.17	.05
Bonds				
Corporate Baa	3.86	4.73	5.28	
Corporate Aaa	3.28	3.99	4.46	
Baa less Aaa	.58	.74	.82	.71
State and local Baa	3.60	4.29	4.31	
State and local Aaa	2.56	3.17	3.34	
Baa less Aaa	1.04	1.12	.97	1.04
Conventional mortgages				
Less Aaa corporate bonds	1.48	1.49	1.63	1.53
Less Aaa state and				
local	2.20	2.31	2.75	2.42

Troughs

	Aug. 1954	April 1958	Feb. 1961	Average
Mortgages				
Conventional	4.74	5.63	5.96	
FHA	4.60	5.61	6.16	
Conv. less FHA	.14	.02	-.20	-.01
Bonds				
Corporate Baa	3.49	4.67	5.07	
Corporate Aaa	2.87	3.60	4.27	
Baa less Aaa	.62	1.07	.80	.83
State and local Baa	2.94	3.78	4.06	
State and local Aaa	1.90	2.70	3.14	
Baa less Aaa	1.04	1.08	.92	1.01
Conventional mortgages				
Less Aaa corporate bonds	1.87	2.03	1.69	1.86
Less Aaa state and				
local	2.84	2.93	2.82	2.86

Note: Mortgage yields are from NBER authorization series, with assumed prepayment of ten years. Bond series are from Moody's.

PART TWO

5

Large Life Insurance Companies in the National Mortgage Market

Life insurance companies are national lenders. This has implications about the kinds of mortgages they acquire, which in turn has implications for the usefulness and limitations of yield series covering life insurance company operations. Mortgages entering the national market at any one time carry a relatively narrow risk and yield dispersion. Hence although the companies represented in our series were not chosen according to principles of scientific sampling, their experience is broadly representative of life insurance companies generally.

As noted earlier, series covering life insurance companies are *not* representative of the residential market as a whole. The national market is, however, the most sensitive component of the residential market as a whole, since the lenders in the market have a wide range of alternative investment opportunities, and shift at the margin from one investment to another. Changes in the national market thus register tendencies operative in local markets, to a greater or lesser degree depending on the extent to which the local market is isolated from outside influences.

Large Life Insurance Companies as National Lenders

National lenders are those that acquire the bulk of their loans outside of their local (home office) area. Table 5-1, drawn from a special survey conducted by the Federal Home Loan Bank Board, classifies a lender as national if 90 per cent or more of his loans in 1961 were outside the lender's local area;[1] otherwise the lender is classified as local. Loans are classified as national or local depending on whether they are made by national or local lenders. Using this definition, 74 per cent of the life insurance companies covered in the survey were classified as national, compared to 8 per cent of mortgage companies and

[1] "Local area" was left to the respondent to define.

TABLE 5-1

Distribution of Conventional Mortgage Loans on One-Family Homes
Approved by National and Local Lenders in 1961

	Life Insurance Companies		Mortgage Companies		Savings and Loan Associations		Commercial Banks		Mutual Savings Banks	
	Number	Per Cent	Number	Per Cent	Number	Per Cent	Number	Per Cent	Number	Per Cent
Total lenders	180	100	751	100	4,318	100	na	na	na	na
national	134	74	66	8	0	0	na	na	na	na
local	46	26	685	92	4,318	100	na	na	na	na
Total loans	5,617	100	4,829	100	51,356	100	35,089	100	8,882	100
national	5,369	96	551	11	0	0	3,275	9	622	7
local	248	4	4,278	89	51,356	100	31,814	91	8,260	93

Note: Coverage was as follows: Life insurance companies holding at least $2.5 million in conventional residential loans as reported in *Bests Life Insurance Reports, 1961*; mortgage companies that were members of the Mortgage Bankers Association or were FHA-approved mortgagees; FSLIC-insured savings and loan associations plus state-insured cooperative banks in Massachusetts; FDIC-insured commercial banks and mutual savings banks. Data cover the first nine months of 1961.
na=not available.

Source: Federal Home Loan Bank Board.

none of the savings and loan associations (data for commercial banks and mutual savings banks were not reported). The life insurance companies that were classified as local were small ones accounting for a very small proportion of total lending by life insurance companies. Thus, 96 per cent of total life insurance company loans in 1961 were accounted for by life insurance companies classified as national lenders, compared to 11 per cent for mortgage companies, 9 per cent for commercial banks, 7 per cent for mutual savings banks, and none for savings and loan associations. The four large companies in our survey would all be classified as national lenders.

Other measures of lender participation in the national market are shown in Tables 5-2 and 5-3, which are drawn from the 1960 Census of Residential Financing and classify outstanding loans in 1960 by whether they are inside or outside the region in which the lender's home office is located. (The traditional census nine-region breakdown is used for this classification.) Thus Table 5-2 indicates that in 1960, 17 per cent of all outstanding first mortgages on single-family homes were held by lenders located in a region different from that of the property. For life insurance companies, however, the figure was 56 per cent, and for all other lenders combined, 8 per cent. The life insurance companies accounted for 58 per cent of all "foreign-held" mortgages. Table 5-3 shows similar data for individual major metropolitan areas. In only one of the seventeen metropolitan areas was the life insurance company share of loans held by outsiders less than 50 per cent. The remainder of these loans was accounted for mainly by mutual savings banks, the Federal National Mortgage Association, and mortgage companies, which are only temporary holders selling most of their loans to life insurance companies and mutual savings banks.

Why are the life insurance companies national lenders? First, they are not subject to legal restrictions on the geographical scope of their mortgage lending, as are savings and loan associations, commercial banks, and (to a somewhat lesser extent) mutual savings banks.[2] Second, most of the larger companies are domiciled in the East where interest rates are generally low; hence, they are constrained to seek the higher interest rates available elsewhere. Third, the insurance side of their business tends to be nationwide, thus creating both internal and external pressures to maintain a broad base of mortgage lending.

[2] See Raymond J. Saulnier, *Urban Mortgage Lending by Life Insurance Companies,* NBER, New York, 1950, p. 24.

TABLE 5-2

First-Mortgage Loans on One-Family Homeowner Mortgaged Properties in 1960, by Type of Holder

| | Per Cent of Mortgages on Properties in Different Region Than Holder | | | | | Life Insurance Company Share of All Mortgages, Held by Outsiders |
	All Holders[a]	Life Insurance Companies	Mutual Savings Banks	Commercial Banks	Savings and Loan Assns.	
All first mortgages	17	56	28	4	2	58
Properties inside SMA	19	57	29	6	2	60
Properties outside SMA	11	50	20	2	2	53
Conventional mortgages	6	40	0	1	1	68
Properties inside SMA	7	44	0	1	b	77
Properties outside SMA	5	22	0	1	2	23
FHA mortgages	34	65	42	6	7	64
Properties inside SMA	35	65	41	6	8	60
Properties outside SMA	30	60	44	7	3	72
VA mortgages	29	61	39	10	7	52
Properties inside SMA	31	61	39	13	8	50
Properties outside SMA	21	61	37	2	4	59

[a]Includes other holders not shown separately.

bLess than 0.5 per cent.

Source: U.S. Census of Housing, 1960, Volume V, Residential Finance, Part 1, Homeowner Properties, pp. 15, 19, 23, 27.

TABLE 5-3

First-Mortgage Loans on One-Family Homeowner Mortgaged Properties
in Selected Metropolitan Areas in 1960

Metropolitan Area	Life Insurance Company Share of All Mortgages Held by Outsiders	Per Cent of Mortgages on Properties in Different Region Than Holder	
		All Holders	Life Insurance Companies
Atlanta	54	40	68
Baltimore	50	13	60
Boston	100	1	35
Buffalo	58	1	10
Chicago	67	10	47
Cleveland	51	13	45
Dallas	73	46	74
Detroit	59	25	48
Los Angeles	54	23	59
Minneapolis	68	9	38
New York	19	1	4
Philadelphia	75	4	21
Pittsburgh	60	4	26
St. Louis	71	18	67
San Francisco	53	27	67
Seattle	69	27	73
Washington	55	39	68

Source: U.S. Census of Housing, 1960, Volume V, *Residential Finance,* Part 1,
Homeowner Properties, Table 5.

Fourth, the assets of the industry are heavily concentrated among a
relatively small number of large companies, which must cultivate a
broad market in order to get their funds invested.[3]

Instruments in the National Market

In general, mortgages entering the national market are obtainable in
relatively large volume and have relatively small risk. Volume is important because the administrative machinery needed to acquire mort-

[3] For data on concentration of mortgage holdings by life insurance companies
and other investors, see J. E. Morton, *Urban Mortgage Lending: Comparative
Markets and Experience,* Princeton University Press for NBER, 1956, pp. 51–53.

gages, whether it is a system of branch offices or a network of local correspondents, is not economical unless it can generate some minimum volume of mortgages. High-risk mortgages do not enjoy a broad market because (1) the institutional lenders that comprise the national market have conservative investment objectives, and (2) these lenders usually are not able to make detailed investigations or maintain the close surveillance that is required on risky loans. The supply of high-risk mortgage loans is thus dominated by local lenders.[4]

These observations suggest the following specific characteristics of the instruments entering the national market. The volume aspect suggests that they are more likely to be secured by newly built houses in tract developments than by existing structures, and more likely to originate within metropolitan areas than outside. The risk aspect suggests that mortgages entering the national market are more likely to be federally underwritten than conventional and, if conventional, are likely to have characteristics considered desirable from the standpoint of risk, such as high borrower income.

These conjectures are broadly consistent with the characteristics of loans acquired by life insurance companies relative to those acquired by other lenders.

1. Mortgages secured by new construction are more likely to enter the national market than mortgages secured by existing structures because construction often generates a package of mortgages that is convenient for national lenders with substantial sums to invest.[5] As shown in Table 5-4, life insurance companies in 1960 had a larger proportion of their outstanding first-mortgage loans secured by new properties than any of the other major lender groups. The FHLBB survey covering first mortgage conventional loans authorized in eighteen metropolitan areas during the period May–December 1963 shows that loans on new properties accounted for about two-thirds of the total for life insurance companies and mortgage companies; one-third for mutual savings banks and savings and loan associations; and one-fourth for commercial banks. The proportion of loans on new properties is prob-

---

[4] This appears to be true generally, at least for small loans. See J. A. Bottomly, "The Premium for Risk as a Determinant of Interest Rates in Underdeveloped Rural Areas," *Quarterly Journal of Economics,* November 1963, pp. 642, 643.

[5] This applies to mortgages generated by tract operations; individual custom-built homes generate only a single mortgage and usually involve construction as well as permanent financing by the same lender. Life insurance companies do not find such loans especially attractive.

TABLE 5-4

First-Mortgage Loans on One-Family Homeowner Mortgaged Properties in 1960:
Per Cent Held Inside Metropolitan Areas and Per Cent Secured
by New Properties, by Type of Holder

	All Holders[a]	Life Insurance Companies	Mutual Savings Banks	Commercial Banks	Savings and Loan Assns.
Per Cent Secured by New Homes[b]					
All first mortgages	43	56	52	39	42
Conventional	40	64	50	41	42
FHA	47	50	52	43	36
VA	48	55	54	28	45
Per Cent Held Inside Metropolitan Areas					
All first mortgages	72	80	87	63	72
Conventional	67	83	79	53	70
FHA	80	78	91	75	78
VA	78	82	91	72	81

[a]Includes other holders not shown separately.

[b]Refers to properties that had never been occupied before being acquired by the current owner-mortgagor.

Source: Same as Table 5-2.

ably higher for the large companies in our survey than for all life insurance companies.

2. Mortgages originated within metropolitan areas are more likely to enter the national market than those originated outside because mortgage credit demands in metropolitan areas are sufficiently large and concentrated to justify the machinery needed to transfer mortgages to the outside. For life insurance companies, this machinery comprises branch offices or correspondent relationships. Referring back to Table 5-2, 19 per cent of mortgages on properties inside metropolitan areas in 1960, but only 11 per cent of mortgages on properties outside metropolitan areas were held by lenders located in another region. Life insurance companies had a somewhat larger share of all mortgages held by outsiders in the case of loans on properties inside than in the case of loans on properties outside metropolitan areas (60 as compared to 53 per cent).

The distribution of total loans between metropolitan and nonmetropolitan areas is, of course, affected by local as well as national lending. Table 5-4 shows that 80 per cent of residential loans held by life insurance companies and 87 per cent of those held by mutual savings banks were on properties in metropolitan areas, as compared to 72 per cent and 63 per cent for savings and loan associations and commercial banks, respectively. A larger proportion of local lending by savings banks is in metropolitan areas than is the case for life insurance companies.

3. Federally underwritten mortgages are more likely to enter the national market than conventional mortgages because federal underwriting implies lower risk and greater uniformity. Table 5-2 showed that 34 per cent of all FHA and 29 per cent of all VA mortgages in 1960 were held outside the region in which the property was located; for conventional mortgages, the figure was only 6 per cent.

Ratios of federally underwritten to total mortgages for individual lender groups, shown in Table 5-5, are affected by the extent of participation in national markets, but other factors are also involved. Commercial banks have higher ratios than savings and loan associations largely because they place a higher value on the greater liquidity of federally underwritten mortgages, while their maximum lending limits on conventional loans are more restrictive. The ratio is higher for mutual savings banks than for life insurance companies because the

TABLE 5-5

Per Cent of Outstanding Loans on One- to Four-Family
Properties Federally Underwritten, Selected Years

	1950	1956	1960
Life insurance companies	67	63	66[b]
Four lenders in NBER survey	84[a]	80	75
Mutual savings banks	57	77	75[b]
Commercial banks	54	52	54[b]
Savings and loan associations	29	24	29[b]

[a]Refers to 1951.

[b]One-unit properties only.

Source: Saul Klaman, The Volume of Mortgage Debt in the Postwar Decade, pp. 74-87; 1960 Census of Residential Finance, p. 12; National Bureau of Economic Research.

savings banks can lend in the national market *only* on an insured or guaranteed basis, whereas life insurance companies can lend in the national market on a conventional basis as well.

Table 5-5 indicates that in 1950, life insurance companies had the highest ratios of federally underwritten to total lending. At that time, mutual savings banks were largely local lenders, limited by law to mortgages in their own or adjoining states. In 1949 and 1950, however, statutes in leading mutual savings banks states were amended to allow these lenders to acquire FHA and VA (but not conventional) mortgages in nonadjoining states, which they did in very substantial volume; by 1956, the relative importance of federally underwritten mortgages in their portfolios exceeded that for life insurance companies.[6] Thus, the higher ratio of federally underwritten holdings for mutual savings banks reflects the fact that *all* nonlocal lending by these institutions is in federally underwritten mortgages (see Table 5-2). Life insurance companies, in contrast, also acquire nonlocal loans on a conventional basis when this is considered advantageous; in 1960, about one-fifth of their nonlocal loans were conventional. Moreover, life insurance companies accounted for two-thirds of all conventional loans held by outsiders.

4. Conventional mortgages entering the national market have characteristics considered favorable from the standpoint of risk. Although no data are available to check this directly, it can be verified indirectly from the characteristics of conventional loans made by life insurance companies. About two-fifths of the conventional loans held by life insurance companies in 1960 were on properties outside the holder's region, compared to negligible proportions for other lenders (Table 5-2). This should be reflected in the over-all characteristics of life insurance company conventional loans as compared to loans made by other lenders.

As indicated in the first three lines of Table 5-6, those who borrow from life insurance companies (on conventional first-mortgage loans) generally have higher incomes than those who borrow from other lenders, and fewer commit themselves to very heavy mortgage payments relative to their income. Life insurance company loans are also more "conventional" in the original meaning of the term. The percentage of borrowers over 65 years of age, not living in husband-wife households, or nonwhite, is lower for life insurance companies than for

---

[6] For further discussion of this episode, see Klaman, *The Postwar Residential Mortgage Market,* pp. 149–156.

TABLE 5-6

Selected Characteristics of Conventional First Mortgages on One-Family
Homeowner Mortgaged Properties, by Type of Lender, 1960

	Life Ins. Cos.	Mutual Savings Banks	Mortgage and Real Est. Cos.	Commercial Banks	Savings and Loan Assns.	Fed. and State Agencies	Individuals	Others	Total
Median income of borrower ($)	9,700	7,400	5,200	6,400	6,600	7,000	5,400	5,000	6,500
Per cent of borrowers with income less than $4,000	7.5	11.0	32.7	17.8	14.5	14.0	27.9	29.5	17.4
Per cent of borrowers with mortgage payments exceeding 30 per cent of income	2.8	2.1	7.1	5.7	5.1	4.9	8.7	11.9	5.6
Per cent of structures built before 1929	8.1	27.0	13.3	36.3	27.0	16.2	40.5	34.3	28.8
Per cent of borrowers 65 years of age and over	4.2	9.1	4.4	6.6	7.1	1.2	7.5	7.9	6.8
Per cent of households "Nonnormal"a	9.8	16.8	11.7	13.8	13.0	9.2	14.9	13.2	13.3
Per cent of borrowers nonwhite	1.8	2.6	13.1	3.5	4.6	2.4	10.3	11.0	5.4
Per cent of mortgages delinquent	2.5	2.8	16.1b	3.7	9.3	5.5	9.0	2.8	7.8
Median interest rate (per cent)	5.0	5.1	6.1	6.0	6.0	4.1	6.0	6.0	5.6

aHouseholds other than "male head, wife present, no nonrelatives."

bMortgages inside SMAs only. Figure given for U.S. clearly is in error.

Source: 1960 Census of Housing, Volume V, *Residential Finance*, Part 1, Homeowner Properties.

other lenders. Also, a relatively small proportion are secured by properties built before 1929.

This tendency of life insurance companies to skim the "best" conventional mortgages is reflected in their refinancing experience. Mortgage borrowers whose credit position has improved through the passage of time often refinance with life insurance companies where their improved status is given recognition in the form of more favorable terms. Data on the purposes of refinancing from the 1950 Census of Residential Financing reveal that almost half of the conventional first mortgages on owner-occupied one-dwelling unit properties refinanced at life insurance companies were for the purpose of securing better terms, whereas this was true of only one-fourth of the refinanced loans of all lenders combined.[7] About three-fifths of the conventional first mortgages refinanced with life insurance companies were held originally by a lender other than the one doing the refinancing, whereas for all lenders combined, this was the case for only about one-third of refinanced mortgages.

Implications for Mortgage-yield Structure

Because they tend to restrict their conventional lending to mortgages having relatively standard characteristics, at the lower end of the risk spectrum, life insurance company loans carry relatively low interest rates, and rate variance is small. Differentials in gross yield between life insurance companies and other lenders on new conventional loans in eighteen metropolitan areas during May–December 1963 are shown in Table 5-7.[8] These differentials are calculated from multiple regression equations in which the type of lender is entered as a dummy variable. The differential marked "adjusted" is calculated from equations which include the average loan-value ratio, property value, maturity, metropolitan area, and purpose of loan.[9] The first figure is

[7] 1950 Census of Housing, Volume IV, *Residential Financing,* Part I, U.S., p. 172. Data on purpose of refinancing were not obtained in the 1960 Census.

[8] The National Bureau's Survey of Urban Mortgage Finance shows that life insurance companies had lower contract rates on home mortgages than savings and loan associations and commercial banks throughout the period 1920–47. See Morton, p. 91.

[9] The interlender yield differentials calculated from regressions that include lender type as a dummy variable may be biased by intercorrelation between lender type and loan characteristics, if the relationship between yield and loan characteristics is not linear. As a check on this possibility, we calculated yield

TABLE 5-7

Differences in Gross Yield Between Life Insurance Companies and Other Major Institutional Lenders
on Conventional First-Mortgage Loans Approved During May-December 1963
(basis points – other lender less life insurance companies)

	Savings and Loan Associations	Commercial Banks	Mortgage Companies	Mutual Savings Banks	R^2
East					
Simple	40 (39)	15 (14)	30 (28)	3 (2)	.23 (.51)
Adjusted	29 (20)	7 (10)	21 (13)	5 (2)	.55 (.89)
Midwest					
Simple	48 (47)	9 (9)	7 (5)	10 (9)	.25 (.74)
Adjusted	28 (17)	-5 (-4)	-1 (-1)	4 (1)	.45 (.85)
South					
Simple	65 (63)	62 (58)	10 (9)	–	.21 (.55)
Adjusted	47 (46)	24 (28)	8 (9)	–	.44 (.84)
West					
Simple	83 (81)	40 (40)	11 (11)	29 (28)	.27 (.66)
Adjusted	62 (58)	3 (23)	5 (9)	19 (22)	.49 (.79)
U.S.					
Simple	65 (63)	11 (11)	12 (11)	-4 (-4)	.33 (.55)
Adjusted	45 (34)	10 (15)	13 (11)	16 (13)	.62 (.91)

Notes to Table 5-7

Note: Rate differences are calculated from multiple regression equations (separately for each region) relating effective yield to type of lender and the following factors: purpose of loan (purchase of new house, purchase of previously occupied house, construction of new house), loan-value ratio, value of property, maturity, and metropolitan area location of property. The "adjusted" yield differences are calculated from equations including *all* the above factors. The simple yield differences are calculated from equations using only type of lender. Figures in parentheses refer to regressions covering pooled averages, each pertaining to a given month (8), type of lender (5), purpose of loan (3), and metropolitan area (18); each average is weighted by the number of cases in the cell. R^2s are adjusted for the reduction in degrees of freedom involved in this procedure. Regional groupings of metropolitan areas are as follows: *East*: Baltimore, Boston, New York, and Philadelphia; *Midwest*: Chicago, Cleveland, Detroit, and Minneapolis; *South*: Atlanta, Memphis, Miami, and New Orleans; *West*: Dallas, Denver, Houston, Los Angeles, San Francisco, and Seattle.

Source: Calculated from data provided by the Federal Home Loan Bank Board.

based on regressions covering individual loans, while the figure in parenthesis is based on regressions covering pooled observations. Life insurance company yields are the lowest of all five lender groups in the U.S. regression, and also in separate regressions covering the South, West, and East, although the differences are smaller after adjustment than before. In the Midwest, life insurance company yields after adjustment don't differ significantly from those of mutual savings banks, commercial banks, or mortgage companies, all of which fall below savings and loan associations.[10]

for each lender group from the regression equation covering that group alone, employing the average characteristics of all lenders. This procedure generated results similar to those shown in Table 5-7 (U.S., Adjusted), with one exception. Using the separate regressions, mutual savings banks had lower rates than life insurance companies. The mutual savings bank regression for the entire U.S., however, has very high standard errors and is not really comparable to the equations for other lenders because the savings banks are represented in only eight of the eighteen metropolitan areas. A more definitive comparison of savings banks with other lenders would be restricted to those eight metropolitan areas.

[10] Whether life insurance company loans actually perform better is not necessarily relevant, and the evidence is difficult to interpret. Census data, which are comparable as between lenders, show life insurance companies with relatively low delinquency rates on conventional mortgages in both 1950 and 1960. Census data are not well suited, however, for measuring such a potentially volatile and erratic characteristic as delinquency. The National Bureau Survey of Urban Mortgage Lending showed life insurance companies to have higher foreclosure rates than commercial banks or savings and loan associations on loans made during the 1920's, but the data are biased by the exclusion of banks and asso-

TABLE 5-8

Variability in Gross Yield on Conventional First Mortgages Approved During May-December 1963, by Type of Lender
(R^2 and standard error of estimate as successive independent variables are added to regression)

Independent Variable	Life Insurance Companies		Mutual Savings Banks		Mortgages Companies		Commercial Banks		Savings and Loan Associations	
	R^2	SE	R^2	SE	R^2	SE	R^2	SE	R^2	SE
Individual Cases										
		.210[a]		.266[a]		.284[a]		.357[a]		.444[a]
Maturity	.03	.207	.10	.252	.07	.274	.10	.339	.02	.439
Loan-value	.03	.207	.20	.239	.21	.252	.14	.330	.11	.420
Property value	.04	.206	.20	.238	.22	.251	.21	.317	.12	.417
Loan purpose (3)	.05	.205	.21	.237	.23	.250	.23	.313	.13	.414
SMSA (18)	.19	.189	.62	.164	.46	.209	.46	.262	.50	.315
Pooled Observations[b]										
		.136[a]		.189[a]		.190[a]		.259[a]		.264[a]
Maturity	.06	.132	.36	.151	.33	.155	.10	.246	.03	.260
Loan-value	.06	.132	.36	.151	.49	.136	.16	.238	.31	.220
Property value	.06	.132	.36	.151	.49	.136	.16	.238	.37	.210
Loan purpose (3)	.07	.131	.42	.144	.50	.134	.22	.229	.44	.200
SMSA (18)	.37	.108	.94	.047	.82	.081	.63	.157	.91	.078

[a]Standard deviation.
[b]See note to Table 5-7.

Source: Calculated from data provided by the Federal Home Loan Bank Board.

Not only do conventional loans by life insurance companies carry relatively low yields, but cross-section yield variability associated with differences in loan and property characteristics (including location), is also relatively small. Table 5-8 shows that yield variability on conventional loans, as measured by the standard deviation, is smaller for life insurance companies than for the four other major lender groups—it is less than half that of savings and loan associations (.21 compared to .44 per cent).

A relatively small proportion of total yield variability on life insurance company loans is explainable by differences in the loan and property characteristics for which data are readily available. Table 5-8 shows that loan maturity, loan-value ratio, property value, and loan purpose collectively account for only 5 per cent of the yield variability of individual life insurance company loans,[11] whereas for other lender groups, these factors account for 13 to 23 per cent of variability. In the pooled observations, the differences are even larger. Life insurance companies are the only major lender group for which the loan-value ratio is not a significant yield determinant.[12]

The quantitatively most important yield determinant for all lender groups in these regressions is the metropolitan area location of property. Again, however, yield variance associated with location is much less important for life insurance companies than for other lenders. The introduction of metropolitan area into the regression covering individual loans raises explained variance to only 19 per cent for life insurance companies compared to 46 to 62 per cent for the other lender groups (Table 5-8). Rate differences between metropolitan areas in the East and areas in the West were smaller in regressions covering life in-

ciations whose experience was so bad that they failed (see Morton, pp. 98–112). Actual loss ratios were lower for the life insurance companies. More recent time series data on life insurance company experience (the Earley manuscript, pp. 4-17 to 4-23), suffer from lack of comparability with data for other lenders, but do not prima facie contradict the presumption that life insurance company loans do better.

[11] Cross-section analysis of individual loans made by the companies in our survey, discussed in Appendix B, shows very similar results.

[12] Relatively high borrower income on life insurance company loans tends to reduce the importance of loan and property characteristics as determinants of risk. In most states, furthermore, life insurance companies are limited to a maximum loan-value ratio of 75 per cent, and in 1963, the companies did not consider this a very risky level. Hence, variability in loan-value ratios below the 75 per cent level on life insurance company loans did not carry much risk variability.

surance company loans than for other lender groups.[13] For example, yield differences for three pairs of metropolitan areas, after taking account of differences in maturity, loan-value ratio, property value, and loan purpose, were as follows (in basis points):

	Life Insurance Companies	Commercial Banks	Savings and Loan Associations
San Francisco less Boston	40	69	103
Los Angeles less Baltimore	35	59	79
Detroit less Philadelphia	21	27	57

SOURCE: Same as Table 5-8.

Implications for Yield Series

The fact that the yield dispersion on mortgages that enter the national market is considerably smaller than the dispersion on all residential mortgages implies much more limited scope for individual lender yield variability, associated with differences in lender policies, than would be true for other lender groups. Some indication of the order of magnitude of the differences that can arise is provided in Table 5-9, which shows the distribution of differences in average quarterly yields between two of the large companies in our survey, separately for conventional and FHA mortgages. The average difference (calculated without regard to sign) was 12.7 basis points for conventionals and 7.6 basis points for FHAs. These differences are larger than those that

[13] One reason for the smaller geographical spread for life insurance companies may be that high-rate areas generate a relatively large volume of high-risk mortgages which do not enter the national market (they are not acquired by life insurance companies), and which are not completely identified by the loan and property characteristics on which we have data. Assume, for example, that some mortgages have a characteristic X which makes them unacceptable to life insurance companies because of high risk, and that X mortgages are more common in high-rate areas. Then local markets for X mortgages will be insulated from national competition by life insurance companies and if there is imperfect competition in local markets, the geographical spread will be larger on X mortgages than on other mortgages. Thus, local lenders who acquire X mortgages will show a wider unadjusted geographical spread than life insurance companies that don't. If the X characteristic could be included in the regressions, the regression covering local lenders would show the same adjusted yield spread as the regression covering life insurance companies. But since X is not identified, its influence is picked up by the metropolitan area coefficient, resulting in a wider geographical yield spread for local lenders.

TABLE 5-9

Differences in Gross Yield
Between Company 4 and
Company 6, Quarterly, 1951-63

Yield Difference in Basis Points	Number of Quarters	
	Conventional	FHA
0-10	24	43
11-20	19	6
21-30	6	3
31-40	2	0
41-50	1	0

Source: National Bureau of Economic Research series.

would arise from sampling error on the assumption that both companies had similar policies,[14] but they are small in absolute terms. When averaged out over four lenders who account for one-third to two-fifths of all life insurance company loans, differences of this magnitude suggest that our series must be fairly representative of life insurance company experience generally.

A comparison of our conventional series with the new FHLBB series that covers over forty companies, during a thirteen-month period when the series overlap, supports this view. The maximum monthly difference between the series was seven basis points and the average for the thirteen months was only two basis points. (For a detailed discussion, see Chapter 9.)

[14] On this assumption, we would expect quarterly yield differences on conventional loans to be on the order of two basis points.

6

Method of Loan Acquisition

In contrast to the series compiled by the Federal Home Loan Bank Board and the Federal Reserve Bank of Chicago, which are restricted to loans originated by the reporting lenders ("direct loans"), the National Bureau series also covers loans acquired from mortgage correspondents ("correspondent loans"); the correspondents are generally mortgage companies which originate loans for sale to "permanent" investors, retaining the servicing for which they receive a fee (expressed as a per cent of the loan balance) as long as the loan is outstanding.[1] In this chapter, we discuss the nature of company transactions with correspondents, the influence of service fees on the gross yield of correspondent loans, and the comparability of direct and correspondent loans.

Relationship of Life Insurance Company to Correspondent

The correspondent is viewed as a borrower rather than as the agent of the life insurance company in a transaction with a third party (builder or mortgagor). From the legal standpoint, at least, the correspondent is free to negotiate the terms on which a mortgage is to be transferred to the company. At a result, the terms and timing of the deal between the company and the correspondent could differ from those of the transaction between the correspondent and the third party. It is true, of course, that the contract rate and other characteristics of the instrument will be the same, since the instrument created (or, rather, authorized to be created) is the same in both transactions. But the price at which the instrument is transferred need not be the same. The finance committee records disclose the price at which the company authorizes purchase of the mortgage from the correspondent, but *not* the price at which the correspondent extends his own commitment, or the time of that commitment.

[1] For a full discussion see Saul B. Klaman, *The Postwar Rise of Mortgage Companies,* Occasional Paper 60, NBER, 1959.

This does not mean that the terms of a transaction between the company and the correspondent are necessarily independent of the terms of the transaction, covering the same instruments, between the correspondent and mortgagor or builder. Although from the legal standpoint the transaction between company and correspondent is a negotiated market transaction, the actual working relationships between them may take a variety of forms, some of which reduce their freedom to bargain for the best terms possible under current market conditions. To the extent that this is the case, the terms of the transaction between the correspondent and the third party may influence the transaction between the correspondent and the company.

Several kinds of company-correspondent relationships may be distinguished in terms of the degree of independence that can be exercised in bargaining on a specific transaction. These relationships differ from company to company, and for any individual company they may differ from one correspondent to another.

First, the relationship may be one of *strict independence*. The company feels free to adjust its buying rate at any time without any notice, and the correspondent is free to offer a loan to another company if he can obtain a better price. If the correspondent extends his own commitment before obtaining a commitment from the company, he does so at his own risk, e.g., if he commits on FHA 5 per cent mortgages at a price of 97 and the company lowers its buying price to 96 before he obtains the company's commitment, the correspondent bears the loss. (Of course, if prices rise in the meantime the correspondent makes a speculative profit.) Correspondents having this kind of relationship with life insurance companies usually deal with a number of companies, and shift offerings from one company to another, depending on the kinds of mortgages they have to sell and on which companies currently have funds to invest. Companies dealing with correspondents on this basis usually do not feel any obligation to provide them with a steady source of funds.

Second, the relationship between company and correspondent may be one of *quasi-independence,* where a continuing relationship causes some modification in their short-run behavior. The company may give the correspondent an *allotment,* permitting him to plan his operations for some period ahead, i.e., the correspondent will be told that the company will accept some specified volume of mortgages during a future period (say, six months or a year). Allotments are not legally binding on the company, offers by the correspondent still have to meet the company's credit requirements, and the company's buying price remains subject to change without notice. Yet behavior is constrained by concern for the relationship. If the company finds it necessary to drop its buying price sharply at a time when a "faithful" correspondent is heavily committed, the company may bail out the correspondent by buying at the higher price in the correspondent's commitment. (If the company adopts this policy, it likely will expect the "faithful" correspondent to pass along any special bargains he may have acquired.) As an alternative, the company may try to soften the impact of a price drop by giving the correspondent short notice (say, a week) that the drop is coming. This involves the hazard to the company that the correspondent will try to dump all its loans on the company, including loans that had been intended for other lenders. (Even if the company is adamant about never bailing out a correspondent or giving notice of a price change, it will feel constrained not to change prices too often or too drastically.)

A third relationship between company and correspondent may be one of virtually *complete dependence*. This arises when the company grants the correspondent precommitment authority. Under such an arrangement, the correspondent is authorized to commit himself at the company's current buying rate up to some maximum amount (e.g., 20 per cent of his annual allotment) without risk. If the company lowers its buying rate after the correspondent extends its own commitment but before he obtains the company's commitment, the company is obligated to accept the loans at the terms of the correspondent's commitment. By the same token, when the company lowers its buying rate, it expects correspondents with commitments outstanding at a higher rate to pass them along.[2] In effect, the correspondent commits the company and for practical purposes becomes the company's de facto agent for as long as the relationship remains intact. Under such arrangements, the terms of the transaction between the correspondent and the company will always be the same as the terms of the transaction between the correspondent and the third party. This type of relationship is most likely to develop when the company provides the sole or largest outlet for a given correspondent.

The implications of various types of company-correspondent relationships for the *timing* of statistical series on correspondent loans were discussed in Chapter 4.

---

[2] The company may or may not reserve the right to refuse mortgages that do not meet its credit standards.

Variability in Service Fees as an Influence on Gross Yield

From the standpoint of mortgage-yield data, correspondent loans have the disadvantage that the recorded yield on the credit transaction may be affected by the terms of the servicing transaction. (The reverse, of course, is also the case.) Saulnier has remarked that "sometimes loan servicing is partly remunerated by a relatively high acquisition fee, and in other cases loan acquisition is remunerated in part by a relatively high servicing fee."[3] The service fee may also be varied to compensate for differences in contract rate. For example, a lender might pay a service fee of ½ per cent on a 6.00 per cent mortgage and only ¼ per cent on a 5.75 per cent mortgage that in other respects was identical.[4] In such case, different gross yields would be recorded for the two mortgages, although the return net of service fee would be the same.

This problem can be viewed from the standpoint of structural (cross-section) analysis and time series analysis. Regarding the structural problem, the service fee is one variable of many affecting gross yield. Differences in service fees can affect gross yield if individual lenders pay different service fees for different loans, or if there are interlender differences in general policy toward service fees. The first effect is illustrated in Table 6-1, which shows gross yield and service fees on loans authorized by one lender in California during February 1960. Of the 215 loans authorized in that month, 198 carried a service fee of ¼ per cent. These loans had gross yields ranging up to 6.12 per cent, but most were concentrated at 5.88 per cent. The remaining seventeen loans all had a service fee of .37 per cent and gross yields of either 6.25 per cent or 6.50 per cent.

Prior to 1959, interlender variability in service fees was small. The standard fee was ½ per cent, and monthly averages were generally within the range of .47 to 51 per cent for all the companies.[5] In 1959, one company dropped its standard service fee to .375 per cent. By in-

---

[3] Saulnier, *Urban Mortgage Lending by Life Insurance Companies,* p. 61.

[4] Such contract-rate differences may arise because correspondents have held loans in inventory over a period of rate change, or because of market imperfections at the origination level.

[5] VA loans, however, occasionally carried lower service fees when the maximum contract rate was far below the market.

TABLE 6-1

Gross Effective Yield and Service Fee on Conventional Mortgages
in California by One Life Insurance Company,
February 1960

Gross Effective Yield	Service Fee	Number of Mortgages
6.50	.37	6
6.25	.37	11
6.12	.25	23
5.90-5.99	.25	11
5.88	.25	163
5.63	.25	1
Total		215

creasing intercompany variability in service fees, this may have increased structural variability in gross yield.[6]

Time series of gross yields could be affected by service fees to the extent that average fees change for individual companies, or shifts occur in the mix as between companies with different average fees. Neither effect could have been of any quantitative importance for United States averages on FHA and conventional loans during the period 1951–58, since the monthly averages for all companies hugged the standard fee of $\frac{1}{2}$ per cent very closely (Chart 6-1). When average service fees fell to a lower level in 1959, month-to-month variability became somewhat greater, as shifts in the mix had a greater effect on the average. The variability was not systematic, however, and cyclical patterns in gross yield were not significantly affected.[7]

The influence of service fees on yield can be avoided, of course, simply by measuring yield net of service fee. Correspondent loans cannot, however, be compared to or combined with direct loans on a net basis because data are not available on servicing costs of direct loans. Correspondent and direct loans can be combined only on a gross yield basis. This raises a question regarding the comparability of gross yields on correspondent and direct loans.

[6] Any increase would have been small, however, since our data do not show a rise in over-all gross yield dispersion after 1959.

[7] It is possible, however, that the average *level* of gross yield on correspondent loans was .10 to .15 per cent lower after 1959 than it would have been if service fees had not fallen.

CHART 6-1

AVERAGE SERVICE FEES ON CORRESPONDENT LOANS,
1951–63

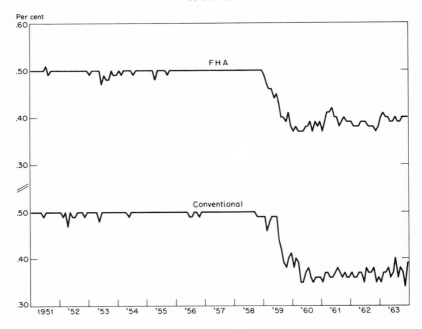

Comparability of Gross Yield on Correspondent and Direct Loans

On direct loans, the costs of servicing are borne by the life insurance company, while on correspondent loans, these costs are borne by the mortgage company. There is evidence to suggest that service fees paid to correspondents are higher than servicing costs of large companies that do their own servicing. Hence, we might expect competition to force gross yields on correspondent loans below those on direct loans, so as to equalize yields net of service costs. As an example assume that (1) the cost of servicing mortgages (including profits adequate to provide a competitive return on capital) is $\frac{1}{4}$ per cent but the service fee is set at $\frac{1}{2}$ per cent by convention, and (2) direct and correspondent loans are alike in every other respect, including contract rate. In such case, we might expect price competition to bring about results such as the following:

	Direct Loan	Correspondent Loan
Contract rate	6.00	6.00
Less: servicing costs	.25	.50
Equals: contract rate net of servicing	5.75	5.50
Plus: fee required to equalize yield	—	.25
Equals: yield net of servicing	5.75	5.75
. . . .		
Gross yield (contract rate plus fees)	6.00	6.25

The gross yield would be larger on correspondent loans by the amount of the "surplus" in the service fee.

On the other hand, net costs of origination are borne by the life insurance company on direct loans, whereas on correspondent loans these costs are borne by the mortgage company.[8] If origination costs (expressed as an annual rate) were exactly equal to the "surplus" in the service fee, competition would tend to equalize gross yields on direct and correspondent loans, as in the following example.

	Direct Loan	Correspondent Loan
Contract rate	6.00	6.00
Less: servicing costs	.25	.50
net cost of origination	.25	—
Equals: contract rate net of servicing and origination	5.50	5.50
Plus: fee required to equalize yield	—	—
Equals: yield net of servicing and origination	5.50	5.50
. . . .		
Gross yield (contract rate plus fees)	6.00	6.00

The upshot is that although gross yields on direct and correspondent loans are not strictly comparable, the elements of noncomparability

[8] Originating loans also generates income, but apparently most mortgage companies do it at a net loss. See Oliver H. Jones, "Mortgage Banking in 1963," *The Mortgage Banker*, December 1964, p. 23.

tend to be offsetting. If the net cost of origination is larger (smaller) than the surplus in service fees paid to correspondents, the gross yield of correspondent loans is biased downward (upward) relative to the gross yield on direct loans.

Gross yields on direct and correspondent loans may also differ because of market imperfections, even if the surplus in the service fee were entirely offset by net origination costs. For the same reason, intercompany differences exist in the net yield on correspondent loans alone. This suggests the following pragmatic test of the appropriateness of combining gross yields on direct and correspondent loans. Such consolidation is appropriate if yield differences between correspondent

CHART 6-2

INTERCOMPANY DIFFERENCES IN NET YIELD ON COR-
RESPONDENT LOANS COMPARED TO DIFFERENCES IN
GROSS YIELD BETWEEN DIRECT AND CORRESPONDENT
LOANS, QUARTERLY, 1951–63

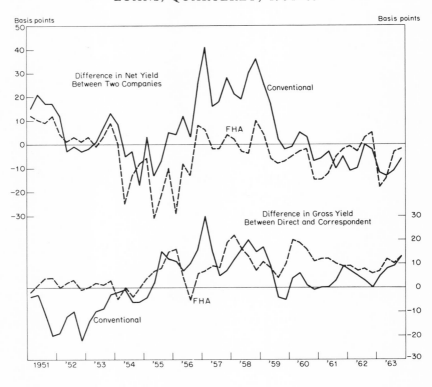

and direct loans are no greater than intercompany yield differences on correspondent loans alone.[9]

This turns out indeed to be the case, as illustrated in Chart 6-2. The upper part of the chart shows differences in net yield on correspondent loans between two companies, while the bottom part shows differences in gross yield between correspondent and direct loans. The differences are calculated quarterly to minimize the effect of sampling error, which on this basis is only slightly larger in the individual company comparisons. It is clear that for both FHA and conventional loans, differences in gross yield between direct and correspondent loans are of the same general order of magnitude or, perhaps, somewhat smaller than differences in net yield on correspondent loans between individual companies. This pragmatic test shows no reason why direct and correspondent loans should not be combined.

[9] The direct-loan sample is not large enough to permit intercompany comparisons on direct loans.

7

The Timing Problem

A mortgage instrument is created over a period of time, through a sequence of steps. This may give rise to a recording lag, the length of which depends on the precise point in the process when the loan characteristics are recorded. The recording lag should be distinguished from the behavioral lags discussed in Chapters 3 and 4. In this chapter, we examine the precise meaning of "transaction date" on a mortgage; consider whether loan attrition affects the timing of authorization series; compare the loan authorization date with the date of approval of the mortgagor's loan application; show how the timing and amplitude of yield series based on date of authorization differs from that of series based on date of disbursement; and analyze the length of residual recording lag in authorization series.

Meaning of Transaction Date

It is useful to view the transaction date as one of a sequence of steps involved in creating the mortgage, as follows[1]:

1a. *Direct Loans:* On tract developments, submission to the lender of preliminary plans for land acquisition, subdivision, etc.
1b. *Correspondent Loans:* Submission of application to correspondent by builder or mortgagor.
2a. *Direct Loans:* Lender approval of preliminary plans for tract development.
2b. *Correspondent Loans:* Correspondent extends commitment to builder or mortgagor.
3. Submission of application to life insurance company by correspondent, builder or mortgagor.
4. Approval of application by an authorized officer of the life insurance company—"conditional transaction date."

[1] This list is far from exhaustive and is designed for the sole purpose of illuminating the timing problem. Steps that could be germane to other purposes but do not affect timing have been left out.

5. Notification of approval by company.
6. Meeting of finance committee—"authorization date."
7. Approval of application of mortgagor if prior application was by a builder or by a correspondent dealing with a builder—"mortgagor approval date."
8. Loan closed, funds disbursed—"closing or disbursement date."

In general the transaction date on any instrument is that date when the terms of the transaction are established on a binding basis. In the case of residential mortgage loans by life insurance companies, with some exceptions that will be explained later, this is the date when an authorized officer of the lending institution approves the application of a correspondent, builder or ultimate borrower (mortgagor)—step 4 in the above list. Such approval represents a commitment to make a loan under specified conditions within some stipulated period (the "commitment period"). If the mortgage is not delivered within the period, the commitment ordinarily lapses unless the lender decides to extend it.

The transaction date hinges on a binding commitment by the lender; the party of the second part is also committed but not quite in the same way. A correspondent obtaining a commitment from a permanent lender, for example, is expected to deliver the mortgage, irrespective of his relationship to the company, whether one of independence or not, but it is understood that delivery may be prevented by circumstances beyond his control. (More correspondents find reasons why they cannot deliver when prices are rising than when they are falling.) On direct loans, it generally is inconvenient for the mortgagor to back out, since it ordinarily means repeating the paperwork involved in originating the instrument and may involve some direct financial loss. Commitments to builders often involve a commitment fee that is forfeited if the builder doesn't deliver. Nevertheless, typically more than 10 per cent of commitments on direct loans never go to closing.

Implications of Commitments Not Taken Down

A question arises as to whether loan commitments not taken down during the commitment period, or commitments taken down with modifications of the original terms, introduce any timing bias in authorization series.

1. It is clear that if a loan disappears forever, as when a builder or mortgagor doesn't carry through the transaction, it can cause no analytical mischief.

2. Lending officers typically will have authority to make minor changes in loan provisions without resubmission to the finance committee. Such cases would not appear again on the finance committee records, and therefore introduce no problem.

3. In some cases, a commitment leads not to a closing but to another commitment. This happens when a builder or correspondent wants a major modification of terms; some commitments to builders, indeed, include provisions for renegotiation of terms in the event that market conditions change during the commitment period. Or a builder or correspondent whose commitment lapses because he cannot deliver within the commitment period may apply for a new commitment.[2] In such cases, a new commitment must be negotiated and appears again on the finance committee records. Renegotiation does not, of course, invalidate the original commitment which would reflect the market at the time it was made. The second observation, however, could be biased if the terms of the old commitment influenced those of the new one.

As far as we could determine, this happens only occasionally; in general, the new commitment is viewed by the participants as a new transaction at the current market price.[3]

Thus, the fact that "authorizations" data include transactions that do not materialize into actual loans at the terms stipulated in the authorization does not affect the timing validity of authorization series.

Significance of the Date of Approval of the Mortgagor's Loan Application

In the case of loans secured by existing houses and loans to owner-builders that will be used to construct a home, approval of the loan application by an authorized officer of the company implies approval of the mortgagor. The transaction date is also the "mortgagor approval

[2] In some cases, the company may extend a lapsed commitment rather than write a new one.

[3] We nevertheless considered it desirable to omit such loans if possible. It turned out to be possible at two of the four companies which identified them separately on the finance committee record as "reapprovals." At the other two companies, they were not identified.

date." When the commitment is to a builder or to a correspondent dealing with a builder, however, the mortgagor is not present at the transaction date. Thus, approval of the mortgagor's loan application occurs some time after the transaction date and before the closing date, shown as step 7 in the list above. The lender's commitment defining the transaction date in such cases means that *when* a buyer-mortgagor is found, the company will make a loan to him at the terms specified, assuming the buyer meets the company's standards. (The lender is honor-bound not to change these standards between the time of the commitment and the time when the buyer arrives on the scene.)

In the series compiled by the Federal Reserve Bank of Chicago and the FHLBB, which only cover direct loans, the transaction date is defined as the date of approval of the borrower's loan application. This means that some of the loans in these surveys are recorded well after the transaction date. In the Chicago survey, this was rectified by throwing out all loans on which the lender reported that a commitment had been outstanding more than thirty days prior to the date of approval of the borrower's loan application. The FHLBB survey does not have such a correction. It should be emphasized that this problem pertains only to the FHLBB series covering the purchase of new homes.

Timing of Authorization and Disbursement Series

Since disbursement is the last step in the process of creating a mortgage instrument, the disbursement date may lag the transaction date by a considerable period. Commitment data compiled by the Life Insurance Association of America covering all residential (including multifamily) loans show that life insurance companies typically expect that less than 10 per cent of their outstanding commitments on a given date will be taken down within one month, less than 20 per cent will be taken down within two months, and about 50 per cent will be taken down within six months.

Some data collected by Klaman covering one large life insurance company show that about half of the loans authorized in a given month were not yet disbursed five months later, and about one-third were not disbursed eight months later (*The Postwar Residential Mortgage Market,* p. 290). As noted earlier, some of these undisbursed loans never go to closing at all; in Klaman's sample attrition amounted to about 14 per cent.

No mechanical adjustment to loan-disbursement data can take account of the authorization-disbursement lag, since the disbursement pattern is not fixed. It is affected, for example, by changes in the mix between mortgages on new and existing properties, and by the direction of interest rate change; when interest rates are falling, for example, the attrition rate rises.

One illustration of how the date of record affects the timing of mortgage rate series is given in Chart 7-1, which compares the quarterly contract rate series on conventional loans compiled by Klaman with our net rate series. Both series apply to four large life insurance companies, but the new series is on an authorization basis and the Klaman series is on a disbursement basis. At each of two clearly defined turning points during the period covered by both series, the authorization series leads the disbursement series by two quarters.

A more definitive and precise comparison of authorization and disbursement series is possible with a unique body of data provided by one of the four companies contributing to our survey. Beginning in 1954, this company began to compile series, with a breakdown by FHA, VA, and conventional loans, on both bases, so that (except

CHART 7-1

CONTRACT RATE ON CONVENTIONAL LOANS BY LIFE
INSURANCE COMPANIES, QUARTERLY, 1951–63

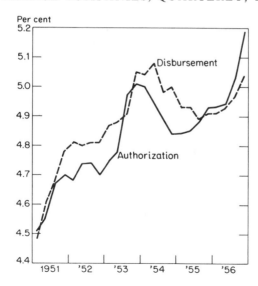

for attrition) the two series cover identical transactions. Charts 7-2, 7-3, and 7-4 show that the closing series lag the authorization series at every turning point. As summarized in Table 7-1, the lags range from one to six months.

We would expect, on a priori grounds that closing series would also have smaller amplitude than authorization series. This is because the rate recorded on loans disbursed in a given month is actually an average of rates authorized over a span of previous months. Thus, the month in which rates reach a cyclical peak in a disbursement series would include cases authorized in earlier months when rates were lower, and similarly at the trough. We would also expect the difference in amplitude between disbursement and authorization series to be smaller when turning points are flat than when they are sharp, because periods of constant rate levels give the disbursement series a chance to "catch up."

CHART 7-2

NET YIELD ON FHA CORRESPONDENT LOANS BY ONE COMPANY, 1954–64: AUTHORIZATION VERSUS DISBURSEMENT BASIS

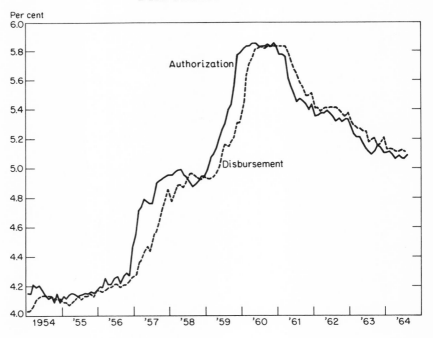

CHART 7-3

NET YIELD ON CONVENTIONAL CORRESPONDENT LOANS
BY ONE COMPANY, 1954–64:
AUTHORIZATION VERSUS DISBURSEMENT BASIS

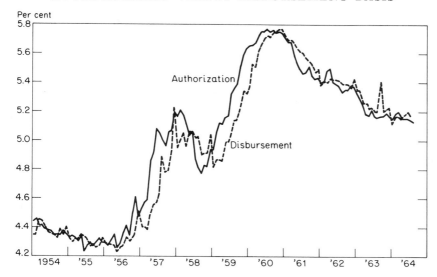

The series shown in Charts 7-2, 7-3, and 7-4 are consistent with these suppositions. The 1954–55 trough and the 1960–61 peak are both flat, so that differences in amplitude between authorizations and disbursement series in the three cyclical movements that include these turning points are quite small (see Table 7-2). The short and sharply reversed cyclical decline in 1958–59, however, has a much greater amplitude in the authorization series.

Residual Lag in Authorization Series

Two types of residual lag in authorization series may be distinguished. First, as already noted, the transaction date as we have defined it—the date of approval by the company of a loan application—precedes the date of record of authorization series, which is the date of finance committee meetings. Second, under some circumstances, the true transaction date must be viewed as preceding the date of approval of the loan application. These problems will be considered in turn.

CHART 7-4

NET YIELD ON ALL RESIDENTIAL CORRESPONDENT
LOANS BY ONE COMPANY, 1954–64:
AUTHORIZATION VERSUS DISBURSEMENT BASIS

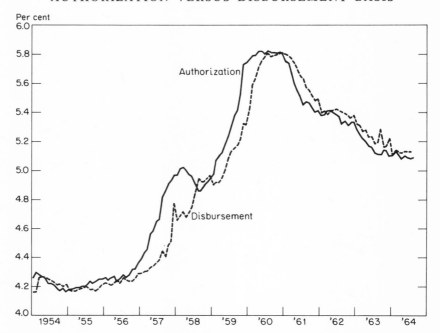

1. The extent of residual recording lag in authorization series arising from the lag between approval of the loan application and the authorization date, depends mainly on the frequency of finance committee meetings. These were held weekly at two of the companies in our survey and twice monthly at the other two.[4] The lag is affected slightly by the speed of communications between the field office where loan approval occurs and the home office where the finance committee meets.

Discussions with company officers and sample studies at each company based on individual loan files indicate that the lag between the loan approval date and the finance committee meeting date is generally less than a month, and the average lag is on the order of half a month.

[4] The frequency of committee meetings did not change at any of the four companies during the 1951–63 period.

TABLE 7-1

Turning Points in Effective Yield:
Authorization and Disbursement Series of One Company

Peak or Trough	Authorization	Disbursement	Authorization Lead (months)
All residential			
T	Jan. 1955	Feb. 1955	1
P	March 1958	Sept. 1958	6
T	Sept. 1958	March 1959	6
P	Nov. 1960	Dec. 1960	1
Conventional			
T	May 1956	June 1956	1
P	Jan. 1958	June 1958	5
T	Sept. 1958	Feb. 1959	5
P	Aug. 1960	Nov. 1960	3
FHA			
T	Jan. 1955	March 1955	2
P	April 1958	Aug. 1958	4
T	Sept. 1958	Feb. 1959	5
P	Nov. 1960	Feb. 1961	3

The results of the sample studies, two for each of the four companies, are summarized in Table 7-3. At two companies, data were available on the date of loan approval (center of the table). The median lag between approval date and the finance committee meeting date was twenty days for both of the samples from Company 1, and twelve and fifteen days for the samples from Company 6. None of the individual loans in these samples lagged more than twenty-eight days. At Company 4, data were available on the date of application and the date a letter of approval was sent to the home office from the field; these dates bracket the date of loan approval, but the notification date ordinarily would be closer. For Company 2, only the date of application was available. These data indicate lags of the same general order of magnitude.

2. Under some circumstances, the true transaction date precedes the date of approval of the loan application, generating a longer lag.

On direct loans, this can happen when a large tract development is involved. Builders planning a large tract typically want some sort of assurance regarding credit availability even before they acquire land

TABLE 7-2

Cyclical Amplitude of Effective Yield
in Authorization and Disbursement Series of One Company
(per cent change)

	Rise 1955-58	Decline 1958-59	Rise 1959-60	Decline 1960-64
All				
Authorization	20.1	2.7	19.2	12.5
Disbursement	18.3	0.1	17.9	11.7
Conventionals				
Authorization	20.8	7.4	19.9	10.7
Disbursement	18.6	3.9	18.9	10.3
FHA				
Authorization	20.9	1.5	19.3	13.3
Disbursement	21.4	0.5	18.2	12.3

Note: Per cent changes are calculated from three-month averages centered at peaks and troughs of each series. Terminal date of 1960 − 64 decline is July 1964 in all series.

or prepare a subdivision. In such cases, it is common to submit tentative plans, and the lender's approval of these plans, which includes a statement of the terms at which credit will be made available if the plans go ahead as stated, constitutes a sort of moral commitment. This is later ratified by the submission and approval of the formal loan application, but the terms in the application hark back to the earlier statement of approval.

Fortunately, data are available for part of the period (1953–61) on the volume of direct loans authorized on large-scale tract developments by the companies in our survey. Such loans constituted less than one-fifth of total authorizations in every year except 1954, when they comprised about two-fifths of the total. From all indications, the figure was less than one-fifth in 1951, 1952, 1962, and 1963. No breakdown is available by type of loan, but company officers indicate that

TABLE 7-3

Distributions of Loans in Samples Drawn from Participating Companies by Number of Days Between Finance Committee Meeting Date and Earlier Stages of the Loan Transaction

Number of Days From Finance Committee Meeting Date	Submission of Application[a]				Loan Approval[b]				Notification of Approval[c]	
	Company 2		Company 4		Company 1		Company 6		Company 4	
	1952-53	1962	1953	1962	1951-52	1962	1953	1962	1953	1962
Less than 5	4		3				17		22	
5-10	5	8	19				23	11	18	
11-15	13	11	8	1	4	3	8	15	1	13
16-20	0	6	4	11	28	24	2	24	3	8
21-25	0		7	6	20	20			4	3
26-30	2		3	6	2				0	9
31-35			0	17					1	17
36-40			2	2					1	
41-45			2	4						
46-50			1	2						
51-55	1		1							
Number of loans in sample	25	25	50	49	54	47	50	50	50	50
Median "lag" (days)	11	12	12	31	20	20	12	15	5	26

[a]Based on date of submission of application to company by correspondent.

[b]Based on date when lending officer approved loan to correspondent or other borrower.

[c]Based on date when letter of approval was sent to home office from field office.

the proportion of tract loans was much higher on FHA and VA loans, which are used more extensively in tract operations, than on conventional loans.

These facts suggest several tests to assess the effect of moral commitments on the timing of direct loan series. First, since the proportion of moral commitments is considerably higher on FHA than on conventional loans, it can be inferred that if moral commitments affect the timing of series, direct FHA yields should be more sluggish than direct conventional yields. This is not in fact the case. At each of six turning points during 1951–63, FHA and conventional loans turned within one month of each other. Table 3-6 (columns 4 and 5) shows that at four of the five turning points in government bond yields, FHA yields were slightly *less* sluggish than conventional yields on direct loans, while at the fifth (October 1957) turning point, there was no appreciable difference. It may be noted that on correspondent loans also there were no significant differences in the timing of conventional and FHA yields.

A second test is to compare the sluggishness of FHA yields at the 1954 trough, when the volume of tract developments was abnormally large, with the 1958 trough. If moral commitments affected the behavior of the series, the rise in yields that began in late 1954 should have been restrained to a greater degree than the rise from the 1958 trough. Table 3-6 indicates that this was not the case either. Mortgage yields were substantially more sluggish at the 1958 trough, both in absolute terms and relative to other market rates.

Neither of these tests is conclusive, since other factors may affect relative timing of FHA and conventional yields, and of mortgage yields versus bond yields. Yet, it does seem safe to conclude that whatever effect moral commitments had on the timing of the direct loan series was quite small.

On correspondent loans, the true transaction date may precede the date of approval of the loan application when the correspondent commits himself to a builder or mortgagor before obtaining a commitment from the company, *and* the correspondent's commitment is binding on the transaction between the correspondent and the company (see the discussion in Chapter 6). In such case, the date of the correspondent's commitment, step 2b in the listing above, is the true transaction date.

Discussions with company officers and correspondents indicate that on precommitted loans by correspondents, the lag between the correspondent's commitment and the company's commitment may run from a week to several months. The impact on the timing of aggregate correspondent loan series, however, depends not only on this lag but on the relative importance of precommitments by correspondents that are binding on the company, *and* on the relative frequency with which the company changes its buying rate. The last factor is relevant because so long as the buying rate is constant, the correspondent's commitment exercises no constraining influence on the company's commitment.

On the other hand, if the company refrains from raising its buying rate under conditions where it would otherwise do so, in order not to burden correspondents who had committed at a lower rate, the correspondent's commitment is de facto binding on the company. It can be argued that in this case, just as in the case where the company raises its rate on new offerings but makes an exception for loans already committed by correspondents, the true transaction date is the date of the correspondent's commitment. As noted in Chapter 4, a relatively stable buying rate may be an alternative to a flexible rate conjoined with precommitment authority granted to correspondents. Alternatively, stable buying rates can be viewed as a behavioral phenomena rather than as a cause of recording lag. In any case, the evidence in Chapter 4 is that correspondent loans do lag direct loans.

8

The Effective Yield Concept

A mortgage transaction almost always involves cash payments between the lender and other parties to the transaction. The contract rate adjusted to take such payments into account is termed an "effective yield." More precisely, it is the rate which, when used to discount the stream of principal and income from the loan, equalizes its present value with the cost of the loan (equal to face amount less net fees received).

$$L - F = \frac{R_1}{1 + Y} + \frac{R_2}{(1 + Y)^2} + \cdots \frac{B}{(1 + Y)^p}$$

where L = face amount of loan
F = net fees received by lender
R = payment of principal and interest, determined by contract rate, maturity, and amortization arrangement
B = balance of loan at time of prepayment
Y = effective yield
p = prepayment period when balance is paid in full

To compute the effective yield thus requires all the information shown in the formula.[1]

The contract rate, contract maturity, and amortization arrangement are specified in the loan contract. Most residential mortgages today are

[1] Strictly speaking, the formula also should include any penalty that the borrower must pay the lender for the privilege of prepaying the loan, which would be represented in the formula by an increment to B in year p. There is no prepayment penalty on VA loans. There is a penalty, equal to 1 per cent of the original principal, for prepayment of an FHA loan within the first ten years of life, but this payment goes to the FHA rather than the lender. The companies in our survey employ a variety of prepayment-penalty formulas on conventional loans, which may vary from loan to loan depending on competitive conditions, the aggressiveness of borrowers, and other factors. We have made no provision for this payment in our calculation of yield because the prepayment provision on individual conventional loans is not shown on the finance committee records. To illustrate the effect on yield, a penalty payment equal to 1½ per cent of the outstanding balance, which would not be unusual, would raise yield by about ten basis points on a twenty-five-year mortgage prepaid after ten years.

amortized by the level monthly payment method, and this is the only method used by the lenders in our survey. Net fees received or paid are a part of the transaction, although not specified in the contract. While the prepayment period is not known at the time the loan is authorized, most loans are prepaid prior to maturity.

In this chapter we discuss a number of questions connected with the fees and charges that may be associated with mortgage loan transactions, including the types of charges that should be considered when calculating the yield. We also investigate the most appropriate assumption regarding prepayment, and the most efficient method of calculating effective yield.

Fees and Charges

Relationship to Yield Concepts

The types of fees and charges that should be included in calculating yield on a direct loan depends on the yield concept desired. If the series are designed to measure borrower cost, the concept most relevant to studies of mortgage credit demand, they would include charges by which the borrower reimburses the lender for expenses connected with the transaction, such as appraisal fees, even though these charges do not increase the lender's net income. On the other hand, fees received by a lender from a third party (as when a builder pays "points" for an FHA or VA loan) would not be included in borrower cost series unless the borrower in some way reimburses the third party (as by paying a higher price for a house). Similarly a "finder's fee" paid by the lender to a broker would not be included.

If the series are designed to measure lenders' net income,[2] the concept most relevant to analysis of the supply of mortgage credit, they would not cover lending expenses reimbursed by the borrower, but would reflect fees the lender paid or received from third parties.

Entanglement with Charges Connected to Property Transfer

Charges associated with directly-originated mortgage loans are often entangled with charges associated with property transfers. Conceptually,

---

[2] By "net income" we mean income net of expenses attributable to a specific loan transaction. All the yield series with which we are concerned in this study are gross of general administrative expenses as well as losses.

the portion of any given charge applicable to the loan transaction should be allocated to the loan, but as a practical matter, it is necessary to take all of it or none.

An appendix to this chapter indicates the amount, if any, of several types of charges to be included in a direct loan series designed to measure borrower cost or lender income.

Direct Versus Correspondent Loans

The problems associated with fees and charges discussed above apply only to direct loans. On correspondent loans, no property transfer is involved. Hence all of the payments involved are associated with the mortgage credit transaction and none with the property transfer (in this sense the correspondent loan is a "purer" transaction). Since the mortgagor is not involved in the transaction, correspondent loan yields can only measure lender income. No significant expenses are connected with correspondent loans, furthermore, so that no distinction arises between net and gross income.

Fees and Charges in the NBER Series

In compiling our historical series, we did not, of course, enjoy the luxury of choosing the fees and charges we wished to include. Our choices, however, may not have differed materially from the practices of the life insurance companies in our study. It is not possible to obtain borrower-cost data from lender records, and the company's practices provide the closest possible approximation to a net income concept.

On correspondent loans, as noted above, fees and charges are necessarily consistent with the net income concept. Ordinarily, only a single payment or price is shown on the finance committee record, and it indicates net income to the lender. A price of ninety-seven, for example, implies net fees received of 3 per cent. Occasionally, the record will show an "origination fee" along with the price, indicating that the company is separately reimbursing the correspondent for some of the latter's net origination costs, but this means merely that the net income has been divided into two components.

On direct loans, the general practice is to record all amounts paid or received as specific consideration for making the loan, and which adjust the lender's *net* income by a like amount. Finance committee records do not show charges that might be connected (in whole or in part) to property transfer or ownership or that are designed to defray lending costs, even though they may in part provide extra net income attributable to the credit extension. This procedure maximizes comparability between direct and correspondent loans. If income designed to reimburse the lender for origination costs were added to fees and charges on direct loans while the costs were not deducted, direct loan yields would have an upward bias relative to yields on correspondent loans.[3]

Finders Fees on Direct Loans

In the National Bureau series, fees paid to a broker are deducted from fees received. The FHLBB and Federal Reserve Bank of Chicago series, in contrast, exclude finders fees; whether this is because they wish to measure borrower cost rather than lender income, or because they do not consider "broker loans" comparable to nonbroker loans, is not clear. Broker loans do tend to have lower yields, but shifts in their relative importance may be an essential part of the market adjustment process that we want to be reflected in time series.

We ran a special tabulation of broker loans for the two cross-section months, June 1953 and February 1960. In the earlier month, fees were paid to a broker on about three-fourths of the direct conventional loans and one-tenth of the direct FHA loans. The gross yield on these loans was .11 and .21 per cent below that on nonbroker loans, for conventionals and FHAs, respectively. In February 1960, broker loans were much less important, were almost entirely conventionals, and carried a yield disadvantage of only .03 per cent. In February 1960, yields were close to peak levels and the companies were not prepared to pay brokers for mortgages unless they could earn a rate closely comparable to that on other (nonbroker) mortgages.

---

[3] Referring to the example on page 125, assume that net origination costs of .25 per cent on direct loans were derived from gross costs of .28 per cent and income of .03 per cent. If the income were included in fees received, the recorded gross yield on direct loans would be 6.03 per cent, compared to 6.00 per cent on correspondent loans, although the yield net of service and net origination costs would be the same for each. The point probably is not of great quantitative importance, however, because charges imposed by large life insurance companies to defray expenses, are small. We obtained data from one lender in our survey for June 1953 on the "origination service charge," a catch-all fee to reimburse the lender for a variety of expenses. If the aggregate of such charges had been added to the lender's income in that month, the effective yield on his direct loans would have risen by less than .01 per cent. This nonrecorded income on direct loans probably varies with market conditions as the incidence of various charges shifts between borrowers and lenders, but evidently this has a very small impact on the yield series for direct loans.

The Prepayment Assumption

The great majority of residential mortgages are prepaid in full prior to maturity. Obviously, it cannot be known at time of authorization when any individual loan will be repaid, but some assumption is required in calculating effective yield.

Differences in effective yield associated with different prepayment assumptions increase proportionately with increases in fees and charges. If net fees received, for example, amount to .50 per cent of the face amount of the loan, the effective yield on a 6 per cent twenty-four-year mortgage is 6.09 per cent if prepaid after eight years, and 6.07 per cent if prepaid after twelve years—a difference of only .02 per cent. If net fees amount to 10 per cent on such a mortgage, however, the effective yields corresponding to the two prepayment assumptions amount to 7.83 and 7.43 per cent—a difference of .40 per cent.

During the period covered by this study, the prepayment assumption was quantitatively important only on FHA and VA mortgages. Because the maximum contract rate on these mortgages is set by law or regulation and is changed infrequently, market adjustments take the form mainly of changes in price, expressed as premiums over or discounts from par. Discounts particularly have at times been sizeable, ranging up to ten points or even more on individual mortgages. In our time series, average monthly discounts for the United States as a whole ranged up to 4 per cent on FHA and up to 6 per cent on VA loans.[4] For conventional loans, in contrast, fees paid generally exceeded fees received but the U.S. average never exceeded 1 per cent.

The approach to the prepayment should be actuarial in nature. Our guess as to when any individual mortgage will be prepaid is worth little, but presumably a reasonable estimate can be made for a large number of similar mortgages, based on termination experience of mortgages made in the past. Two questions will be discussed with respect to this experience. First assuming past termination experience can be extrapolated, is it appropriate to use average life as the prepayment assumption? Second, should the prepayment assumption be related to the face maturity?

Since yield is not a linear function of mortgage life (see Chapter 4), the entire distribution of lives and not merely the average is relevant

---

[4] For some regions and states, of course, average discounts were higher.

to the average yield for a group of mortgages. Assume, for example, that we have a group of twenty-five-year 6 per cent mortgages priced at ninety-four and all are prepaid after ten years; the yield for each mortgage, and for the group is 6.92 per cent. If prepayments are evenly distributed between five, ten and fifteen years, the average life remains ten years, but the average yield rises to 7.06 per cent. This average yield assumes, however, that the interest, amortization and prepaid balance on the five-year mortgage are reinvested at the yield on the five-year mortgage, and similarly for the ten- and fifteen-year mortgages. On the more appropriate assumption that all flows are reinvested at the average calculated yield, the average is about 7.00 per cent.

Thus, when mortgages carry discounts, the use of average life as the prepayment assumption tends to understate yields; when mortgages carry premiums, this procedure overstates yields.

To determine the actual quantitative importance of this bias, we calculated the appropriately weighted average yield for 6 per cent mortgages of varying maturity and discount, on the assumptions that (a) the distribution of lives was the same as that for equivalent maturity FHA home mortgages made between 1935 and 1965, and (b) all flows are reinvested at the average yield. This yield is shown in column 3 of Table 8-1.[5] Column 4 compares this yield with the yield calculated on the assumption of prepayment at half the face maturity, which is approximately equal to the average life (see Table 8-2). The understatement of yield from using average life increases with the discount and reaches .25–.33 per cent when discounts are 10 points. Thus the use of average life as the prepayment assumption introduces a significant downward bias in the estimate of yield.

Should the prepayment assumption be related to the face maturity, a procedure used both by the Federal Reserve Bank of Chicago and by the Federal Home Loan Bank Board?[6] Table 8-2 shows that on FHA and VA mortgages, average life has been equal roughly to half the face

[5] The computer program required to calculate these yields was written by Anthony Curley of the University of Pennsylvania.

[6] In the Federal Reserve Bank of Chicago survey, prepayment was assumed to occur after eight years for mortgages maturing in less than twenty years, and after twelve years for mortgages with longer maturities. The Federal Home Loan Bank Board originally calculated yield on the assumption that loans are prepaid after a period equal to half the face maturity. Later, however, the FHLBB adopted the same procedure as the National Bureau of Economic Research, namely, a uniform assumption of ten years.

TABLE 8-1

Effective Yield on 6 Per Cent Contract Rate Mortgages Using Average Life
and Distribution of Lives, at Varying Maturities and Discounts

Discount (points) (1)	Yield at Average Life[a] (2)	Yield Using Distribution of Lives[b] (3)	Difference (Col 3-Col 2) (4)
		20 Year Mortgages	
2	6.31	6.37	.06
4	6.64	6.76	.12
6	6.97	7.16	.19
8	7.31	7.57	.26
10	7.66	7.99	.33
12	8.02	8.44	.42
14	8.40	8.89	.49
		25 Year Mortgages	
2	6.26	6.31	.05
4	6.53	6.64	.11
6	6.81	6.97	.16
8	7.10	7.32	.22
10	7.39	7.67	.28
12	7.69	8.04	.35
14	8.01	8.42	.41
		30 Year Mortgages	
2	6.23	6.28	.05
4	6.46	6.56	.10
6	6.71	6.85	.14
8	6.95	7.15	.20
10	7.21	7.46	.25
12	7.48	7.79	.31
14	7.75	8.12	.37

[a]Assumed to equal half the face maturity.

[b]FHA experience covering Section 203 mortgages during 1935-65.

TABLE 8-2

Estimated Life Expectancy of FHA and VA
Mortgages, by Maturity
(years)

Maturity	Average Life
FHA	
Less than 13 years	5.9
13-17 years	7.6
18-22 years	9.5
23-25 years	11.8
26-30 years	14.7
VA	
Less than 15 years	8.3
20 years	10.9
25 years	13.8
30 years	16.6

Note: FHA experience 1935 − 62 was on Section 203 mortgages only. VA experience 1944 − 60 was on primary home loans.

Source: 1964 *Annual Report of the Housing and Home Finance Agency*, p. 173; "Probable Life Expectancy of GI Home Mortgages," Veterans Administration (mimeograph).

maturity. Whether this relationship or any relationship of life to maturity should be employed depends partly on whether the relationship is likely to be stable.

This question can be approached by asking what determines the difference in life between mortgages of different face maturity. For simplicity, assume the mortgages have maturities of two and three years, respectively. The average life of the two-year mortgage is

$$L_2 = R_1 + 2R_2$$

where L_2 is average life, R_1 is the retirement rate in the first year (per cent of the original group of mortgages), and R_2 is the retirement rate in the second year. Since R_2 equals $1 - R_1$, this can be written

$$L_2 = 2 - R_1$$

Similarly for the three year mortgage,

$$L_3 = 3 - 2R_1' - R_2'$$

where R_1' and R_2' are retirement rates in the first and second years, respectively.

Thus,

$$L_3 - L_2 = 1 - 2R_1' - R_2' + R_1$$

The difference in life is positively related to the prematurity retirement rate on two-year mortgages and negatively related to the prematurity retirement rates on three-year mortgages. (Henceforth the term "retirement rates" refers to prematurity rates.) The retirement rates on the longer mortgages, however, carry more weight. Any uniform reduction in retirement rates will increase the difference in life between the long and short mortgage. This means that with a given relationship between retirement rates on longs and on shorts, the difference in life is affected by changes in the *general* level of retirement rates.

If we posit a "normal" level of retirement rates, the actual difference in life between long and short mortgages can be divided into three components: (1) the difference attributable to the difference in face maturity at normal retirement rates, which are assumed to be the same for long and short mortgages; (2) the difference attributable to the divergence between actual and normal retirement rates, still assuming the same rates for all mortgages (this component could be either positive or negative); and (3) the difference that is due to higher retirement rates on the shorter mortgages.

It seems likely that the second component has been positive, i.e., the actual retirement rates underlying the termination experience shown in Table 8-2 have been below normal because of the high level of assumptions during the period covered by that experience. (An assumption occurs when a property is transferred, but the existing mortgage remains in force; the new owner assumes the obligation.) The *1960 Census of Residential Financing* showed that one of every six outstanding mortgages on one-unit homeowner properties in 1960 had been assumed from previous owners. Assumption rates probably have been abnormally high because of the upward ratcheting of interest rates in the period since World War II. Termination of this trend would imply a rise in over-all retirement rates and consequently, a reduction in the differences in life between short and long mortgages. Since there is no way to determine normal retirement rates, there is no way of determining the quantitative importance of the changing trend; however, the major part of the difference in life between short and long mortgages is due to higher retirement rates on short mortgages (component 3).

Component 3 can be measured statistically from existing data covering termination experience of FHA mortgages. The actual difference in life between twenty- and twenty-five-year mortgages is 2.25 years, while the difference attributable to different retirement rates is 1.61 or 2.08 years,[7] depending on whether we equalize retirement rates at the

---

[7] Following the logic employed above

$$L_{25} = R_1' + 2R_2' + 3R_3' + \ldots 24R_{24}' + 25(1 - R_1' - R_2' - \ldots R_{24}')$$
$$L_{20} = R_1 + 2R_2 + 3R_3 + \ldots 19R_{19} + 20(1 - R_1 - R_2 - \ldots R_{19})$$

The actual difference in life $L_{25} - L_{20}$ is

$$L_{25} - L_{20} = 5 - 24R_1' - 23R_2' - \ldots R_{24}' + 19R_1 + 18R_2 + \ldots R_{19}$$

We then obtain a calculated difference in life $(L_{25} - L_{20})^c$ on the assumption that $R_1' = R_1 = R_1''$, $R_2' = R_2 = R_2''$ etc. Combining the Rs and subtracting

$$(L_{25} - L_{20})^c = 5 - 5R_{20}'' - 4R_{21}'' - 3R_{22}''$$
$$-2R_{23}'' - R_{24}'' - 5(R_1'' + R_2'' + \ldots R_{19}'')$$

The difference in life attributable to differences in retirement rates is the difference between actual life and life calculated on the assumption that retirement rates are the same.

$$L_{25} - L_{20} - (L_{25} - L_{20})^c = -24R_1' - 23R_2'$$
$$- \ldots R_{24}' + 19R_1 + 18R_2 + \ldots R_{19} + 5R_{20}'' + 4R_{21}''$$
$$+ 3R_{22}'' + 2R_{23}'' + R_{24}'' + 5(R_1'' + R_2'' + \ldots R_{19}'')$$

Since the only estimates of R_{20}'', $R_{21}'' \ldots R_{24}''$ are R_{20}', $R_{21}' \ldots R_{24}'$, we assume these to be equal, which reduces the expression.

$$L_{25} - L_{20} - (L_{25} - L_{20})^c = -24R_1' - 23R_2' - \ldots 6R_{19}'$$
$$+ 19R_1 + 18R_2 + \ldots R_{19} + 5(R_1'' + R_2'' \ldots R_{19}'')$$

R_1'', R_2'', etc. in this expression can be assumed equal either to R_1', $R_2'\ldots$ or R_1, $R_2 \ldots$. These two assumptions provide two estimates of the difference in life attributable to different retirement rates on long- and short-maturity mortgages.

level of those on the twenty-five-year mortgage or at the level of rates on the twenty-year mortgage.

The higher retirement rates on shorter mortgages reflect lower assumption rates.[8] The shorter mortgages are less attractive to home purchasers and are therefore less frequently assumed. This is partly for structural reasons. Loan balances are smaller on short-maturity loans, because they are paid down at a faster rate and because original loan values are smaller.[9] In addition, however, a transient element is involved. Over the period covered by the termination experience, interest rates were lower on the short-maturity mortgages because a larger proportion of them came from the early post-World War II period when interest rates were low.

Thus, two of the three components of the difference in life between long and short mortgages have been affected by the upward trend in interest rates. This raises a serious question regarding the stability of the relationship between mortgage life and face maturity.

In this study it was decided to use a uniform prepayment assumption rather than base the prepayment assumption on the face maturity. In addition to our question about the stability of the relationship between face maturity and mortgage life, we were influenced by pragmatic considerations of the ease in handling data; we found that variable prepayment assumptions introduce needless complexities into analytical uses of the data. A uniform assumption is easier to work with in the sense that it is usually a simple matter to determine the effect on results of a shift in assumption. This is true for both time series and cross-section analysis.

The assumption is ten years. No defense of this particular figure will be given. All our tabulations include the information needed to recompute the effective yield on a different assumption.[10] For analytical purposes, it is important to be aware of the implications of different assumptions. For time series analysis, for example, it is important to note the following:

1. If expected mortgage life increased with maturities over the post-World War II period, our assumption of a fixed prepayment period

[8] Although different retirement rates conceivably could reflect different turnover rates, there is no reason why turnover should be related to maturity of outstanding mortgages.

[9] On a cross-section basis, loan-value ratios and maturities tend to be positively correlated.

[10] The average effective yield for a group of loans calculated from the weighted average contract rate, net fees received, and maturity of the group is virtually the same as the weighted average of each individual effective yield.

results in a small upward bias in the secular trend of yields, the size of the bias depending on the level of discounts in the terminal years. For example, assuming that the "correct" prepayment assumption is half of the face maturity, the bias in the NBER-FHA series over the period 1951–63 associated with the extension of average maturity from 21 to 29 years amounts to .06–.12 per cent for discounts of 2 and 4 points respectively. The bias in the FHA secondary market series associated with an extension of maturity from 20 to 30 years over the period 1949–67 amounts to .16–.21 per cent for discounts of 5 and 7 points. Using a prepayment equal to $\frac{4}{10}$ of maturity, these possible biases fall to .02–.04 and .05–.10 per cent respectively.

2. The assumption of a uniform short prepayment period will raise the level of any time series and widen its cyclical amplitude relative to a series that embodies a uniform longer prepayment period, or a prepayment period that bears some fixed relationship to face maturity. The cyclical decline and rise in the FHA secondary market series during 1960–66 are reduced, respectively, from .85 to .81 per cent, and from 1.56 to 1.38 per cent if yields are calculated on the assumption that prepayment occurs after a period equal to half the face maturity. Using the $\frac{4}{10}$ of maturity assumption, the change in yields is only .03 per cent smaller in each phase.

The Computation of Effective Yield

The effective yield on a given mortgage can be obtained from the *Prepayment Mortgage Yield Table for Monthly Payment Mortgages*.[11] Since most cases involve an interpolation between the values shown in the book, this is a time-consuming operation when the number of loans is very large. It turned out also that the mathematical routine used in calculating effective yield when programmed for machine tabulation used an inordinate amount of machine time. As a result, we finally adopted an empirical, and easily programmed, formula which provides a close approximation to the yield shown in the yield book.[12] Table 8-3

[11] Second edition, Boston, 1962; hereafter referred to as the "yield book."

[12] This formula, which is a variant of one developed by Charles Torrance, formerly of the Federal Home Loan Bank Board, is as follows:

$$E = C + 2D(1/M + .0025C + .001M) - D/10M$$

where E = effective rate
       C = contract rate
       M = maturity (in years)
       D = discount (in points below par)

TABLE 8-3

Differences in Effective Yield Between Yield Book and Formula
(ten-year prepayment)

Price	10 Years Maturity			15 Years Maturity			20 Years Maturity			25 Years Maturity			30 Years Maturity		
	4%	5%	6%	4%	5%	6%	4%	5%	6%	4%	5%	6%	4%	5%	6%
99.5	.01	.01	.01	.01	.01	.00	.01	.00	.00	.00	.01	.01	.00	.00	.01
99.0	.02	.02	.02	.02	.01	.02	.01	.01	.01	.01	.01	.01	.01	.01	.01
98.5	.03	.02	.02	.02	.02	.02	.01	.01	.02	.01	.01	.01	.02	.01	.01
98.0	.03	.03	.03	.02	.02	.02	.01	.01	.02	.01	.01	.01	.02	.02	.02
97.5	.04	.04	.04	.02	.02	.02	.02	.02	.03	.02	.01	.02	.02	.02	.02
97.0	.04	.04	.04	.03	.04	.03	.02	.02	.03	.01	.02	.02	.02	.03	.02
96.5	.05	.04	.05	.03	.04	.03	.01	.02	.02	.01	.01	.02	.02	.03	.03
96.0	.04	.05	.05	.04	.04	.04	.02	.02	.02	.02	.02	.02	.03	.02	.03
95.5	.05	.05	.05	.04	.04	.04	.02	.02	.02	.02	.01	.02	.03	.03	.03
95.0	.05	.06	.05	.03	.04	.04	.02	.02	.03	.01	.02	.02	.03	.03	.03
94.5	.05	.05	.05	.04	.04	.05	.01	.02	.02	.02	.02	.02	.03	.03	.03
94.0	.05	.05	.05	.04	.04	.05	.01	.02	.02	.01	.02	.02	.02	.03	.03
93.5	.05	.05	.05	.04	.04	.04	.01	.02	.02	.02	.02	.02	.02	.03	.03
93.0	.04	.05	.05	.04	.04	.05	.01	.01	.02	.01	.01	.01	.02	.02	.03
92.5	.04	.04	.05	.04	.04	.04	.00	.01	.02	.01	.02	.01	.03	.03	.03
92.0	.03	.04	.04	.03	.03	.04	.00	.01	.01	.00	.01	.01	.02	.02	.02
91.5	.03	.04	.04	.03	.03	.04	.00	.00	.01	.00	.00	.01	.02	.03	.02
91.0	.02	.03	.03	.02	.03	.03	.00	.00	.00	.01	.00	.01	.02	.02	.02
90.5	.02	.02	.03	.02	.03	.03	.02	.01	.01	.01	.01	.01	.01	.03	.02
90.0	.01	.01	.02	.02	.03	.03	.02	.01	.01	.02	.01	.01	.01	.01	.01

shows differences in yield between the formula and the yield book for various values of discount, contract rate, and maturity. The largest difference is .05 per cent, and within the range of maturities where most observations fall (twenty to thirty years), the deviation is not more than .03 per cent. The errors, furthermore, are not systematically related to the maturity, the discount, or the contract rate.

This formula was used to calculate effective yield on each individual loan, from which weighted averages were then computed. As a check, the averages for the U.S. were recomputed from the yield book, using the average maturity, discount, and contract rate in each month. The differences between the book averages and those obtained from the program are shown in Table 8-4. On FHA loans the deviation is two basis points or less in 120 of 156 months, and only in one month is it as large as five basis points. For all practical purposes, therefore, it makes no difference whether the series used is calculated from the program or obtained from the yield book.

Nevertheless, anyone using our data on FHA loans who wishes to recalculate yield employing a different prepayment assumption should take account of the small difference between yield as calculated from the formula given above and yield as shown in the yield book. All the yield series shown in Appendix C are calculated from the formula.

TABLE 8-4

Deviation Between Yields Calculated in Program and
Yields Obtained from Yield Book, U.S. Averages
for FHA and VA Mortgages, 1951 — 63

Deviation (basis points)	FHA (months)	VA (months)
0	30	16
1	37	41
2	53	46
3	30	38
4	5	15
5	1	0
	156	156

Appendix:
Types of Fees and Charges on Direct Loans

Costs of Services Connected to Property Ownership.[18]

Certain costs of property ownership are usually prepaid at the time a mortgage is closed. These include property taxes and insurance designed to protect the owner—principally title, fire, and hazard insurance. Costs of property ownership should not be included in the effective rate on mortgage loans. If prepaid items are held in escrow by the lender, however, the interest on these funds is really an added cost of mortgage credit, as well as added income to the lender. To the extent that insurance is designed to protect the lender rather than the borrower, moreover, the charge is also part of the cost of credit, although it would not ordinarily be net income to the lender.

Costs of Property Transfer

These costs, which should also be excluded from the effective rate, include charges for state and federal stamps on the deed, and the conveyancing fee for recording the deed. They also include the property survey and appraisal report if these are for the borrower rather than the lender.

Costs of Services Connected to Credit Extension

These charges, which offset specified expenses of mortgage lending, include closing (or attorney's fee), credit report, appraisal report and property survey when required by the lender, and title or other insurance designed for the lender's protection. These charges are part of the cost of credit to the borrower. Ordinarily, they would constitute gross income, but not net income to the lender. Part of such charges could constitute net income, however, if priced by the lender above cost, or if the lender obtains a brokerage fee from a third party who provides the service.

On the other hand, some expenses incurred by the lender are not

---

[18] A further discussion of various types of charges can be found in *Closing Costs and Settlement Payments in the Jacksonville, Florida, Mortgage Market,* Housing Research Paper 22, Housing and Home Finance Agency, November 1952; and in John M. Ducey and Kenneth R. Berliant, *Loan Closing Costs on Single-Family Homes,* Institute of Urban Life, Chicago, May 1965.

reimbursed, and the lender generally pays to put a loan on the books. This is sometimes termed the "net origination cost."

Mortgage Service Charge

It is general practice for lenders to charge borrowers a fee, often 1 per cent of the loan or some flat dollar amount, to cover various miscellaneous costs of mortgage lending. Both the VA and FHA allow lenders to charge borrowers a 1 per cent fee to cover a number of expense items that cannot be charged for separately.[14] This charge differs from those under Costs of Services, above, only in not being related to a specific service. Like the others, this charge is clearly a cost to the borrower, but the extent to which it constitutes net income to the lender probably varies from case to case.

Points

When a lender pays less than face value for a mortgage ("discounts" it), or receives a premium, fee, or commision for granting the loan, which amounts to the same thing, his net income is increased. The distinguishing characteristic of points is that they do not even ostensibly purport to defray expenses, so that they represent net income to the lender.[15]

Points, however, may or may not represent a cost to the borrower, depending on who pays them, the borrower or the home seller. Regulations under the federal underwriting programs prohibit direct payment of points by borrowers, but home sellers (including builders) have generally been allowed to pay them as needed, and in many cases they have no doubt passed them along to borrowers in the form of a higher price.

Finder's Fee

Lenders sometimes pay a real estate or mortgage broker a fee for steering loans to them. These fees should be *deducted* from the effective rate if we are measuring return to the lender, but ignored if we are measuring cost to the borrower.

---

[14] A list of these miscellaneous charges will be found in *Closing Costs and Settlement Payments in the Jacksonville, Florida, Mortgage Market*, p. 12.

[15] Included in this category is the "commitment fee," which is retained by the lender even if the loan is not closed. From the standpoint of authorization data, commitment fees are indistinguishable from other sources of net income. From the standpoint of data on closings, however, commitment fees swell the lender's over-all net income without being included in the income attributable to any specific loan.

Brokerage Fee

On the other hand, sometimes borrowers will pay a fee to a broker for help in obtaining a loan. This should be considered a cost of credit, but it is not income to the lender.

Conceptually, we can aim at an effective rate series that measures cost to the borrower or net income to the lender. (By net income we mean net of costs connected to the specific loan transaction; the series would, of course, be gross of general administrative and operating expenses.) A gross income series would be identical to a borrower cost series except for the cost of services that the lender chooses to turn over to subcontractors. Since it is of no analytical interest whether the lender chooses to appraise a property himself or to have an outside appraiser do it for him, a gross income series has little merit.

The items that conceptually belong in cost and net income series can be summarized as follows:

	Coverage of Item in Series	
	Cost	Net Income
Interest on prepaid costs of property ownership when held in escrow by lender	All	All
Title and hazard insurance when required by, and designed to protect, lender	All	Only brokerage fee or commission earned by lender
Mortgage service charge, closing fee, credit report, and appraisal and property survey when required by lender	All	Only the part of charge above cost of service
Points, premiums, commissions, etc.	Portion paid by borrower directly or in price of house	All
Finder's fee	None	All
Brokerage fee	All	None

9

Reliability and Limitations of the Data

The new time series compiled for this study are subject to a number of independent checks. First, we have two checks on the extent to which the series accurately represent the experience of the participating companies. One check is a complete census of all loans made by participating companies in June 1953 and February 1960. The second is a set of yield series compiled by one company covering all its authorized loans; these company series are closely comparable to our sample series.

The new FHLBB data, which cover a larger number of companies, provide a broader check of how well the companies in our series represent the experience of life insurance companies generally. This check is limited to conventional loans during a one-year overlap period. Finally, the new NBER FHA series can be compared to the secondary market series based on quotations reported by the Federal Housing Administration.

Comparison with Benchmarks

For two months, June 1953 and February 1960, we compiled a complete census of loans made by participating companies. Later, when the time series sample was collected, these two months were treated in the same way as every other month. Appendix Tables 9-1 and 9-2 compare items calculated from the census and the sample for each company and loan type, in absolute terms and relative to standard errors. There are eight comparisons apiece for FHA and conventional loans (four companies on each of the two dates), and four comparisons for VA loans, or twenty in all.[1] Differences are calculated for four loan items, making a total of eighty comparisons between census and sample values. Summary data are shown in Tables 9-1 and 9-2. In general, the

[1] Only two companies authorized VA loans in February 1960. Three companies authorized VA loans in June 1953, but data were not available for one of them when we took the census. These loans later became available for the time series, but we did not find it advantageous to complete the census.

TABLE 9-1

Distribution of Ratios to Standard Errors of Differences
Between Census and Sample Values for Selected Loan Items,
February 1960 and June 1953 Combined
(number of cases)

	Ratio to Standard Error				
	1.0 or less	1.1-2.0	2.1-3.0	More than 3.0	Total
Gross yield	12	4	2	2	20
Value of property	14	4	2		20
Loan-value ratio	16	4			20
Maturity	13	6	1		20
Total	55	18	5	2	80
Per cent	69	22	6	3	100

Source: Appendix Tables 9-1 and 9-2.

comparison of census and sample values supports the validity of the sampling procedures used.

The distribution of differences between census and sample values by their ratio to standard errors is very close to what sampling theory would lead us to expect (Table 9-1). In 69 per cent of the cases (fifty-five of eighty cases), the difference between the census and sample value was one standard error or less; the theoretical expectation is 68 per cent. The difference was between one and two standard errors in 22 per cent of the cases (eighteen of eighty cases), compared to the theoretical expectation of 27 per cent. In only two of the eighty cases did the census-sample difference exceed three standard errors.

Table 9-2 shows the absolute difference in gross yield between census and sample values for the twenty samples. Eight of the differences were less than .005 per cent (that is, less than one basis point rounded), while only one exceeded .03 per cent. This was one of several cases where the number of loans fell well short of the sample target so that the census and sample values theoretically should have been the same. In fact, more loans were recorded in the sample than in the census. This is because the census was done first, and by the time we took the sample, our procedures were more thorough and our work force better

TABLE 9-2

Comparison of Gross Yield from Census and Sample,
by Type of Mortgage and Company

	Gross Yield			Number of Loans	
	Census	Sample	Census less Sample	Census	Sample
February 1960					
Conventionals					
1	6.07	6.04	.03	1178	124
2	5.87	5.86	.01	14	16
4	6.10	6.10	.00	390	116
6	5.98	6.00	-.02	787	127
FHA					
1	6.40	6.40	.00	888	124
2	5.75[a]	5.75[a]	.00	7	8
4	6.26	6.26	.00	142	118
6	6.22	6.22	.00	2618	110
VA					
1	6.01	6.00	.01	755	125
6	5.90	5.92	-.02	15	20
June 1953					
Conventionals					
1	4.64	4.64	.00	2052	111
2	4.80	4.80	.00	33	34
4	4.84	4.82	.02	180	113
6	4.87[a]	4.88[a]	-.01	919	121
FHA					
1	4.52	4.53	-.01	1362	108
2	4.45	4.35	.10[b]	14	19
4	4.49	4.50	-.01	333	118
6	4.50	4.50	.00	1639	118
VA					
1	4.52	4.55	-.03	134	114
4	4.50	4.49	.01[b]	74	71

[a]Contract rate.

[b]More than three times the standard error.

Source: Appendix Tables 9-1 and 9-2.

trained; as a result, at one company loans were unearthed that had been overlooked in the census. In these cases, therefore, the sample values are correct.

Comparison of Sample Yields Covering One Company with Yields on All Loans by That Company

One of the companies in our sample, for its own use, began in 1954 to calculate an effective yield (net of service fee) on all its authorized loans with breakdowns by type of loan. Although these series are not completely comparable with ours, the differences are small and do not invalidate their use to test the reliability of our procedures. The two main differences between the series are that the company series include Canadian loans, while the NBER series do not: and the yield is cal-

CHART 9-1

NET YIELD ON CONVENTIONAL CORRESPONDENT LOANS
BY ONE COMPANY, 1954–63:
SAMPLE VERSUS UNIVERSE SERIES

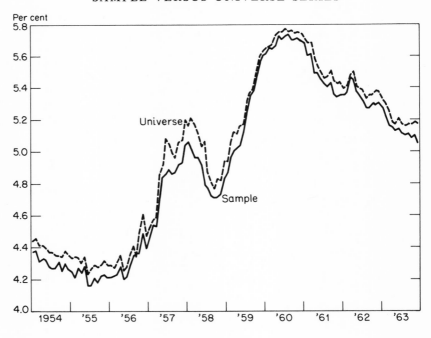

CHART 9-2

NET YIELD ON FHA CORRESPONDENT LOANS
BY ONE COMPANY, 1954–63:
SAMPLE VERSUS UNIVERSE SERIES

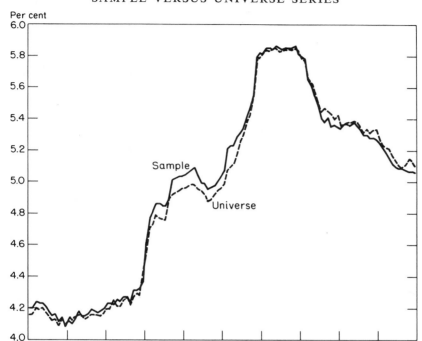

culated differently in the two series.[2] For this test, we plotted time
series of census and sample values (Charts 9-1, 9-2, and 9-3), and
compiled frequency distributions of the differences between census and
sample values (Table 9-3).

Mainly because Canadian loans were included, the company series
on conventional loans averaged about .08 percentage points higher than
the National Bureau series (Chart 9-1). Therefore, we raised the
Bureau series by a uniform .08 percentage points before calculating
monthly differences. In about two-thirds of the observations the yield
difference was .03 percentage points or less and in only five months was
the difference greater than .08 percentage points (Table 9-3). These

[2] The company assumes a fixed maturity rather than the actual, and shifts its
prepayment assumption.

CHART 9-3

NET YIELD ON VA CORRESPONDENT LOANS
BY ONE COMPANY, 1954–63:
SAMPLE VERSUS UNIVERSE SERIES

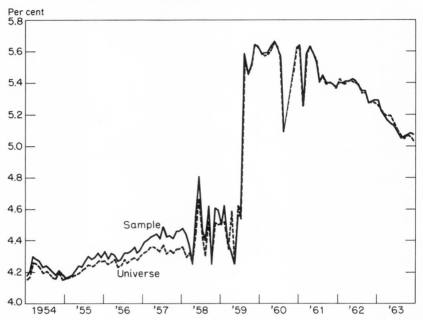

differences are somewhat larger than those that would be expected from sampling error alone. (The median monthly standard deviation of .231 per cent implies a standard error of .02 percentage points, suggesting that about two-thirds of the differences should be within .02 rather than within .03 percentage points.) This probably reflects the difference in coverage, the effects of which are only partly eliminated by the over-all adjustment in yield level.

On FHA and VA mortgages, differences between the Bureau series and the company series are somewhat larger than on conventionals (Table 9-3). The yield difference is .03 percentage points or less in 65 of 120 months for FHAs, and in 69 of 117 months for VAs,[3] as compared to 78 of 120 months for conventionals. The difference is larger than .08 per cent in fourteen months for both FHAs and VAs as compared to five months for conventionals. This is due partly to the greater

[3] The Bureau series on VA loans is reduced a uniform .03 percentage points before calculating differences.

TABLE 9-3

Frequency Distribution of Monthly Differences in Net Effective Yield
Between NBER Sample Series and Company Universe Series
for One Company, 1954 – 63

Percentage Points	Conventional		FHA		VA	
	Number	Cum. Total	Number	Cum. Total	Number	Cum. Total
.00	19	19	6	6	9	9
.01	25	44	24	30	14 (2)	23
.02	21	65	18	48	19 (2)	42
.03	13	78	17	65	27 (12)	69
.04	14	92	15	80	15 (5)	84
.05	10	102	5	85	11 (4)	95
.06	7	109	5	90	2	97
.07	3	112	10	100	5 (1)	102
.08	3	115	6	106	1 (1)	103
.09	0		7	113	5 (3)	108
.10	1	116	3	116	0	
.11	0		2	118	0	
.12	1	117	0		2 (2)	110
.13	1	118	2	120	3 (3)	113
.14	1	119			0	
.15	0				1 (1)	114
.18	0				2 (2)	116
.19	1	120			0	
.23					1 (1)	117

Note: Differences are calculated after adjustment for conventionals (sample series) raised .08 percentage points), and VAs (sample series reduced .03 percentage points). Figures in parentheses refer to VA loans during the period December 1957-May 1961, when the sample was very thin. In three months, there were no observations.

impact on federally underwritten mortgages of the methods used to calculate gross yield. The company changed its assumption regarding average maturity and prepayment several times during 1954–63, and this resulted in shifts in the level of the company series relative to the Bureau's sample series.

VA loans accounted for nine of the fifteen yield differences of .12 per cent or more. All nine of these cases occurred during the period December 1957–May 1961, when the total number of VA loans authorized by the company fell short of the target, coverage was (theoretically) complete, and there should have been no sampling error. Part of the explanation is that discounts were relatively large in the complete coverage months, so that the different maturity and prepayment assumptions had a larger effect. Probably the main reason, however, is that there were so few loans that small differences in loan coverage or recording errors had a substantial effect on the averages. In several cases that we were able to check, we found the recording error to be in the company series rather than in ours.

The frequency distribution of yield differences between the company and Bureau series are probably less significant than the pattern of differences over time; a given frequency distribution could have very different implications for the reliability and usefulness of sample series, depending upon how the differences are distributed over time. In this respect, Charts 9-1, 9-2, and 9-3 are reassuring. Although the relative levels of the sample series and company series change over the period, cyclical movements correspond very closely. The sample series, furthermore, are no more erratic than the company series. This constitutes strong evidence that our sample series accurately portray the experience of the companies participating in our survey.

Comparison with FHLBB Series

The third test is a comparison of our series on conventional mortgages with the new Federal Home Loan Bank Board series during 1963, when the series overlap. This is not a rigorous test because the series are not strictly comparable, yet their relationship is of considerable interest. We want to know the extent to which the differences in comparability actually affect the recorded yields, and whether the series can appropriately be spliced.

The most important differences in the series are as follows.

1. *Sample.* The FHLBB sample is somewhat larger and more variable, as shown on the lowermost two lines of Table 9-4. During 1963, it ranged from 351 to 767 loans per month while the National Bureau sample ranged from 305 to 381. The FHLBB series is drawn from forty-four companies, but not all of them have reported consistently; the National Bureau series covers four companies. The FHLBB sample is "proportional" in the sense that individual lenders contribute loans roughly in proportion to their relative importance, while the NBER aimed at a sample of equal absolute size for each lender.

2. *Coverage.* The FHLBB series only covers direct loans, while the National Bureau series includes direct and correspondent loans.

3. *Fees and Charges.* The FHLBB survey includes fees received by lenders but not fees paid, while the National Bureau series includes both, netting one against the other. As a result, the National Bureau series generally shows a small negative figure, while the FHLBB series shows a small positive figure. The difference between them, expressed as per cent of face loan amount, was .38 per cent in 1963 (see Table 9-4), the equivalent of about six basis points in yield.

4. *Purpose of Loan.* A larger proportion of the loans in the NBER series than in the FHLBB series is for the purpose of buying newly built homes. The NBER series does not have a "purpose of loan" breakdown, however, while the FHLBB series has a threefold break.

Despite these differences, the loan characteristics in the two series are remarkably similar. The contract rate averaged about .04 per cent higher in the Bureau series during 1963, with monthly differences ranging from .07 per cent to − .01 per cent. Similarly, average effective rate in the two series differed by only .02 per cent; property value by less than $1,000; loan-value ratio by two percentage points; and maturity by seven months. With the exception of the loan-value ratio, these differences between the series are smaller than some of the erratic month-to-month changes in both series.

These results reflect the relative homogeneity of conventional mortgage loans authorized by life insurance companies, as discussed in Chapter 2. They lend support to the assumption underlying our study that a series covering a small number of national lenders would provide an accurate picture of life insurance company lending in general.

Comparability between the National Bureau and the FHLBB series is even closer if the latter is limited to loans covering newly built homes, since the National Bureau series is heavily weighted by such loans. As indicated in Table 9-5 (based on Table 9-4 and Appendix Table 9-3), the differences in average contract rate, property value, loan-value ratio, and maturity between the National Bureau and FHLBB series are smaller on this basis than using the over-all FHLBB series.

Strict comparability in effective yield is not possible because of the different definition of fees and charges. It is analytically neater to use the contract rate for both series. In practice, however, it makes little difference whether contract rate or effective yield is used because fees and charges are very small. Effective yield in the Bureau series turns out to be virtually identical to contract rate in the FHLBB series on

TABLE 9-4

Characteristics of Conventional Loans Authorized by Life Insurance Companies in 1963,
NBER and FHLBB series

	Jan.	Feb.	March	April	May	June	July
Contract rate (%)							
NBER	5.65	5.63	5.59	5.58	5.54	5.57	5.56
FHLBB	5.58	5.59	5.54	5.52	5.55	5.52	5.53
Difference	.07	.04	.05	.06	-.01	.05	.03
Fees and charges							
NBER	-.28	-.08	-.29	-.26	-.18	-.25	-.22
FHLBB	.16	.17	.20	.15	.22	.18	.17
Difference	-.44	-.25	-.49	-.41	-.40	-.43	-.39
Effective rate (%)							
NBER	5.61	5.61	5.55	5.54	5.51	5.53	5.53
FHLBB	5.60	5.60	5.56	5.54	5.58	5.54	5.54
Difference	.01	.01	-.01	.00	-.07	-.01	-.01
Value of property ($)							
NBER	27349	28783	28150	27864	27486	27092	26982
FHLBB	28980	27822	28433	28621	28189	29153	28723
Difference	-1631	961	-283	-757	-703	-2061	-1741
Loan-value (%)							
NBER	70.5	70.4	70.5	70.3	69.5	70.4	70.3
FHLBB	67.3	69.1	68.6	68.0	67.7	68.5	68.1
Difference	3.2	1.3	1.9	2.3	1.8	1.9	2.2
Maturity (mos.)							
NBER	307	310	307	312	307	309	313
FHLBB	302	300	304	299	303	306	300
Difference	5	10	3	13	4	3	13
Number of loans							
NBER	323	367	347	363	354	305	357
FHLBB	385	460	539	579	670	639	767

[a]Unweighted.

Aug.	Sept.	Oct.	Nov.	Dec.	1963 Average[a]
5.52	5.55	5.55	5.52	5.50	5.56
5.50	5.50	5.49	5.49	5.51	5.52
.02	.05	.06	.03	-.01	.04
-.21	-.19	-.24	-.24	.01	-.20
.17	.18	.15	.18	.18	.18
-.38	-.37	-.39	-.42	-.17	-.38
5.48	5.52	5.51	5.48	5.50	5.53
5.52	5.52	5.51	5.51	5.53	5.55
-.04	.00	.00	-.03	-.03	-.02
27166	27307	27923	28358	27817	27689
28700	28693	28626	28638	29358	28660
-1534	-1386	-703	-280	-1541	-971
70.1	70.0	70.3	70.3	68.7	70.1
68.8	67.7	67.7	68.7	67.5	68.1
1.3	2.3	2.6	1.6	1.2	2.0
314	306	318	314	309	310
308	304	300	306	303	303
6	2	18	8	6	7
355	381	359	314	342	347
678	571	612	351	523	564

TABLE 9-5

Characteristics of Conventional Loans Authorized by Life Insurance
Companies, NBER and FHLBB Series, 1963 Annual Averages

	Contract Rate (per cent)	Fees and Charges (per cent)	Effective Rate (per cent)	Property Value (dollars)	Loan-Value (per cent)	Maturity (months)
FHLBB						
all	5.52	.18	5.55	28660	68.1	303
newly built	5.54	.17	5.55	28074	68.6	312
construction	5.51	.18	5.53	29631	67.5	300
previously occupied	5.54	.18	5.56	28521	68.1	292
NBER	5.56	-.20	5.53	27689	70.1	310
NBER less FHLBB (all)	.04	-.38	-.02	-971	2.0	7
NBER less FHLBB (newly built)	.02	-.37	-.02	-385	1.5	-2

newly built homes, because a slightly higher contract rate in the Bureau series during 1963 was offset by the inclusion of fees paid. A pragmatic case can be made, therefore, for splicing effective yield in the Bureau series with contract rate in the FHLBB series (the procedure used in this study).

Comparison with FHA Secondary Market Series

The Bureau series on FHA mortgage yields were compared with the FHA secondary market series based on quotations reported by that agency. The FHA series has been widely used, but it has always been somewhat suspect because the underlying quotations are based on *opinions* of FHA insuring-office directors about the prices at which mortgages are trading in market areas of insuring office cities. A priori, the National Bureau series are thus more soundly based than the secondary market series, so that comparison of the two constitutes more a test of the latter than the former.

Sometime ago one of the authors commented on the secondary market series as follows:

Although economists are apt to be skeptical toward such data, the writer has come to the conclusion that they reflect the prevailing state of the market with considerable accuracy. In the first place, although the quotations are not actual offers to buy or sell they are nevertheless the opinions of persons who must be considered experts with respect to conditions in their local markets (these are the directors of FHA insuring offices). Secondly, the procedure of taking a simple unweighted average of quotations from 60 to 70 such offices solves in a fashion the most difficult part of the problem of maintaining from month to month an underlying security of fixed yield-determining characteristics. The structural variation in yields associated with location does not influence the movement of the series over time. Unfortunately, the same cannot be said for the terms of the mortgage (down payment and maturity). Until 1956 respondents were instructed to report the price of "typical transactions," which left the question of maturity and down payment an open one. It is not believed, however, that this constitutes a major source of error in the series. . . .[4]

In addition to a fundamental difference in the source of quotations, other differences in the two series are as follows.

[4] Guttentag, "Some Studies of the Post-World War II Residential Construction and Mortgage Markets," pp. 68–70.

1. Terms on the Bureau series pertain to the characteristics of mortgages currently authorized. In contrast, no terms were specified in the secondary market series prior to January 1957, the series covering "typical transactions." During 1957–63, the secondary market series refer to new home mortgages with 10 per cent down payment and twenty-five year maturities. In 1957 maturities on the Bureau series were a little longer and loan-value ratios a little lower than those specified in the secondary market series, but the terms in the Bureau series became increasingly liberal during the balance of this period. This may explain why the secondary market yield series is generally higher in the early part of the 1951–63 period while the Bureau series is higher at the end of the period (Chart 9-4). The shift is very gradual, however, and does not affect their comparative cyclical behavior.

2. The secondary market series always pertains to mortgages carrying the current maximum allowable contract rate, whereas the Bureau series sometimes includes mortgages at rates other than the current

CHART 9-4

GROSS YIELD AND CONTRACT RATE ON FHA LOANS,
1951–63

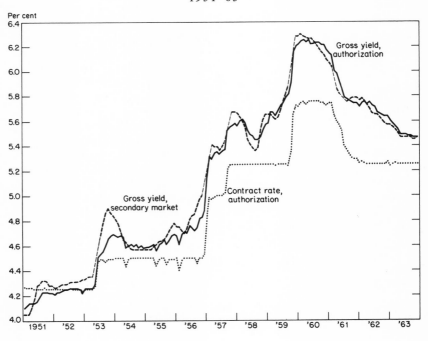

maximum. The number of such mortgages, however, is very small except in the period immediately following a change in the maximum rate. As shown in Chart 9-4, the contract rate in the Bureau series hugs the maximum allowable rate with only minor deviations. During these periods of transition, the FHA does not report secondary market prices, as indicated by the light dashed lines in the chart.[5]

3. The National Bureau series covers new commitments, implying actual delivery of the instrument sometime in the future, while the secondary market series pertains to "immediate delivery" transactions, sometimes referred to as "over-the-counter" transactions. The difference is one of degree, since commitment periods may be quite short in some cases (as on loans secured by existing houses), while "immediate delivery" may involve a month or more between the transaction and delivery dates. Nevertheless, the average delivery time is no doubt considerably longer in the Bureau series.[6]

4. The NBER series is weighted by the loan volume of the individual lenders covered by the series (see Appendix A), while the secondary market series is weighted by "the probable volume of secondary market sales in the jurisdiction of each of the insuring offices throughout the country."

5. The lender groups covered are different. Whereas the Bureau series covers only large life insurance companies, the secondary market series apparently is weighted heavily by mutual savings banks, which are most active in over-the-counter purchases. Beyond this is a difference in market relationships and organization. Because of their investment in branch organization or correspondent relationships, large life insurance companies tend to maintain continuity in their over-all mortgage investing. Savings banks, in contrast, while maintaining continuity in their local lending, are in and out of the national market, depending on their available funds.[7] It was argued in Chapter 4 that this probably

[5] To provide a continuous secondary market series, we have interpolated values for these months based on FNMA quotations. The complete series is given in Appendix Table 9-4.

[6] The secondary market series is dated as of the first day of the stated month, while the Bureau series covers transactions throughout the month; this implies a recording lead in the Bureau series of about fifteen days. On the other hand, this lead tends to be offset by the short recording lag in the Bureau series between the date of approval of the loan application and the date of finance committee meeting.

[7] For further discussion of differences in modus operandi between life insurance companies and mutual savings banks, see Klaman, *The Postwar Residential Mortgage Market*, pp. 137–156.

CHART 9-5

GROSS YIELD ON FHA MORTGAGES, 1951–63:
AUTHORIZATION SERIES ON DIRECT LOANS
VERSUS SECONDARY MARKET SERIES

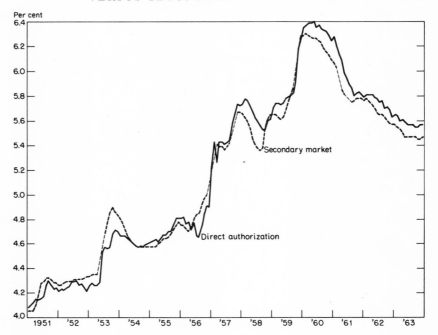

accounts for the greater cyclical sensitivity of the secondary market series.

The secondary market and National Bureau series are compared in Chart 9-4, which shows the Bureau series on all FHA loans, and Chart 9-5, which shows the Bureau series on direct loans only.[8]

In general, these statistical comparisons defend the view expressed earlier that the secondary market series reflects the state of the market with considerable accuracy. Cyclical correspondence between the series is quite close, particularly when the authorization series is limited to

[8] To make the National Bureau and secondary market series as comparable as possible, gross yields in the Bureau series have been recomputed from the yield book using the average discount, contract rate, and maturity for each month. The secondary market series is calculated on an assumed twenty-five-year maturity (see Appendix Table 9-4). The assumed prepayment period is ten years for both series.

direct loans, as in Chart 9-5. Several intracyclical movements in the secondary market series have only a dim counterpart in the Bureau's series on all loans but do show up in the direct loan series. During the entire 1951–63 period, there is only one persistent movement of four months or longer in the direct loan series—the brief decline in the second half of 1952—that does not have a counterpart in the secondary market series. There is not a single such movement in the secondary market series that does not have a counterpart in the direct loan series.

APPENDIX TABLE 9-1

Sample and Total Loans Authorized by Each of Four Life Insurance Companies
in February 1960: Comparison of Selected Items, Total United States

	Company 1			Company 4		Company 6			Company 2	
	FHA	VA	Conv.	FHA	Conv.	FHA	VA	Conv.	FHA	Conv.
Number of loans										
(T)	888	755	1178	142	390	2618	15	787	7	14
(S)	124	125	124	118	116	110	20	127	8	16
Gross yield (%)										
T	6.40	6.01	6.07	6.26	6.10	6.22	5.90	5.98	5.75[b]	5.87
S	6.40	6.00	6.04	6.26	6.10	6.22	5.92	6.00	5.75[b]	5.86
T-S	.00	.01	.03	.00	.00	.00	-.02	-.02	.00	.01
std. dev. (T)	.293	.075	.164	.097	.158	.079	.200	.190	.169	.323
std. error[a]	.026	.007	.015	.009	.015	.008	.044	.017	.060	.081
(T-S) ÷ std. error	.00	1.4	2.0	.00	.00	.00	0.5	1.2	.00	0.1
Value of property ($)										
T	15835	17073	25467	16233	25268	16045	19308	23384	13843	25234
S	15512	17010	25184	16413	25634	16139	18013	23708	13362	26363
T-S	323	63	283	-180	-366	-94	1295	-324	481	-1129
std. dev. (T)	3135	1849	7643	3281	8993	3676	4331	7665	3612	8375
std. error	282	165	689	301	832	350	962	678	1281	2094
(T-S) ÷ std. error	1.1	0.4	0.4	0.6	0.4	0.3	1.3	0.5	0.4	0.5

Loan-value (%)									
T	92.3	99.7	69.9	90.2	69.5	92.0	88.1	69.1	91.5	63.9
S	92.7	99.8	69.9	90.0	69.1	91.9	90.1	69.3	92.1	59.9
T-S	-0.4	-0.1	.00	0.2	0.4	0.1	-2.0	-0.2	-0.6	4.0
std. dev. (T)	5.22	2.57	8.77	6.76	8.73	4.39	8.06	8.33	4.01	12.38
std. error	0.57	.23	.79	.62	.81	.42	1.79	.74	1.42	3.10
(T-S) ÷ std. error	0.8	0.5	0.0	0.3	0.5	0.2	1.1	0.3	0.4	1.3
Maturity (mos.)									
T	346.5	358.8	285.6	334.4	281.9	346.3	352.9	279.7	352.9	262.2
S	344.2	358.2	286.8	335.8	285.2	340.4	354.4	281.3	331.5	256.1
T-S	2.3	0.6	-1.2	-1.4	-3.3	5.9	-1.5	-1.6	21.4	6.1
std. dev. (T)	29.75	5.27	33.02	30.73	36.12	32.38	20.40	37.30	21.00	43.01
std. error	2.68	.47	2.97	2.82	3.33	3.08	4.53	3.30	7.44	10.75
(T-S) ÷ std. error	0.9	1.3	0.4	0.5	1.0	1.9	0.3	0.5	2.9	0.6

[a] Standard deviation of all loans divided by the square root of the sample size.

[b] Contract rate.

T=total.

S=sample.

APPENDIX TABLE 9-2

Sample and Total Loans Authorized by Each of Four Life Insurance Companies in June 1953: Comparison of Selected Items, Total United States

	Company 1			Company 4			Company 6		Company 2	
	FHA	VA	Conv.	FHA	VA	Conv.	Conv.	FHA	Conv.	FHA
Number of loans										
(T)	1362	134	2052	333	74	180	919	1639	33	14
(S)	108	114	111	118	71	113	121	118	34	19
Gross yield (%)										
T	4.52	4.52	4.64	4.49	4.50	4.84	4.87[b]	4.50	4.80	4.45
S	4.53	4.55	4.64	4.50	4.49	4.82	4.88[b]	4.50	4.80	4.35
T-S	-.01	-.03	.00	-.01	.01	.02	-.01	.00	.00	-.10
std. dev. (T)	.116	.152	.209	.048	.027	.143	.241	.115	.132	.103
std. error[a]	.011	.014	.019	.004	.003	.013	.022	.011	.023	.023
(T-S) ÷ std. error	0.9	2.1	0.0	2.5	3.3	1.5	0.5	0.0	.00	4.3
Value of property ($)										
T	11862	13620	19937	12214	12799	20993	19089	10610	20795	10293
S	11704	13099	19560	11757	12766	20046	17751	10382	20584	10450
T-S	158	521	377	457	33	947	1338	228	211	-157
std. dev. (T)	2869	3283	7594	2156	2367	7095	6728	2435	5094	2080
std. error	276	307	723	198	282	669	612	223	878	473
(T-S) ÷ std. error	0.6	1.7	0.5	2.3	0.1	1.4	2.2	1.0	0.2	0.3

Loan-value(%)									
T	80.7	91.1	65.6	80.5	86.8	62.3	62.2	84.1	61.9	84.9
S	81.5	91.5	65.9	80.8	86.8	61.1	62.0	84.5	61.9	84.9
T-S	-0.8	-0.4	-0.3	-0.3	0.0	1.2	0.2	-0.4	0.0	0.0
std. dev. (T)	6.99	8.86	9.08	5.36	5.23	7.00	5.95	6.91	5.01	5.31
std. error	.67	.83	.86	.49	.62	.66	.54	.63	.86	1.21
(T-S) ÷ std. error	1.2	0.5	0.3	0.6	0.0	1.8	0.4	0.6	0.0	0.0

Maturity (mos.)									
T	251.4	268.9	224.9	248.6	266.6	229.6	223.4	255.6	222.6	271.3
S	255.6	262.8	228.6	249.7	268.3	227.1	222.4	254.6	222.9	274.8
T-S	-4.2	6.1	3.7	1.1	1.7	2.5	1.0	1.0	-0.3	-3.5
std. dev. (T)	26.42	32.44	26.57	22.75	29.82	24.71	25.41	29.62	23.84	30.00
std. error	2.5	3.0	2.5	2.1	3.6	2.3	2.3	2.7	4.1	6.8
(T-S) ÷ std. error	1.7	2.0	1.5	0.5	0.5	1.1	0.4	0.4	0.1	0.5

[a] Standard deviation of all loans divided by the square root of the sample size.
[b] Contract rate.
T=total.
S=sample.

APPENDIX TABLE 9-3

Characteristics of Conventional Loans Authorized by Life Insurance Companies in 1963:
NBER Series and FHLBB Series on Newly Built Homes

	Jan.	Feb.	March	April	May	June	July
Contract rate (%)							
NBER	5.65	5.63	5.59	5.58	5.54	5.57	5.56
FHLBB	5.59	5.59	5.55	5.51	5.57	5.53	5.55
difference	.06	.04	.04	.07	-.03	.04	.01
Fees and charges (%)							
NBER	-.28	-.08	-.29	-.26	-.18	-.25	-.22
FHLBB	.16	.16	.19	.14	.20	.19	.18
difference	-.44	-.24	-.48	-.40	-.38	-.44	-.40
Effective rate (%)							
NBER	5.61	5.61	5.55	5.54	5.51	5.53	5.53
FHLBB	5.61	5.6C	5.57	5.52	5.59	5.56	5.56
difference	.00	.01	-.02	.02	-.08	-.03	-.03
Value of property ($)							
NBER	27349	28783	28150	27864	27486	27092	26982
FHLBB	28728	27965	28057	27520	27938	28691	27507
difference	-1379	818	93	344	-452	-1599	-525
Loan-value (%)							
NBER	70.5	70.4	70.5	70.3	69.5	70.4	70.3
FHLBB	68.5	69.5	70.1	68.7	68.1	69.2	68.3
difference	2.0	.9	.4	1.6	1.4	1.2	2.0
Maturity (mos.)							
NBER	307	310	307	312	307	309	313
FHLBB	317	313	316	305	314	319	305
difference	-10	-3	-9	7	-7	-10	8
Number of loans							
NBER	323	367	347	363	354	305	357
FHLBB	178	199	227	210	309	249	297

[a]Unweighted.

Aug.	Sept.	Oct.	Nov.	Dec.	1963 Average[a]
5.52	5.55	5.55	5.52	5.50	5.56
5.51	5.51	5.51	5.49	5.52	5.54
.01	.04	.04	.03	-.02	.02
-.21	-.19	-.24	-.24	-.01	-.20
.17	.17	.15	.15	.16	.17
-.38	-.36	-.39	-.39	ᵣ.15	-.37
5.48	5.52	5.51	5.48	5.50	5.53
5.53	5.53	5.52	5.51	5.54	5.55
-.05	-.01	-.01	-.03	-.04	-.02
27166	27307	27923	28358	27817	27689
27869	28651	27422	27549	28999	28074
-703	-1344	501	809	-1182	-385
70.1	70.0	70.3	70.3	68.7	70.1
69.3	67.4	67.9	68.7	67.5	68.6
.8	2.6	2.4	1.6	1.2	1.5
314	306	318	314	309	310
317	310	312	310	308	312
-3	-4	6	4	1	-2
355	381	359	314	342	347
292	242	229	184	218	236

APPENDIX TABLE 9-4

Secondary Market Yields on FHA (Section 203) Home Mortgages, for Immediate Delivery, 1948 – 66

	Jan.	Feb.	March	April	May	June	July	Aug.	Sept.	Oct.	Nov.	Dec.
1948 (4.50)	4.15	4.19	4.22	4.26	4.28	4.29	4.29	4.29	4.29	4.30	4.32	4.32
1949	4.33	4.33	4.33	4.33	4.33	4.32	4.33	4.32	4.32	4.30	4.30	4.30
1950	4.30	4.29	4.29	4.28	(4¼	)	4.07	4.05	4.05	4.05	4.05	4.05
1951	4.05	4.05	4.05	4.10	4.18	4.28	4.29	4.32	4.32	4.31	4.28	4.28
1952	4.26	4.26	4.28	4.29	4.29	4.29	4.31	4.31	4.31	4.31	4.32	4.33
1953	4.33	4.35	4.35	4.35	4.40[e] (4½	4.66[e])	4.68	4.77	4.86	4.90	4.86	4.84
1954	4.81	4.78	4.71	4.65	4.63	4.60	4.58	4.57	4.57	4.57	4.57	4.57
1955	4.57	4.57	4.57	4.60	4.61	4.64	4.64	4.65	4.68	4.72	4.75	4.78
1956	4.75	4.75	4.72	4.70	4.74	4.81	4.85	4.85	4.92	4.97	5.00	5.09[e]
1957	5.26[e] (5	5.36[e])	5.41	5.39	5.39	5.36	5.39	5.42	5.56[e] (5¼	5.64[e])	5.67	5.67
1958	5.66	5.63	5.60	5.54	5.45	5.41	5.38	5.36	5.38	5.53	5.62	5.65
1959	5.65	5.65	5.63	5.62	5.63	5.69	5.76	5.81	5.87	6.18[e] (5¾	6.28[e])	6.28
1960	6.28	6.30	6.28	6.27	6.26	6.26	6.24	6.23	6.18	6.15	6.13	6.09
1961	6.08	6.03	6.03[e] (5½)	5.85	5.81	5.79[e] (5¼	5.77[e])	5.75	5.76	5.78	5.78	5.78
1962	5.76	5.78	5.75	5.73	5.70	5.66	5.65	5.65	5.63	5.60	5.58	5.57
1963	5.57	5.55	5.53	5.50	5.47	5.47	5.47	5.47	5.47	5.45	5.45	5.47
1964	5.47	5.47	5.47	5.47	5.47	5.47	5.47	5.47	5.47	5.47	5.47	5.47
1965	5.45	5.45	5.45	5.45	5.45	5.45	5.45	5.45	5.47	5.48	5.51	5.54
1966	5.68	5.77	5.89[e] (5½)	6.10	6.36[e] (5¾)	6.44	6.59	6.67	6.77	6.81[e] (6)	6.99[e]	7.01
1967	6.97	6.78	6.58	6.44	6.36	6.55	6.64	6.68	6.77	6.79	6.83	6.97

Note to Appendix Table 9-4

Yields are derived from FHA field office opinions on secondary market prices for Section 203 home mortgages, and pertain to the first day of the month. Figures in parentheses show the contract rate to which the figures apply. Beginning March 1, 1956, data have been weighted to reflect the probable volume of transactions in regional areas, but this did not affect the national average on that date. Beginning in 1958, quotations refer to "new home mortgages," whereas before that the reference was to "home mortgages." Starting January 1957, quotations refer to mortgages having 10 per cent down payment and twenty-five-year maturity. Prior to that, no terms were specified. Beginning December 1966, quotations refer to thirty-year mortgages and "minimum" down payment. Breaks in the series occur at times of change in maximum allowable rate when prices are not reported. Rates during these months (labeled "e") are interpolations based on FNMA quotations. Prices are converted into yields on the assumption of a twenty-five maturity (thirty years beginning December 1966) and ten-year prepayment.

APPENDIXES

Appendix A

The Mechanics of Data Collection

This appendix provides detailed information on the mechanics involved in compiling the new series.

Selection of Companies

The decision to draw our data from the records of large life insurance companies was dictated by our data requirements and limited resources. Large life insurance companies acquire residential mortgages on a nationwide basis, their records are generally in good order and reasonably accessible, and the size of their operations makes it possible to draw a relatively large number of observations per institution. No other

TABLE A-1

Percentage of Total Residential Loans Held by Life Insurance
Companies Accounted for by Four Companies in Survey

	All Loans	FHA	VA	Conventional
1963	39.8	43.8	53.9	28.4
1962	39.8	44.1	55.3	27.0
1961	39.5	44.0	55.4	25.9
1960	39.3	43.8·	55.7	24.3
1959	39.0	43.1	56.6	22.5
1958	39.7	43.1	57.0	22.3
1957	40.3	43.6	57.1	22.2
1956	40.7	44.3	56.6	22.5
1955	40.5	44.7	56.1	22.5
1954	41.1	47.4	56.6	23.3
1953	40.6	47.3	57.7	22.9
1952	40.5	45.4	58.4	20.6
1951	40.8	44.6	56.9	21.2

Source: Life Insurance Association of America, NBER Survey.

approach to the task of acquiring monthly data covering a reasonably long span of time and having a broad geographical basis was even remotely feasible.

The specific companies chosen were determined by their accessibility and convenience. We began with six companies, but two were found to have gaps in their historical records and had to be dropped from the time series. The four remaining companies accounted for 39 to 41 per cent of outstanding loans on one- to four-family properties held by all life insurance companies throughout the 1951–63 period (see Table A-1). On new loans acquired, the share of the four companies on an annual basis ranged from 31 to 43 per cent and was somewhat higher on FHA and VA than on conventional loans (Table A-2).

TABLE A-2

Percentage of Total Residential Loans Acquired by Life
Insurance Companies Accounted for by
Four Companies in Survey

	All Loans	FHA	VA	Conventional
1963	35.2	39.8	36.0	31.9
1962	37.3	42.4	50.7	30.0
1961	35.2	42.4	39.1	29.0
1960	37.0	45.4	29.5	31.4
1959	32.1	41.9	38.7	23.2
1958	30.8	39.4	48.7	21.5
1957	34.0	35.4	59.4	20.2
1956	38.0	39.2	56.5	21.6
1955	35.4	28.1	55.8	17.6
1954	38.5	42.7	50.9	25.1
1953	35.4	na	na	na
1952	34.7	na	na	na
1951	43.1	na	na	na

na=Data not available.
Source: Life Insurance Association of America, NBER Survey.

Selection of Data

Virtually no choice was exercised in the specific items of information recorded for each loan. The finance committee records for the four companies in the sample contain the following information, and we took it all except city location.[1]

1. Date of committee meeting.
2. Code identification of lender.
3. City and state location of property.
4. Amount of loan.
5. Property value.
6. Maturity of loan.
7. Type of loan (whether FHA, VA or conventional).
8. Method of acquisition (whether originated directly by the company or acquired through a correspondent).
9. Contract interest rate.
10. Fees received by lender.
11. Fees paid by lender.
12. Service fee (on correspondent loans only).

The above comprises the data input recorded on IBM cards.

In the case of one of the four companies, some of the above information was not available in the finance committee minutes but was available in another type of internal record—a listing of loans offered the company by correspondents. For this company, we had to match these two records to obtain all the data.

Information in addition to that listed above (such as purpose of loan, income of borrower, etc.) was available only in individual file folders which could not be matched with finance committee records. For all practical purposes, therefore, it was not available.

Recording and Checking Data

The items of information listed above were transcribed on either work sheets or optical scan cards, from which IBM cards were punched and

[1] The reason for this will be discussed under Classification of Property Location, below.

verified. A print-out of the data was then checked against the original source. In addition, a reasonableness check was built into the program, as follows:

	Conventional	FHA	VA
Contract rate—Max. (%)	15.00	5.75	5.25
Min. (%)	3.00	3.00	3.00
Maturity—Max. (mos.)	480	480	480
Min. (mos.)	60	60	60
Loan-value—Max. (%)	85	110	130
Min. (%)	25	25	25
Loan amount—Max. ($)	100,000	35,000	70,000
Min. ($)	2,500	2,500	2,500
Fees paid—Max. (%)	5.00	5.00	5.00
Fees received—Max. (%)	15.00	15.00	15.00
Service fee—Max. (%)	1.00	1.00	1.00

The function of the reasonableness check was to insure against residual errors large enough to affect the results. For example, if a contract rate of 6.00 per cent was incorrectly punched as 60.00 per cent, the average rate in a cell containing this observation and ninety-nine others would be raised by about .50 per cent, a serious error. The card containing this error would, however, fail the reasonableness check and be thrown out.

Census Spot Checks

As a preliminary step, before compiling the time series on a sample basis, we obtained complete coverage of loans authorized by six companies during February 1960, and by five companies during June 1953; in each month, data were collected on about 7,100 individual loans. The main purposes of compiling these two censuses were (1) to aid in designing the sample (see below); (2) to determine the feasibility of obtaining data on metropolitan areas (see below); (3) to serve as an ex post facto check on the sample after it was drawn (see Chapter 9); and (4) to use in analysis of yield determinants, for the light this could shed on the market in which the participating lenders operate (see Appendix B).

As it turned out, the census also gave us the opportunity to refine our data-collection procedures. While checking out discrepancies between the census and the sample, in cases where they should have been exactly the same, we found that the census, rather than the sample, was in error.

Sampling Procedure

It would have been extremely wasteful to record all the loans authorized by the participating companies every month; a sampling procedure was required. We set a quota of 120 loans of each type (FHA, VA, and conventional) at each of the four companies for each month. If a given company authorized less than 120 loans of a given type, we took all of their loans of that type. For example, if a company authorized 360 conventional loans, 240 FHA loans, and 100 VA loans in a given February, we took every third conventional, every second FHA, and every VA loan. Since we had only estimates of the total number of each loan type for each company, the procedure was subject to error; sometimes we collected more than 120 loans, at other times we collected less. We resampled, however, only when the number fell well short of the quota.

Stratification

In general, the case for stratification by a given factor N with strata 1, 2, 3 . . . depends on (1) the need for separate series classified by N; (2) the extent to which observations are equally distributed among the strata 1, 2, 3 . . . (stratification permits relatively heavy sampling in thin strata); (3) the cost of stratification (in the case at hand, this depended mainly on whether or not the original data were sorted by the factor N); and (4) the availability of strata weights—in our case a breakdown of aggregate loan volume into strata 1, 2, 3 . . . —for the calculation of weighted totals.

We stratified by loan type (FHA, VA, and conventional) and by company. There would have been some advantages in stratifying by region as well, but they were not as compelling, and the additional costs would have been prohibitive.

We stratified by loan type to produce separate series for each type of mortgage. Had we not stratified by type, only the conventional sample would have been large enough over the entire period. (Even with stratification, the VA sample was very thin during several years.) Monthly data were available on the volume of authorized loans for each type of mortgage, permitting calculation of weighted totals for all mortgages. At three companies, loans were sorted on the finance

TABLE A-3

Distribution of Loans and Estimated Sampling Error of Gross Yield by Type of Loan and Region

| | Per Cent Distribution of Loans[a] | | Estimated Range of Standard Error[d] | | | |
| | | | Monthly[b] | | Quarterly[c] | |
	Conventional	FHA	Conventional	FHA	Conventional	FHA
9-Region Classification						
New England	2.6	1.4	.03-.10	.05-.14	.02-.06	.03-.08
Middle Atlantic	14.6	4.4	.01-.04	.03-.08	.01-.03	.02-.05
South Atlantic	9.9	16.0	.02-.05	.01-.04	.01-.03	.01-.02
West South Central	16.5	12.6	.01-.04	.02-.05	.01-.02	.01-.03
East South Central	4.9	9.8	.03-.08	.02-.05	.01-.04	.01-.03
East North Central	14.5	18.5	.01-.04	.01-.04	.01-.03	.01-.02
West North Central	8.9	7.4	.02-.06	.02-.06	.01-.03	.01-.04
Pacific	23.8	22.3	.01-.03	.01-.04	.01-.02	.01-.02
Mountain	4.2	7.5	.03-.08	.02-.06	.02-.05	.01-.04
Total	100.0	100.0				
4-Region Classification						
East	17.2	5.8	.01-.04	.02-.07	.01-.02	.01-.04
South	31.3	38.5	.01-.03	.01-.03	.01-.02	.01-.02
North Central	23.4	25.8	.01-.03	.01-.03	.01-.02	.01-.02
West	28.0	29.8	.01-.03	.01-.03	.01-.02	.01-.02
Total	100.0	100.0				

Notes to Table A-3

[a]Based on combined June 1953 and February 1960 cross sections.

[b]Assumed sample of 330 loans.

[c]Assumed sample of 990 loans.

[d]Assumed standard deviations of 0.1 and 0.3 per cent. Standard errors are rounded.

---

committee record by type of mortgage, facilitating stratification by type. At one company, the various types were intermixed on the records, and this raised the sampling cost at that company.

The case for stratification by individual companies was not as compelling, but since the data came to us already sorted in this way, no extra costs were involved. Company volume data were, of course, available for constructing weighted totals.

Stratification by location of property would have been of value because coverage is quite thin in the Middle Atlantic and particularly in the New England states. Had we stratified by location, we could also have obtained series for some metropolitan areas. The costs, however, would have been prohibitive because the companies do not record region or metropolitan area on their finance committee records, and do not sort their loans by location. Furthermore, aggregate volume figures were not available for constructing weighted totals. As it was, the geographical distribution of loans was adequate to permit a number of reliable regional series.

Drawing the Sample

As noted, a sample was drawn of every n^{th} loan where $n = U/120$ and U is the total number of loans of a given type at a given company. The principal alternative procedure, which has been used in other loan surveys including that of the FHLBB, is to take *all* the loans authorized by a given lender during a specified *part* of the month (the first five working days, for example). This procedure was rejected mainly because it was inconsistent with stratification by type of loan.

Sample Size

The target sample of 120 loans of each type for each company was considered roughly consistent with the goal of providing quarterly FHA and conventional series with a seven- to nine-region break and monthly series with a three- to four-region break. Some of the data used in arriving at this judgment are shown in Tables A-3 and A-4, which are based on the June 1953 and February 1960 cross sections.

TABLE A-4

Standard Deviation of Gross Yield by Type of Loan and Region
(per cent)

	February 1960			June 1953		
	Conventional	FHA	VA	Conventional	FHA	VA
9-Region Classification						
New England	.368	.082	a	.270	.150	a
Middle Atlantic	.176	.101	a	.204	.095	.160
South Atlantic	.118	.199	.107	.226	.080	.053
West South Central	.190	.395	.010	.223	.092	.127
East South Central	.095	.162	.342	.171	.071	.116
East North Central	.156	.116	.088	.229	.102	.216
West North Central	.173	.098	.023	.169	.095	.098
Pacific	.194	.063	.003	.174	.113	.117
Mountain	.215	.106	a	.156	.146	a
4-Region Classification						
East	.214	.099	a	.228	.146	.144
South	.164	.268	.199	.222	.085	.124
North Central	.165	.110	.084	.207	.101	.153
West	.203	.071	.003	.172	.127	.115
Total U.S.	.196	.189	.109	.236	.111	.141

aLess than twenty-five loans.

TABLE A-5

Distribution of Months and Quarters by Size of Sample for
FHA, VA, and Conventional Loans, 1951 − 63
(number of months or quarters)

Number of Loans In Sample	FHA	VA	Conventional
Monthly			
More than 400	107	45	21
300-399	47	16	131
200-299	2	55	4
100-199	0	14	0
50-99	0	8	0
Less than 50	0	18	0
Total	156	156	156
Quarterly			
More than 1,200	38	16	6
900-1,199	14	3	45
600-899	0	19	1
300-599	0	6	0
150-299	0	3	0
50-149	0	4	0
Less than 50	0	1	0
Total	52	52	52

We estimated that our sample target would provide a minimum of
330 loans of each type per month, and 990 per quarter.[2] We distributed
these by regions in line with the June 1953 and February 1960 combined distributions, shown in the first two columns of Table A-3. We
then calculated a range of standard errors for each region, monthly and
quarterly, as shown in the right-hand portion of Table A-3; the smaller
figure in each case assumes a standard deviation of 0.1, and the larger
figure is based on a standard deviation of 0.3. As shown in Table A-4,

[2] As it turned out, the FHA sample fell short of 330 loans in three of the
156 months, while the conventional sample fell short in seventeen months. Only
in four months, however, did the conventional sample fall below 300 loans, as
shown in Table A-5. In contrast, the VA sample was below 330 loans in more
than two-thirds of the months, and fell below fifty loans in eighteen months.
The quarterly FHA sample did not fall short of 990 loans in any quarter; the
conventional sample fell slightly short in three quarters.

fifty-five of the seventy-eight deviations calculated from the two cross sections were in this range, twenty were less than .1, and only three exceeded .3 per cent.

Assuming a standard error of .04 per cent is a reasonable, although admittedly a completely arbitrary, definition of "reliability," the distribution of standard errors is consistent with reliable monthly series on a three- to four-region basis, and quarterly series on a seven- to nine-region basis.

Tabulation Program

Several loan characteristics were computed as part of the tabulation program and were not part of the data input.

1. Net Discount: fees received less fees paid, expressed as a per cent of the loan amount.

2. Loan-to-value ratio.

3. Effective yield: contract rates adjusted for net fees received (or paid), as explained in Chapter 8.

4. Net yield on correspondent loans: effective yield net of the correspondent's service fee, on mortgages originated by correspondents.

Our tabulation program involved calculation of weighted and unweighted averages and standard deviations for the major loan characteristics, with breakdowns by type of loan and by direct and correspondent serviced, as illustrated in Table A-6. These data were calculated separately for each of thirteen regions (the census nine-region break and the census four-region break), eight states and U.S. total, or twenty-two location-of-property categories. All of this was done for each of the four companies included in the time series, as well as for the four companies combined, and was, of course, replicated for every month and quarter during 1951–63. The entire output thus consisted of several thousands of tables of the type illustrated in Table A-6.

Weighting

In the census, the program for all-company totals was identical to the program for the individual companies. For the sample, however, a weighting routine was needed because the samples did not reflect the relative importance of the separate companies. For use in the weighting routine, we compiled data on the aggregate volume of each type of loan authorized by each company in each month and quarter. Such data were not available for regions or states, but the sample provided data on average loan size and number of loans that could be used as the basis for an estimate.

More precisely, four weights were used as follows.

1. V, the United States volume of a given type of loan for a given company (derived independently of the sample from company records); used for all average loan characteristics except loan size in U.S. totals.

2. $V \div L_u$, where L_u is the sample average loan size for a given type of loan for a given company in the United States; used for average loan size in U.S. totals.

3. $(V \div L_u)(N_j \div N_u)$, where N_j is the sample number of loans of a given type by a given company in a region or state, and N_u is the same for the United States; used for average loan size in regions and states.

4. $(V \div L_u)(N_j \div N_u)L_j = V\left(\dfrac{N_j}{N_u} \times \dfrac{L_j}{L_u}\right)$, where L_j is the sample average loan size for a given type of loan for a given company in a region or state; used for average loan characteristics except loan size in regions and states.

Weights 3 and 4 used for regions and states make maximum use of the information available from both the aggregate data and the sample to estimate relative loan volume or number of loans by region. Thus, weight 4 adjusts each company's aggregate U.S. loan volume figure by a factor that measures, for that company, the percentage of the U.S. total accounted for by a given region, as indicated by the sample. The smaller the number of loans in the region, of course, the weaker is the statistical foundation of the adjustment factor.

Classification of Property Location

At the outset of the study, we investigated the feasibility of obtaining data for metropolitan areas. In taking the February 1960 and June 1953 cross sections, we coded loans that fell within eighteen major metropolitan areas. We found that the expense of obtaining reliable quarterly data for the largest eight of these metropolitan areas was substantially higher than the expense of obtaining reliable series for

TABLE A-6

Company 4, Region 13

	Number of Loans	Amt. of Loan		Value of Prop.		Loan-Value Ratio			Term to Maturity		
		Mean	Std. Dev.	Mean	Std. Dev.	Mean	Wtd. Mean	Std. Dev.	Mean	Wtd. Mean	Std. Dev.
Conventional loans											
direct	0	0	0	0	0	0	0	0	0	0	0
correspondent											
serviced	108	20579	4973	29495	6752	70.0	70.5	6.97	288.2	290.2	27.42
both	108	20579	4973	29495	6752	70.0	70.5	6.97	288.2	290.2	27.42
FHA loans											
direct	0	0	0	0	0	0	0	0	0	0	0
correspondent											
serviced	54	15872	3164	17417	3759	91.6	91.6	6.16	343.3	345.6	33.50
both	54	15872	3164	17417	3759	91.6	91.6	6.16	343.3	345.6	33.50
VA loans											
direct	0	0	0	0	0	0	0	0	0	0	0
correspondent											
serviced	3	16033	2899	18181	2532	87.7	88.5	5.25	360.0	360.0	0
both	3	16033	2899	18181	2532	87.7	88.5	5.25	360.0	360.0	0
All loans											
direct	0	0	0	0	0	0	0	0	0	0	0
correspondent											
serviced	165	18956	4961	25337	8207	77.4	76.5	12.21	307.6	306.4	39.66
both	165	18956	4961	25337	8207	77.4	76.5	12.21	307.6	306.4	39.66

Table A-6 (concluded)

	Contract Rate			Discount			Gross Yield			Net Yield		
	Mean	Wtd. Mean	Std. Dev.	Mean	Wtd. Mean	Std. Dev.	Mean	Wtd. Mean	Std. Dev.	Mean	Wtd. Mean	Std. Dev.
Conventional loans												
direct	0	0	0	0	0	0	0	0	0	0	0	0
correspondent serviced	5.77	5.76	0.078	0	0	0	5.77	5.76	0.078	5.27	5.27	0.069
both	5.77	5.76	0.078	0	0	0	5.77	5.76	0.078	0	0	0
FHA loans												
direct	0	0	0	0	0	0	0	0	0	0	0	0
correspondent serviced	5.25	5.25	0.034	3.99	4.02	0.677	5.86	5.86	0.096	5.36	5.36	0.096
both	5.25	5.25	0.034	3.99	4.02	0.677	5.86	5.86	0.096	0	0	0
VA loans												
direct	0	0	0	0	0	0	0	0	0	0	0	0
correspondent serviced	5.25	5.25	0.001	4.00	4.00	-0.000	5.85	5.85	-0.000	5.35	5.35	0.001
both	5.25	5.25	0.001	4.00	4.00	-0.000	5.85	5.85	-0.000	0	0	0
All loans												
direct	0	0	0	0	0	0	0	0	0	0	0	0
correspondent serviced	5.59	5.62	0.252	1.38	1.16	1.937	5.80	5.79	0.094	5.30	5.29	0.088
both	5.59	5.62	0.252	1.38	1.16	1.937	5.80	5.79	0.094	0	0	0

the eight largest states. In part, this was because of the much greater concentration of loans by states. The largest eight metropolitan areas accounted for only 14 per cent of total loans in 1960 and 20 per cent in 1953, whereas the eight largest states accounted for 47 and 48 per cent in the two months, respectively. Hence, metropolitan area series would have required a substantially larger sample.[3] To obtain metropolitan area data, moreover, turned out to be extremely burdensome because only the city and state were recorded on the finance committee records. We thus reluctantly abandoned the effort to obtain metropolitan area series, and recorded only the state location of property. This permitted the calculation of separate series for those states with enough cases, and for desired regional groupings of states.

We used the June 1953 and February 1960 data to explore a number of possibilities of regional groupings, including the eightfold classification suggested for general-purpose economic data by Ullman and Klove.[4] The intraregional yield variance for this classification was slightly smaller than for the conventional census nine-region grouping. The difference, however, did not seem large enough to offset the loss of historical continuity and comparability with other series on the nine-region basis.

Loan Coverage

In general, the time series cover first-mortgage loans on residential one- to four-family properties. Some categories of loans, however, create special problems that warrant discussion.

Construction Loans

Short-term advances to builders were not included in the survey. Life insurance companies do not ordinarily make such loans. They sometimes, however, will make construction financing available to a builder under a permanent mortgage which will later be assumed by the home purchaser. In such cases, two sets of terms ordinarily will appear on the finance committee record for a given loan, one applicable to the builder and the other to the final buyer (the former are invariably more

---

[3] As noted above, stratification by any locational category was not feasible.

[4] Morris B. Ullman and Robert C. Klove, "The Geographic Area and Regional Economic Research," in *Regional Income,* Studies in Income and Wealth, 21, Princeton University Press for NBER, 1957, p. 108.

restrictive). We took the terms applicable to the final buyer. Long-term loans to an individual constructing his own house are also included.

Substitution Loans

Loans that replace an existing loan by the same borrower were excluded from the survey when we could identify them. There are strong a priori grounds for believing that if the contract rate on the outstanding loan differs from the current market rate, the new loan will not be at the current market rate. For example, if a borrower with a $10,000 balance remaining on a 5 per cent loan wishes an additional $10,000 at a time when market rates are 6 per cent, the lender should be willing to give him a new $20,000 first mortgage at $5\frac{1}{2}$ per cent, since this implies a 6 per cent rate on the increment.

At two companies, we were unable to exclude substitution loans because they were not identified separately on the finance committee record. The possible bias is small because such loans constitute a small proportion of the total—probably less than 5 per cent at the companies involved.[5]

Reapprovals

Loans to replace previous loan commitments that were not taken down were excluded from the survey when they could be identified on the finance committee record (identification was not possible at two companies). The exclusions were more for sampling convenience than for analytical reasons. Where reapprovals were listed separately, it would have been awkward to include them in the sample. As noted in Chapter 7, reapprovals ordinarily are viewed by the participants as a new transaction at the current market rate.

Multiple Commitments

A multiple commitment is an arrangement whereby a lender promises to make some variable proportion of FHA, VA and conventional loans,

[5] Interestingly enough, lending officers at one company indicated that when old loans were below the current market rate, substitution loans were made at the market rate and were not a weighted average of the current and the old rate; this would imply a rate on the increment above the current market rate. This may happen because of borrower ignorance, or because the borrower is blocked in some way from refinancing with another lender—by a heavy prepayment penalty, for example. In such case, the only alternative might be a second mortgage which is not generally available from institutional sources and which carry very heavy rates.

each at specified terms, up to some maximum limit of either FHA, VA, or both. For example, the lender may agree to make sixty mortgage loans on the following basis: conventional loans at 6 per cent for any part of the sixty; up to forty FHA loans at $5\frac{3}{4}$ per cent priced at ninety-nine; and up to twenty VA loans at $5\frac{1}{4}$ per cent priced at ninety-five. When all the houses are sold, the breakdown might be thirty-five conventionals, fifteen FHAs, and five VAs, this distribution falling within the limits set by the lender.

In a simpler variant of this procedure, the original commitment covers only one type of loan (say, conventional), and when buyers are found, the commitment is modified by changing that type of mortgage to other types at a comparable rate. The company must specifically approve these modifications, the terms of which hark back to the original commitment, but the new loans do not appear again on the finance committee records.

Multiple commitments of the first or "complex" type were omitted from the sample. This was partly a matter of sampling convenience, since the companies making these arrangements did not list them with their other loans. In addition, we suspected that the terms on each type of mortgage might be influenced by the fact that they were part of a package. For example, a lender might be willing to accept a certain number of VA loans at a moderate discount if he could obtain a certain number of conventional loans at an attractive rate; he would not necessarily be willing to take an individual VA loan on the same terms. We avoided this problem by excluding these multiple commitments from the sample.

The simple type of multiple commitment, however, was not separately identified in the finance committee record and was included in the sample. In such case, the terms on the single type of mortgage included in the commitment are necessarily at the market.

Because of the exclusions referred to, there are small differences between the sample coverage and the volume data used in weighting. At two companies we excluded substitution loans and loans in multiple commitments from the sample but the net increment on substitution loans and all multiple commitment loans were included in the volume data, for these companies. These differences in coverage between the sample and the volume data, however, were small.

Special Problems in Connection with the VA Loan Series

The new series on VA loans are biased by three separate although related factors. First, during part of the 1951–63 period, the VA sample was too thin to be reliable. Table A-5 shows that in eighteen separate months, the VA sample was less than fifty loans, and in eight more it was between fifty and one hundred. In contrast, the conventional and FHA samples never fell below two hundred loans. The months of thin VA coverage were concentrated in the years 1958–60 when life insurance companies sharply reduced their VA lending.

Second, during certain periods the VA series did not truly reflect the market. This problem was discussed in Chapter 4 and requires no elaboration here.

Third, during 1959–60 one company acquired VA loans from correspondents in trade for government securities, and recorded the mortgage price as par, although the securities were then selling well below par.[6]

Incomplete Data on Fees and Charges

One of the companies in our survey did not record fees and charges on individual conventional loans during the period January 1951–September 1953. Our program interpreted fees and charges on these loans as zero, so that all conventional yields calculated for this period were incorrect and later had to be recomputed by hand.

The company with incomplete finance committee records did have *aggregate* monthly data on fees and charges on conventional loans.[7] This permitted accurate recalculation of U.S. totals for the four companies without great difficulty. For regions and states, however, we had no basis for such a recalculation. Tests run with data for the same company indicated that net discounts varied greatly from one region to another, so that the average net discount over the U.S. could not

[6] Such transactions occurred every month during August–November 1959 and February–November 1960. This company also acquired some FHA loans in the same way, which caused us to make an adjustment in the FHA series (see below).

[7] These data included nonresidential as well as residential loans, but some tests indicated that net discounts on this total were very close to discounts on residential loans alone.

be used without introducing substantial error. As a result, we recalculated gross yield on conventional loans for regions and states using three companies instead of four.

A similar problem arose in the data for 1959–60. After the tabulations were run, a check of time series for individual companies showed that yields on FHA loans were substantially lower for one company than for the others in certain months during 1959–60. Inquiries disclosed that the company with atypical yields acquired FHAs during these months by swapping government bonds from their portfolio. The mortgages were recorded as having been acquired at par even though at the time the bonds were selling at substantial discounts from par. As a result for the month in which the swaps took place we recalculated yield and net discount for three companies instead of four.

Appendix B

Cross-Section Analysis of Loans by Life Insurance Companies in the Time Series

Before the time series data were collected on a sample basis, we obtained complete coverage of residential loans authorized by six companies in February 1960 (some 7,100 loans), and by five companies in June 1953 (7,200 loans). These censuses were taken to aid in designing the sample and the tabulation program, and to use as a benchmark check of the sample data when it became available.

As a guide to the tabulation program, the June 1953 and February 1960 censuses were subjected to regression analysis of factors associated with yield. It was recognized that because of the limited number of transaction characteristics for which data were available, no very adequate explanation of yield determinants would be possible. The objective, however, was to assess the desirability of holding constant in the time series those characteristics for which data were available, not to study the cross-section problem in depth. For this purpose, the question was only whether there was appreciable cross-section yield variability associated with these characteristics.

We were aware at the outset, of course, that yield might vary between the three different types of mortgages (FHA, VA, and conventional). But since we were committed to obtaining separate time series for each type of mortgage the intertype yield differences were not analyzed with the benchmark data, which provide inadequate perspective on this problem in any case. Rather the focus was on other yield determinants which were examined within the separate types of mortgages, with particular emphasis on conventional mortgages where the influence of risk figured to be largest.

The following variables were employed in this analysis.

Dependent	Independent
1. Contract rate	1. Loan-value ratio
2. Gross yield (contract rate adjusted to take account of net fees received or paid)	2. Maturity
	3. Value of property
3. Net yield (gross yield net of correspondent service fee, on correspondent loans only)	4. Volume of activity by individual lender (1)
	5. Volume of activity by individual lender (2)
	6. Individual company
	7. Region of country
	8. Metropolitan area (as opposed to nonmetropolitan area)

On several runs, the first three independent variables were dummied —that is, the variable was broken into three or four groups each of which was entered as a separate independent variable in the regression. This practice illuminates the nature of the underlying functional relationship between yield and the independent variable involved— whether the relationship is linear or some nonlinear form; it assures that a low coefficient obtained when the independent variable is in its original form indicates a low order of relationship and not an incorrectly specified equation.[1] The specific groups used for dummying are shown in the note to Table B-2.[2]

[1] Suppose, for example, the underlying relationship between yield and maturity is U-shaped; yield declines with rising maturity up to some point and then rises. A linear regression in which maturity is entered in its original form might show an insignificant coefficient for the maturity, but the inference from this that there was no relationship, would be incorrect. The "true" relationship would be revealed by entering the maturity in dummy form.

[2] Note that for each dummied variable, the number of independent variables included in the regression is always one less than the number of dummy groups, and the absolute size of each coefficient shows the yield or rate for the group *relative to the group left out.* This means that the absolute size of dummy coefficients depends on the purely arbitrary choice of which group is left out. As a general practice, it is not advisable to leave out a thin group because this may make the absolute size of the coefficients unstable from one cross section to another. In the regressions shown here, the groups left out are as follows: for property value, maturity, and loan-value ratio, the highest valued group; for companies, Company 1, and for regions, New England. The last choice turned out to be a poor one, because New England was the thinnest of the regions. Thus, in running the February 1960 FHA cross section with risk variables in dummy form we decided to exclude some 232 loans which were not Section 203 home mortgages, and which had been included in the regression with risk variables in their original form. The exclusion of these loans reduced the number of loans in New England from twenty-six to six, and sharply altered all the

The so-called risk variables—loan-value ratio, maturity, and property value—explained very little of the variation in yield in the two cross sections examined. As an illustration, Table B-1 covering conventional loans in February 1960 shows that these variables in combination explained only 1 per cent of total variance in gross yield.

The most important factors underlying yield variability in these data turned out to be the geographical region in which the property was located, and the individual lender making the loan. The addition of individual company to the regression shown in Table B-1 raised the explained variance from 5 to 25 per cent, and the further addition of geographical region and nonmetropolitan area location raised it to 43 per cent. Some of the individual company and regional coefficients were quite sizable, furthermore. Gross yields on conventional mortgages in the mountain region, for example, were forty-four basis points higher than yields in New England in February 1960.[3]

The main concern was the absolute size of the coefficients for each of the risk variables, rather than their relative importance in explaining yield variance. (The latter might be expected to be small in national data with marked regional yield differentials.)

The loan-value ratio, when it was included in a linear multiple regression equation as a single independent variable, had a very small effect on the gross yield of conventional mortgages as shown below (drawn from Tables B-2 and B-3).

	Per Cent	
	1953	1960
b-coefficient	.0016	.0007
Standard error	.0004	.0004
Standard deviation	9.0	8.2
Change in yield per change of one standard deviation in loan-value ratio	.014	.006

The change in yield associated with a change of one standard deviation in the loan-value ratio amounted to less than .02 per cent in 1953, although the coefficient was more than three times its standard error.

---

regional coefficients relative to New England, although leaving them largely unchanged relative to each other (see Table B-2).

[3] As explained in Chapter 2, the importance of region and individual lender as yield determinants did not call for a regression-type yield-adjustment procedure for the time series because the lender-regional mix was stable over time. Furthermore, our series are cross classified by region.

TABLE B-1

Stepwise Regression: Determinants of Gross Effective Yield on Conventional
Loans Authorized by Six Life Insurance Companies, February 1960

	Variables Included at Reduction							
	Loan-Value (%) (1)	Value ($) (2)	Maturity (Mos.) (3)	No. Conventional Loans (4)	No. Total Loans (5)	Indiv. Co. (10)	Region (18)	Nonmet. Area (19)
R^2	.002	.003	.005	.011	.049	.250	.428	.432
Constant	6.00	5.98	5.93	5.93	5.94	5.94	5.79	5.76
b=coefficients[a]								
(1) Loan-value	.0010 (.0004)	.0011 (.0004)	.0006 (.0004)	.0008 (.0005)	.0008 (.0005)	.0012 (.0004)	.0008 (.0004)	.0007 (.0004)
(2) Value[b]		.056 (.048)	.050 (.048)	.063 (.048)	.020 (.047)	-.069 (.040)	-.105 (.038)	-.093 (.038)
(3) Maturity[c]			.286 (.116)	.309 (.116)	.253 (.114)	.132 (.102)	.053 (.089)	.048 (.089)
(4) No. Conv. Loans[c]				-.236 (.059)	.730 (.110)	.685 (.114)	.258 (.120)	.303 (.120)
(5) No. Total Loans[c]					-.288 (.028)	-.165 (.031)	-.207 (.028)	-.205 (.028)
(6) Company 2						-.131 (.046)	-.160 (.041)	-.160 (.040)
(7) Company 3						.199 (.014)	.143 (.013)	.148 (.013)

(8) Company 4	.044 (.010)	.015 (.009)	.015 (.009)
(9) Company 5	.405 (.021)	.304 (.020)	.308 (.019)
(10) Company 6	-.062 (.010)	-.081 (.009)	-.082 (.009)
(11) Mid. Atlantic		.133 (.023)	.145 (.023)
(12) So. Atlantic		.221 (.023)	.226 (.023)
(13) West So. Central		.321 (.023)	.328 (.023)
(14) East So. Central		.184 (.024)	.184 (.023)
(15) East No. Central		.230 (.023)	.236 (.024)
(16) West No. Central		.281 (.024)	.284 (.023)
(17) Pacific		.358 (.024)	.365 (.025)
(18) Mountain		.440 (.025)	.444 (.024)
(19) Nonmet. area			.030 (.025) (.007)

Average	68.6	24,865	281.3	60.2	163.8
Standard deviation	9.1	8,081	35.4	65.2	255.6

Notes to Table B-1

Note: The number of loans is 2628. The average and standard deviation of the gross yield are 6.07 per cent and .196 per cent, respectively.

^aStandard errors are given in parentheses.

^bDivided by 100,000.

^cDivided by 1,000.

In 1960, the coefficient was of borderline significance. On FHA and VA mortgages, more sizable b-coefficients were obtained on early reductions, but in every case they declined sharply with the addition of individual company and region to the regression. At the final reduction, none of the coefficients were as much as twice the size of their standard error (Table B-4).

The loan-value ratio was also tested by the dummy procedure. The largest dummy coefficients were obtained on conventional mortgages in June 1953 as follows.

Loan-Value Ratio	b	Standard Error
70.0% and over (left out of regression)	.00%	.00%
65.0 to 69.9	.035	.010
60.0 to 64.9	.044	.011
Less than 60.0	−.009	.011

Somewhat surprisingly, the dummy procedure shows yield rising with loan-value ratio and then declining. In all probability this reflects our inability to make any distinction between new and existing properties in these data, or to take account of borrower characteristics. Although two of the dummy coefficients are statistically significant (there were 3,367 loans in this cross section), they are very small in absolute size. Use of the dummy form adds a negligible amount to the R^2.

The results for property value and maturity were in broad outline very similar. The regression coefficient for property value was usually statistically significant but invariably small. Thus, on conventional loans in 1953, the coefficient was about six times its standard error, but it implied a yield difference for a change in value of $10,000 of only .03 per cent. The association of yield with maturity was even weaker.

It was thus concluded that for the life insurance companies in our group, variability in terms does not carry the risk variability and associated interest-rate variability characteristic of some other lenders.

Two volume-of-lending variables were included in the regressions for experimental purposes. One was the total number of the specific type

TABLE B-2

Multiple Regression: Determinants of Effective Yield and Contract Rate on Conventional Loans Authorized by Six Life Insurance Companies, February 1960 (final reduction)

Independent Variables	Gross Yield		Gross Yield		Contract Rate		Net Yield[c]	
	b-coefficient	Std. Error	b-coefficient	Std. Error	b-coefficient	Std. Error	b-coefficient	Std. Error
Loan-value	.0007	.0004					.0014	.0005
dummy 1			-.017	.008	-.007	.008		
2			-.007	.008	.005	.008		
(lowest) 3			-.030	.009	-.022	.009		
Value[a]	-.093	.038					.031	.050
dummy 1			.016	.010	.017	.009		
2			.026	.009	.024	.009		
(lowest) 3			.022	.012	.022	.011		
Maturity[b]	.048	.089					.055	.117
dummy 1			-.053	.022	-.045	.021		
2			-.045	.023	-.039	.021		
(lowest) 3			-.063	.025	-.060	.024		
No. conv. loans[b]	.303	.120					-.830	.427
No. total loans[b]	-.205	.028	-.155	.017	-.091	.016	.126	.094

(continued)

Table B-2 (concluded)

Independent Variables	Gross Yield		Gross Yield		Contract Rate		Net Yield[c]	
	b-coefficient	Std. Error	b-coefficient	Std. Error	b-coefficient	Std. Error	b-coefficient	Std. Error
Company 2	-.160	.040	-.178	.042	-.166	.039	.156	.062
Company 3	.148	.013	.136	.012	.142	.011	.519	.047
Company 4	.015	.0009	.009	.009	.017	.008	.355	.047
Company 5	.308	.019	.291	.019	.264	.018	.655	.050
Company 6	-.082	.0009	-.092	.008	-.085	.007	.376	.048
Mid. Atlantic	.145	.023	.151	.023	.121	.021	.347	.031
So. Atlantic	.226	.023	.229	.023	.212	.021	.400	.031
West So. Central	.328	.023	.335	.023	.308	.022	.447	.031
East So. Central	.184	.024	.187	.024	.171	.023	.367	.035
East No. Central	.236	.023	.242	.023	.224	.021	.435	.031
West No. Central	.284	.025	.286	.024	.224	.022	.427	.032
Pacific	.365	.024	.385	.023	.411	.022	.550	.032
Mountain	.444	.025	.442	.025	.409	.024	.586	.034
Nonmet. area	.030	.007	.028	.007	.030	.006	.047	.009
R^2	.432		.435		.473		.447	
Constant	5.76		5.85		5.85		4.68	
N	2628		2599		2599		1461	
Yield or rate:								
average	6.071		6.071		6.080		5.659	
std. dev.	.196		.196		.190		.200	

Notes to Table B-2

^aDivided by 100,000.
^bDivided by 1,000.
^cCorrespondent loans only.
Note: Dummy groups are as follows:

	Loan-Value Ratio (%)	Maturity (months)	Property Value ($)
	February 1960		
Conventional	72.5 and over	More than 300	More than 32,500
	67.5-72.4	241-300	25,000-32,500
	62.5-67.4	240	17,500-24,999
	Less than 62.5	Less than 240	Less than 17,500
FHA	95.0 and over	360	More than 20,000
	90.0-94.9	Less than 360	15,000-20,000
	85.0-89.9		10,000-14,999
	Less than 85.0		Less than 10,000
	June 1953		
Conventional	70.0 and over	241 and over	More than 32,500
	65.0-69.9	181-240	25,000-32,500
	60.0-64.9	180 and less	17,500-24,999
	Less than 60.0		Less than 17,500
FHA	87.5 and over	300 and over	More than 15,000
	82.5-87.4	240-299	12,500-15,000
	77.5-82.4	Less than 240	10,000-12,499
	Less than 77.5		Less than 10,000

TABLE B-3

Multiple Regression: Determinants of Effective Yield and Contract Rate
on Conventional Loans Authorized by Six Life Insurance Companies,
June 1953
(final reduction)

Independent Variables	Gross Yield		Contract Rate		Gross Yield		Contract Rate	
	b-coefficient	Std. Error	b-coefficient	Std. Error	b-coefficient	Std. Error	b-coefficient	Std. Error
Loan-value	.0016	.0004	.0014	.0004				
dummy 1					.035	.010	.046	.010
2					.044	.011	.050	.011
(lowest) 3					-.009	.011	-.002	.011
Value[a]	-.319	.048	-.408	.048				
dummy 1					-.034	.016	-.022	.016
2					.023	.015	.043	.015
(lowest) 3					.051	.015	.078	.017
Maturity[b]	-.223	.124	-.586	.123				
dummy 1					-.012	.017	-.033	.017
2					-.015	.019	-.009	.019
(lowest) 3								
No. conv. loans[b]	-.420	.088	-.455	.087	-.385	.090	-.431	.089
No. total loans[b]	.533	.082	.541	.081	.531	.083	.554	.082

	(1)		(2)		(3)		(4)	
Company 2	.185	.034	.185	.033	.173	.033	.172	.033
Company 3	.221	.017	.212	.017	.138	.017	.128	.017
Company 4	.199	.016	.191	.016	.099	.016	.087	.016
Company 5	c	c	c	c	c	c	c	c
Company 6	.184	.009	.171	.009	.040	.009	.024	.009
Mid. Atlantic	.103	.019	.097	.019	.127	.019	.117	.019
So. Atlantic	.237	.020	.228	.020	.246	.020	.234	.020
West So. Central	.278	.020	.274	.020	.292	.020	.285	.020
East So. Central	.190	.023	.185	.023	.231	.023	.224	.023
East No. Central	.164	.019	.155	.019	.178	.109	.167	.019
West No. Central	.212	.020	.210	.019	.174	.019	.172	.019
Pacific	.284	.022	.260	.022	.330	.022	.306	.022
Mountain	.346	.024	.338	.024	.382	.024	.371	.024
Nonmet. area	.013	.007	.013	.007	.032	.007	.033	.007
R^2	.393		.401		.320		.331	
Constant	4.41		4.37		4.63		4.48	
N	3367		3367		3367		3367	
Yield or rate:								
average	4.74		4.74		4.83		4.83	
std. dev.	.236		.236		.222		.222	

Note: See note to Table B-2 for dummy groups.

[a]Divided by 100,000.

[b]Divided by 1,000.

[c]Company had no loans of the given type.

TABLE B-4

Determinants of Gross Effective Yield on FHA and VA Loans Authorized
by Six Life Insurance Companies, February 1960 and June 1953
(final reduction)

Independent Variables	February 1960				June 1953			
	FHA		VA		FHA		VA	
	b-coefficient	Std. Error	b-coefficient	Std. Error	b-coefficient	Std. Error	b-coefficient	Std. Error
Loan-value								
dummy 1	.0011	.0006	-.0007	.0004	-.005	.007	.0001	.0010
2	-.015	.006			-.0002	.007		
(lowest) 3	-.022	.008			-.007	.008		
Value[a]								
dummy 1	-.018	.089	-.151	.060	.026	.007	-.498	.275
2	-.001	.011			.024	.007		
(lowest) 3	.006	.012			.018	.009		
Maturity[b]								
dummy 1	-.173	.075	-.534	.188	.027	.005	.003	.205
(lowest) 2	.006	.006			-.071	.012		

	(1)		(2)		(3)		(4)		(5)	
No. FHA or VA loans[b]	-.123	.081	.080	.012	-1.56	.058	1.04	.050	1.77	.646
No. total loans[b]	.170	.062			.949	.073	-.327	.028	-1.32	.194
Company 2	-.603	.050	-.608	.051	d	d	-.026	.027	d	d
Company 3	d	d	d	d	.812	.013	d	d	-.023	.026
Company 4	-.125	.013	-.125	.013	.298	.033	-.015	.007	-.181	.027
Company 5	.249	.014	.246	.014	d	d	d	d	d	d
Company 6	-.182	.006	-.185	.006	-.051	.010	-.027	.004	d	d
Mid. Atlantic	-.004	.028	.182	.056	.254	.034	.034	.012	.179	.046
So. Atlantic	.096	.027	.283	.055	.558	.031	.042	.008	.141	.045
West So. Central	.135	.027	.323	.055	.508	.033	.075	.008	.183	.045
East So. Central	.110	.027	.293	.055	.533	.033	.092	.009	.159	.042
East No. Central	.117	.027	.305	.055	.912	.033	.040	.007	.229	.047
West No. Central	.061	.027	.252	.055	.587	.032	.076	.009	.164	.040
Pacific	.136	.028	.323	.055	.487	.034	.056	.008	.257	.050
Mountain	.170	.028	.360	.056	.595	.033	.069	.011	d	d
Nonmet. area	.030	.006	.028	.006	.061	.008	-.033	.004	-.029	.016
R^2	.405		.403		.932		.225		.385	
Constant	6.205		6.062		5.63		4.420		4.575	
N	3756[c]		3524		779		3348		343	
Yield, average	6.269		6.268		6.017		4.511		4.573	
Yield, std. dev.	.169		.174		.109		.112		.142	

[a] Divided by 100,000.
[b] Divided by 1,000.
[c] Includes 232 loans that were not Section 203 home mortgages.
[d] Company had no loans of the given type.

of loan covered by the regression authorized by the individual lender in the state in which the property securing the loan was located. The second variable was the total number of *all* types of loans authorized by the individual lender in the state in which the property securing the given loan was located. The coefficients for the two-volume measures were generally significant, but because of high intercorrelation between them, they showed different signs when used together. Another problem with these variables is that lenders presumably will lend more heavily in areas where rates are high, generating a positive relationship that runs counter to the negative relationship we are seeking. Introduction of regional dummies eliminates a part, but probably not all, of the positive relationship. Volume coefficients decline sharply with the introduction of region, as noted in Table B-1.

The results were interesting enough to indicate further experimentation. Results might be improved by making the geographic area used in the volume measure coordinate with the area used to define rate differences. This implies either defining the loan volume in terms of nine regions rather than fifty states or dummying the fifty states rather than the nine regions. A second approach is to extend the cross section to cover a longer period, dummying the months to take account of changing market conditions and introducing volume figures for each month. This would take into account the influence of changing volume over time, as well as the differential effect of volume by individual lenders at a given point in time.

Appendix C

Data

All the series shown in this appendix were compiled in the NBER Survey and cover the period 1951–63. The FHLBB conventional loan series used in this study is shown in Appendix Table 3-1, while the FHA secondary market series is shown in Appendix Table 9-4.

The yield shown in the tables below assume prepayment in ten years. The yield is calculated from the formula shown on page 154, note 12, and differs slightly from the yield shown in *Mortgage Yield Table for Monthly Payment Mortgages* (Boston Financial Company).

Regional grouping of states used in the tables below are as follows:

EAST

New England

Maine
New Hampshire
Vermont
Massachusetts
Rhode Island
Connecticut

Middle Atlantic

New York
New Jersey
Pennsylvania

SOUTH

South Atlantic

Maryland
District of Columbia
Delaware
Virginia
West Virginia
North Carolina
South Carolina
Georgia
Florida

West South Central

Texas
Oklahoma
Arkansas
Louisiana

East South Central

Kentucky
Tennessee
Alabama
Mississippi

NORTH CENTRAL

East North Central

Ohio
Indiana
Illinois
Michigan
Wisconsin

West North Central

Minnesota
Iowa
Missouri
North Dakota
South Dakota
Nebraska
Kansas

WEST

Pacific

Washington
California
Oregon

Mountain

Idaho
Wyoming
Colorado
New Mexico
Arizona
Utah
Nevada
Montana

TABLE C-1

Characteristics of Conventional Mortgage Loans on Residential (1-4 Family) Properties by Four Life Insurance Companies, 1951-63, United States

Gross Yield[a]

	1951	1952	1953	1954	1955	1956	1957	1958	1959	1960	1961	1962	1963
Jan.	4.34	4.53	4.60	4.87	4.72	4.79	5.26	5.67	5.52	6.01	6.02	5.74	5.61
Feb.	4.31	4.50	4.61	4.84	4.71	4.80	5.39	5.69	5.59	6.04	5.96	5.76	5.61
March	4.36	4.56	4.60	4.83	4.73	4.81	5.47	5.66	5.60	6.06	5.94	5.78	5.55
April	4.37	4.57	4.60	4.81	4.72	4.81	5.52	5.63	5.62	6.06	5.85	5.78	5.54
May	4.39	4.64	4.62	4.81	4.72	4.80	5.48	5.57	5.64	6.09	5.83	5.76	5.51
June	4.40	4.61	4.68	4.77	4.71	4.82	5.49	5.50	5.67	6.08	5.81	5.71	5.53
July	4.45	4.65	4.76	4.75	4.74	4.87	5.48	5.49	5.68	6.10	5.78	5.68	5.53
Aug.	4.56	4.60	4.85	4.74	4.78	4.89	5.47	5.45	5.73	6.09	5.77	5.66	5.48
Sept.	4.55	4.60	4.84	4.76	4.74	4.93	5.52	5.38	5.74	6.07	5.79	5.66	5.52
Oct.	4.56	4.61	4.86	4.72	4.79	5.00	5.60	5.38	5.81	6.07	5.76	5.66	5.51
Nov.	4.53	4.55	4.86	4.68	4.81	5.12	5.64	5.43	5.94	6.03	5.74	5.65	5.48
Dec.	4.54	4.51	4.87	4.72	4.80	5.14	5.67	5.51	5.97	6.01	5.75	5.64	5.50

Standard Deviation - Gross Yield

	1951	1952	1953	1954	1955	1956	1957	1958	1959	1960	1961	1962	1963
Jan.				0.188	0.217	0.186	0.266	0.276	0.277	0.279	0.138	0.154	0.167
Feb.				0.158	0.202	0.206	0.286	0.167	0.245	0.181	0.172	0.143	0.217
March				0.157	0.253	0.187	0.283	0.198	0.286	0.189	0.164	0.132	0.154
April				0.171	0.212	0.224	0.250	0.169	0.196	0.291	0.174	0.133	0.162
May				0.187	0.225	0.168	0.244	0.166	0.231	0.180	0.160	0.150	0.147
June				0.176	0.208	0.205	0.219	0.217	0.166	0.183	0.169	0.167	0.163
July				0.198	0.204	0.218	0.202	0.202	0.194	0.161	0.162	0.166	0.134
Aug.				0.203	0.201	0.224	0.210	0.236	0.209	0.164	0.147	0.156	0.148
Sept.				0.207	0.276	0.261	0.196	0.224	0.223	0.177	0.165	0.156	0.145
Oct.			0.204	0.198	0.193	0.268	0.216	0.243	0.190	0.181	0.167	0.154	0.168
Nov.			0.199	0.226	0.210	0.289	0.182	0.257	0.259	0.134	0.164	0.158	0.209
Dec.			0.201	0.178	0.209	0.298	0.181	0.227	0.188	0.159	0.145	0.135	0.279

(continued)

Table C-1 (continued)

	1951	1952	1953	1954	1955	1956	1957	1958	1959	1960	1961	1962	1963
Contract Rate													
Jan.	4.52	4.68	4.76	5.02	4.86	4.94	5.35	5.76	5.58	6.04	6.05	5.77	5.65
Feb.	4.48	4.64	4.76	4.99	4.82	4.93	5.46	5.75	5.63	6.06	5.99	5.79	5.63
March	4.53	4.71	4.75	4.98	4.85	4.94	5.52	5.74	5.66	6.09	5.97	5.81	5.59
April	4.54	4.71	4.75	4.95	4.85	4.93	5.55	5.68	5.67	6.10	5.89	5.80	5.58
May	4.56	4.78	4.77	4.95	4.85	4.94	5.53	5.63	5.70	6.12	5.86	5.80	5.54
June	4.56	4.73	4.81	4.90	4.84	4.95	5.54	5.55	5.71	6.10	5.84	5.75	5.57
July	4.60	4.77	4.91	4.90	4.87	5.00	5.53	5.53	5.71	6.12	5.80	5.72	5.56
Aug.	4.71	4.73	5.01	4.88	4.90	5.02	5.53	5.51	5.77	6.11	5.81	5.71	5.52
Sept.	4.70	4.73	4.98	4.91	4.86	5.05	5.58	5.44	5.77	6.09	5.82	5.71	5.55
Oct.	4.71	4.75	5.01	4.85	4.92	5.10	5.67	5.44	5.85	6.09	5.78	5.71	5.55
Nov.	4.68	4.70	5.01	4.82	4.94	5.22	5.71	5.48	5.97	6.05	5.76	5.69	5.52
Dec.	4.71	4.65	5.02	4.87	4.93	5.23	5.73	5.57	5.99	6.03	5.78	5.69	5.50
Net Discount													
Jan.				-0.96	-0.84	-0.93	-0.58	-0.53	-0.33	-0.19	-0.19	-0.17	-0.28
Feb.				-0.89	-0.72	-0.82	-0.39	-0.37	-0.29	-0.14	-0.21	-0.20	-0.08
March				-0.87	-0.78	-0.80	-0.32	-0.47	-0.36	-0.17	-0.19	-0.19	-0.29
April				-0.87	-0.76	-0.78	-0.21	-0.33	-0.33	-0.22	-0.23	-0.17	-0.26
May				-0.88	-0.80	-0.84	-0.29	-0.34	-0.36	-0.16	-0.22	-0.22	-0.18
June				-0.76	-0.79	-0.81	-0.33	-0.28	-0.30	-0.12	-0.19	-0.26	-0.25
July				-0.89	-0.72	-0.82	-0.36	-0.25	-0.21	-0.13	-0.12	-0.27	-0.22
Aug.				-0.87	-0.79	-0.78	-0.36	-0.39	-0.22	-0.08	-0.21	-0.29	-0.21
Sept.				-0.93	-0.82	-0.78	-0.40	-0.36	-0.22	-0.12	-0.18	-0.30	-0.19
Oct.			-0.90	-0.84	-0.82	-0.63	-0.43	-0.33	-0.27	-0.13	-0.15	-0.33	-0.24
Nov.			-0.89	-0.83	-0.82	-0.61	-0.44	-0.31	-0.16	-0.12	-0.16	-0.31	-0.24
Dec.			-0.92	-0.92	-0.81	-0.58	-0.37	-0.36	-0.16	-0.13	-0.18	-0.35	0.01

(continued)

Table C-1 (continued)

Maturity (months)

	1951	1952	1953	1954	1955	1956	1957	1958	1959	1960	1961	1962	1963
Jan.	216.3	223.6	221.6	224.6	241.8	241.1	247.9	255.6	275.0	282.4	287.2	290.1	307.3
Feb.	214.1	222.9	222.2	224.9	243.8	244.4	254.2	263.2	275.3	284.7	284.7	300.9	310.3
March	216.3	221.5	222.4	224.9	242.3	251.5	254.4	259.6	274.4	283.7	280.0	299.3	306.8
April	217.5	226.4	223.9	225.8	248.2	245.3	253.6	263.1	274.2	284.6	284.2	303.0	312.2
May	212.5	217.9	224.5	228.3	241.1	249.5	246.3	265.0	280.5	288.0	287.1	308.7	307.1
June	215.5	219.7	226.9	225.3	245.2	243.7	254.8	266.9	278.8	281.5	286.4	304.1	309.2
July	216.8	220.1	222.3	235.1	247.7	243.4	257.5	260.9	281.5	284.6	284.1	303.4	313.3
Aug.	217.7	222.0	224.0	235.0	242.5	243.7	252.3	263.7	281.8	283.3	288.4	303.6	313.9
Sept.	216.4	221.9	227.1	234.0	244.1	238.3	252.0	273.7	277.8	285.7	291.2	307.5	306.1
Oct.	217.7	221.1	220.5	234.7	245.1	250.2	257.4	270.5	282.2	284.0	293.6	306.9	317.5
Nov.	218.4	219.9	219.2	243.1	242.4	249.0	258.6	269.9	281.0	285.6	292.8	303.3	313.7
Dec.	223.6	222.3	224.6	245.8	245.3	254.3	255.7	281.0	283.6	284.5	296.4	312.6	308.7

Standard Deviation - Maturity

	1951	1952	1953	1954	1955	1956	1957	1958	1959	1960	1961	1962	1963
Jan.	30.99	25.36	28.10	28.17	36.86	35.29	36.99	38.74	40.75	36.13	29.66	47.34	40.99
Feb.	28.10	26.96	27.40	26.55	35.73	38.26	36.16	36.62	41.41	33.13	35.08	39.18	47.17
March	29.62	27.36	24.01	29.60	39.58	36.65	40.09	39.97	40.70	30.56	36.63	45.48	50.26
April	29.35	24.61	26.56	30.71	41.19	38.77	36.93	36.71	41.78	33.08	37.07	44.80	46.75
May	32.25	31.29	26.18	24.80	39.28	40.29	43.05	43.50	35.89	28.24	32.74	44.34	46.93
June	28.25	28.89	24.35	28.56	38.29	38.53	44.03	42.35	38.93	35.60	33.63	43.76	46.31
July	28.25	29.08	26.66	31.79	36.71	35.32	37.06	45.09	37.28	29.86	35.84	54.57	46.54
Aug.	26.74	28.67	27.13	33.19	36.35	39.11	39.67	41.04	36.69	33.96	43.03	51.89	47.67
Sept.	28.50	26.19	24.47	34.28	37.48	36.00	46.13	38.73	42.34	32.57	45.78	48.90	55.09
Oct.	30.40	26.27	29.42	34.90	38.83	36.52	40.16	39.67	37.63	35.93	42.86	44.87	46.45
Nov.	30.68	30.50	30.09	37.78	39.01	38.26	34.87	44.87	35.92	32.72	45.61	47.92	45.29
Dec.	33.83	32.41	25.66	42.37	39.38	37.47	38.93	35.09	33.70	34.23	43.90	52.51	53.63

(continued)

Table C-1 (continued)

Loan-Value Ratio

	1951	1952	1953	1954	1955	1956	1957	1958	1959	1960	1961	1962	1963
Jan.	62.8	61.8	63.9	63.4	64.5	63.4	66.0	64.8	66.0	69.3	69.5	67.8	70.5
Feb.	63.2	61.9	64.9	63.6	65.1	63.4	65.3	67.0	67.3	69.5	70.6	69.4	70.4
March	62.5	61.6	63.9	63.3	64.9	65.8	65.2	66.4	67.3	69.7	68.8	69.3	70.5
April	63.0	61.5	63.8	63.6	65.8	64.8	64.4	67.1	66.2	69.5	69.1	70.0	70.3
May	63.0	61.8	64.7	64.5	64.3	64.9	63.6	65.7	67.5	69.2	69.4	70.6	69.5
June	62.8	61.7	64.6	64.2	64.4	64.4	65.0	65.8	68.2	69.3	69.2	69.8	70.4
July	61.7	62.6	64.1	64.6	64.9	63.5	63.6	65.8	68.4	70.0	69.2	69.8	70.3
Aug.	61.6	62.6	63.8	63.4	65.3	64.5	63.9	66.0	69.2	69.8	69.6	69.7	70.1
Sept.	61.4	63.2	63.2	63.9	64.4	64.3	63.9	67.6	69.2	70.6	70.0	69.7	70.0
Oct.	61.7	63.0	63.5	62.7	64.8	63.5	65.3	66.3	69.2	70.1	69.4	69.8	70.3
Nov.	62.9	63.7	63.9	64.6	65.0	64.2	65.9	65.7	69.3	69.2	70.2	69.3	70.3
Dec.	62.7	64.1	64.5	64.6	64.5	65.3	65.2	67.5	69.5	69.8	69.1	70.1	68.7

Standard Deviation - Loan-Value Ratio

	1951	1952	1953	1954	1955	1956	1957	1958	1959	1960	1961	1962	1963
Jan.	8.30	7.40	6.96	7.37	8.59	8.42	8.37	8.77	8.97	7.44	8.42	10.13	7.38
Feb.	8.39	8.03	7.50	9.52	8.25	8.61	7.75	6.92	9.50	8.10	7.25	9.44	7.93
March	7.29	8.07	7.53	7.90	9.58	8.90	9.29	7.29	7.77	8.53	8.02	8.01	7.93
April	7.44	8.39	8.55	7.26	7.57	8.81	8.36	8.06	8.90	7.92	9.17	8.28	8.41
May	7.04	7.49	7.93	7.79	8.27	8.97	8.19	7.96	8.50	7.91	7.34	7.71	8.74
June	8.84	7.81	8.20	7.55	8.43	8.69	8.00	8.14	7.10	8.28	9.15	8.51	7.92
July	8.99	7.21	7.41	9.07	8.38	8.64	8.76	8.63	8.53	6.58	9.07	10.87	8.83
Aug.	7.01	7.88	6.26	8.50	8.12	8.32	9.89	8.79	8.27	8.57	8.41	9.07	7.80
Sept.	7.79	7.53	7.41	8.11	8.04	8.67	8.08	8.50	7.65	7.54	7.61	8.97	8.90
Oct.	7.84	7.76	8.21	8.07	8.00	8.29	9.83	8.78	8.04	7.02	8.75	7.63	7.80
Nov.	7.56	7.84	8.31	8.69	8.28	9.42	8.85	8.03	8.57	8.67	7.78	9.07	9.44
Dec.	7.12	8.89	7.15	9.45	9.61	8.17	8.36	8.38	8.50	7.79	8.67	8.77	11.26

(continued)

Table C-1 (continued)

Number of Loans

	1951	1952	1953	1954	1955	1956	1957	1958	1959	1960	1961	1962	1963
Jan.	334	350	389	357	329	410	366	358	325	365	349	356	323
Feb.	239	347	303	308	292	421	309	370	340	383	372	380	367
March	263	394	348	441	303	385	319	349	418	371	372	377	347
April	317	449	384	370	324	421	380	351	398	370	396	367	363
May	378	425	371	468	370	389	372	366	379	360	371	365	354
June	359	401	379	433	341	404	360	364	391	386	390	380	305
July	347	339	388	366	408	376	361	379	365	375	372	362	357
Aug.	361	412	350	411	400	366	363	352	365	373	376	371	355
Sept.	356	413	373	393	397	379	375	397	407	380	387	391	381
Oct.	362	389	381	362	408	360	363	375	392	355	373	350	359
Nov.	342	356	410	390	445	347	365	327	364	365	381	374	314
Dec.	279	339	380	303	360	382	354	365	404	346	365	355	342

Mean Loan Size

	1951	1952	1953	1954	1955	1956	1957	1958	1959	1960	1961	1962	1963
Jan.	10,114	10,549	11,180	11,509	13,206	13,873	14,211	14,480	16,020	17,018	16,872	17,674	19,029
Feb.	10,667	11,209	11,478	12,424	13,428	13,437	15,257	15,781	16,179	16,959	18,299	18,389	19,887
March	10,556	10,852	11,874	12,291	12,883	13,495	14,457	15,185	17,056	17,442	18,205	18,137	19,495
April	10,425	10,682	11,466	11,948	13,864	13,565	14,662	15,892	16,453	17,170	17,411	18,289	19,218
May	11,097	10,376	11,803	12,384	12,840	14,271	14,060	14,989	16,267	17,001	18,110	18,323	18,747
June	10,453	10,358	12,110	13,006	12,762	13,904	14,215	15,669	17,012	16,545	17,646	18,863	18,785
July	10,947	10,634	11,966	12,312	12,938	13,750	14,111	15,262	17,328	17,730	17,682	18,056	18,599
Aug.	10,273	11,054	11,286	12,201	13,495	14,342	14,796	15,766	17,264	16,739	17,782	18,970	18,676
Sept.	10,342	11,116	11,672	12,195	13,431	13,547	14,685	16,011	17,687	17,222	17,681	18,648	18,728
Oct.	10,709	11,025	11,421	12,686	13,090	13,783	14,939	15,656	16,986	16,455	17,850	18,903	19,309
Nov.	10,780	11,326	11,869	13,147	13,665	14,112	15,414	15,605	16,235	16,763	18,029	18,653	19,442
Dec.	10,789	11,128	12,197	12,967	13,542	14,616	14,355	16,231	17,374	17,681	17,765	18,754	18,482

(continued)

Table C-1 (continued)

Gross Yield[a]

	1951	1952	1953	1954	1955	1956	1957	1958	1959	1960	1961	1962	1963
I	4.34	4.53	4.60	4.85	4.72	4.80	5.37	5.67	5.58	6.04	5.97	5.76	5.59
II	4.39	4.60	4.64	4.80	4.72	4.81	5.49	5.57	5.64	6.08	5.83	5.75	5.53
III	4.51	4.61	4.80	4.75	4.75	4.90	5.49	5.44	5.72	6.09	5.78	5.67	5.51
IV	4.55	4.56	4.86	4.70	4.80	5.09	5.63	5.44	5.90	6.03	5.75	5.65	5.50

Standard Deviation - Gross Yield

	1951	1952	1953	1954	1955	1956	1957	1958	1959	1960	1961	1962	1963
I				0.166	0.228	0.196	0.295	0.224	0.266	0.218	0.163	0.145	0.186
II				0.179	0.214	0.202	0.240	0.183	0.198	0.227	0.169	0.154	0.158
III				0.201	0.232	0.237	0.204	0.226	0.212	0.166	0.158	0.159	0.143
IV			0.201	0.204	0.205	0.293	0.195	0.244	0.216	0.160	0.159	0.150	0.225

Contract Rate

	1951	1952	1953	1954	1955	1956	1957	1958	1959	1960	1961	1962	1963
I	4.51	4.68	4.75	5.00	4.84	4.93	5.44	5.75	5.63	6.07	6.00	5.79	5.62
II	4.55	4.74	4.78	4.94	4.85	4.94	5.54	5.62	5.70	6.11	5.86	5.78	5.56
III	4.67	4.74	4.97	4.89	4.88	5.03	5.55	5.49	5.75	6.10	5.81	5.71	5.54
IV	4.70	4.70	5.01	4.84	4.93	5.18	5.70	5.50	5.93	6.05	5.77	5.70	5.52

Net Discount,

	1951	1952	1953	1954	1955	1956	1957	1958	1959	1960	1961	1962	1963
I				-0.90	-0.78	-0.85	-0.43	-0.45	-0.32	-0.17	-0.19	-0.19	-0.22
II				-0.84	-0.80	-0.81	-0.28	-0.31	-0.33	-0.17	-0.21	-0.22	-0.23
III				-0.90	-0.77	-0.79	-0.38	-0.33	-0.22	-0.11	-0.17	-0.28	-0.20
IV			-0.90	-0.86	-0.82	-0.60	-0.41	-0.34	-0.20	-0.12	-0.16	-0.33	-0.15

(continued)

Table C-1 (continued)

	1951	1952	1953	1954	1955	1956	1957	1958	1959	1960	1961	1962	1963
Maturity (months)													
I	215.6	222.6	222.0	224.9	242.8	245.5	251.7	259.6	274.9	284.0	284.0	296.9	307.9
II	215.3	221.6	225.2	226.6	244.7	246.4	251.6	265.1	277.8	284.6	285.9	305.4	309.2
III	217.3	221.3	224.9	235.6	245.3	241.9	253.9	266.6	280.3	284.6	288.3	304.9	311.0
IV	219.7	221.2	221.2	240.8	244.5	251.4	257.3	274.3	282.5	284.8	294.5	307.7	313.2
Standard Deviation - Maturity													
I	29.66	26.68	26.70	28.18	37.35	36.73	38.01	38.50	41.39	33.05	33.70	44.10	46.52
II	30.19	28.43	25.63	27.77	40.06	39.29	41.16	41.17	39.07	32.74	34.46	44.44	47.17
III	27.60	28.00	25.69	33.27	36.86	36.93	41.32	42.16	39.10	32.29	41.76	51.81	50.32
IV	31.89	29.51	28.65	38.56	39.01	37.42	38.13	39.95	35.81	34.25	44.21	49.20	48.92
Loan-Value Ratio													
I	62.8	61.7	64.2	63.5	64.8	64.2	65.4	66.0	66.9	69.6	69.7	68.8	70.4
II	62.9	61.7	64.4	64.2	64.9	64.7	64.3	66.3	67.3	69.3	69.3	70.1	70.0
III	61.6	62.9	63.9	64.1	64.8	64.1	63.9	66.6	69.0	70.1	69.6	69.7	70.1
IV	62.3	63.6	64.0	64.0	64.8	64.4	65.5	66.6	69.3	69.7	69.6	69.7	69.7
Standard Deviation - Loan-Value Ratio													
I	7.99	7.87	7.37	8.23	8.86	8.69	8.64	7.81	8.68	7.89	7.92	9.26	7.84
II	7.85	7.82	8.27	7.69	8.11	8.87	8.21	8.08	8.23	8.08	8.55	8.22	8.39
III	7.94	7.48	7.15	8.59	8.19	8.55	8.91	8.66	8.10	7.62	8.42	9.65	8.58
IV	7.55	8.19	7.96	8.71	8.61	8.71	9.02	8.39	8.29	7.90	8.38	8.52	9.71

(continued)

Table C-1 (continued)

	1951	1952	1953	1954	1955	1956	1957	1958	1959	1960	1961	1962	1963
							Number of Loans						
I	836	1,091	1,040	1,106	924	1,216	994	1,077	1,083	1,119	1,093	1,113	1,037
II	1,054	1,275	1,134	1,271	1,035	1,214	1,112	1,081	1,168	1,116	1,157	1,112	1,022
III	1,064	1,164	1,111	1,170	1,205	1,121	1,099	1,128	1,137	1,128	1,135	1,124	1,093
IV	983	1,084	1,171	1,055	1,213	1,089	1,082	1,067	1,160	1,066	1,119	1,079	1,015
							Mean Loan Size						
I	10,435	10,874	11,541	12,054	13,161	13,574	14,633	15,153	16,416	17,215	17,847	18,073	19,443
II	10,688	10,486	11,764	12,399	13,104	13,938	14,329	15,515	16,622	16,922	17,824	18,556	18,896
III	10,516	10,953	11,693	12,348	13,271	13,863	14,555	15,678	17,408	17,227	17,750	18,598	18,684
IV	10,770	11,155	11,832	12,910	13,416	14,216	14,895	15,845	17,019	16,940	17,940	18,829	19,034

[a]Data for one company during the period January 1951-September 1953 were partly estimated from aggregate data covering that company. The standard deviation was thus not available for that period.

TABLE C-2

Characteristics of FHA Mortgage Loans on Residential (1-4 Family)
Properties by Four Life Insurance Companies, 1951-63, United States

	1951	1952	1953	1954	1955	1956	1957	1958	1959	1960	1961	1962	1963
						Gross Yield							
Jan.	4.08	4.20	4.26	4.68	4.60	4.70	5.16	5.58	5.61	6.23	6.17	5.74	5.63
Feb.	4.10	4.23	4.26	4.68	4.59	4.63	5.34	5.62	5.69	6.27	6.16	5.77	5.61
March	4.12	4.23	4.26	4.69	4.61	4.71	5.31	5.63	5.70	6.29[a]	6.03	5.78	5.58
April	4.13	4.24	4.26	4.67	4.61	4.72	5.36	5.61	5.69	6.27[a]	6.00	5.78	5.56
May	4.13	4.25	4.30	4.59	4.56	4.71	5.37	5.55	5.71	6.28[a]	5.94	5.78	5.50
June	4.14	4.25	4.52	4.61	4.62	4.77	5.35	5.51	5.74	6.24	5.86	5.75	5.50
July	4.19	4.26	4.53	4.61	4.62	4.76	5.38	5.50	5.77	6.25	5.80	5.74	5.51
Aug.	4.23	4.26	4.56	4.60	4.66	4.73	5.39	5.47	5.81	6.26	5.79	5.70	5.50
Sept.	4.23	4.26	4.60	4.62	4.62	4.76	5.54	5.47	5.84[a]	6.25	5.80	5.69	5.49
Oct.	4.22	4.26	4.67	4.58	4.65	4.84	5.56	5.49	5.93[a]	6.25[a]	5.77	5.69	5.49
Nov.	4.22	4.25	4.69	4.61	4.69	4.85	5.59	5.55	6.18[a]	6.25	5.77	5.67	5.48
Dec.	4.22	4.23	4.70	4.58	4.71	4.90	5.60	5.59	6.23	6.20	5.76	5.66	5.48
					Standard Deviation - Gross Yield								
Jan.	0.111	0.092	0.062	0.146	0.100	0.141	0.290	0.124	0.175	0.206	0.154	0.120	0.148
Feb.	0.086	0.086	0.084	0.127	0.116	0.274	0.185	0.139	0.171	0.128	0.136	0.112	0.132
March	0.087	0.080	0.059	0.149	0.135	0.169	0.158	0.131	0.165	0.139	0.168	0.107	0.124
April	0.095	0.069	0.063	0.111	0.111	0.143	0.136	0.125	0.169	0.247	0.151	0.120	0.123
May	0.102	0.050	0.107	0.221	0.216	0.152	0.113	0.115	0.161	0.149	0.157	0.109	0.141
June	0.097	0.050	0.122	0.138	0.134	0.143	0.121	0.111	0.155	0.131	0.136	0.099	0.119
July	0.096	0.071	0.086	0.142	0.116	0.149	0.137	0.106	0.139	0.110	0.224	0.120	0.107
Aug.	0.104	0.052	0.122	0.120	0.132	0.143	0.144	0.115	0.140	0.132	0.123	0.121	0.111
Sept.	0.113	0.132	0.171	0.147	0.216	0.214	0.110	0.120	0.237	0.110	0.146	0.129	0.108
Oct.	0.100	0.089	0.158	0.100	0.143	0.152	0.119	0.111	0.249	0.152	0.123	0.113	0.109
Nov.	0.097	0.081	0.157	0.104	0.190	0.152	0.121	0.144	0.300	0.181	0.127	0.132	0.139
Dec.	0.108	0.117	0.160	0.116	0.156	0.165	0.124	0.153	0.156	0.238	0.141	0.096	0.159

(continued)

TABLE C-2 (continued)

Contract Rate

	1951	1952	1953	1954	1955	1956	1957	1958	1959	1960	1961	1962	1963
Jan.	4.27	4.25	4.25	4.50	4.50	4.50	4.84	5.25	5.25	5.71	5.74	5.26	5.24
Feb.	4.26	4.25	4.25	4.50	4.50	4.40	4.98	5.25	5.25	5.74	5.74	5.27	5.25
March	4.26	4.25	4.25	4.50	4.50	4.48	4.97	5.25	5.25	5.75	5.65	5.26	5.26
April	4.26	4.25	4.25	4.50	4.50	4.50	4.99	5.25	5.24	5.73	5.60	5.25	5.25
May	4.25	4.25	4.28	4.43	4.44	4.50	5.00	5.25	5.25	5.75	5.57	5.25	5.25
June	4.25	4.26	4.47	4.49	4.49	4.50	5.00	5.25	5.25	5.75	5.52	5.25	5.25
July	4.25	4.25	4.49	4.50	4.50	4.50	5.00	5.25	5.25	5.75	5.40	5.25	5.25
Aug.	4.25	4.25	4.49	4.50	4.50	4.50	5.02	5.25	5.25	5.75	5.37	5.25	5.25
Sept.	4.27	4.25	4.47	4.50	4.45	4.46	5.21	5.25	5.24	5.75	5.33	5.25	5.25
Oct.	4.25	4.25	4.49	4.50	4.49	4.50	5.25	5.25	5.35	5.74	5.30	5.25	5.25
Nov.	4.25	4.25	4.49	4.50	4.49	4.50	5.25	5.25	5.65	5.74	5.29	5.25	5.25
Dec.	4.25	4.23	4.49	4.50	4.49	4.53	5.25	5.25	5.72	5.72	5.29	5.27	5.25

Net Discount

	1951	1952	1953	1954	1955	1956	1957	1958	1959	1960	1961	1962	1963
Jan.	-1.21	-0.30	0.04	1.18	0.66	1.32	2.07	2.14	2.36	3.42	2.77	3.18	2.59
Feb.	-1.06	-0.13	0.07	1.15	0.61	1.49	2.30	2.42	2.92	3.41	2.72	3.31	2.37
March	-0.89	-0.16	0.05	1.24	0.75	1.51	2.18	2.47	2.95	3.52[a]	2.44	3.45	2.12
April	-0.87	-0.07	0.07	1.14	0.78	1.50	2.44	2.34	2.95	3.50[a]	2.63	3.38	2.08
May	-0.79	-0.01	0.10	1.01	0.83	1.44	2.45	1.96	3.08	3.47[a]	2.40	3.49	1.69
June	-0.71	0.03	0.28	0.82	0.88	1.85	2.30	1.70	3.27	3.25	2.25	3.34	1.69
July	-0.40	0.02	0.26	0.76	0.84	1.74	2.47	1.65	3.46	3.30	2.68	3.23	1.69
Aug.	-0.13	0.07	0.45	0.67	1.06	1.55	2.46	1.42	3.70	3.33	2.83	2.97	1.64
Sept.	-0.25	0.08	0.87	0.78	1.17	1.99	2.11	1.45	4.01[a]	3.29[a]	3.10	2.92	1.63
Oct.	-0.17	0.09	1.14	0.54	1.05	2.25	2.07	1.60	3.87[a]	3.28	3.16	2.88	1.59
Nov.	-0.18	0.00	1.32	0.71	1.39	2.34	2.21	2.01	3.53[a]	3.13	3.16	2.76	1.54
Dec.	-0.22	-0.05	1.38	0.54	1.43	2.45	2.30	2.26	3.35		3.16	2.61	1.55

(continued)

TABLE C-2 (continued)

Maturity (months)

	1951	1952	1953	1954	1955	1956	1957	1958	1959	1960	1961	1962	1963
Jan.	266.0	250.4	254.0	259.8	306.1	292.3	300.0	306.3	330.7	341.8	342.3	349.9	346.9
Feb.	258.8	252.3	251.4	260.2	308.0	292.7	285.1	305.6	332.1	341.1	344.1	347.7	352.0
March	255.7	253.2	254.9	263.8	309.9	299.7	296.1	308.0	331.0	344.2	343.4	348.1	352.9
April	253.4	252.0	254.1	266.4	310.6	296.3	308.1	311.6	334.6	347.8	345.2	351.5	352.1
May	250.2	248.1	248.7	267.6	309.0	297.1	304.7	321.3	333.7	344.7	346.3	347.5	354.0
June	251.8	248.2	254.7	276.6	313.4	300.3	303.4	325.1	334.5	345.5	346.5	347.0	352.6
July	246.3	249.3	253.1	277.7	306.2	302.6	302.3	328.2	341.2	344.6	342.7	348.1	349.3
Aug.	245.6	246.3	254.0	273.9	306.5	311.8	305.9	333.7	337.4	337.0	344.7	347.6	351.8
Sept.	245.5	250.0	260.7	293.6	304.7	297.9	300.7	328.2	338.0	341.6	344.4	347.0	352.1
Oct.	247.9	256.7	260.3	292.4	301.1	298.0	302.0	330.7	340.4	345.5	346.1	349.6	354.5
Nov.	252.6	254.1	258.7	301.8	304.5	303.2	305.4	330.4	340.8	343.0	346.6	345.8	353.7
Dec.	245.4	251.6	263.4	299.4	302.1	301.4	302.1	328.9	345.7	342.9	346.6	355.1	351.4

Standard Deviation - Maturity

	1951	1952	1953	1954	1955	1956	1957	1958	1959	1960	1961	1962	1963
Jan.	31.53	30.04	28.81	29.85	38.50	30.57	38.07	37.93	37.89	35.53	34.91	30.47	37.40
Feb.	31.31	26.44	25.92	30.15	40.69	31.38	43.34	36.13	39.67	38.41	30.57	29.86	32.20
March	32.46	30.63	34.28	30.20	40.01	35.55	34.16	35.02	41.56	32.96	31.98	29.89	29.74
April	29.73	28.09	32.20	31.26	38.32	35.01	32.76	33.59	41.46	27.71	30.54	25.62	30.63
May	25.19	23.71	29.04	35.36	41.51	34.04	33.72	40.14	37.95	33.93	31.16	28.68	29.57
June	26.43	27.79	29.57	32.93	39.67	35.92	36.94	38.13	37.17	28.38	30.25	33.56	32.18
July	24.26	26.09	27.42	35.52	40.72	33.22	36.38	37.78	31.83	32.45	34.33	32.89	37.65
Aug.	24.36	22.71	28.48	34.21	39.83	36.35	34.05	39.29	37.46	38.87	31.95	35.33	34.71
Sept.	23.06	26.22	30.62	36.42	38.95	42.53	29.64	36.30	36.53	30.38	34.70	36.49	32.12
Oct.	22.12	29.56	29.20	43.92	37.24	35.24	30.34	39.50	34.07	35.44	33.61	32.24	32.15
Nov.	27.99	27.73	29.38	45.02	37.01	36.79	34.78	39.36	33.77	38.77	32.76	39.80	32.61
Dec.	24.45	31.40	31.91	41.16	33.60	35.55	33.18	44.87	32.39	34.15	31.72	34.87	35.87

(continued)

TABLE C-2 (continued)

Loan-Value Ratio

	1951	1952	1953	1954	1955	1956	1957	1958	1959	1960	1961	1962	1963
Jan.	83.3	81.3	82.0	81.0	85.1	85.0	83.5	89.7	91.7	92.1	92.7	94.1	93.7
Feb.	82.3	81.0	81.5	81.2	85.6	84.7	83.1	89.7	91.9	92.0	92.5	93.8	94.0
March	82.4	81.1	82.9	80.8	86.0	84.3	83.7	90.3	92.2	92.1	92.9	93.7	94.0
April	82.6	80.9	82.1	80.7	85.7	83.7	83.3	89.8	91.9	91.8	92.6	93.4	94.2
May	80.8	81.0	81.2	82.2	86.7	83.6	84.5	90.9	92.4	91.6	93.2	93.8	93.7
June	81.8	81.2	82.6	81.4	86.4	84.6	85.1	91.1	92.4	92.2	92.3	93.8	93.1
July	80.0	80.5	82.1	80.8	86.6	84.6	85.1	90.9	92.6	93.2	93.2	93.7	92.9
Aug.	80.2	81.2	81.8	80.9	85.9	84.6	85.7	92.0	92.7	93.3	92.2	93.3	93.0
Sept.	80.5	81.5	80.8	84.7	86.3	84.1	87.7	91.3	92.0	93.2	93.5	93.6	93.6
Oct.	80.5	81.7	81.5	84.7	86.0	83.7	88.3	91.1	92.4	92.7	92.8	94.0	93.3
Nov.	80.8	82.1	81.1	85.0	85.3	83.9	89.0	91.3	92.0	92.7	93.6	93.1	93.7
Dec.	80.8	80.4	81.9	85.2	85.9	83.0	88.6	91.3	91.8	92.7	93.6	93.9	93.8

Standard Deviation - Loan-Value Ratio

	1951	1952	1953	1954	1955	1956	1957	1958	1959	1960	1961	1962	1963
Jan.	8.36	7.12	6.89	6.49	5.77	6.03	6.11	5.69	6.53	5.25	5.37	4.80	4.49
Feb.	7.61	7.12	6.87	6.82	6.44	6.50	6.63	5.50	5.85	4.43	4.45	4.09	3.76
March	7.75	6.80	7.36	5.85	6.63	6.36	5.87	5.08	5.57	4.33	4.40	4.22	4.03
April	7.75	7.58	7.65	6.53	6.74	7.59	6.62	5.53	6.16	4.79	5.17	4.57	4.10
May	8.23	7.46	7.08	6.26	6.05	7.42	5.91	5.45	5.31	5.51	4.27	4.35	4.85
June	7.91	7.32	6.05	6.55	6.72	5.40	5.31	6.01	4.83	5.46	5.38	3.85	5.78
July	7.78	8.42	7.43	6.71	6.64	5.80	5.86	6.59	4.84	4.13	4.88	5.16	6.80
Aug.	7.60	7.26	6.66	7.15	5.92	5.31	5.71	4.96	4.43	4.33	6.40	6.32	7.09
Sept.	7.54	7.06	6.96	7.22	5.73	6.01	6.16	6.14	4.64	3.87	4.54	4.45	4.53
Oct.	7.42	7.22	6.79	6.94	5.99	5.77	6.25	6.32	4.39	5.50	5.81	3.76	5.64
Nov.	7.32	7.52	6.57	6.71	6.00	5.98	6.54	6.29	4.93	4.51	4.04	7.11	4.01
Dec.	6.87	8.27	5.56	7.03	6.41	6.78	6.79	6.14	5.20	4.49	3.76	5.74	3.97

(continued)

TABLE C-2 (continued)

	1951	1952	1953	1954	1955	1956	1957	1958	1959	1960	1961	1962	1963
Number of Loans													
Jan.	397	452	454	401	469	422	384	419	438	373	338	356	455
Feb.	302	425	440	374	414	441	226	485	473	360	480	380	378
March	262	462	477	452	486	437	386	474	492	410	482	368	448
April	407	438	462	387	491	409	370	490	509	371	553	441	421
May	423	433	388	408	542	411	373	501	508	382	508	509	393
June	433	431	363	452	399	353	385	490	473	401	493	498	363
July	384	474	402	400	476	366	417	481	447	367	422	430	441
Aug.	400	450	384	431	439	395	384	457	404	407	417	485	415
Sept.	431	452	450	418	500	366	408	498	493	331	406	496	459
Oct.	458	471	412	417	507	424	373	412	497	454	356	495	541
Nov.	482	422	400	468	469	392	375	391	482	380	395	371	399
Dec.	415	437	384	472	480	389	364	394	402	400	382	368	412
Mean Loan Size													
Jan.	7,865	8,524	8,912	9,761	11,019	11,120	11,775	12,872	13,508	14,313	14,004	14,536	14,037
Feb.	7,926	8,566	9,243	9,786	11,118	11,310	11,698	13,037	13,687	14,665	14,632	15,170	14,219
March	8,060	8,606	8,740	9,833	11,001	11,393	11,949	12,951	13,591	14,623	14,653	15,045	14,710
April	8,132	8,442	8,819	9,769	11,164	11,341	12,136	13,020	13,469	14,911	14,386	15,165	14,366
May	8,338	8,610	9,484	9,733	10,847	11,412	12,065	13,311	13,274	14,868	14,228	14,612	14,414
June	8,409	8,703	9,192	9,781	10,727	11,678	12,437	13,344	13,761	14,551	14,292	14,744	14,936
July	8,364	8,490	9,262	9,858	11,013	11,919	12,548	13,543	13,688	14,153	14,382	14,929	14,939
Aug.	8,461	8,787	9,636	9,922	11,124	11,629	12,272	13,716	13,828	14,209	14,426	14,341	14,254
Sept.	8,596	8,669	9,777	10,121	11,057	11,491	13,098	13,491	13,862	14,509	14,211	14,718	14,596
Oct.	8,472	8,789	9,534	10,556	11,342	11,877	13,347	13,689	13,832	14,251	14,589	14,784	14,596
Nov.	8,480	8,722	9,647	11,148	11,397	12,217	13,196	13,481	14,193	14,409	14,501	14,533	14,768
Dec.	8,617	8,940	9,718	10,693	11,263	11,880	12,998	13,662	14,353	14,661	14,875	13,986	14,693

(continued)

TABLE C-2 (continued)

	1951	1952	1953	1954	1955	1956	1957	1958	1959	1960	1961	1962	1963
Gross Yield													
I	4.10	4.22	4.26	4.68	4.60	4.66	5.26	5.61	5.67	6.26	6.11	5.76	5.61
II	4.13	4.25	4.36	4.63	4.59	4.74	5.36	5.55	5.72	6.27[a]	5.94	5.76	5.52
III	4.22	4.26	4.57	4.61	4.63	4.75	5.43	5.48	5.81[a]	6.25	5.80	5.71	5.50
IV	4.22	4.25	4.69	4.59	4.68	4.86	5.58	5.55	6.11[a]	6.23[a]	5.77	5.68	5.49
Standard Deviation - Gross Yield													
I	0.097	0.087	0.068	0.141	0.119	0.223	0.230	0.132	0.175	0.169	0.163	0.114	0.138
II	0.096	0.062	0.151	0.166	0.173	0.148	0.125	0.121	0.163	0.188	0.153	0.110	0.129
III	0.107	0.092	0.130	0.136	0.168	0.173	0.152	0.114	0.175	0.118	0.169	0.125	0.108
IV	0.101	0.097	0.159	0.108	0.164	0.158	0.122	0.146	0.279	0.197	0.130	0.124	0.137
Contract Rate													
I	4.26	4.25	4.25	4.50	4.50	4.45	4.94	5.25	5.25	5.73	5.71	5.27	5.25
II	4.26	4.25	4.34	4.47	4.47	4.50	5.00	5.25	5.25	5.74	5.57	5.25	5.25
III	4.26	4.25	4.49	4.50	4.48	4.48	5.08	5.25	5.25	5.75	5.36	5.25	5.25
IV	4.25	4.24	4.49	4.50	4.49	4.51	5.25	5.25	5.57	5.74	5.29	5.25	5.25
Net Discount													
I	-1.07	-0.20	0.05	1.20	0.68	1.44	2.15	2.35	2.77	3.43	2.66	3.31	2.36
II	-0.79	0.01	0.15	1.00	0.84	1.62	2.40	2.00	3.09	3.43[a]	2.45	3.40	1.82
III	-0.24	0.06	0.52	0.73	1.03	1.75	2.34	1.52	3.75[a]	3.31	2.88	3.04	1.65
IV	-0.18	0.02	1.29	0.60	1.27	2.36	2.19	1.97	3.83[a]	3.25[a]	3.16	2.83	1.56

(continued)

TABLE C-2 (continued)

	1951	1952	1953	1954	1955	1956	1957	1958	1959	1960	1961	1962	1963
Maturity (months)													
I	260.7	251.9	253.5	261.4	308.0	294.8	296.5	306.6	331.4	342.4	343.1	348.4	351.0
II	251.9	249.5	251.9	270.8	310.9	297.8	305.4	319.4	333.9	346.2	346.0	348.6	352.7
III	245.6	248.7	255.2	281.1	306.0	304.2	302.9	329.8	339.2	341.1	344.1	347.4	351.2
IV	248.7	254.2	260.7	298.1	302.1	300.9	303.2	329.8	342.2	343.8	346.5	350.8	353.4
Standard Deviation - Maturity													
I	32.04	29.21	31.16	30.17	39.74	33.05	37.73	36.33	39.68	35.69	32.52	30.12	33.06
II	27.29	26.13	30.18	33.53	40.00	35.05	34.77	37.73	38.92	30.01	30.84	29.70	30.93
III	23.71	25.34	28.70	36.17	39.78	38.13	33.95	37.54	35.28	34.29	33.50	35.08	34.88
IV	25.10	29.49	30.14	43.43	36.08	36.09	32.88	41.56	33.58	37.09	32.67	35.19	33.59
Loan-Value Ratio													
I	82.7	81.2	82.1	80.9	85.6	84.6	83.6	89.9	91.9	92.1	92.6	93.9	93.9
II	81.7	81.0	82.0	81.5	86.3	84.0	84.3	90.6	92.2	91.9	92.7	93.6	93.7
III	80.2	81.1	81.5	82.0	86.3	84.4	86.2	91.4	92.4	93.2	92.9	93.5	93.2
IV	80.7	81.4	81.4	85.0	85.7	83.5	88.6	91.3	92.1	92.7	93.3	93.7	93.6
Standard Deviation - Loan-Value Ratio													
I	7.92	6.98	7.12	6.38	6.25	6.27	5.91	5.43	5.99	4.71	4.77	4.35	4.12
II	8.06	7.40	7.02	6.36	6.44	6.97	6.01	5.67	5.49	5.26	4.86	4.27	4.91
III	7.65	7.56	7.02	7.28	6.09	5.70	6.03	5.93	4.68	4.13	5.40	5.27	6.13
IV	7.19	7.72	6.34	6.90	6.12	6.24	6.55	6.25	4.83	4.83	4.66	5.25	4.68

(continued)

TABLE C-2 (continued)

	1951	1952	1953	1954	1955	1956	1957	1958	1959	1960	1961	1962	1963
Number of Loans													
I	961	1,339	1,371	1,227	1,369	1,300	996	1,378	1,403	1,143	1,300	1,104	1,281
II	1,263	1,302	1,213	1,247	1,432	1,173	1,128	1,481	1,490	1,154	1,554	1,448	1,177
III	1,215	1,376	1,236	1,249	1,415	1,127	1,209	1,436	1,344	1,105	1,245	1,411	1,315
IV	1,355	1,330	1,196	1,357	1,456	1,205	1,112	1,197	1,381	1,234	1,133	1,234	1,352
Mean Loan Size													
I	7,955	8,570	8,940	9,797	11,037	11,284	11,835	12,935	13,596	14,500	14,458	14,925	14,351
II	8,288	8,591	9,170	9,776	10,912	11,464	12,204	13,222	13,502	14,783	14,320	14,835	14,640
III	8,476	8,654	9,552	9,974	11,066	11,682	12,658	13,578	13,811	14,289	14,337	14,672	14,586
IV	8,533	8,833	9,645	10,795	11,356	11,966	13,174	13,604	14,126	14,407	14,638	14,518	14,699

[a]Data cover only three companies.

TABLE C-3

Characteristics of Conventional Mortgage Loans on Residential (1-4 Family)
Properties by Four Life Insurance Companies, 1951-63, Correspondent Loans,
United States

	1951	1952	1953	1954	1955	1956	1957	1958	1959	1960	1961	1962	1963
						Gross Yield[a]							
Jan.	4.39	4.68	4.67	4.88	4.75	4.74	5.08	5.63	5.41	5.98	6.01	5.71	5.62
Feb.	4.35	4.64	4.69	4.88	4.72	4.71	5.22	5.61	5.45	6.03	5.96	5.71	5.56
March	4.36	4.64	4.69	4.83	4.77	4.75	5.25	5.54	5.54	6.04	5.96	5.78	5.50
April	4.35	4.64	4.67	4.83	4.73	4.79	5.35	5.52	5.54	6.02	5.85	5.76	5.49
May	4.42	4.67	4.68	4.80	4.73	4.74	5.40	5.46	5.58	6.07	5.84	5.71	5.47
June	4.47	4.65	4.73	4.78	4.66	4.75	5.40	5.39	5.64	6.07	5.80	5.67	5.48
July	4.55	4.67	4.79	4.77	4.67	4.80	5.42	5.33	5.69	6.10	5.77	5.68	5.48
Aug.	4.64	4.64	4.88	4.77	4.71	4.86	5.43	5.30	5.77	6.09	5.75	5.64	5.44
Sept.	4.61	4.66	4.93	4.80	4.64	4.86	5.48	5.28	5.76	6.05	5.78	5.64	5.47
Oct.	4.67	4.69	4.88	4.75	4.73	4.92	5.53	5.27	5.83	6.05	5.71	5.67	5.44
Nov.	4.70	4.69	4.88	4.74	4.74	5.03	5.55	5.34	5.95	6.06	5.70	5.64	5.43
Dec.	4.70	4.67	4.89	4.75	4.71	5.02	5.68	5.44	5.99	6.02	5.70	5.65	5.42
						Standard Deviation - Gross Yield[a]							
Jan.				0.218	0.187	0.208	0.322	0.240	0.307	0.315	0.136	0.169	0.199
Feb.				0.207	0.210	0.267	0.375	0.231	0.288	0.195	0.184	0.166	0.224
March				0.184	0.210	0.204	0.324	0.245	0.279	0.218	0.181	0.172	0.195
April				0.201	0.213	0.218	0.273	0.203	0.236	0.376	0.208	0.171	0.214
May				0.237	0.290	0.218	0.259	0.210	0.304	0.156	0.203	0.230	0.186
June				0.189	0.236	0.225	0.230	0.251	0.182	0.171	0.200	0.218	0.199
July				0.222	0.247	0.217	0.244	0.246	0.220	0.141	0.193	0.201	0.150
Aug.				0.191	0.192	0.237	0.245	0.265	0.242	0.150	0.195	0.195	0.165
Sept.				0.209	0.312	0.279	0.245	0.276	0.275	0.191	0.209	0.201	0.157
Oct.			0.233	0.212	0.201	0.293	0.243	0.242	0.241	0.197	0.200	0.205	0.185
Nov.			0.239	0.307	0.218	0.348	0.251	0.300	0.270	0.171	0.192	0.185	0.211
Dec.			0.234	0.181	0.239	0.366	0.242	0.271	0.168	0.212	0.178	0.184	0.180

(continued)

TABLE C-3 (continued)

Contract Rate

	1951	1952	1953	1954	1955	1956	1957	1958	1959	1960	1961	1962	1963
Jan.	4.57	4.80	4.83	5.05	4.90	4.89	5.21	5.73	5.48	6.01	6.05	5.73	5.65
Feb.	4.54	4.77	4.84	5.05	4.86	4.85	5.30	5.69	5.52	6.06	5.99	5.75	5.59
March	4.55	4.76	4.83	4.99	4.92	4.90	5.32	5.61	5.60	6.06	5.99	5.81	5.53
April	4.53	4.77	4.82	5.00	4.89	4.92	5.40	5.58	5.61	6.11	5.89	5.79	5.52
May	4.59	4.81	4.84	4.96	4.85	4.88	5.46	5.53	5.65	6.09	5.87	5.74	5.51
June	4.62	4.77	4.88	4.93	4.77	4.89	5.46	5.45	5.69	6.12	5.83	5.71	5.51
July	4.68	4.81	4.96	4.92	4.81	4.94	5.48	5.39	5.72	6.11	5.79	5.70	5.50
Aug.	4.75	4.78	5.03	4.92	4.84	4.99	5.50	5.36	5.79	6.08	5.78	5.66	5.48
Sept.	4.71	4.80	5.09	4.95	4.78	5.01	5.54	5.34	5.79	6.09	5.81	5.67	5.50
Oct.	4.79	4.83	5.05	4.89	4.86	5.05	5.61	5.33	5.86	6.09	5.74	5.69	5.47
Nov.	4.80	4.83	5.03	4.88	4.88	5.16	5.62	5.40	5.98	6.09	5.73	5.67	5.48
Dec.	4.84	4.81	5.07	4.90	4.86	5.11	5.75	5.51	6.01	6.05	5.73	5.68	5.45

Net Discount

	1951	1952	1953	1954	1955	1956	1957	1958	1959	1960	1961	1962	1963
Jan.				-0.99	-0.93	-0.92	-0.76	-0.58	-0.46	-0.17	-0.23	-0.16	-0.21
Feb.				-0.99	-0.85	-0.87	-0.53	-0.45	-0.49	-0.14	-0.20	-0.23	-0.21
March				-0.94	-0.90	-0.96	-0.41	-0.42	-0.39	-0.12	-0.19	-0.21	-0.20
April				-1.00	-0.94	-0.80	-0.32	-0.36	-0.40	-0.23	-0.22	-0.20	-0.19
May				-0.95	-0.73	-0.83	-0.38	-0.38	-0.40	-0.22	-0.19	-0.18	-0.22
June				-0.92	-0.67	-0.82	-0.34	-0.34	-0.30	-0.14	-0.17	-0.26	-0.22
July				-0.96	-0.82	-0.83	-0.36	-0.35	-0.20	-0.13	-0.14	-0.15	-0.15
Aug.				-0.91	-0.79	-0.81	-0.40	-0.38	-0.14	-0.12	-0.17	-0.14	-0.24
Sept.				-0.91	-0.85	-0.86	-0.39	-0.37	-0.16	-0.18	-0.17	-0.17	-0.18
Oct.			-1.04	-0.88	-0.83	-0.75	-0.44	-0.36	-0.17	-0.21	-0.19	-0.15	-0.20
Nov.			-0.88	-0.88	-0.85	-0.80	-0.43	-0.37	-0.14	-0.23	-0.18	-0.20	-0.35
Dec.			-1.03	-0.95	-0.89	-0.59	-0.38	-0.46	-0.12	-0.24	-0.23	-0.21	-0.15

(continued)

TABLE C-3 (continued)

Loan-Value Ratio

	1951	1952	1953	1954	1955	1956	1957	1958	1959	1960	1961	1962	1963
Jan.	61.4	60.8	62.6	62.1	62.2	60.9	61.1	62.0	61.4	68.7	68.6	66.6	70.0
Feb.	61.2	60.3	62.1	62.2	61.5	61.1	60.9	62.9	61.0	69.2	70.6	67.6	69.1
March	61.4	60.6	62.3	61.9	61.3	62.0	60.4	62.0	62.3	69.8	69.0	68.1	68.6
April	61.7	60.8	62.0	62.7	61.3	62.2	61.5	61.4	61.0	70.0	68.9	70.3	68.5
May	61.5	61.1	61.5	63.2	62.2	59.8	62.1	61.5	63.2	69.4	68.6	69.2	68.1
June	60.2	60.5	61.8	62.7	61.4	60.7	62.0	62.5	66.8	69.5	68.3	68.6	69.6
July	60.3	61.7	61.4	62.5	61.3	59.8	61.8	61.8	67.9	69.9	68.3	68.4	69.3
Aug.	59.4	60.9	63.0	62.7	61.1	61.6	60.6	60.7	69.0	69.7	68.6	67.8	68.8
Sept.	59.2	61.8	62.4	62.1	61.6	61.3	61.4	61.9	68.6	70.4	69.2	68.7	69.2
Oct.	60.0	62.1	62.4	61.3	61.9	60.9	60.4	61.6	68.4	69.7	69.1	69.3	68.4
Nov.	60.5	61.6	62.5	61.4	61.3	61.1	61.5	61.1	69.3	69.6	69.7	68.6	69.7
Dec.	62.8	61.7	61.9	62.2	60.5	60.5	62.0	62.9	69.5	70.3	68.2	68.4	66.4

Maturity (months)

	1951	1952	1953	1954	1955	1956	1957	1958	1959	1960	1961	1962	1963
Jan.	208.5	220.6	219.9	223.6	221.8	228.9	230.6	242.8	266.7	278.2	283.5	275.9	289.0
Feb.	202.7	217.6	220.6	225.9	226.8	231.2	238.1	251.2	262.5	282.8	281.3	288.2	283.8
March	208.6	220.0	218.8	225.5	218.5	234.0	243.9	245.5	265.6	282.2	279.8	282.3	282.1
April	206.4	223.0	219.4	223.1	225.4	227.2	237.9	250.5	265.7	281.2	282.9	288.4	284.0
May	200.8	214.3	217.9	230.3	220.9	226.3	232.8	249.8	271.1	286.0	284.9	284.9	282.8
June	209.7	218.3	223.3	226.1	230.5	227.9	235.0	260.8	274.4	279.6	284.4	285.1	292.4
July	217.5	213.8	215.7	226.8	233.7	228.1	241.7	241.7	278.5	280.5	279.9	282.5	288.9
Aug.	210.6	218.2	222.5	228.4	232.9	232.7	237.9	246.3	276.9	282.2	278.6	279.6	293.0
Sept.	209.8	217.3	226.0	224.4	228.6	228.8	234.0	258.5	268.3	282.5	277.5	286.8	287.4
Oct.	210.5	214.9	225.7	226.5	230.3	234.1	241.0	257.6	278.0	281.1	283.7	281.9	294.2
Nov.	215.3	213.8	217.4	220.2	231.1	232.3	241.4	254.5	280.4	285.6	280.3	284.1	293.4
Dec.	221.1	219.6	222.6	222.8	231.4	235.5	247.6	271.4	281.7	280.7	282.7	280.7	286.6

(continued)

TABLE C-3 (continued)

	1951	1952	1953	1954	1955	1956	1957	1958	1959	1960	1961	1962	1963
						Number of Loans							
Jan.	213	251	252	239	224	283	241	241	203	242	229	250	205
Feb.	128	226	191	205	196	295	189	260	216	259	247	252	249
March	156	285	225	316	190	255	190	250	286	243	275	253	245
April	218	331	258	260	215	299	261	247	271	243	263	242	244
May	272	312	252	290	262	261	240	246	253	239	253	251	243
June	243	305	268	319	224	287	235	239	276	259	252	252	204
July	235	239	266	252	280	263	244	252	261	246	253	254	234
Aug.	253	290	247	281	296	246	238	229	243	248	248	246	239
Sept.	246	300	264	266	277	249	254	254	285	250	261	258	261
Oct.	256	284	267	237	286	236	251	253	277	247	253	253	240
Nov.	231	259	295	234	324	224	260	203	251	243	258	248	211
Dec.	177	236	264	202	263	247	237	238	277	220	237	252	236
						Mean Loan Size							
Jan.	9,813	10,094	10,311	11,407	11,884	13,555	12,502	13,746	15,547	16,145	15,647	17,394	18,079
Feb.	10,105	10,417	10,493	12,107	12,041	12,448	14,195	14,791	14,970	16,641	17,250	17,538	17,828
March	10,223	10,601	11,457	12,514	11,345	12,365	13,944	14,645	15,983	16,922	17,283	17,756	17,684
April	9,952	10,506	11,406	11,625	12,364	12,306	14,203	14,829	15,665	16,660	16,883	17,737	17,372
May	9,931	10,200	11,238	12,016	11,232	12,950	13,053	14,274	14,965	16,222	17,524	17,112	17,653
June	10,328	10,196	11,101	11,711	12,255	13,021	13,881	15,066	16,404	15,728	16,270	17,193	17,801
July	10,577	10,206	10,979	11,123	12,154	12,629	13,870	14,465	16,499	16,766	17,180	17,471	17,460
Aug.	10,349	10,783	10,944	12,256	12,582	13,225	13,466	15,210	16,402	15,753	17,055	17,260	17,241
Sept.	9,981	10,875	10,767	11,385	12,582	12,865	13,407	14,933	16,316	16,499	16,757	17,556	17,537
Oct.	10,518	10,858	10,731	12,263	12,332	13,093	14,096	14,498	15,840	16,152	17,883	17,668	17,722
Nov.	10,743	11,121	11,435	11,553	12,699	12,729	14,571	14,650	15,863	16,083	17,423	17,678	18,370
Dec.	10,211	10,926	11,433	11,610	11,894	13,355	14,231	15,470	16,562	17,306	16,931	18,166	17,348

(continued)

TABLE C-3 (continued)

Net Yield

	1951	1952	1953	1954	1955	1956	1957	1958	1959	1960	1961	1962	1963
Jan.	3.89	4.18	4.17	4.38	4.25	4.24	4.58	5.13	4.92	5.60	5.66	5.34	5.27
Feb.	3.85	4.15	4.19	4.38	4.22	4.21	4.72	5.11	4.99	5.63	5.59	5.35	5.19
March	3.86	4.14	4.19	4.33	4.27	4.25	4.72	5.04	5.06	5.65	5.59	5.42	5.13
April	3.85	4.17	4.17	4.33	4.23	4.29	4.85	5.02	5.05	5.67	5.49	5.39	5.11
May	3.92	4.17	4.20	4.31	4.23	4.24	4.90	4.96	5.09	5.72	5.48	5.34	5.11
June	3.98	4.16	4.23	4.28	4.16	4.26	4.90	4.89	5.15	5.70	5.43	5.32	5.11
July	4.05	4.18	4.29	4.27	4.17	4.31	4.92	4.83	5.25	5.72	5.39	5.30	5.08
Aug.	4.14	4.14	4.38	4.27	4.21	4.36	4.93	4.80	5.35	5.73	5.38	5.27	5.08
Sept.	4.11	4.16	4.43	4.30	4.14	4.36	4.98	4.78	5.37	5.70	5.42	5.27	5.08
Oct.	4.17	4.19	4.38	4.25	4.23	4.43	5.03	4.78	5.45	5.69	5.34	5.29	5.07
Nov.	4.20	4.20	4.38	4.24	4.24	4.53	5.05	4.85	5.55	5.70	5.34	5.29	5.09
Dec.	4.20	4.17	4.39	4.25	4.21	4.52	5.18	4.95	5.58	5.66	5.34	5.29	5.03

Standard Deviation - Net Yield

	1951	1952	1953	1954	1955	1956	1957	1958	1959	1960	1961	1962	1963
Jan.				0.218	0.187	0.208	0.322	0.240	0.311	0.304	0.158	0.170	0.207
Feb.				0.207	0.210	0.266	0.375	0.231	0.297	0.194	0.186	0.167	0.237
March				0.184	0.210	0.209	0.324	0.245	0.279	0.205	0.187	0.185	0.198
April				0.201	0.213	0.217	0.273	0.207	0.240	0.384	0.215	0.190	0.221
May				0.234	0.290	0.217	0.258	0.210	0.304	0.167	0.199	0.230	0.190
June				0.189	0.234	0.225	0.230	0.253	0.177	0.172	0.211	0.216	0.203
July				0.222	0.247	0.208	0.240	0.246	0.226	0.137	0.206	0.197	0.153
Aug.				0.191	0.192	0.237	0.245	0.265	0.240	0.149	0.212	0.190	0.161
Sept.				0.209	0.312	0.279	0.245	0.276	0.287	0.190	0.231	0.198	0.161
Oct.			0.233	0.212	0.201	0.296	0.243	0.244	0.256	0.212	0.206	0.202	0.180
Nov.			0.239	0.307	0.218	0.353	0.251	0.301	0.268	0.193	0.195	0.185	0.203
Dec.			0.234	0.182	0.239	0.366	0.241	0.272	0.161	0.236	0.181	0.182	0.173

(continued)

TABLE C-3 (continued)

	1951	1952	1953	1954	1955	1956	1957	1958	1959	1960	1961	1962	1963
Gross Yield													
I	4.37	4.65	4.68	4.86	4.74	4.73	5.17	5.59	5.48	6.02	5.97	5.73	5.56
II	4.41	4.65	4.69	4.80	4.71	4.76	5.38	5.46	5.59	6.05	5.83	5.72	5.48
III	4.60	4.66	4.87	4.78	4.67	4.84	5.45	5.30	5.74	6.08	5.77	5.65	5.46
IV	4.69	4.68	4.88	4.74	4.73	4.98	5.58	5.35	5.93	6.04	5.70	5.65	5.43
Standard Deviation - Gross Yield													
I			0.228	0.204	0.205	0.232	0.348	0.241	0.294	0.248	0.173	0.172	0.214
II			0.232	0.216	0.253	0.223	0.260	0.227	0.243	0.259	0.206	0.211	0.200
III			0.288	0.208	0.263	0.248	0.247	0.263	0.249	0.162	0.200	0.200	0.158
IV		0.242	0.236	0.236	0.218	0.342	0.253	0.272	0.235	0.193	0.191	0.192	0.193
Contract Rate													
I	4.55	4.78	4.83	5.02	4.89	4.88	5.27	5.67	5.55	6.04	6.01	5.76	5.59
II	4.58	4.79	4.84	4.96	4.84	4.90	5.44	5.52	5.65	6.08	5.86	5.75	5.51
III	4.72	4.80	5.03	4.93	4.80	4.98	5.52	5.36	5.77	6.10	5.79	5.68	5.49
IV	4.81	4.83	5.05	4.89	4.87	5.10	5.66	5.42	5.95	6.08	5.74	5.68	5.47
Net Discount													
I	-0.09	-0.05	-0.11	-0.96	-0.89	-0.91	-0.57	-0.48	-0.44	-0.14	-0.21	-0.20	-0.21
II	-0.12	-0.11	-0.12	-0.96	-0.79	-0.82	-0.36	-0.37	-0.36	-0.20	-0.19	-0.22	-0.21
III	-0.10	-0.12	-0.05	-0.93	-0.82	-0.83	-0.40	-0.37	-0.17	-0.14	-0.16	-0.16	-0.19
IV	-0.04	-0.11	-0.98	-0.90	-0.86	-0.72	-0.44	-0.41	-0.14	-0.23	-0.20	-0.19	-0.23

(continued)

TABLE C-3 (continued)

	1951	1952	1953	1954	1955	1956	1957	1958	1959	1960	1961	1962	1963
Loan-Value Ratio													
I	61.3	60.6	62.3	62.1	61.6	61.3	60.4	62.3	61.6	69.3	69.4	67.5	69.2
II	61.1	60.8	61.8	62.9	61.7	60.9	61.8	61.9	63.8	69.6	68.6	69.4	68.6
III	59.6	61.5	62.3	62.4	61.4	61.3	61.4	61.6	68.6	70.0	68.7	68.3	69.1
IV	61.0	61.8	62.3	61.6	61.3	60.8	61.5	62.1	69.1	69.8	69.0	68.7	68.1
Maturity (months)													
I	206.6	219.5	219.6	225.1	222.8	231.5	235.9	246.5	264.8	281.1	281.5	282.3	284.7
II	205.7	218.4	220.3	226.9	225.6	227.4	235.9	253.8	270.5	282.1	284.0	286.5	286.1
III	213.3	216.3	221.8	226.8	232.0	230.8	238.4	249.2	274.7	281.8	278.8	283.2	289.8
IV	215.0	216.0	221.7	223.5	231.3	233.6	244.1	262.2	280.0	282.5	282.2	282.2	291.4
Number of Loans													
I	497	762	668	760	610	833	620	751	705	744	751	755	699
II	733	948	778	869	701	847	736	732	800	741	768	745	691
III	734	829	777	799	853	758	736	735	789	744	762	758	734
IV	664	779	826	673	873	707	748	694	805	710	748	753	687
Mean Loan Size													
I	10,049	10,385	10,724	12,019	11,752	12,811	13,545	14,417	15,504	16,582	16,830	17,567	17,830
II	10,057	10,294	11,243	11,779	11,948	12,774	13,710	14,728	15,811	16,201	16,921	17,403	17,592
III	10,240	10,631	10,885	11,591	12,441	12,985	13,560	14,850	16,365	16,335	17,051	17,457	17,436
IV	10,503	10,958	11,204	11,821	12,335	13,062	14,359	14,880	16,103	16,467	17,462	17,830	17,774

(continued)

TABLE C-3 (continued)

Net Yield

	1951	1952	1953	1954	1955	1956	1957	1958	1959	1960	1961	1962	1963
I	3.87	4.15	4.18	4.36	4.24	4.23	4.67	5.09	5.00	5.63	5.61	5.37	5.19
II	3.91	4.16	4.20	4.30	4.21	4.26	4.88	4.96	5.10	5.70	5.47	5.36	5.11
III	4.10	4.16	4.37	4.28	4.17	4.34	4.95	4.80	5.32	5.72	5.39	5.28	5.08
IV	4.19	4.19	4.38	4.24	4.23	4.49	5.08	4.86	5.53	5.68	5.34	5.29	5.06

Standard Deviation - Net Yield

	1951	1952	1953	1954	1955	1956	1957	1958	1959	1960	1961	1962	1963
I			0.228	0.204	0.205	0.233	0.348	0.241	0.298	0.239	0.181	0.177	0.221
II			0.233	0.215	0.252	0.222	0.260	0.228	0.243	0.265	0.211	0.215	0.205
III			0.288	0.208	0.263	0.245	0.245	0.263	0.258	0.160	0.218	0.196	0.159
IV		0.244	0.236	0.237	0.218	0.344	0.253	0.273	0.238	0.214	0.196	0.192	0.188

[a]Data for one company during the period January 1951-September 1953 were partly estimated from aggregate data covering that company. The standard deviation was thus not available for that period.

TABLE C-4

Characteristics of FHA Mortgage Loans on Residential (1-4 Family)
Properties by Four Life Insurance Companies, 1951-63, Correspondent Loans,
United States

Gross Yield

	1951	1952	1953	1954	1955	1956	1957	1958	1959	1960	1961	1962	1963
Jan.	4.10	4.20	4.25	4.70	4.58	4.69	5.15	5.54	5.58	6.18	6.14	5.73	5.62
Feb.	4.10	4.24	4.25	4.70	4.58	4.61	5.26	5.56	5.67	6.22[a]	6.14	5.75	5.59
March	4.13	4.24	4.26	4.71	4.60	4.70	5.31	5.57	5.68	6.22[a]	6.00	5.75	5.56
April	4.12	4.23	4.26	4.70	4.61	4.71	5.36	5.57	5.67	6.21[a]	5.96	5.74	5.53
May	4.13	4.25	4.30	4.55	4.54	4.71	5.36	5.52	5.70	6.23[a]	5.90	5.76	5.47
June	4.15	4.25	4.50	4.62	4.62	4.77	5.34	5.49	5.72	6.22	5.85	5.74	5.48
July	4.23	4.26	4.51	4.62	4.62	4.77	5.36	5.48	5.76	6.22	5.78	5.72	5.48
Aug.	4.19	4.25	4.55	4.61	4.65	4.74	5.38	5.44	5.81	6.22	5.76	5.67	5.47
Sept.	4.18	4.27	4.63	4.63	4.61	4.76	5.52	5.44	5.84[a]	6.22	5.79	5.67	5.47
Oct.	4.19	4.26	4.64	4.59	4.64	4.83	5.53	5.47	5.92[a]	6.23[a]	5.75	5.66	5.46
Nov.	4.21	4.25	4.66	4.61	4.66	4.84	5.54	5.54	6.18[a]	6.22	5.75	5.65	5.46
Dec.	4.19	4.25	4.71	4.56	4.69	4.90	5.54	5.58	6.19	6.18	5.74	5.65	5.46

Standard Deviation - Gross Yield

	1951	1952	1953	1954	1955	1956	1957	1958	1959	1960	1961	1962	1963
Jan.	0.099	0.093	0.042	0.103	0.108	0.135	0.282	0.081	0.174	0.198	0.143	0.120	0.161
Feb.	0.072	0.053	0.030	0.113	0.116	0.275	0.153	0.091	0.183	0.083	0.124	0.118	0.136
March	0.093	0.056	0.038	0.159	0.137	0.170	0.140	0.080	0.179	0.099	0.163	0.115	0.121
April	0.094	0.056	0.051	0.104	0.111	0.134	0.131	0.102	0.175	0.251	0.139	0.125	0.119
May	0.113	0.028	0.096	0.289	0.224	0.139	0.105	0.097	0.168	0.109	0.138	0.118	0.140
June	0.120	0.028	0.115	0.153	0.134	0.132	0.109	0.094	0.170	0.082	0.135	0.102	0.118
July	0.090	0.065	0.071	0.161	0.111	0.133	0.115	0.092	0.150	0.083	0.239	0.121	0.105
Aug.	0.110	0.026	0.119	0.139	0.128	0.128	0.147	0.102	0.147	0.112	0.117	0.123	0.106
Sept.	0.098	0.138	0.142	0.161	0.220	0.208	0.090	0.093	0.230	0.074	0.139	0.116	0.105
Oct.	0.102	0.081	0.140	0.100	0.135	0.128	0.083	0.095	0.272	0.143	0.120	0.110	0.104
Nov.	0.113	0.016	0.146	0.110	0.181	0.140	0.084	0.120	0.314	0.110	0.130	0.110	0.140
Dec.	0.108	0.023	0.138	0.112	0.146	0.151	0.077	0.144	0.133	0.216	0.131	0.118	0.103

(continued)

TABLE C-4 (continued)

Contract Rate

	1951	1952	1953	1954	1955	1956	1957	1958	1959	1960	1961	1962	1963
Jan.	4.27	4.25	4.25	4.50	4.50	4.50	4.84	5.25	5.25	5.72	5.74	5.26	5.24
Feb.	4.27	4.25	4.25	4.50	4.50	4.39	4.97	5.25	5.25	5.74	5.74	5.26	5.25
March	4.26	4.25	4.25	4.49	4.49	4.48	4.97	5.25	5.25	5.75	5.65	5.26	5.25
April	4.26	4.25	4.25	4.50	4.50	4.50	4.99	5.25	5.24	5.73	5.60	5.25	5.25
May	4.25	4.25	4.29	4.37	4.42	4.49	5.00	5.25	5.25	5.75	5.58	5.25	5.25
June	4.25	4.26	4.46	4.49	4.49	4.50	5.00	5.25	5.25	5.75	5.52	5.25	5.25
July	4.26	4.25	4.49	4.49	4.50	4.50	5.01	5.25	5.25	5.75	5.38	5.26	5.25
Aug.	4.25	4.25	4.49	4.49	4.50	4.50	5.02	5.25	5.25	5.74	5.37	5.25	5.25
Sept.	4.28	4.25	4.49	4.50	4.44	4.45	5.22	5.25	5.25	5.75	5.34	5.25	5.25
Oct.	4.25	4.25	4.49	4.50	4.49	4.50	5.25	5.25	5.37	5.74	5.29	5.25	5.25
Nov.	4.25	4.25	4.49	4.50	4.48	4.50	5.25	5.25	5.67	5.75	5.29	5.26	5.25
Dec.	4.25	4.25	4.49	4.49	4.49	4.54	5.24	5.25	5.74	5.72	5.29	5.25	5.25

Net Discount

	1951	1952	1953	1954	1955	1956	1957	1958	1959	1960	1961	1962	1963
Jan.	-1.09	-0.34	0.02	1.33	0.60	1.25	2.02	1.89	2.19	3.01[a]	2.59	3.09	2.49
Feb.	-1.07	-0.09	0.03	1.35	0.52	1.42	1.84	2.02	2.77	3.10	2.58	3.20	2.21
March	-0.82	-0.08	0.06	1.50	0.70	1.47	2.23	2.10	2.80	3.10[a]	2.29	3.29	2.09
April	-0.86	-0.07	0.05	1.33	0.79	1.42	2.40	2.11	2.85	3.19[a]	2.36	3.26	1.88
May	-0.80	-0.02	0.05	1.21	0.80	1.46	2.41	1.81	3.01	3.20[a]	2.07	3.36	1.49
June	-0.70	-0.02	0.23	0.88	0.83	1.85	2.26	1.55	3.09	3.06	2.21	3.22	1.50
July	-0.20	-0.04	0.12	0.87	0.79	1.84	2.31	1.50	3.36	3.09	2.65	3.05	1.51
Aug.	-0.36	-0.03	0.39	0.78	0.99	1.62	2.33	1.26	3.68	3.10	2.61	2.80	1.49
Sept.	-0.68	0.09	0.89	0.86	1.14	2.04	1.97	1.24	3.92[a]	3.08	3.03	2.80	1.49
Oct.	-0.41	0.05	0.97	0.60	0.97	2.19	1.85	1.46	3.64[a]	3.18[a]	3.04	2.69	1.37
Nov.	-0.25	0.01	1.09	0.76	1.21	2.26	1.87	1.90	3.35[a]	3.03	3.07	2.61	1.37
Dec.	-0.36	0.01	1.44	0.43	1.33	2.41	1.91	2.15	2.97	3.03	3.00	2.61	1.37

(continued)

TABLE C-4 (continued)

Loan-Value Ratio

	1951	1952	1953	1954	1955	1956	1957	1958	1959	1960	1961	1962	1963
Jan.	85.6	81.1	82.4	82.0	86.2	85.1	83.6	89.7	91.9	92.2	92.5	94.1	93.6
Feb.	83.6	81.5	82.2	81.1	86.3	84.8	83.4	90.0	92.3	91.7	92.5	93.9	94.0
March	83.4	81.9	83.3	81.9	86.6	84.3	83.5	90.5	92.1	92.0	93.2	93.9	94.0
April	83.7	81.1	83.1	81.9	86.3	83.8	83.3	90.0	92.0	91.9	92.6	93.3	94.2
May	81.8	81.4	82.4	83.5	87.1	83.7	84.6	91.1	92.7	91.4	93.7	93.9	93.6
June	82.5	81.3	83.6	81.8	86.5	85.0	85.0	91.3	92.7	92.3	92.2	93.9	93.0
July	81.1	80.5	83.2	81.5	86.8	84.8	85.2	91.0	92.9	93.3	93.2	93.7	92.7
Aug.	80.5	81.6	82.4	82.1	86.4	84.8	85.7	92.1	92.9	93.4	92.3	93.3	92.8
Sept.	81.8	81.9	81.8	86.2	86.4	84.4	88.3	91.6	92.2	93.4	93.8	93.4	93.5
Oct.	81.6	82.0	83.0	86.7	86.4	84.0	88.2	91.4	92.8	92.7	92.8	93.9	93.1
Nov.	81.0	83.1	82.4	86.3	85.6	84.1	88.9	91.5	92.1	93.1	93.6	92.8	93.7
Dec.	81.7	80.3	81.5	85.8	85.9	83.0	88.5	91.7	91.7	93.0	93.6	93.4	93.8

Maturity (months)

	1951	1952	1953	1954	1955	1956	1957	1958	1959	1960	1961	1962	1963
Jan.	266.2	247.8	256.2	264.6	310.9	292.5	301.7	308.6	329.0	341.2	343.0	350.0	342.1
Feb.	261.3	249.3	258.4	264.0	312.9	293.0	294.5	308.9	331.0	340.0	344.3	346.4	349.4
March	256.7	252.0	254.7	268.3	313.9	301.4	297.6	312.8	331.4	342.8	344.2	346.3	350.9
April	252.1	253.2	258.7	272.1	311.1	297.5	309.5	315.2	334.1	351.4	346.0	351.2	348.1
May	250.6	245.9	251.4	275.2	312.1	298.9	306.3	323.3	333.5	345.9	345.3	345.1	351.8
June	253.5	248.7	254.0	277.6	314.8	301.8	304.8	327.4	331.1	345.7	346.0	346.7	350.4
July	247.8	248.3	254.7	287.5	307.7	304.0	306.7	330.0	342.0	344.6	342.4	343.9	345.5
Aug.	248.2	246.3	256.1	283.7	308.6	315.7	309.0	334.3	337.1	336.4	345.9	346.5	348.6
Sept.	251.4	251.1	257.5	302.7	305.8	200.9	303.3	330.3	339.7	342.1	344.0	343.2	351.2
Oct.	249.1	253.5	264.7	308.5	301.4	298.6	303.9	330.2	338.8	346.7	346.3	348.7	352.1
Nov.	252.4	253.6	257.2	306.8	302.8	303.6	305.8	330.7	338.7	342.3	346.3	340.8	351.5
Dec.	249.5	248.8	258.5	303.2	303.2	302.8	304.4	325.3	342.6	343.8	345.9	345.1	349.8

(continued)

TABLE C-4 (continued)

	1951	1952	1953	1954	1955	1956	1957	1958	1959	1960	1961	1962	1963
						Number of Loans							
Jan.	255	332	329	291	343	304	269	296	323	253	302	253	311
Feb.	191	319	339	255	307	320	140	371	354	236	355	254	272
March	158	348	336	332	364	320	271	357	372	286	383	251	339
April	309	323	359	262	391	294	274	375	384	247	436	324	309
May	312	331	291	297	425	304	314	375	378	256	387	374	271
June	326	333	257	338	301	248	280	369	365	282	374	370	240
July	274	369	251	294	353	249	293	366	338	241	290	307	332
Aug.	300	351	258	308	344	273	259	336	278	282	287	361	294
Sept.	323	355	332	307	382	255	278	368	360	207	288	368	328
Oct.	342	366	304	298	388	303	268	299	383	340	246	375	423
Nov.	354	316	293	326	359	253	268	276	363	259	269	247	280
Dec.	283	335	285	338	369	249	242	277	277	282	258	248	297
						Mean Loan Size							
Jan.	7,765	8,303	8,846	9,614	10,728	11,098	11,777	12,909	13,366	14,215	14,004	14,476	13,972
Feb.	8,035	8,467	8,987	9,649	11,085	11,327	12,192	13,020	13,452	14,779	14,650	15,200	14,119
March	8,027	8,418	8,851	9,605	10,822	11,386	12,109	12,785	13,397	14,605	14,523	15,004	14,747
April	8,215	8,514	8,672	9,552	10,921	11,302	12,246	12,910	13,253	15,047	14,351	15,330	14,543
May	8,275	8,456	9,037	9,393	10,814	11,362	12,129	13,273	13,066	14,940	14,056	14,507	14,251
June	8,471	8,699	8,885	9,633	10,637	11,651	12,481	13,243	13,437	14,559	14,237	14,648	14,787
July	8,219	8,424	9,042	9,799	10,904	11,898	12,627	13,461	13,576	14,150	14,363	14,836	14,843
Aug.	8,376	8,723	9,406	9,756	11,002	11,625	12,281	13,747	13,725	14,225	14,278	14,242	14,143
Sept.	8,428	8,639	9,415	9,990	10,967	11,469	13,075	13,326	13,505	14,483	14,064	14,626	14,430
Oct.	8,281	8,712	9,232	10,389	11,309	11,637	13,391	13,467	13,643	14,167	14,529	14,925	14,556
Nov.	8,483	8,484	9,456	10,994	11,286	12,093	13,002	13,410	13,968	14,069	14,527	14,434	14,750
Dec.	8,706	8,797	9,546	10,526	11,247	11,883	12,756	13,398	14,387	14,632	14,735	14,517	14,649

(continued)

TABLE C-4 (continued)

Net Yield

	1951	1952	1953	1954	1955	1956	1957	1958	1959	1960	1961	1962	1963
Jan.	3.60	3.70	3.76	4.20	4.08	4.19	4.65	5.04	5.09	5.81	5.77	5.34	5.22
Feb.	3.60	3.74	3.75	4.21	4.08	4.11	4.76	5.06	5.20	5.84	5.75	5.37	5.18
March	3.63	3.74	3.76	4.21	4.10	4.20	4.81	5.07	5.22	5.85a	5.59	5.37	5.16
April	3.62	3.73	3.76	4.20	4.13	4.21	4.86	5.07	5.21	5.84a	5.55	5.36	5.13
May	3.63	3.75	3.80	4.05	4.04	4.21	4.86	5.02	5.26	5.86a	5.48	5.37	5.08
June	3.65	3.75	4.03	4.12	4.12	4.27	4.84	4.99	5.27	5.84	5.45	5.35	5.09
July	3.72	3.76	4.02	4.13	4.12	4.27	4.86	4.98	5.33	5.84	5.38	5.33	5.08
Aug.	3.70	3.75	4.07	4.11	4.15	4.24	4.88	4.94	5.41	5.83	5.38	5.29	5.08
Sept.	3.68	3.77	4.15	4.13	4.12	4.26	5.02	4.94	5.44a	5.85	5.40	5.29	5.08
Oct.	3.69	3.76	4.14	4.09	4.14	4.33	5.03	4.97	5.53a	5.84a	5.35	5.27	5.06
Nov.	3.71	3.75	4.17	4.11	4.16	4.34	5.04	5.04	5.77a	5.84	5.36	5.28	5.06
Dec.	3.69	3.75	4.22	4.06	4.19	4.40	5.04	5.08	5.81	5.79	5.35	5.27	5.06

Standard Deviation - Net Yield

	1951	1952	1953	1954	1955	1956	1957	1958	1959	1960	1961	1962	1963
Jan.	0.099	0.094	0.067	0.103	0.108	0.136	0.280	0.083	0.186	0.199	0.153	0.112	0.172
Feb.	0.072	0.053	0.030	0.112	0.118	0.275	0.146	0.092	0.204	0.090	0.148	0.113	0.152
March	0.100	0.056	0.045	0.159	0.137	0.171	0.140	0.100	0.178	0.103	0.173	0.112	0.139
April	0.095	0.056	0.065	0.116	0.125	0.134	0.131	0.101	0.181	0.257	0.165	0.120	0.127
May	0.113	0.029	0.108	0.290	0.225	0.139	0.105	0.097	0.186	0.114	0.166	0.119	0.150
June	0.112	0.028	0.152	0.153	0.134	0.132	0.109	0.094	0.199	0.085	0.157	0.101	0.114
July	0.084	0.065	0.097	0.160	0.112	0.134	0.115	0.091	0.182	0.082	0.245	0.115	0.094
Aug.	0.116	0.026	0.135	0.139	0.127	0.128	0.147	0.113	0.149	0.124	0.126	0.120	0.103
Sept.	0.098	0.138	0.142	0.161	0.224	0.208	0.090	0.093	0.247	0.069	0.138	0.116	0.094
Oct.	0.105	0.081	0.140	0.102	0.135	0.128	0.084	0.095	0.294	0.170	0.107	0.107	0.096
Nov.	0.113	0.016	0.146	0.110	0.181	0.138	0.085	0.130	0.348	0.115	0.124	0.110	0.134
Dec.	0.108	0.023	0.139	0.112	0.146	0.152	0.077	0.151	0.140	0.225	0.124	0.116	0.086

(continued)

TABLE C-4 (continued)

	1951	1952	1953	1954	1955	1956	1957	1958	1959	1960	1961	1962	1963
						Loan-Value Ratio							
I	84.2	81.6	82.6	81.6	86.4	84.7	83.6	90.1	92.1	92.0	92.8	94.0	93.9
II	82.6	81.3	83.1	82.4	86.7	84.2	84.3	90.8	92.4	91.8	92.8	93.7	93.6
III	81.2	81.3	82.3	83.2	86.5	84.7	86.4	91.6	92.7	93.3	93.1	93.4	93.1
IV	81.5	81.8	82.3	86.3	85.9	83.6	88.5	91.5	92.2	93.0	93.3	93.4	93.5
						Maturity (months)							
I	261.7	249.6	256.0	266.0	312.6	295.4	301.0	310.0	330.5	341.4	343.6	347.5	348.0
II	252.3	249.6	254.0	275.4	312.6	299.3	307.0	321.9	332.8	347.7	345.5	347.7	350.0
III	249.1	248.6	255.8	291.3	307.5	307.0	306.2	331.2	340.0	341.1	344.3	344.5	348.7
IV	250.4	252.1	260.5	305.9	302.2	302.0	304.6	328.6	340.0	344.5	346.2	345.0	351.4
						Number of Loans							
I	604	999	1,004	878	1,014	944	680	1,024	1,049	775	1,040	758	922
II	947	987	907	897	1,117	846	868	1,119	1,127	785	1,197	1,068	820
III	897	1,075	841	909	1,079	777	830	1,070	976	730	865	1,036	954
IV	979	1,017	882	962	1,116	805	778	852	1,023	881	773	870	1,000
						Mean Loan Size							
I	7,951	8,413	8,894	9,622	10,873	11,280	12,008	12,895	13,407	14,486	14,376	14,891	14,326
II	8,316	8,559	8,885	9,560	10,807	11,425	12,284	13,142	13,253	14,847	14,230	14,827	14,580
III	8,343	8,601	9,301	9,845	10,959	11,667	12,674	13,516	13,633	14,291	14,232	14,576	14,458
IV	8,473	8,674	9,430	10,618	11,311	11,859	13,050	13,424	13,979	14,273	14,583	14,635	14,668

(continued)

TABLE C-4 (continued)

Gross Yield

	1951	1952	1953	1954	1955	1956	1957	1958	1959	1960	1961	1962	1963
I	4.11	4.22	4.26	4.71	4.59	4.65	5.25	5.56	5.65	6.20	6.09	5.74	5.59
II	4.13	4.24	4.35	4.63	4.58	4.73	5.35	5.53	5.70	6.23[a]	5.91	5.75	5.49
III	4.20	4.26	4.56	4.62	4.62	4.75	5.42	5.45	5.80[a]	6.22	5.78	5.69	5.48
IV	4.20	4.25	4.67	4.59	4.66	4.85	5.53	5.53	6.10[a]	6.21[a]	5.75	5.65	5.46

Standard Deviation - Gross Yield

	1951	1952	1953	1954	1955	1956	1957	1958	1959	1960	1961	1962	1963
I	0.092	0.071	0.040	0.131	0.121	0.224	0.210	0.085	0.184	0.147	0.157	0.118	0.143
II	0.101	0.038	0.137	0.204	0.179	0.137	0.116	0.103	0.172	0.166	0.143	0.116	0.129
III	0.102	0.088	0.123	0.154	0.170	0.163	0.144	0.097	0.176	0.091	0.172	0.121	0.105
IV	0.107	0.051	0.144	0.109	0.154	0.141	0.082	0.129	0.284	0.171	0.127	0.113	0.115

Contract Rate

	1951	1952	1953	1954	1955	1956	1957	1958	1959	1960	1961	1962	1963
I	4.27	4.25	4.25	4.49	4.50	4.44	4.93	5.25	5.25	5.74	5.70	5.26	5.25
II	4.25	4.25	4.33	4.45	4.46	4.49	5.00	5.25	5.25	5.74	5.57	5.25	5.25
III	4.26	4.25	4.49	4.50	4.48	4.48	5.08	5.25	5.25	5.75	5.36	5.25	5.25
IV	4.25	4.25	4.49	4.50	4.49	4.51	5.25	5.25	5.59	5.74	5.29	5.25	5.25

Net Discount

	1951	1952	1953	1954	1955	1956	1957	1958	1959	1960	1961	1962	1963
I	-1.00	-0.16	0.04	1.42	0.61	1.38	2.08	2.01	2.61	3.04	2.51	3.20	2.26
II	-0.79	-0.04	0.11	0.15	0.81	1.61	2.35	1.83	2.98	3.17[a]	2.25	3.28	1.63
III	-0.42	0.01	0.45	0.83	0.99	1.83	2.19	1.34	3.66[a]	3.09	2.78	2.88	1.49
IV	-0.34	0.03	1.19	0.60	1.14	2.30	1.88	1.84	3.34[a]	3.07[a]	3.03	2.64	1.38

(continued)

TABLE C-4 (continued)

	1951	1952	1953	1954	1955	1956	1957	1958	1959	1960	1961	1962	1963
						Net Yield							
I	3.61	3.72	3.76	4.21	4.09	4.15	4.75	5.06	5.17	5.83	5.70	5.36	5.18
II	3.63	3.74	3.86	4.13	4.09	4.23	4.85	5.03	5.25	5.85[a]	5.50	5.36	5.10
III	3.70	3.76	4.08	4.12	4.12	4.26	4.92	4.95	5.40[a]	5.84	5.39	5.30	5.08
IV	3.70	3.75	4.18	4.09	4.16	4.35	5.03	5.03	5.71[a]	5.82[a]	5.35	5.27	5.06
					Standard Deviation - Net Yield								
I	0.100	0.071	0.051	0.131	0.122	0.224	0.207	0.094	0.198	0.149	0.172	0.113	0.157
II	0.105	0.038	0.160	0.206	0.183	0.137	0.116	0.103	0.191	0.172	0.166	0.115	0.132
III	0.102	0.089	0.134	0.154	0.172	0.163	0.144	0.101	0.194	0.094	0.177	0.119	0.097
IV	0.108	0.051	0.145	0.110	0.154	0.141	0.082	0.135	0.307	0.185	0.119	0.111	0.106

[a]Data cover only three companies.

TABLE C-5

Characteristics of Conventional Mortgage Loans on Residential (1-4 Family) Properties by Four Life Insurance Companies, 1951-63, Direct Loans, United States

Gross Yield

	1951	1952	1953	1954	1955	1956	1957	1958	1959	1960	1961	1962	1963
Jan.	4.32	4.44	4.54	4.85	4.71	4.82	5.34	5.70	5.65	6.04	6.03	5.79	5.60
Feb.	4.30	4.44	4.56	4.85	4.70	4.85	5.49	5.72	5.67	6.05	5.96	5.80	5.64
March	4.37	4.51	4.54	4.83	4.70	4.84	5.59	5.72	5.64	6.08	5.92	5.79	5.57
April	4.38	4.49	4.54	4.79	4.72	4.82	5.57	5.66	5.67	6.11	5.85	5.79	5.57
May	4.37	4.58	4.58	4.81	4.72	4.83	5.52	5.61	5.68	6.11	5.81	5.79	5.54
June	4.38	4.52	4.64	4.77	4.76	4.85	5.52	5.60	5.69	6.10	5.82	5.73	5.57
July	4.41	4.61	4.73	4.75	4.78	4.92	5.49	5.57	5.66	6.09	5.80	5.68	5.56
Aug.	4.53	4.55	4.81	4.72	4.83	4.92	5.48	5.54	5.71	6.09	5.79	5.68	5.53
Sept.	4.52	4.54	4.79	4.70	4.84	4.97	5.53	5.42	5.73	6.09	5.79	5.67	5.57
Oct.	4.52	4.54	4.85	4.69	4.83	5.03	5.62	5.45	5.80	6.09	5.79	5.65	5.56
Nov.	4.47	4.44	4.84	4.67	4.86	5.18	5.67	5.50	5.89	6.00	5.79	5.65	5.54
Dec.	4.47	4.40	4.86	4.71	4.85	5.20	5.66	5.55	5.95	6.00	5.79	5.64	5.58

Standard Deviation - Gross Yield

	1951	1952	1953	1954	1955	1956	1957	1958	1959	1960	1961	1962	1963
Jan.	0.209	0.227	0.209	0.146	0.232	0.162	0.187	0.295	0.162	0.209	0.140	0.105	0.137
Feb.	0.234	0.170	0.186	0.137	0.197	0.150	0.153	0.123	0.165	0.164	0.158	0.102	0.210
March	0.180	0.202	0.189	0.133	0.276	0.172	0.179	0.138	0.281	0.165	0.139	0.077	0.113
April	0.203	0.195	0.204	0.137	0.211	0.227	0.218	0.141	0.145	0.149	0.136	0.090	0.119
May	0.193	0.239	0.226	0.132	0.175	0.142	0.227	0.121	0.157	0.195	0.117	0.078	0.097
June	0.187	0.228	0.209	0.169	0.160	0.193	0.206	0.126	0.149	0.197	0.111	0.102	0.112
July	0.218	0.268	0.151	0.177	0.159	0.206	0.188	0.115	0.159	0.176	0.120	0.141	0.114
Aug.	0.190	0.237	0.212	0.207	0.194	0.211	0.186	0.160	0.177	0.178	0.078	0.127	0.118
Sept.	0.209	0.239	0.257	0.193	0.194	0.235	0.176	0.185	0.182	0.158	0.088	0.120	0.114
Oct.	0.211	0.195	0.176	0.180	0.174	0.250	0.202	0.221	0.157	0.153	0.122	0.120	0.130
Nov.	0.196	0.308	0.154	0.186	0.191	0.223	0.135	0.194	0.190	0.079	0.086	0.130	0.190
Dec.	0.186	0.321	0.177	0.175	0.174	0.237	0.156	0.185	0.200	0.064	0.082	0.112	0.329

(continued)

TABLE C-5 (continued)

Contract Rate

	1951	1952	1953	1954	1955	1956	1957	1958	1959	1960	1961	1962	1963
Jan.	4.49	4.60	4.69	5.00	4.83	4.97	5.42	5.78	5.68	6.08	6.05	5.82	5.65
Feb.	4.46	4.58	4.71	4.97	4.80	4.97	5.54	5.77	5.69	6.07	5.99	5.83	5.64
March	4.53	4.66	4.70	4.97	4.81	4.95	5.63	5.80	5.70	6.11	5.95	5.82	5.63
April	4.54	4.65	4.70	4.91	4.83	4.94	5.60	5.71	5.71	6.14	5.89	5.81	5.62
May	4.53	4.71	4.73	4.95	4.85	4.96	5.56	5.67	5.73	6.13	5.85	5.83	5.57
June	4.54	4.64	4.77	4.88	4.91	4.98	5.57	5.63	5.73	6.11	5.86	5.77	5.61
July	4.58	4.72	4.87	4.88	4.91	5.05	5.55	5.60	5.70	6.12	5.82	5.73	5.60
Aug.	4.68	4.66	4.96	4.86	4.93	5.04	5.54	5.60	5.75	6.10	5.83	5.74	5.55
Sept.	4.69	4.67	4.92	4.85	4.96	5.09	5.59	5.47	5.77	6.10	5.83	5.73	5.60
Oct.	4.68	4.67	4.98	4.82	4.96	5.12	5.69	5.50	5.85	6.10	5.81	5.72	5.60
Nov.	4.64	4.59	4.99	4.79	4.98	5.25	5.74	5.54	5.93	6.00	5.81	5.71	5.56
Dec.	4.63	4.55	5.00	4.85	4.97	5.29	5.72	5.60	5.98	6.00	5.82	5.70	5.56

Net Discount

	1951	1952	1953	1954	1955	1956	1957	1958	1959	1960	1961	1962	1963
Jan.	-1.08	-0.96	-0.94	-0.94	-0.79	-0.94	-0.49	-0.49	-0.19	-0.22	-0.14	-0.18	-0.33
Feb.	-0.95	-0.89	-0.93	-0.86	-0.65	-0.79	-0.31	-0.34	-0.17	-0.14	-0.21	-0.17	-0.01
March	-0.95	-0.92	-0.95	-0.81	-0.70	-0.72	-0.26	-0.49	-0.32	-0.21	-0.19	-0.16	-0.35
April	-0.98	-0.96	-0.99	-0.74	-0.68	-0.77	-0.18	-0.32	-0.28	-0.19	-0.23	-0.14	-0.30
May	-0.96	-0.80	-0.98	-0.82	-0.84	-0.85	-0.24	-0.32	-0.33	-0.11	-0.25	-0.24	-0.15
June	-0.98	-0.72	-0.79	-0.67	-0.91	-0.80	-0.33	-0.23	-0.31	-0.07	-0.22	-0.25	-0.26
July	-0.98	-0.72	-0.83	-0.84	-0.78	-0.81	-0.36	-0.20	-0.23	-0.13	-0.10	-0.32	-0.26
Aug.	-0.91	-0.68	-0.91	-0.85	-0.68	-0.77	-0.34	-0.39	-0.27	-0.05	-0.24	-0.37	-0.17
Sept.	-1.01	-0.77	-0.75	-0.95	-0.73	-0.72	-0.41	-0.36	-0.25	-0.05	-0.21	-0.37	-0.20
Oct.	-0.96	-0.84	-0.77	-0.80	-0.80	-0.57	-0.43	-0.31	-0.31	-0.04	-0.12	-0.42	-0.26
Nov.	-1.02	-0.97	-0.90	-0.81	-0.80	-0.48	-0.43	-0.26	-0.28	0.00	-0.13	-0.40	-0.13
Dec.	-1.00	-0.91	-0.85	-0.91	-0.77	-0.57	-0.36	-0.31	-0.18	0.00	-0.14	-0.38	-0.18

(continued)

TABLE C-5 (continued)

	1951	1952	1953	1954	1955	1956	1957	1958	1959	1960	1961	1962	1963
Loan-Value Ratio													
Jan.	63.5	62.5	65.3	64.7	65.8	65.2	68.3	66.5	71.0	70.2	70.6	69.5	70.9
Feb.	63.9	62.7	66.8	63.9	67.1	64.6	67.7	68.6	70.9	69.8	70.6	71.0	71.2
March	63.2	62.3	64.9	64.4	67.2	67.5	68.0	68.4	70.4	69.6	68.7	70.3	71.7
April	63.9	62.2	65.2	64.5	68.0	66.1	65.2	68.8	69.5	69.0	69.2	69.8	71.2
May	63.8	63.4	66.8	65.6	65.5	66.6	64.4	67.5	69.9	69.1	70.1	71.2	70.5
June	63.5	63.9	65.9	65.1	67.3	65.7	66.2	68.6	69.2	68.9	70.5	70.8	71.0
July	62.1	63.5	65.9	66.1	67.3	66.0	64.1	67.7	68.9	70.0	70.2	70.5	70.9
Aug.	62.5	65.0	66.0	63.7	68.1	66.2	65.2	69.3	69.3	69.8	70.6	70.9	71.4
Sept.	62.4	64.3	63.7	66.1	67.3	65.8	64.7	69.8	69.5	70.7	71.0	70.2	70.7
Oct.	62.4	64.0	64.6	64.0	67.3	64.6	66.7	68.9	69.7	70.6	69.7	70.0	71.7
Nov.	63.7	65.2	65.1	65.8	67.5	66.5	67.5	69.2	69.5	68.9	70.9	69.9	70.8
Dec.	62.6	65.5	66.0	65.8	66.6	67.8	66.2	70.0	69.5	69.3	69.9	70.5	70.9
Maturity (months)													
Jan.	220.6	225.5	223.6	225.6	253.2	250.2	255.8	263.5	284.1	288.5	291.4	311.1	321.6
Feb.	218.4	225.3	223.2	224.5	253.1	250.7	263.1	267.9	282.5	286.5	288.0	312.7	325.6
March	221.2	222.5	224.7	224.4	256.4	259.0	260.3	266.1	280.0	284.6	280.1	315.2	322.4
April	224.3	229.4	227.0	228.2	259.2	254.2	259.0	267.0	279.5	287.9	285.3	313.8	327.2
May	218.8	225.3	228.7	226.6	253.0	257.7	253.0	271.5	286.1	289.7	288.7	320.2	325.7
June	217.1	222.3	228.6	224.8	259.7	249.5	262.6	272.0	282.0	284.4	289.1	320.0	322.4
July	216.6	226.8	226.9	240.9	256.2	254.1	261.9	269.9	284.9	288.3	288.3	314.9	330.2
Aug.	220.2	227.1	228.5	238.2	248.7	249.8	257.9	274.2	285.6	284.3	297.2	317.9	333.9
Sept.	219.5	225.6	227.8	245.3	260.6	244.7	257.8	279.7	283.2	289.3	307.1	319.7	323.9
Oct.	222.0	227.1	215.9	242.6	257.5	256.9	262.4	277.7	284.4	287.7	301.8	319.6	334.5
Nov.	219.4	224.3	220.4	251.1	250.0	260.2	264.6	281.5	284.8	285.3	309.4	319.5	333.1
Dec.	225.2	223.9	225.8	256.2	252.7	263.8	258.3	286.4	285.1	288.7	308.9	323.1	330.6

(continued)

TABLE C-5 (continued)

	1951	1952	1953	1954	1955	1956	1957	1958	1959	1960	1961	1962	1963
						Number of Loans							
Jan.	121	99	137	118	105	127	125	117	122	123	120	106	118
Feb.	111	121	112	103	96	126	120	110	124	124	125	128	118
March	107	109	123	125	113	130	129	99	132	128	97	124	102
April	99	118	126	110	109	122	119	104	127	127	133	125	119
May	106	113	119	178	108	128	132	120	126	121	118	114	111
June	116	96	111	114	117	117	125	125	115	127	138	128	101
July	112	100	122	114	128	113	117	127	104	129	119	108	123
Aug.	108	122	103	130	104	120	125	123	122	125	128	125	116
Sept.	110	113	109	127	120	130	121	143	122	130	126	133	120
Oct.	106	105	114	125	122	124	112	122	115	108	120	97	119
Nov.	111	97	115	156	121	123	105	124	113	122	123	126	103
Dec.	102	103	116	101	97	135	117	127	127	126	128	103	106
						Mean Loan Size							
Jan.	10,304	10,883	12,353	11,618	14,121	14,123	15,162	14,954	16,566	18,456	18,535	18,102	19,839
Feb.	10,888	11,639	12,246	12,522	14,330	13,972	15,884	16,176	16,966	17,288	19,460	19,252	21,312
March	10,756	11,037	12,160	12,136	14,056	14,040	14,769	15,469	17,804	17,779	19,386	18,520	20,848
April	10,782	10,841	11,509	12,298	14,721	14,324	14,764	16,252	16,982	17,735	17,904	18,680	20,430
May	11,839	10,768	12,195	12,701	14,025	14,799	14,619	15,275	17,141	17,715	18,554	18,990	19,678
June	10,489	10,670	12,672	13,851	13,293	14,256	14,346	16,211	17,468	17,854	19,855	20,470	19,676
July	11,050	11,162	12,751	13,338	13,465	14,474	14,169	15,671	18,391	18,743	18,219	18,355	19,376
Aug.	10,270	11,450	12,418	12,163	14,089	15,076	15,401	16,126	17,976	17,846	18,427	20,167	20,279
Sept.	10,522	11,320	12,331	13,312	14,470	14,064	15,143	16,482	18,619	18,109	18,884	19,362	20,003
Oct.	10,742	11,190	12,138	13,133	13,817	14,091	15,224	16,394	17,648	16,845	17,824	19,598	20,657
Nov.	10,792	11,497	12,209	13,810	14,404	15,218	15,735	16,415	18,056	17,371	18,898	19,558	20,593
Dec.	11,044	11,249	12,690	13,685	14,618	15,359	14,395	16,661	18,118	18,102	18,605	18,908	19,687

(continued)

TABLE C-5 (continued)

	1951	1952	1953	1954	1955	1956	1957	1958	1959	1960	1961	1962	1963
Gross Yield													
I	4.33	4.46	4.54	4.84	4.70	4.84	5.47	5.71	5.65	6.06	5.97	5.80	5.61
II	4.38	4.53	4.59	4.79	4.73	4.83	5.53	5.62	5.68	6.11	5.83	5.77	5.56
III	4.49	4.56	4.78	4.72	4.82	4.94	5.50	5.50	5.70	6.09	5.80	5.68	5.55
IV	4.49	4.46	4.85	4.68	4.85	5.14	5.65	5.50	5.88	6.03	5.79	5.65	5.56
Standard Deviation - Gross Yield													
I	0.211	0.201	0.196	0.139	0.240	0.162	0.202	0.205	0.212	0.183	0.152	0.096	0.162
II	0.194	0.225	0.217	0.146	0.183	0.190	0.219	0.132	0.153	0.182	0.123	0.093	0.111
III	0.213	0.249	0.213	0.194	0.183	0.219	0.184	0.170	0.175	0.171	0.097	0.129	0.117
IV	0.198	0.284	0.170	0.182	0.181	0.250	0.168	0.204	0.196	0.115	0.098	0.122	0.229
Contract Rate													
I	4.49	4.61	4.70	4.98	4.82	4.97	5.53	5.78	5.69	6.09	6.00	5.82	5.64
II	4.54	4.67	4.74	4.92	4.86	4.96	5.57	5.67	5.73	6.13	5.87	5.80	5.60
III	4.65	4.68	4.91	4.86	4.93	5.06	5.56	5.56	5.74	6.10	5.82	5.73	5.58
IV	4.65	4.61	4.99	4.82	4.97	5.22	5.72	5.55	5.92	6.03	5.81	5.71	5.57
Net Discount													
I	-0.99	-0.92	-0.94	-0.87	-0.71	-0.81	-0.36	-0.44	-0.23	-0.19	-0.18	-0.17	-0.22
II	-0.97	-0.83	-0.92	-0.75	-0.81	-0.81	-0.25	-0.29	-0.31	-0.12	-0.23	-0.21	-0.24
III	-0.97	-0.72	-0.83	-0.88	-0.73	-0.77	-0.37	-0.32	-0.25	-0.08	-0.18	-0.36	-0.21
IV	-1.00	-0.91	-0.84	-0.83	-0.79	-0.54	-0.41	-0.29	-0.25	-0.01	-0.13	-0.40	-0.08

(continued)

TABLE C-5 (continued)

	1951	1952	1953	1954	1955	1956	1957	1958	1959	1960	1961	1962	1963
					Loan-Value Ratio								
I	63.5	62.5	65.6	64.3	66.7	65.8	68.0	67.8	70.7	69.9	70.0	70.3	71.2
II	63.7	63.1	65.9	65.1	67.0	66.2	65.3	68.3	69.6	69.0	70.0	70.6	70.9
III	62.3	64.3	65.2	65.3	67.5	66.0	64.7	69.0	69.2	70.2	70.6	70.5	71.0
IV	62.9	64.9	65.2	65.2	67.2	66.4	66.8	69.4	69.5	69.6	70.2	70.1	71.2
					Maturity (months)								
I	220.0	224.4	223.9	224.8	254.3	253.3	259.8	265.8	282.1	286.5	286.9	313.1	323.3
II	219.9	225.9	228.1	226.5	257.3	254.0	258.1	270.3	282.5	287.3	287.7	318.0	325.2
III	218.7	226.5	227.7	241.6	255.5	249.4	259.1	274.9	284.6	287.4	297.8	317.7	329.3
IV	222.1	225.1	220.8	249.7	253.4	260.5	261.7	282.0	284.8	287.3	306.8	320.7	332.8
					Number of Loans								
I	339	329	372	346	314	383	374	326	378	375	342	358	338
II	321	327	356	402	334	367	376	349	368	375	389	367	331
III	330	335	334	371	352	363	363	393	348	384	373	366	359
IV	319	305	345	382	340	382	334	373	355	356	371	326	328
					Mean Loan Size								
I	10,641	11,212	12,256	12,074	14,162	14,045	15,260	15,525	17,133	17,841	19,115	18,656	20,659
II	11,022	10,765	12,102	12,909	13,996	14,470	14,573	15,901	17,190	17,767	18,786	19,418	19,946
III	10,619	11,320	12,512	12,916	13,995	14,531	14,920	16,110	18,323	18,238	18,519	19,339	19,878
IV	10,857	11,309	12,347	13,559	14,254	14,902	15,091	16,492	17,948	17,469	18,446	19,362	20,324

TABLE C-6

Characteristics of FHA Mortgage Loans on Residential (1-4 Family)
Properties by Four Life Insurance Companies, 1951-63, Direct Loans,
United States

Gross Yield

	1951	1952	1953	1954	1955	1956	1957	1958	1959	1960	1961	1962	1963
Jan.	4.06	4.21	4.26	4.67	4.61	4.82	5.26	5.76	5.73	6.38	6.30	5.83	5.68
Feb.	4.09	4.23	4.27	4.66	4.64	4.84	5.45	5.80	5.77	6.40	6.23	5.83	5.67
March	4.11	4.22	4.26	4.66	4.64	4.77	5.28	5.79	5.77	6.42	6.16	5.84	5.62
April	4.14	4.24	4.27	4.65	4.61	4.79	5.46	5.74	5.77	6.42	6.11	5.83	5.64
May	4.14	4.25	4.30	4.62	4.65	4.72	5.45	5.70	5.77	6.43	6.02	5.83	5.61
June	4.14	4.30	4.53	4.60	4.68	4.78	5.43	5.64	5.81	6.39	5.96	5.81	5.59
July	4.16	4.30	4.57	4.59	4.68	4.68	5.44	5.61	5.82	6.40	5.92	5.79	5.59
Aug.	4.27	4.30	4.58	4.58	4.71	4.68	5.45	5.59	5.83	6.38	5.89	5.79	5.59
Sept.	4.30	4.26	4.57	4.59	4.71	4.77	5.60	5.55	5.85	6.35	5.83	5.73	5.57
Oct.	4.26	4.27	4.69	4.57	4.77	4.87	5.68	5.54	5.94	6.35	5.84	5.75	5.58
Nov.	4.23	4.24	4.72	4.60	4.83	4.92	5.75	5.62	6.20	6.32	5.85	5.72	5.59
Dec.	4.23	4.21	4.70	4.60	4.83	4.92	5.74	5.64	6.29	6.27	5.83	5.66	5.59

Standard Deviation - Gross Yield

	1951	1952	1953	1954	1955	1956	1957	1958	1959	1960	1961	1962	1963
Jan.	0.116	0.090	0.088	0.171	0.083	0.163	0.342	0.120	0.117	0.149	0.127	0.078	0.089
Feb.	0.094	0.097	0.109	0.132	0.108	0.142	0.176	0.086	0.100	0.129	0.149	0.048	0.096
March	0.075	0.090	0.075	0.131	0.124	0.143	0.240	0.115	0.082	0.100	0.134	0.048	0.122
April	0.094	0.080	0.077	0.111	0.111	0.164	0.182	0.107	0.109	0.118	0.120	0.066	0.091
May	0.080	0.075	0.118	0.104	0.147	0.206	0.155	0.109	0.108	0.165	0.163	0.054	0.071
June	0.080	0.101	0.127	0.098	0.111	0.206	0.202	0.109	0.087	0.228	0.121	0.062	0.077
July	0.092	0.097	0.095	0.099	0.127	0.194	0.166	0.101	0.082	0.102	0.100	0.099	0.065
Aug.	0.084	0.074	0.123	0.088	0.134	0.200	0.115	0.096	0.102	0.136	0.089	0.067	0.076
Sept.	0.092	0.115	0.187	0.090	0.132	0.234	0.150	0.135	0.247	0.140	0.171	0.149	0.082
Oct.	0.081	0.098	0.167	0.101	0.153	0.209	0.140	0.129	0.193	0.126	0.106	0.093	0.068
Nov.	0.086	0.121	0.158	0.098	0.168	0.204	0.067	0.209	0.241	0.264	0.062	0.172	0.072
Dec.	0.105	0.146	0.173	0.117	0.177	0.250	0.087	0.163	0.167	0.298	0.157	0.086	0.261

(continued)

TABLE C-6 (continued)

	1951	1952	1953	1954	1955	1956	1957	1958	1959	1960	1961	1962	1963
Contract Rate													
Jan.	4.26	4.25	4.25	4.50	4.50	4.50	4.84	5.25	5.26	5.68	5.75	5.28	5.25
Feb.	4.25	4.25	4.26	4.50	4.50	4.50	5.00	5.25	5.26	5.75	5.75	5.29	5.25
March	4.26	4.25	4.25	4.51	4.50	4.50	4.99	5.25	5.25	5.75	5.65	5.27	5.29
April	4.28	4.25	4.25	4.50	4.50	4.50	4.99	5.25	5.25	5.75	5.59	5.26	5.25
May	4.25	4.25	4.27	4.50	4.50	4.51	5.00	5.25	5.25	5.75	5.55	5.25	5.25
June	4.25	4.25	4.48	4.50	4.50	4.50	5.00	5.25	5.25	5.73	5.52	5.25	5.25
July	4.25	4.25	4.50	4.50	4.50	4.50	5.00	5.25	5.25	5.75	5.49	5.25	5.25
Aug.	4.25	4.25	4.49	4.50	4.50	4.50	5.00	5.25	5.25	5.75	5.35	5.25	5.25
Sept.	4.26	4.25	4.45	4.50	4.50	4.50	5.18	5.25	5.23	5.75	5.32	5.25	5.25
Oct.	4.25	4.25	4.49	4.50	4.50	4.50	5.25	5.25	5.31	5.75	5.32	5.25	5.25
Nov.	4.25	4.24	4.49	4.50	4.50	4.50	5.25	5.24	5.59	5.73	5.31	5.24	5.25
Dec.	4.26	4.22	4.50	4.50	4.50	4.50	5.25	5.25	5.69	5.72	5.27	5.27	5.25
Net Discount													
Jan.	-1.30	-0.28	0.07	1.08	0.75	2.16	2.71	3.31	3.17	4.63	3.55	3.60	2.86
Feb.	-1.06	-0.14	0.11	1.04	0.89	2.24	2.90	3.58	3.39	4.29	3.17	3.63	2.82
March	-0.98	-0.20	0.05	0.98	0.95	1.80	1.86	3.53	3.43	4.40	3.33	3.79	2.22
April	-0.91	-0.08	0.10	0.95	0.76	1.93	3.03	3.20	3.39	4.37	3.46	3.84	2.58
May	-0.77	0.01	0.15	0.82	0.98	1.44	2.91	2.95	3.43	4.46	3.07	3.82	2.40
June	-0.72	0.31	0.34	0.68	1.24	1.89	2.81	2.56	3.69	4.30	2.90	3.72	2.25
July	-0.57	0.28	0.48	0.57	1.20	1.19	2.88	2.35	3.79	4.25	2.82	3.59	2.26
Aug.	0.10	0.33	0.52	0.53	1.40	1.17	2.98	2.22	3.84	4.08	3.55	3.58	2.25
Sept.	0.27	0.04	0.84	0.55	1.42	1.78	2.68	1.98	4.10	3.98	3.40	3.22	2.14
Oct.	0.09	0.14	1.31	0.48	1.81	2.46	2.82	1.91	4.19	3.92	3.50	3.28	2.17
Nov.	-0.14	-0.02	1.47	0.66	2.21	2.86	3.25	2.52	4.01	3.83	3.63	3.19	2.25
Dec.	-0.15	-0.10	1.33	0.68	2.18	2.78	3.20	2.58	3.95	3.59	3.75	2.60	2.28

(continued)

TABLE C-6 (continued)

	1951	1952	1953	1954	1955	1956	1957	1958	1959	1960	1961	1962	1963
						Loan-Value Ratio							
Jan.	81.7	81.2	81.2	80.4	83.2	84.2	83.1	89.5	90.7	92.1	93.6	94.1	93.8
Feb.	81.6	80.8	80.9	81.3	83.7	83.8	82.7	88.9	90.8	92.7	92.4	93.4	94.1
March	81.0	80.6	82.4	79.8	84.1	83.8	85.2	89.6	92.4	92.4	91.1	93.4	94.1
April	80.0	80.7	80.7	79.8	83.9	83.3	83.2	89.1	91.6	91.5	92.4	93.4	94.1
May	79.0	80.3	79.8	80.9	84.9	82.9	83.8	90.0	91.2	92.4	92.1	93.4	93.9
June	80.2	80.6	81.6	80.8	85.6	82.0	85.3	89.7	91.7	91.6	92.6	93.6	93.5
July	79.1	80.3	80.3	79.6	84.7	83.4	84.7	90.4	91.8	92.8	92.8	93.7	93.5
Aug.	80.1	80.2	81.1	79.5	83.7	83.3	85.9	91.3	91.7	92.9	92.2	93.6	93.7
Sept.	78.8	80.4	80.0	80.5	85.3	83.2	85.2	90.5	91.6	92.8	92.5	94.1	94.0
Oct.	79.2	81.4	80.3	82.1	83.2	83.0	88.5	90.6	91.8	92.6	93.1	94.2	93.8
Nov.	80.7	80.9	80.4	83.8	83.9	82.2	89.3	90.7	91.7	91.9	93.4	94.0	93.9
Dec.	80.3	80.6	82.1	84.4	85.3	83.0	88.9	90.4	92.0	91.5	93.7	94.2	93.9
						Maturity (months)							
Jan.	265.7	251.7	250.1	256.4	298.4	290.2	284.1	295.6	338.7	343.7	339.5	349.5	359.7
Feb.	257.0	253.8	245.6	258.1	292.3	289.7	273.0	296.3	335.9	344.2	343.1	351.3	359.7
March	254.7	253.8	254.9	259.0	296.4	289.1	286.9	294.5	329.7	347.4	338.6	352.0	358.3
April	256.4	250.8	247.3	261.2	309.1	289.7	283.5	298.5	336.5	336.8	343.9	352.8	361.9
May	249.4	251.4	245.4	259.8	294.1	287.5	287.9	307.3	334.4	340.9	348.3	353.8	361.9
June	247.6	245.3	254.8	274.8	304.6	290.0	285.7	311.0	342.5	344.8	351.1	347.5	359.2
July	245.1	254.4	250.4	260.2	296.5	294.5	291.4	320.7	338.9	344.1	344.0	356.8	360.8
Aug.	242.7	246.6	251.3	261.5	295.6	288.9	293.2	331.3	338.8	339.6	340.9	351.7	364.8
Sept.	238.3	246.7	263.1	267.6	294.3	285.7	290.6	323.0	334.9	339.8	346.0	357.0	355.5
Oct.	246.3	260.6	257.0	272.3	298.8	296.0	295.6	331.9	343.3	340.5	345.5	351.5	360.8
Nov.	252.6	254.8	259.8	296.9	311.8	301.0	304.2	328.9	345.8	344.6	348.1	360.1	362.8
Dec.	243.6	253.5	266.6	294.3	294.6	288.9	296.9	338.5	350.6	339.3	349.4	359.1	357.9

(continued)

TABLE C-6 (continued)

Number of Loans

	1951	1952	1953	1954	1955	1956	1957	1958	1959	1960	1961	1962	1963
Jan.	142	120	125	110	126	118	115	123	115	120	36	103	144
Feb.	111	106	101	119	107	121	86	114	119	124	125	126	106
March	104	114	141	120	122	117	115	117	120	124	99	117	109
April	98	115	103	125	100	115	96	115	125	124	117	117	112
May	111	102	97	111	117	107	59	126	130	126	121	135	122
June	107	98	106	114	98	105	105	121	108	119	119	128	123
July	110	105	151	106	123	117	124	115	109	126	132	123	109
Aug.	100	99	126	123	95	122	125	121	126	125	130	124	121
Sept.	108	97	118	111	118	111	130	130	133	124	118	128	131
Oct.	116	105	108	119	119	121	105	113	114	114	110	120	118
Nov.	128	106	107	142	110	139	107	115	119	121	126	124	119
Dec.	132	102	99	134	111	140	122	117	125	118	124	120	115

Mean Loan Size

	1951	1952	1953	1954	1955	1956	1957	1958	1959	1960	1961	1962	1963
Jan.	7,927	8,606	9,031	9,825	11,514	11,373	11,681	12,709	14,221	14,562	13,981	14,847	14,206
Feb.	7,856	8,617	9,464	9,860	11,224	11,126	11,105	13,079	14,475	14,351	14,577	15,083	14,525
March	8,105	8,715	8,626	10,092	11,666	11,465	11,019	13,409	14,222	14,673	15,454	15,144	14,609
April	7,942	8,377	9,047	9,944	12,004	11,547	10,511	13,452	14,492	14,519	14,468	14,604	13,947
May	8,463	8,898	10,051	10,095	10,987	11,636	11,402	13,602	14,346	14,587	14,559	14,907	15,028
June	8,237	8,729	9,507	10,110	11,334	11,873	11,950	13,987	14,576	14,522	14,778	15,040	15,421
July	8,487	8,815	9,643	9,959	11,780	12,051	12,354	13,905	14,010	14,151	14,463	15,127	15,192
Aug.	8,561	8,917	9,935	10,147	11,808	11,636	12,238	13,558	14,227	14,148	14,926	14,723	14,715
Sept.	8,811	8,761	10,096	10,511	12,053	11,584	13,188	13,918	14,583	14,592	14,891	14,960	15,263
Oct.	8,688	8,886	9,775	10,740	11,647	12,748	13,188	14,222	14,191	14,630	14,770	14,518	14,705
Nov.	8,480	9,061	9,758	11,312	11,928	13,069	13,828	13,807	14,749	15,181	14,375	14,816	14,847
Dec.	8,578	9,038	9,831	10,917	11,372	11,855	13,573	14,346	14,299	14,754	15,404	13,855	14,874

(continued)

TABLE C-6 (continued)

Gross Yield

	1951	1952	1953	1954	1955	1956	1957	1958	1959	1960	1961	1962	1963
I	4.09	4.22	4.26	4.66	4.63	4.81	5.32	5.78	5.76	6.40	6.21	5.83	5.66
II	4.14	4.26	4.37	4.63	4.65	4.77	5.44	5.69	5.78	6.41	6.03	5.82	5.61
III	4.24	4.29	4.57	4.58	4.70	4.70	5.50	5.58	5.83	6.38	5.88	5.77	5.58
IV	4.24	4.24	4.70	4.59	4.81	4.91	5.72	5.60	6.15	6.31	5.84	5.71	5.59

Standard Deviation - Gross Yield

	1951	1952	1953	1954	1955	1956	1957	1958	1959	1960	1961	1962	1963
I	0.100	0.093	0.090	0.145	0.107	0.152	0.278	0.110	0.102	0.128	0.149	0.059	0.106
II	0.085	0.089	0.164	0.106	0.130	0.196	0.185	0.116	0.104	0.176	0.152	0.061	0.082
III	0.108	0.099	0.137	0.092	0.132	0.215	0.162	0.115	0.166	0.128	0.128	0.114	0.076
IV	0.093	0.126	0.166	0.106	0.168	0.224	0.106	0.175	0.253	0.244	0.116	0.129	0.160

Contract Rate

	1951	1952	1953	1954	1955	1956	1957	1958	1959	1960	1961	1962	1963
I	4.26	4.25	4.25	4.50	4.50	4.50	4.94	5.25	5.25	5.72	5.71	5.28	5.26
II	4.26	4.25	4.34	4.50	4.50	4.50	5.00	5.25	5.25	5.74	5.55	5.25	5.25
III	4.25	4.25	4.48	4.50	4.50	4.50	5.07	5.25	5.24	5.75	5.39	5.25	5.25
IV	4.25	4.24	4.49	4.50	4.50	4.50	5.25	5.25	5.54	5.73	5.30	5.25	5.25

Net Discount

	1951	1952	1953	1954	1955	1956	1957	1958	1959	1960	1961	1962	1963
I	-1.13	-0.21	0.07	1.03	0.86	2.07	2.46	3.47	3.33	4.44	3.28	3.68	2.65
II	-0.79	0.07	0.20	0.82	0.99	1.76	2.91	2.89	3.49	4.38	3.14	3.79	2.40
III	-0.07	0.22	0.60	0.55	1.33	1.37	2.84	2.18	3.92	4.10	3.25	3.46	2.21
IV	-0.07	0.01	1.37	0.61	2.06	2.71	3.10	2.34	4.05	3.78	3.63	3.04	2.23

(continued)

TABLE C-6 (continued)

	1951	1952	1953	1954	1955	1956	1957	1958	1959	1960	1961	1962	1963
Loan-Value Ratio													
I	81.4	80.9	81.5	80.5	83.6	83.9	83.7	89.4	91.3	92.4	92.0	93.6	94.0
II	79.7	80.5	80.7	80.5	84.8	82.8	84.3	89.6	91.5	91.8	92.4	93.5	93.8
III	79.3	80.3	80.5	79.8	84.6	83.3	85.3	90.7	91.7	92.9	92.5	93.8	93.7
IV	80.1	80.9	80.9	83.5	84.1	82.7	88.9	90.6	91.8	92.0	93.5	94.1	93.9
Maturity (months)													
I	259.8	253.1	250.6	257.9	295.9	289.7	282.1	295.5	334.7	345.1	340.9	351.0	359.3
II	250.9	249.3	249.3	265.2	302.4	289.1	285.4	305.8	337.6	340.8	347.8	351.4	360.9
III	242.0	249.3	254.5	263.1	295.5	289.9	291.7	324.9	337.4	341.2	343.6	355.2	260.2
IV	247.5	256.3	261.0	288.8	301.7	295.5	298.9	333.2	346.7	341.6	347.8	356.9	360.5
Number of Loans													
I	357	340	367	349	355	356	316	354	354	368	260	346	359
II	316	315	306	350	315	327	260	362	363	369	357	380	357
III	318	301	395	340	336	350	379	366	368	375	380	375	361
IV	376	313	314	395	340	400	334	345	358	353	360	364	352
Mean Loan Size													
I	7,958	8,646	8,995	9,929	11,479	11,319	11,283	13,060	14,307	14,528	14,828	15,033	14,423
II	8,225	8,655	9,525	10,046	11,418	11,681	11,294	13,683	14,465	14,543	14,602	14,859	14,824
III	8,620	8,831	9,872	10,207	11,884	11,758	12,602	13,795	14,291	14,296	14,754	14,937	15,058
IV	8,579	8,995	9,787	11,006	11,648	12,547	13,533	14,126	14,414	14,860	14,850	14,401	14,808

TABLE C-7

Characteristics of Conventional Mortgage Loans on Residential (1-4 Family)
Properties by Four Life Insurance Companies, 1951-63, East

	1951	1952	1953	1954	1955	1956	1957	1958	1959	1960	1961	1962	1963
Gross Yield[a]													
I	4.20	4.37	4.44	4.78	4.52	4.66	5.15	5.51	5.38	5.90	5.87	5.70	5.49
II	4.31	4.47	4.46	4.73	4.60	4.67	5.28	5.43	5.44	5.95	5.70	5.68	5.50
III	4.39	4.48	4.67	4.62	4.54	4.70	5.32	5.32	5.49	5.96	5.68	5.63	5.50
IV	4.40	4.32	4.75	4.55	4.62	4.81	5.46	5.28	5.71	5.94	5.70	5.56	5.44
Standard Deviation - Gross Yield													
I				0.149	0.255	0.295	0.377	0.250	0.277	0.239	0.176	0.159	0.177
II				0.217	0.265	0.269	0.275	0.223	0.209	0.181	0.206	0.216	0.140
III				0.249	0.331	0.260	0.243	0.286	0.225	0.143	0.178	0.198	0.161
IV			0.216	0.243	0.265	0.238	0.232	0.232	0.267	0.203	0.166	0.184	0.199
Contract Rate													
I	4.37	4.51	4.56	4.92	4.64	4.80	5.22	5.58	5.42	5.90	5.87	5.70	5.50
II	4.48	4.58	4.58	4.83	4.70	4.78	5.33	5.48	5.46	5.96	5.70	5.68	5.51
III	4.54	4.57	4.77	4.74	4.66	4.80	5.38	5.37	5.51	5.96	5.69	5.64	5.51
IV	4.58	4.49	4.88	4.67	4.73	4.91	5.51	5.31	5.73	5.94	5.70	5.58	5.45
Net Discount													
I				-0.86	-0.76	-0.85	-0.41	-0.41	-0.22	-0.02	-0.02	-0.02	-0.08
II				-0.60	-0.65	-0.70	-0.33	-0.31	-0.13	-0.02	-0.01	-0.03	-0.10
III				-0.72	-0.73	-0.62	-0.36	-0.34	-0.12	-0.02	-0.02	-0.10	-0.09
IV			-0.81	-0.77	-0.65	-0.65	-0.27	-0.17	-0.13	-0.03	-0.01	-0.11	-0.05

(continued)

TABLE C-7 (continued)

	1951	1952	1953	1954	1955	1956	1957	1958	1959	1960	1961	1962	1963
Loan-Value Ratio													
I	62.0	60.4	63.2	65.4	64.9	62.3	63.4	64.5	65.2	68.8	68.8	67.3	70.0
II	61.9	61.1	64.8	64.3	64.1	61.3	62.7	64.8	67.3	67.8	68.0	69.2	70.8
III	60.4	62.6	63.2	62.9	63.0	61.9	60.9	65.8	67.2	69.8	67.6	68.6	69.7
IV	61.3	64.0	64.3	63.0	62.0	62.5	64.0	66.8	68.7	69.3	67.9	68.1	66.2
Maturity (months)													
I	221.3	223.5	228.4	228.2	255.9	248.7	260.6	256.7	269.1	285.6	283.5	299.9	301.6
II	219.8	227.8	229.4	223.6	251.5	237.5	246.6	258.3	281.2	285.9	286.1	302.2	321.3
III	222.1	226.7	228.5	239.5	252.2	240.3	254.2	260.1	275.7	287.9	291.4	305.0	312.0
IV	219.2	227.1	225.9	250.5	242.3	261.7	260.0	276.8	280.4	285.4	298.4	315.8	308.7
Number of Loans													
I	140	161	162	136	161	151	173	152	205	159	131	179	121
II	154	250	226	187	187	167	221	157	188	167	162	165	135
III	203	195	178	187	151	187	188	131	186	165	198	166	124
IV	150	192	153	169	162	189	161	202	179	152	168	141	153
Mean Loan Size													
I	10,917	11,437	12,260	12,512	14,124	14,822	14,863	15,650	16,035	17,290	18,863	19,357	20,558
II	11,500	10,389	12,177	12,660	12,630	13,601	13,834	15,039	17,135	18,682	19,027	20,466	21,791
III	10,726	11,195	13,041	13,050	13,839	14,155	14,778	16,691	18,299	18,749	18,392	18,497	20,460
IV	11,989	11,391	12,356	13,488	13,801	15,030	15,087	15,988	17,296	18,210	19,545	19,573	19,008

[a]During the period January 1951-September 1953 the data cover only three companies.

TABLE C-8

Characteristics of Conventional Mortgage Loans on Residential (1-4 Family)
Properties by Four Life Insurance Companies, 1951-63, South

	1951	1952	1953	1954	1955	1956	1957	1958	1959	1960	1961	1962	1963
							Gross Yield[a]						
I	4.36	4.54	4.55	4.84	4.80	4.83	5.43	5.72	5.60	6.05	5.95	5.76	5.57
II	4.41	4.56	4.64	4.79	4.76	4.82	5.49	5.58	5.69	6.09	5.83	5.77	5.55
III	4.59	4.57	4.83	4.75	4.80	4.98	5.50	5.43	5.78	6.08	5.76	5.70	5.52
IV	4.58	4.55	4.85	4.72	4.85	5.16	5.68	5.49	5.93	6.03	5.74	5.68	5.53
						Standard Deviation - Gross Yield							
I				0.138	0.190	0.187	0.248	0.283	0.276	0.170	0.163	0.137	0.137
II				0.145	0.182	0.229	0.203	0.162	0.173	0.253	0.131	0.108	0.148
III				0.162	0.217	0.242	0.162	0.219	0.163	0.149	0.122	0.144	0.129
IV			0.163	0.158	0.213	0.285	0.156	0.254	0.168	0.090	0.143	0.143	0.309
							Contract Rate						
I	4.54	4.71	4.73	4.98	4.90	4.94	5.49	5.75	5.64	6.06	5.96	5.77	5.60
II	4.57	4.72	4.80	4.93	4.87	4.93	5.53	5.62	5.73	6.09	5.84	5.78	5.58
III	4.73	4.72	4.99	4.90	4.90	5.07	5.56	5.47	5.80	6.07	5.77	5.73	5.54
IV	4.74	4.73	5.00	4.85	4.96	5.23	5.75	5.53	5.94	6.02	5.75	5.72	5.54
							Net Discount						
I				-0.86	-0.65	-0.66	-0.38	-0.23	-0.27	-0.05	-0.07	-0.08	-0.19
II				-0.88	-0.69	-0.66	-0.27	-0.22	-0.28	0.01	-0.10	-0.10	-0.20
III				-0.89	-0.63	-0.61	-0.40	-0.27	-0.15	0.04	-0.07	-0.19	-0.12
IV			-0.88	-0.80	-0.67	-0.45	-0.40	-0.25	-0.05	0.01	-0.08	-0.26	-0.07

(continued)

TABLE C-8 (continued)

	1951	1952	1953	1954	1955	1956	1957	1958	1959	1960	1961	1962	1963
Loan-Value Ratio													
I	63.3	62.9	65.4	63.9	67.1	65.9	67.9	68.7	68.5	70.9	70.4	69.5	70.8
II	64.0	62.2	65.3	64.8	67.0	66.5	66.2	68.2	68.5	69.8	70.0	71.2	70.3
III	62.6	63.7	65.0	66.5	66.9	66.2	65.9	68.5	70.5	71.1	70.3	70.1	70.4
IV	63.8	64.6	64.9	65.7	67.8	66.6	68.5	67.4	70.9	70.8	70.2	71.1	70.1
Maturity (months)													
I	215.6	224.9	222.9	228.1	245.1	253.5	259.3	270.5	280.2	284.4	285.1	301.2	308.9
II	220.0	226.6	225.5	231.0	249.3	252.4	257.0	271.5	280.0	280.9	284.0	307.2	304.2
III	213.4	223.6	222.5	238.1	252.5	246.2	260.3	273.2	283.7	285.3	289.7	304.2	312.0
IV	219.9	223.1	223.6	241.1	251.8	260.6	265.8	277.4	286.9	285.3	298.8	306.3	315.4
Number of Loans													
I	259	391	335	395	238	365	297	303	356	385	341	308	319
II	319	456	324	431	286	355	294	357	389	313	331	329	275
III	359	411	350	368	362	276	311	396	358	320	325	299	332
IV	306	366	396	327	360	286	280	327	344	360	336	320	301
Mean Loan Size													
I	10,944	10,867	12,092	11,916	13,085	13,597	14,829	15,346	16,196	17,059	17,373	17,733	19,060
II	11,107	10,605	12,217	12,550	13,763	13,967	14,937	15,952	16,196	15,784	17,065	17,512	18,066
III	10,815	11,105	12,066	12,405	13,485	14,130	14,671	15,822	17,344	17,537	17,243	18,254	18,012
IV	10,855	11,460	12,229	12,988	13,889	14,410	15,728	15,477	16,515	16,653	17,219	18,685	18,234

[a]During the period January 1951-September 1953 the data cover only three companies.

TABLE C-9

Characteristics of Conventional Mortgage Loans on Residential (1-4 Family)
Properties by Four Life Insurance Companies, 1951-63, North Central

	1951	1952	1953	1954	1955	1956	1957	1958	1959	1960	1961	1962	1963
Gross Yield[a]													
I	4.31	4.49	4.56	4.82	4.73	4.81	5.39	5.66	5.64	6.03	5.97	5.77	5.57
II	4.40	4.55	4.62	4.77	4.71	4.85	5.51	5.56	5.68	6.04	5.81	5.74	5.51
III	4.49	4.57	4.77	4.73	4.76	4.90	5.50	5.44	5.76	6.05	5.76	5.64	5.49
IV	4.48	4.47	4.82	4.70	4.82	5.12	5.64	5.47	5.91	6.00	5.74	5.63	5.49
Standard Deviation - Gross Yield													
I				0.133	0.213	0.172	0.275	0.160	0.191	0.142	0.132	0.123	0.171
II				0.146	0.210	0.146	0.170	0.160	0.155	0.177	0.149	0.118	0.152
III				0.193	0.219	0.160	0.176	0.214	0.158	0.105	0.141	0.152	0.156
IV			0.110	0.199	0.173	0.256	0.168	0.203	0.167	0.140	0.135	0.131	0.168
Contract Rate													
I	4.52	4.64	4.70	4.95	4.83	4.93	5.45	5.72	5.68	6.04	5.98	5.78	5.60
II	4.53	4.73	4.74	4.87	4.83	4.96	5.55	5.60	5.71	6.04	5.82	5.75	5.52
III	4.66	4.71	4.88	4.85	4.86	5.01	5.54	5.47	5.77	6.05	5.76	5.67	5.50
IV	4.65	4.64	4.95	4.81	4.93	5.18	5.68	5.53	5.93	6.00	5.75	5.66	5.49
Net Discount													
I				-0.72	-0.64	-0.74	-0.35	-0.40	-0.26	-0.07	-0.08	-0.07	-0.19
II				-0.63	-0.76	-0.69	-0.21	-0.24	-0.19	0.04	-0.09	-0.07	-0.07
III				-0.72	-0.64	-0.66	-0.25	-0.18	-0.08	-0.02	-0.06	-0.19	-0.07
IV			-0.79	-0.68	-0.73	-0.42	-0.26	-0.36	-0.16	-0.02	-0.05	-0.23	-0.01

(continued)

TABLE C-9 (continued)

	1951	1952	1953	1954	1955	1956	1957	1958	1959	1960	1961	1962	1963
Loan-Value Ratio													
I	62.0	60.9	63.3	61.7	63.3	63.0	64.5	65.1	67.1	68.3	69.6	68.9	70.0
II	62.8	61.5	63.0	63.0	63.4	64.3	63.7	65.5	67.2	68.9	68.8	69.9	69.7
III	60.9	61.8	61.8	62.7	63.6	63.3	63.3	65.4	68.1	69.7	69.4	69.7	69.8
IV	60.9	62.2	62.2	62.4	63.4	64.1	64.6	66.5	67.9	68.3	69.2	69.5	70.2
Maturity (months)													
I	219.5	222.9	222.8	222.5	242.8	243.7	250.3	266.2	273.0	280.8	279.3	293.6	303.5
II	214.8	223.2	225.4	223.3	242.4	251.7	254.5	270.3	276.3	285.7	281.2	305.0	307.9
III	221.0	221.8	224.5	235.8	241.2	244.6	256.8	271.0	277.7	282.9	281.8	304.0	310.6
IV	221.9	223.6	221.2	243.9	245.4	251.2	261.5	273.3	280.6	281.5	286.2	300.8	310.3
Number of Loans													
I	148	199	204	204	237	359	278	296	258	297	287	293	266
II	192	236	239	272	280	285	336	310	287	338	350	300	303
III	197	237	222	246	385	317	306	327	282	346	362	336	323
IV	196	216	250	252	365	318	312	320	331	308	345	288	265
Mean Loan Size													
I	9,381	11,045	11,513	12,170	13,331	12,776	14,064	15,032	15,887	16,219	16,714	16,682	17,118
II	10,148	10,169	11,004	12,879	12,774	13,808	13,929	14,703	15,681	15,298	16,817	17,051	17,531
III	10,149	11,013	11,341	11,948	12,907	13,330	14,467	14,730	15,530	15,717	16,643	17,643	17,291
IV	9,954	10,523	11,289	12,807	12,966	13,481	14,101	15,236	16,446	15,569	16,546	17,489	17,270

[a]During the period January 1951-September 1953 the data cover only three companies.

TABLE C-10

Characteristics of Conventional Mortgage Loans on Residential (1-4 Family)
Properties by Four Life Insurance Companies, 1951-63, West

	1951	1952	1953	1954	1955	1956	1957	1958	1959	1960	1961	1962	1963
Gross Yield[a]													
I	4.45	4.51	4.66	4.91	4.82	4.81	5.41	5.71	5.63	6.10	6.04	5.79	5.65
II	4.48	4.68	4.70	4.87	4.82	4.82	5.63	5.64	5.70	6.17	5.92	5.78	5.54
III	4.54	4.84	4.87	4.83	4.80	4.94	5.57	5.52	5.79	6.22	5.90	5.69	5.52
IV	4.54	4.63	4.97	4.81	4.81	5.18	5.67	5.49	5.97	6.15	5.79	5.68	5.51
Standard Deviation - Gross Yield													
I				0.196	0.132	0.128	0.242	0.151	0.210	0.268	0.148	0.144	0.213
II				0.188	0.129	0.133	0.203	0.173	0.127	0.220	0.124	0.152	0.173
III			0.233	0.165	0.110	0.213	0.190	0.165	0.162	0.157	0.117	0.136	0.132
IV				0.144	0.122	0.238	0.182	0.207	0.202	0.126	0.173	0.118	0.147
Contract Rate													
I	4.57	4.76	4.92	5.09	5.00	5.01	5.51	5.83	5.72	6.18	6.11	5.86	5.70
II	4.61	4.88	4.92	5.06	5.00	5.00	5.69	5.73	5.80	6.25	6.01	5.87	5.61
III	4.70	4.95	5.13	5.02	4.99	5.13	5.65	5.62	5.86	6.28	5.98	5.78	5.59
IV	4.79	4.89	5.14	5.00	5.00	5.33	5.78	5.59	6.04	6.22	5.87	5.77	5.57
Net Discount													
I				-1.09	-1.14	-1.18	-0.59	-0.75	-0.54	-0.46	-0.44	-0.45	-0.30
II				-1.12	-1.16	-1.14	-0.33	-0.55	-0.64	-0.53	-0.54	-0.55	-0.44
III				-1.18	-1.16	-1.18	-0.51	-0.60	-0.44	-0.41	-0.50	-0.56	-0.44
IV			-1.05	-1.16	-1.17	-0.92	-0.66	-0.57	-0.41	-0.45	-0.46	-0.59	-0.38

(continued)

TABLE C-10 (continued)

	1951	1952	1953	1954	1955	1956	1957	1958	1959	1960	1961	1962	1963
						Loan-Value Ratio							
I	63.2	61.7	63.9	63.5	64.1	64.1	64.3	64.8	65.8	69.6	69.6	69.0	70.6
II	62.4	61.8	64.1	64.4	64.1	64.5	63.9	64.8	65.7	70.1	69.9	69.8	69.6
III	62.1	62.9	64.5	64.1	64.4	64.3	63.8	65.5	69.3	69.6	70.5	70.0	70.3
IV	62.6	63.2	63.9	64.4	64.1	64.0	63.9	65.3	69.6	70.1	70.4	69.2	70.6
						Maturity (months)							
I	209.1	219.0	217.2	221.6	226.6	235.6	236.1	244.0	273.7	285.2	286.5	294.0	312.4
II	207.3	209.7	221.6	226.3	233.9	238.8	245.1	251.6	273.8	286.0	291.8	305.9	307.9
III	215.0	213.0	225.5	230.7	236.4	236.4	242.0	255.4	281.8	283.1	292.2	306.5	310.2
IV	218.2	212.2	216.1	230.0	235.8	233.8	242.1	268.8	281.6	287.5	295.8	311.0	315.6
						Number of Loans							
I	289	340	339	371	288	341	246	326	264	278	334	333	331
II	389	333	345	381	282	407	261	257	304	298	314	318	309
III	305	321	361	369	307	341	294	274	311	297	250	323	314
IV	331	310	372	307	326	296	329	218	306	246	270	330	296
						Mean Loan Size							
I	10,299	10,478	10,690	11,887	12,197	13,768	14,857	14,853	17,714	18,305	18,690	18,911	21,313
II	10,134	10,677	11,596	11,709	13,033	14,177	14,530	16,159	17,775	18,503	18,937	20,088	19,514
III	10,269	10,500	10,861	12,194	13,124	13,992	14,360	16,056	18,428	17,560	19,350	20,014	20,091
IV	10,535	11,195	11,538	12,519	13,173	14,217	14,786	17,177	17,940	18,133	19,343	19,901	21,378

[a]During the period January 1951-September 1953 the data cover only three companies.

TABLE C-11

Characteristics of FHA Mortgage Loans on Residential (1-4 Family) Properties by Four Life Insurance Companies, 1951-63, East

	1951	1952	1953	1954	1955	1956	1957	1958	1959	1960	1961	1962	1963
Gross Yield													
I	4.04	4.19	4.22	4.64	4.49	4.54	5.03	5.42	5.38	6.06	5.88	5.55	5.42
II	4.08	4.24	4.28	4.58	4.50	4.53	5.23	5.40	5.42	6.06	5.72	5.54	5.39
III	4.18	4.25	4.55	4.50	4.51	4.61	5.25	5.33	5.51	6.06	5.62	5.49	5.36
IV	4.18	4.19	4.64	4.50	4.52	4.64	5.39	5.35	5.81	6.05[a]	5.55	5.49	5.34
Standard Deviation - Gross Yield													
I	0.087	0.096	0.074	0.116	0.096	0.154	0.228	0.077	0.094	0.130	0.150	0.109	0.165
II	0.086	0.048	0.151	0.199	0.112	0.116	0.124	0.070	0.131	0.352	0.137	0.096	0.103
III	0.150	0.180	0.173	0.074	0.089	0.139	0.133	0.093	0.140	0.104	0.121	0.120	0.113
IV	0.120	0.081	0.144	0.064	0.107	0.154	0.094	0.103	0.251	0.259	0.089	0.111	0.103
Contract Rates													
I	4.25	4.26	4.25	4.50	4.49	4.47	4.91	5.25	5.25	5.75	5.69	5.26	5.26
II	4.26	4.25	4.32	4.45	4.48	4.49	4.99	5.25	5.25	5.71	5.54	5.25	5.26
III	4.25	4.25	4.47	4.50	4.49	4.50	5.08	5.25	5.25	5.75	5.36	5.25	5.26
IV	4.25	4.25	4.49	4.50	4.49	4.51	5.25	5.25	5.52	5.72	5.29	5.26	5.25
Net Discount													
I	-1.36	-0.48	-0.19	0.95	0.02	0.44	0.78	1.14	0.83	2.00	1.24	1.91	1.06
II	-1.18	-0.05	-0.26	0.83	0.13	0.29	1.59	1.02	1.09	2.28	1.24	1.94	0.86
III	-0.51	-0.02	0.52	-0.03	0.17	0.70	1.12	0.52	1.70	2.08	1.73	1.56	0.69
IV	-0.48	-0.41	1.04	-0.01	0.24	0.87	0.90	0.64	1.92	2.14[a]	1.73	1.54	0.60

(continued)

TABLE C-11 (continued)

	1951	1952	1953	1954	1955	1956	1957	1958	1959	1960	1961	1962	1963
Loan-Value Ratio													
I	84.9	82.2	80.9	80.7	85.8	83.6	83.1	89.6	90.7	90.6	93.8	92.5	92.4
II	77.5	82.1	80.1	81.1	86.9	82.3	84.1	89.2	91.9	91.6	92.6	92.6	91.1
III	77.6	81.6	81.1	79.5	86.4	85.3	85.4	91.2	92.3	92.9	90.1	92.2	83.2
IV	79.8	81.2	80.2	85.4	85.7	83.2	90.0	91.1	90.5	92.1	91.3	93.3	93.3
Maturity (months)													
I	256.3	266.4	257.6	262.6	334.4	307.3	309.8	317.9	337.6	343.7	347.7	349.4	344.3
II	266.3	267.1	257.9	270.3	336.5	305.9	324.1	337.4	326.7	341.6	343.4	353.8	354.3
III	262.0	256.4	271.1	289.0	338.2	320.6	316.2	338.8	345.0	346.3	344.4	342.0	343.3
IV	264.5	259.6	272.4	322.4	325.8	317.6	321.2	318.1	338.0	327.5	348.9	345.4	340.7
Number of Loans													
I	63	126	83	104	91	132	114	148	105	41	60	61	53
II	40	92	127	56	139	86	107	145	124	75	84	62	52
III	50	73	104	56	98	109	116	90	85	46	70	55	45
IV	43	85	137	52	151	125	105	59	53	84	53	62	39
Mean Loan Size													
I	7,617	8,129	8,899	9,937	11,260	10,743	11,577	12,708	13,840	14,473	14,516	14,402	14,529
II	8,484	7,986	9,069	9,309	10,305	11,158	12,029	13,239	13,385	14,229	14,701	13,635	14,191
III	8,044	7,873	9,410	9,726	11,185	11,251	12,303	13,596	14,036	14,760	14,412	14,460	13,891
IV	8,271	8,987	9,652	10,732	11,120	11,556	12,479	13,126	13,257	13,725	14,684	14,474	14,666

[a]Data covers only three companies.

TABLE C-12

Characteristics of FHA Mortgage Loans on Residential (1-4 Family)
Properties by Four Life Insurance Companies, 1951-63, South

	1951	1952	1953	1954	1955	1956	1957	1958	1959	1960	1961	1962	1963
Gross Yield													
I	4.09	4.22	4.25	4.72	4.62	4.65	5.29	5.62	5.67	6.28	6.09	5.78	5.62
II	4.14	4.25	4.35	4.63	4.60	4.77	5.36	5.56	5.71	6.27	5.95	5.77	5.53
III	4.22	4.26	4.59	4.58	4.63	4.79	5.45	5.49	5.81	6.27	5.80	5.72	5.52
IV	4.24	4.24	4.71	4.60	4.69	4.87	5.60	5.57	6.09[a]	6.23[a]	5.78	5.70	5.51
Standard Deviation - Gross Yield													
I	0.077	0.066	0.067	0.144	0.123	0.252	0.226	0.129	0.154	0.156	0.160	0.100	0.126
II	0.089	0.051	0.147	0.179	0.191	0.134	0.124	0.112	0.142	0.152	0.153	0.108	0.141
III	0.092	0.085	0.130	0.133	0.183	0.155	0.148	0.099	0.176	0.121	0.178	0.125	0.103
IV	0.085	0.084	0.157	0.109	0.134	0.130	0.108	0.138	0.334	0.234	0.138	0.094	0.152
Contract Rate													
I	4.25	4.25	4.25	4.50	4.50	4.42	4.94	5.25	5.25	5.73	5.70	5.26	5.26
II	4.25	4.25	4.33	4.47	4.46	4.49	4.99	5.25	5.25	5.75	5.58	5.25	5.25
III	4.25	4.25	4.49	4.50	4.47	4.48	5.08	5.25	5.24	5.75	5.36	5.25	5.25
IV	4.25	4.25	4.49	4.50	4.50	4.51	5.25	5.25	5.53	5.73	5.29	5.25	5.25
Net Discount													
I	-1.06	-0.18	-0.01	1.41	0.79	1.52	2.28	2.41	2.74	3.60	2.55	3.43	2.40
II	-0.72	0.01	0.14	1.06	0.92	1.86	2.40	2.03	3.07	3.44	2.45	3.44	1.88
III	-0.19	0.05	0.68	0.55	1.05	2.11	2.42	1.60	3.72	3.41	2.89	3.11	1.77
IV	-0.08	-0.07	1.38	0.70	1.32	2.41	2.32	2.13	3.67[a]	3.25[a]	3.27	2.95	1.73

(continued)

TABLE C-12 (continued)

	1951	1952	1953	1954	1955	1956	1957	1958	1959	1960	1961	1962	1963
						Loan-Value Ratio							
I	83.1	82.0	83.4	82.3	86.9	85.9	84.3	90.9	92.4	92.7	92.9	94.2	94.6
II	83.6	82.0	83.1	82.7	87.6	85.1	85.0	91.5	92.5	92.0	93.3	93.3	93.9
III	80.8	82.0	83.4	82.6	87.4	85.5	87.1	91.7	92.6	93.6	93.3	93.8	94.2
IV	81.9	82.3	83.3	86.2	86.8	85.0	89.7	91.7	93.0	93.0	93.8	94.4	93.7
						Maturity (months)							
I	258.0	251.0	254.4	262.2	301.7	294.7	294.4	307.9	329.5	338.8	340.9	349.1	358.9
II	248.0	248.4	251.9	265.5	305.2	298.7	303.4	320.1	335.4	349.0	347.7	352.3	357.2
III	242.3	249.9	258.3	274.2	301.6	308.4	299.9	327.8	338.7	341.9	346.6	352.7	354.8
IV	250.7	252.2	261.7	288.9	297.9	299.3	301.8	330.5	343.7	341.8	350.1	354.9	357.6
						Number of Loans							
I	393	558	610	551	461	492	397	599	614	413	571	507	586
II	469	573	537	535	576	454	523	660	707	454	671	606	532
III	512	682	515	510	632	365	481	701	613	448	571	615	514
IV	588	589	533	507	588	446	499	535	648	471	571	528	456
						Mean Loan Size							
I	7,996	8,492	8,583	9,306	10,483	10,869	11,385	12,700	13,399	13,914	14,257	15,004	13,782
II	8,140	8,338	8,860	9,083	10,189	11,194	11,700	12,954	13,271	14,554	13,760	14,738	14,182
III	8,320	8,335	9,074	9,561	10,832	11,824	12,159	13,374	13,673	13,849	14,061	14,386	14,412
IV	8,287	8,550	9,121	10,087	11,228	11,486	13,100	13,468	13,571	14,298	14,376	14,130	14,392

[a]Data covers only three companies.

TABLE C-13

Characteristics of FHA Mortgage Loans on Residential (1-4 Family)
Properties by Four Life Insurance Companies, 1951-63, North Central

	1951	1952	1953	1954	1955	1956	1957	1958	1959	1960	1961	1962	1963
						Gross Yield							
I	4.09	4.23	4.28	4.68	4.59	4.69	5.31	5.63	5.74	6.24	6.15	5.75	5.60
II	4.12	4.25	4.38	4.63	4.60	4.76	5.38	5.56	5.78	6.27[a]	5.94	5.74	5.51
III	4.23	4.27	4.55	4.65	4.64	4.79	5.45	5.47	5.85[a]	6.25	5.80	5.69	5.48
IV	4.23	4.26	4.70	4.60	4.70	4.90	5.62	5.55	6.15	6.24	5.76	5.67	5.47
						Standard Deviation - Gross Yield							
I	0.108	0.102	0.070	0.131	0.101	0.199	0.227	0.105	0.129	0.221	0.119	0.092	0.112
II	0.093	0.088	0.149	0.151	0.155	0.136	0.114	0.107	0.110	0.181	0.127	0.077	0.134
III	0.117	0.070	0.127	0.145	0.168	0.162	0.132	0.106	0.128	0.123	0.113	0.091	0.105
IV	0.118	0.124	0.135	0.106	0.192	0.146	0.099	0.127	0.192	0.111	0.110	0.157	0.144
						Contract Rate							
I	4.26	4.25	4.25	4.50	4.50	4.47	4.94	5.25	5.25	5.73	5.70	5.26	5.25
II	4.25	4.25	4.34	4.49	4.48	4.50	5.00	5.25	5.25	5.74	5.54	5.25	5.25
III	4.27	4.25	4.49	4.50	4.48	4.48	5.07	5.25	5.25	5.75	5.34	5.25	5.25
IV	4.25	4.24	4.50	4.50	4.48	4.51	5.24	5.25	5.62	5.75	5.29	5.25	5.25
						Net Discount							
I	-1.11	-0.12	0.20	1.16	0.62	1.51	2.45	2.49	3.25	3.37	2.90	3.24	2.35
II	-0.88	0.04	0.22	0.95	0.81	1.74	2.52	2.06	3.52	3.43[a]	2.59	3.24	1.75
III	0.27	0.11	0.44	1.02	1.07	2.07	2.52	1.47	4.00[a]	3.31	3.07	2.88	1.55
IV	-0.12	0.17	1.33	0.65	1.42	2.64	2.47	1.95	3.49	3.21	3.11	2.82	1.43

(continued)

TABLE C-13 (continued)

	1951	1952	1953	1954	1955	1956	1957	1958	1959	1960	1961	1962	1963
						Loan-Value Ratio							
I	81.3	79.9	79.6	79.4	84.2	83.6	82.1	88.3	91.4	92.0	91.2	93.4	93.1
II	80.4	80.1	80.4	80.3	84.8	83.2	82.9	89.1	91.5	91.8	92.3	93.6	93.6
III	80.4	79.9	80.0	81.3	85.0	83.0	84.4	90.6	91.8	93.2	92.7	93.4	93.6
IV	80.3	80.8	79.1	83.8	84.4	82.3	86.6	90.1	92.1	91.9	93.2	92.7	93.5
						Maturity (months)							
I	265.5	248.1	248.7	259.7	300.7	289.5	293.3	307.4	334.3	339.2	340.0	345.8	345.9
II	252.0	247.3	247.2	276.6	303.9	292.3	302.8	316.0	336.5	342.5	342.9	344.6	351.7
III	246.2	245.8	254.5	285.7	298.9	294.9	300.7	329.5	340.5	339.7	342.2	346.2	350.4
IV	247.0	260.2	263.7	297.8	298.8	296.7	305.3	329.2	337.6	343.2	340.2	351.9	353.3
						Number of Loans							
I	243	348	353	278	513	411	253	383	438	364	280	260	292
II	369	386	301	367	494	351	280	358	424	400	375	338	296
III	399	404	410	342	446	305	390	381	387	378	337	388	358
IV	419	405	287	448	482	389	318	362	345	341	298	338	505
						Mean Loan Size							
I	7,999	8,729	9,370	10,403	11,408	11,673	12,503	13,623	13,854	14,123	14,127	14,670	14,719
II	8,437	8,977	9,726	10,575	11,639	11,750	12,977	13,654	13,989	14,227	14,334	14,743	14,793
III	8,678	9,114	9,925	10,478	11,402	11,907	13,429	13,888	14,017	14,144	14,541	14,798	14,799
IV	8,680	9,170	10,215	11,429	11,670	12,528	13,657	14,021	13,991	14,087	14,702	14,653	14,805

[a]Data cover only three companies.

TABLE C-14

Characteristics of FHA Mortgage Loans on Residential (1-4 Family)
Properties by Four Life Insurance Companies, 1951-63, West

	1951	1952	1953	1954	1955	1956	1957	1958	1959	1960	1961	1962	1963
	Gross Yield												
I	4.13	4.21	4.26	4.65	4.63	4.70	5.28	5.67	5.73	6.28	6.16	5.82	5.64
II	4.16	4.24	4.37	4.62	4.62	4.72	5.40	5.62	5.76	6.29	5.98	5.82	5.56
III	4.22	4.26	4.55	4.62	4.67	4.72	5.48	5.53	5.86	6.28	5.85	5.77	5.52
IV	4.18	4.25	4.67	4.58	4.72	4.90	5.59	5.56	6.17a	6.28a	5.82	5.71	5.50
	Standard Deviation - Gross Yield												
I	0.109	0.093	0.061	0.136	0.124	0.215	0.171	0.108	0.138	0.091	0.136	0.047	0.129
II	0.104	0.035	0.152	0.163	0.176	0.133	0.094	0.097	0.140	0.103	0.135	0.065	0.087
III	0.099	0.110	0.103	0.115	0.141	0.172	0.132	0.103	0.113	0.051	0.178	0.093	0.093
IV	0.088	0.046	0.182	0.106	0.125	0.131	0.077	0.152	0.216	0.177	0.074	0.095	0.094
	Contract Rate												
I	4.28	4.25	4.25	4.50	4.50	4.45	4.94	5.25	5.25	5.74	5.71	5.27	5.24
II	4.27	4.25	4.35	4.47	4.46	4.49	5.00	5.25	5.25	5.74	5.58	5.25	5.25
III	4.26	4.26	4.49	4.50	4.48	4.49	5.09	5.25	5.25	5.75	5.40	5.25	5.25
IV	4.25	4.25	4.48	4.50	4.49	4.51	5.25	5.25	5.60	5.74	5.30	5.26	5.25
	Net Discount												
I	-1.00	-0.26	0.04	0.96	0.86	1.62	2.24	2.70	3.17	3.54	2.94	3.67	2.63
II	-0.73	-0.03	0.19	1.00	1.09	1.55	2.65	2.46	3.41	3.56	2.64	3.75	2.03
III	-0.25	0.01	0.38	0.79	1.26	1.56	2.53	1.87	4.06	3.49	3.02	3.43	1.80
IV	-0.44	0.04	1.18	0.52	1.53	2.61	2.24	2.07	3.76a	3.52a	3.40	2.96	1.66

(continued

TABLE C-14 (continued)

	1951	1952	1953	1954	1955	1956	1957	1958	1959	1960	1961	1962	1963
						Loan-Value Ratio							
I	82.8	81.0	82.7	80.5	86.2	84.7	84.5	90.3	92.6	91.8	92.9	94.2	94.1
II	81.5	80.0	82.4	81.4	86.7	83.8	85.0	91.3	93.0	91.8	92.5	94.2	94.1
III	79.2	80.7	80.6	82.5	86.4	84.3	87.4	91.9	92.9	92.8	93.5	93.7	93.7
IV	79.1	80.4	81.5	85.1	85.8	82.7	88.5	92.2	91.3	93.3	93.4	93.9	93.7
						Maturity (months)							
I	261.2	254.7	256.6	261.8	320.0	297.6	297.2	295.8	326.2	348.8	345.7	349.2	346.5
II	254.7	250.6	256.6	270.5	321.8	301.4	303.0	311.1	328.1	347.5	347.0	347.0	348.2
III	247.4	249.1	244.2	283.3	312.6	300.7	304.6	330.7	336.0	340.3	342.7	343.4	348.8
IV	246.1	244.9	251.5	305.3	301.6	301.6	291.1	332.6	345.4	349.3	347.0	345.8	350.8
						Number of Loans							
I	262	307	325	294	304	265	232	248	246	325	389	276	350
II	385	251	248	289	223	282	218	318	235	225	424	442	297
III	254	217	207	341	239	348	222	264	259	233	267	353	398
IV	305	251	239	350	235	245	190	241	335	338	211	306	352
						Mean Loan Size							
I	7,929	8,625	9,181	9,979	11,158	11,583	11,989	12,649	13,416	15,610	14,814	15,216	14,795
II	8,282	8,827	9,100	9,917	11,260	11,592	12,400	13,282	13,291	15,616	14,865	15,234	15,153
III	8,496	8,997	9,954	10,054	10,916	11,523	12,672	13,592	13,696	14,936	14,481	14,936	14,769
IV	8,824	8,847	9,935	10,885	11,179	12,290	13,056	13,448	15,219	14,933	14,956	14,928	14,971

[a]Data cover only three companies.

TABLE C-15

Characteristics of Conventional Mortgage Loans on Residential (1-4 Family)
Properties by Four Life Insurance Companies, 1951-63, New England

	1951	1952	1953	1954	1955	1956	1957	1958	1959	1960	1961	1962	1963
Gross Yield[a]													
I	4.17	4.46	4.45	4.60	4.27	4.36	4.97	5.40	5.23	5.76	5.77	5.62	5.49
II	4.20	4.53	4.38	4.49	4.32	4.35	5.09	5.37	5.34	5.92	5.61	5.61	5.50
III	4.35	4.40	4.79	4.39	4.28	4.45	5.14	5.19	5.38	5.91	5.64	5.63	5.42
IV	4.43	4.29	4.54	4.37	4.34	4.64	5.34	5.20	5.62	5.82	5.66	5.59	5.40
Standard Deviation - Gross Yield													
I				0.235	0.210	0.335	0.484	0.371	0.402	0.429	0.317	0.238	0.250
II				0.247	0.283	0.237	0.313	0.340	0.349	0.266	0.309	0.358	0.191
III				0.197	0.381	0.273	0.239	0.440	0.359	0.246	0.280	0.233	0.248
IV			0.279	0.172	0.310	0.342	0.321	0.310	0.488	0.335	0.301	0.266	0.224
Contract Rate													
I	4.25	4.31	4.53	4.75	4.40	4.48	5.06	5.48	5.26	5.78	5.81	5.64	5.54
II	4.32	4.37	4.45	4.63	4.43	4.46	5.20	5.42	5.36	5.93	5.63	5.63	5.59
III	4.34	4.35	4.56	4.50	4.41	4.57	5.25	5.24	5.41	5.93	5.66	5.68	5.46
IV	4.48	4.38	4.67	4.49	4.48	4.77	5.44	5.23	5.64	5.84	5.67	5.64	5.43
Net Discount													
I				-0.89	-0.84	-0.77	-0.58	-0.56	-0.19	-0.13	-0.23	-0.12	-0.35
II				-0.84	-0.74	-0.68	-0.69	-0.33	-0.11	-0.05	-0.12	-0.11	-0.59
III				-0.71	-0.82	-0.69	-0.70	-0.36	-0.17	-0.10	-0.08	-0.33	-0.28
IV			-0.80	-0.78	-0.84	-0.80	-0.60	-0.18	-0.16	-0.16	-0.08	-0.35	-0.21

(continued)

TABLE C-15 (continued)

	1951	1952	1953	1954	1955	1956	1957	1958	1959	1960	1961	1962	1963
Loan-Value Ratio													
I	62.6	59.0	62.7	62.9	62.7	61.3	62.7	65.7	63.3	64.3	68.1	69.5	69.7
II	61.9	55.5	61.8	64.0	61.7	59.8	63.9	62.6	66.4	66.0	65.4	68.2	71.5
III	59.1	59.7	60.8	64.3	61.9	62.8	61.7	66.6	67.6	70.8	67.2	71.9	72.0
IV	60.3	62.6	64.1	65.1	60.6	61.1	64.6	64.4	67.6	70.5	69.5	70.8	68.7
Maturity (months)													
I	225.1	227.0	225.1	215.5	247.8	237.0	261.7	253.1	265.6	282.5	262.4	284.4	277.6
II	226.8	232.5	222.1	218.7	245.0	238.4	257.0	250.6	275.6	273.0	281.2	283.1	309.1
III	231.3	216.7	229.9	245.3	236.7	232.1	262.5	266.4	276.5	276.7	291.1	315.8	299.8
IV	220.9	226.3	235.3	266.7	238.6	253.3	263.0	267.9	261.6	279.3	277.7	303.8	319.9
Number of Loans													
I	45	31	37	23	33	35	44	32	53	22	15	40	30
II	35	32	53	37	26	36	48	38	49	25	24	30	24
III	68	24	25	35	36	47	38	32	43	21	29	27	20
IV	34	19	27	38	30	50	44	45	29	26	24	31	27
Mean Loan Size													
I	10,759	11,739	11,858	11,524	13,226	13,536	15,814	16,865	16,504	15,550	23,107	18,611	21,988
II	11,275	11,195	11,351	12,437	12,476	12,238	15,475	15,124	18,692	20,468	19,007	21,729	22,397
III	10,839	11,738	12,463	12,290	14,138	15,995	17,970	16,949	19,583	22,167	21,127	22,240	20,495
IV	10,455	10,451	12,706	12,752	12,083	15,381	15,773	16,778	18,517	18,983	21,458	19,900	21,606

[a]During the period January 1951–September 1953 the data cover only three companies.

TABLE C-16

Characteristics of Conventional Mortgage Loans on Residential (1-4 Family)
Properties by Four Life Insurance Companies, 1951-63, Middle Atlantic

	1951	1952	1953	1954	1955	1956	1957	1958	1959	1960	1961	1962	1963
Gross Yield[a]													
I	4.21	4.37	4.43	4.81	4.58	4.75	5.21	5.55	5.44	5.92	5.88	5.72	5.49
II	4.32	4.46	4.47	4.78	4.64	4.76	5.35	5.45	5.47	5.96	5.72	5.70	5.50
III	4.40	4.49	4.67	4.68	4.65	4.79	5.39	5.35	5.52	5.97	5.69	5.63	5.52
IV	4.40	4.32	4.79	4.61	4.69	4.86	5.51	5.30	5.73	5.97	5.71	5.55	5.45
Standard Deviation - Gross Yield													
I				0.100	0.226	0.198	0.320	0.188	0.190	0.175	0.140	0.120	0.143
II				0.176	0.229	0.201	0.226	0.173	0.130	0.146	0.173	0.135	0.120
III			0.169	0.216	0.230	0.189	0.208	0.200	0.160	0.108	0.138	0.187	0.132
IV				0.232	0.190	0.172	0.167	0.206	0.187	0.115	0.128	0.148	0.189
Contract Rate													
I	4.41	4.55	4.58	4.95	4.70	4.89	5.27	5.61	5.48	5.92	5.88	5.72	5.48
II	4.51	4.62	4.61	4.87	4.74	4.87	5.38	5.50	5.50	5.96	5.72	5.70	5.50
III	4.59	4.61	4.80	4.80	4.76	4.89	5.43	5.41	5.54	5.97	5.69	5.63	5.52
IV	4.60	4.50	4.93	4.73	4.79	4.96	5.53	5.33	5.75	5.97	5.71	5.56	5.45
Net Discount													
I				-0.86	-0.74	-0.87	-0.36	-0.37	-0.23	0.00	0.01	0.00	0.02
II				-0.54	-0.63	-0.70	-0.21	-0.31	-0.14	-0.02	0.00	-0.01	0.01
III			-0.81	-0.72	-0.69	-0.60	-0.23	-0.33	-0.10	0.00	-0.01	-0.03	-0.05
IV				-0.77	-0.61	-0.60	-0.15	-0.17	-0.12	0.01	0.00	-0.03	-0.01

(continued)

TABLE C-16 (continued)

	1951	1952	1953	1954	1955	1956	1957	1958	1959	1960	1961	1962	1963
Loan-Value Ratio													
I	61.8	60.7	63.4	65.7	65.5	62.7	63.6	64.1	65.9	69.5	68.9	66.7	70.1
II	61.9	61.9	65.4	64.3	64.4	61.7	62.2	65.4	67.6	68.2	68.5	69.5	70.7
III	60.8	63.1	63.6	62.5	63.5	61.5	60.6	65.6	67.1	69.5	67.6	67.7	69.2
IV	61.5	64.1	64.4	62.3	62.3	62.9	63.8	67.4	68.9	69.0	67.6	67.3	65.5
Maturity (months)													
I	220.2	222.9	229.6	230.2	258.1	252.2	259.6	257.7	270.3	286.0	286.8	303.9	310.4
II	218.6	227.1	230.9	224.7	252.4	237.3	243.0	260.4	283.1	288.7	287.0	307.5	324.1
III	219.6	228.2	228.3	237.9	258.7	243.3	251.0	258.2	275.4	290.4	291.4	302.0	314.6
IV	218.9	227.1	223.9	244.9	243.2	264.2	259.0	278.8	284.3	287.1	302.3	319.3	305.6
Number of Loans													
I	95	130	125	113	128	116	129	120	152	137	116	139	91
II	119	218	173	150	161	131	173	119	139	142	138	135	111
III	135	171	153	152	115	140	150	99	143	144	169	139	104
IV	116	173	126	131	132	139	117	157	150	126	144	110	126
Mean Loan Size													
I	10,965	11,387	12,411	12,677	14,378	15,247	14,580	15,332	15,870	17,564	18,330	19,562	20,078
II	11,540	10,276	12,358	12,708	12,651	14,041	13,351	15,016	16,655	18,329	19,031	20,138	21,657
III	10,696	11,119	13,130	13,260	13,717	13,573	13,832	16,616	17,969	18,142	17,878	17,670	20,453
IV	12,285	11,476	12,284	13,759	14,278	14,928	14,855	15,825	17,063	18,011	19,226	19,478	18,387

[a]During the period January 1951-September 1953 the data cover only three companies.

TABLE C-17

Characteristics of Conventional Mortgage Loans on Residential (1-4 Family)
Properties by Four Life Insurance Companies, 1951-63, South Atlantic

	1951	1952	1953	1954	1955	1956	1957	1958	1959	1960	1961	1962	1963
Gross Yield[a]													
I	4.37	4.54	4.55	4.78	4.70	4.75	5.32	5.68	5.47	6.00	5.90	5.72	5.56
II	4.43	4.60	4.65	4.74	4.68	4.78	5.40	5.54	5.62	6.06	5.81	5.76	5.54
III	4.55	4.59	4.76	4.72	4.72	4.86	5.44	5.36	5.71	6.03	5.74	5.69	5.51
IV	4.49	4.53	4.79	4.70	4.75	5.06	5.62	5.36	5.89	6.01	5.71	5.67	5.50
Standard Deviation - Gross Yield													
I				0.103	0.154	0.169	0.273	0.165	0.366	0.142	0.133	0.153	0.146
II				0.135	0.155	0.169	0.198	0.169	0.173	0.124	0.130	0.123	0.157
III				0.154	0.193	0.208	0.175	0.245	0.182	0.103	0.114	0.152	0.139
IV			0.122	0.159	0.207	0.237	0.140	0.255	0.144	0.073	0.158	0.143	0.266
Contract Rate													
I	4.54	4.71	4.72	4.92	4.81	4.86	5.42	5.73	5.51	6.02	5.91	5.72	5.60
II	4.59	4.72	4.78	4.86	4.81	4.89	5.45	5.57	5.67	6.05	5.83	5.77	5.58
III	4.69	4.73	4.91	4.85	4.83	4.96	5.52	5.40	5.73	6.02	5.75	5.73	5.54
IV	4.67	4.70	4.91	4.83	4.88	5.15	5.70	5.40	5.89	6.01	5.71	5.72	5.54
Net Discount													
I				-0.82	-0.64	-0.70	-0.59	-0.32	-0.24	-0.07	-0.06	0.00	-0.27
II				-0.71	-0.78	-0.66	-0.31	-0.18	-0.29	0.03	-0.13	-0.07	-0.25
III				-0.82	-0.71	-0.62	-0.48	-0.24	-0.09	0.05	-0.08	-0.21	-0.19
IV			-0.74	-0.77	-0.77	-0.57	-0.46	-0.23	-0.01	0.01	-0.05	-0.29	-0.21

(continued)

TABLE C-17 (continued)

	1951	1952	1953	1954	1955	1956	1957	1958	1959	1960	1961	1962	1963
Loan-Value Ratio													
I	60.8	60.5	62.2	60.7	64.6	64.3	66.9	68.2	66.8	70.1	71.2	68.5	71.3
II	62.2	60.1	61.2	62.3	66.2	64.8	64.6	67.6	68.8	69.5	70.4	71.7	70.2
III	61.3	62.0	63.1	64.7	64.3	64.8	65.2	67.6	69.4	71.1	70.0	70.7	70.0
IV	62.6	63.5	62.9	63.5	64.7	65.4	67.5	66.0	71.0	71.2	69.7	70.9	69.3
Maturity (months)													
I	212.9	224.3	225.7	226.9	233.1	252.9	260.1	272.7	279.0	286.1	286.3	290.9	304.3
II	219.3	227.4	227.1	230.1	244.4	250.9	260.0	269.3	282.4	283.6	285.6	303.3	298.9
III	212.9	223.6	219.6	233.6	246.3	241.9	265.8	268.9	278.4	284.2	283.8	302.5	306.5
IV	216.1	225.8	219.4	227.2	242.9	258.7	267.5	275.6	287.6	284.7	297.6	305.0	310.6
Number of Loans													
I	119	141	126	118	114	186	149	153	150	147	161	141	149
II	117	159	94	161	145	190	174	169	162	122	141	165	131
III	145	153	130	181	190	132	163	202	166	150	153	153	171
IV	119	157	133	158	172	161	160	154	162	171	156	164	160
Mean Loan Size													
I	10,138	10,853	11,214	12,171	13,408	13,332	14,596	15,801	15,923	17,260	16,803	17,610	18,805
II	10,618	10,720	11,763	12,309	13,778	13,708	14,881	15,906	16,570	15,294	16,931	17,534	17,777
III	10,683	10,650	11,841	11,656	12,607	13,530	14,864	15,857	17,107	17,862	16,903	18,309	17,436
IV	11,730	10,879	11,743	12,154	12,993	14,444	15,986	15,228	16,932	16,411	17,335	19,142	17,999

[a]During the period January 1951-September 1953 the data cover only three companies.

TABLE C-18

Characteristics of Conventional Mortgage Loans on Residential (1-4 Family) Properties by Four Life Insurance Companies, 1951-63, West South Central

	1951	1952	1953	1954	1955	1956	1957	1958	1959	1960	1961	1962	1963
Gross Yield[a]													
I	4.36	4.56	4.56	4.88	4.88	4.93	5.54	5.76	5.66	6.13	6.05	5.78	5.59
II	4.42	4.57	4.67	4.83	4.88	4.90	5.55	5.63	5.76	6.13	5.89	5.78	5.57
III	4.64	4.60	4.91	4.80	4.94	5.07	5.54	5.52	5.85	6.19	5.79	5.69	5.55
IV	4.65	4.60	4.90	4.76	4.92	5.34	5.77	5.63	6.01	6.05	5.77	5.69	5.56
Standard Deviation - Gross Yield													
I				0.153	0.189	0.169	0.160	0.417	0.155	0.185	0.191	0.126	0.132
II				0.146	0.160	0.323	0.167	0.156	0.137	0.351	0.134	0.091	0.137
III				0.161	0.212	0.222	0.130	0.146	0.129	0.162	0.120	0.147	0.137
IV			0.181	0.150	0.169	0.229	0.145	0.160	0.154	0.128	0.133	0.154	0.114
Contract Rate													
I	4.55	4.73	4.73	5.02	4.98	5.00	5.54	5.77	5.70	6.13	6.07	5.81	5.60
II	4.57	4.75	4.84	5.00	4.96	4.98	5.57	5.67	5.79	6.13	5.91	5.81	5.59
III	4.79	4.73	5.04	4.95	4.99	5.14	5.56	5.55	5.88	6.18	5.80	5.71	5.56
IV	4.79	4.78	5.05	4.88	5.00	5.38	5.79	5.66	6.03	6.06	5.78	5.71	5.57
Net Discount													
I				-0.89	-0.63	-0.45	-0.03	-0.05	-0.25	0.00	-0.11	-0.19	-0.09
II				-1.01	-0.53	-0.47	-0.10	-0.24	-0.14	0.00	-0.14	-0.15	-0.16
III				-0.92	-0.33	-0.46	-0.14	-0.23	-0.20	0.04	-0.06	-0.14	-0.08
IV			-0.95	-0.80	-0.47	-0.28	-0.13	-0.17	-0.12	-0.05	-0.08	-0.13	-0.04

(continued)

TABLE C-18 (continued)

	1951	1952	1953	1954	1955	1956	1957	1958	1959	1960	1961	1962	1963
Loan-Value Ratio													
I	65.1	64.7	67.4	66.2	69.4	69.7	69.4	69.3	70.4	71.6	69.2	69.5	71.1
II	65.3	63.9	67.6	66.9	68.4	70.1	68.8	69.0	68.9	69.5	69.5	70.5	70.7
III	63.8	64.8	66.3	68.7	70.1	67.7	67.0	70.2	71.7	71.5	71.4	68.4	71.1
IV	65.1	65.7	66.9	68.3	71.1	68.9	70.6	69.2	71.5	70.0	70.0	71.4	72.6
Maturity (months)													
I	216.7	224.9	225.4	232.4	254.5	257.0	256.9	259.8	277.8	281.5	282.3	296.8	308.4
II	219.2	226.5	226.3	233.9	259.6	255.5	244.7	267.2	277.7	275.0	286.3	303.7	305.7
III	213.4	225.4	225.7	243.3	253.7	254.9	249.7	270.9	286.5	281.8	292.2	302.0	315.9
IV	220.9	228.0	228.0	249.2	256.3	261.2	260.2	272.2	284.6	283.9	289.2	298.4	320.3
Number of Loans													
I	105	197	163	234	91	110	93	93	138	163	90	91	98
II	157	228	177	215	91	91	72	115	137	127	96	83	79
III	162	202	183	153	109	84	89	122	112	99	92	72	75
IV	147	160	215	129	122	67	82	108	126	94	106	80	68
Mean Loan Size													
I	11,863	11,188	12,675	11,979	13,043	14,431	16,250	15,504	16,633	17,206	17,814	17,704	19,886
II	11,372	10,497	12,308	12,698	13,917	15,242	16,297	16,583	16,629	15,929	17,698	17,769	18,496
III	11,140	11,309	12,266	13,159	14,568	15,532	14,499	16,430	18,313	17,067	17,592	18,163	18,477
IV	10,563	11,696	12,829	13,726	15,511	15,722	16,271	16,575	16,076	17,856	17,576	18,442	19,579

[a]During the period January 1951-September 1953 the data cover only three companies.

TABLE C-19

Characteristics of Conventional Mortgage Loans on Residential (1-4 Family) Properties by Four Life Insurance Companies, 1951-63, East South Central

	1951	1952	1953	1954	1955	1956	1957	1958	1959	1960	1961	1962	1963
Gross Yield[a]													
I	4.31	4.48	4.52	4.80	4.73	4.85	5.43	5.73	5.70	5.99	5.93	5.78	5.57
II	4.30	4.46	4.55	4.75	4.71	4.81	5.60	5.60	5.70	6.06	5.80	5.76	5.55
III	4.46	4.48	4.75	4.66	4.73	5.03	5.56	5.48	5.77	6.05	5.76	5.71	5.52
IV	4.52	4.43	4.83	4.64	4.89	5.18	5.68	5.56	5.89	6.02	5.76	5.69	5.55
Standard Deviation - Gross Yield													
I				0.094	0.103	0.167	0.252	0.103	0.190	0.096	0.112	0.106	0.118
II				0.120	0.171	0.142	0.166	0.137	0.159	0.134	0.103	0.092	0.140
III				0.130	0.161	0.234	0.155	0.182	0.101	0.137	0.129	0.128	0.095
IV			0.134	0.147	0.229	0.347	0.132	0.219	0.177	0.058	0.096	0.126	0.471
Contract Rate													
I	4.50	4.65	4.73	4.94	4.85	5.01	5.54	5.79	5.76	6.01	5.94	5.80	5.60
II	4.54	4.62	4.73	4.90	4.84	4.96	5.68	5.64	5.76	6.06	5.80	5.78	5.57
III	4.64	4.64	4.96	4.81	4.88	5.17	5.65	5.53	5.80	6.05	5.77	5.74	5.53
IV	4.73	4.58	4.99	4.78	5.03	5.24	5.81	5.62	5.89	6.01	5.78	5.75	5.51
Net Discount													
I				-0.84	-0.78	-0.98	-0.71	-0.37	-0.37	-0.10	-0.06	-0.11	-0.17
II				-0.89	-0.77	-0.98	-0.51	-0.26	-0.42	0.00	-0.02	-0.10	-0.16
III				-0.93	-0.98	-0.84	-0.61	-0.38	-0.18	0.02	-0.08	-0.19	-0.03
IV			-0.94	-0.88	-0.88	-0.37	-0.82	-0.40	-0.02	0.06	-0.12	-0.39	0.24

(continued)

TABLE C-19 (continued)

	1951	1952	1953	1954	1955	1956	1957	1958	1959	1960	1961	1962	1963
Loan-Value Ratio													
I	64.5	62.5	65.4	62.9	64.8	62.8	67.2	68.7	67.6	70.6	70.1	71.1	69.1
II	62.0	61.7	63.5	63.5	66.2	64.9	65.5	68.4	67.7	70.8	69.6	70.9	69.8
III	61.2	63.5	64.7	61.7	67.2	66.2	65.4	68.0	70.9	70.7	69.8	70.9	70.7
IV	62.4	62.8	62.8	61.7	66.9	66.2	66.8	67.9	69.5	71.0	71.4	71.3	69.4
Maturity (months)													
I	220.9	226.0	209.6	214.3	241.2	248.3	263.3	284.9	286.8	287.1	286.0	321.5	319.4
II	224.4	225.0	221.2	224.3	241.5	251.4	272.0	281.7	279.2	288.1	279.2	318.5	311.9
III	214.7	217.1	216.2	227.9	263.4	239.6	265.3	287.8	290.2	291.5	296.9	309.9	318.8
IV	226.0	196.4	218.2	246.7	261.4	265.1	272.9	288.4	289.3	287.7	313.8	319.7	321.7
Number of Loans													
I	35	53	46	43	33	69	55	57	68	75	90	76	72
II	45	69	53	55	50	74	48	73	90	64	94	81	65
III	52	56	37	34	63	60	59	72	80	71	80	74	86
IV	40	49	48	40	66	58	38	65	56	95	74	76	73
Mean Loan Size													
I	10,468	9,849	12,244	11,075	12,384	12,803	12,721	14,157	15,867	16,442	17,958	17,955	18,570
II	11,105	10,677	12,499	12,636	13,439	12,890	13,004	15,223	15,118	16,411	16,663	17,182	18,115
III	9,967	11,517	11,817	11,634	13,776	13,224	14,562	14,898	16,340	17,372	17,473	18,249	18,776
IV	9,937	12,211	11,485	12,690	12,726	12,640	13,990	14,651	16,293	15,949	16,552	17,949	17,537

[a]During the period January 1951-September 1953 the data cover only three companies.

TABLE C-20

Characteristics of Conventional Mortgage Loans on Residential (1-4 Family)
Properties by Four Life Insurance Companies, 1951-63, East North Central

	1951	1952	1953	1954	1955	1956	1957	1958	1959	1960	1961	1962	1963
Gross Yield[a]													
I	4.30	4.48	4.57	4.83	4.75	4.81	5.41	5.66	5.67	6.02	5.97	5.77	5.55
II	4.38	4.57	4.60	4.78	4.72	4.86	5.52	5.58	5.71	6.04	5.80	5.72	5.49
III	4.47	4.56	4.77	4.75	4.77	4.91	5.51	5.44	5.77	6.04	5.74	5.60	5.47
IV	4.50	4.48	4.83	4.70	4.82	5.12	5.65	5.49	5.89	5.99	5.73	5.60	5.47
Standard Deviation - Gross Yield													
I				0.134	0.189	0.179	0.285	0.163	0.202	0.153	0.121	0.133	0.173
II				0.151	0.219	0.161	0.166	0.169	0.158	0.186	0.161	0.136	0.163
III				0.202	0.227	0.168	0.192	0.231	0.152	0.097	0.148	0.153	0.169
IV			0.109	0.206	0.176	0.262	0.175	0.196	0.162	0.146	0.153	0.134	0.156
Contract Rate													
I	4.49	4.61	4.73	4.96	4.86	4.93	5.47	5.74	5.72	6.03	5.98	5.78	5.57
II	4.51	4.74	4.75	4.89	4.84	4.97	5.56	5.62	5.74	6.02	5.81	5.73	5.50
III	4.65	4.70	4.89	4.87	4.87	5.01	5.56	5.49	5.79	6.04	5.75	5.63	5.48
IV	4.65	4.64	4.97	4.82	4.94	5.19	5.70	5.55	5.92	5.99	5.73	5.63	5.46
Net Discount													
I				-0.75	-0.69	-0.72	-0.40	-0.49	-0.26	-0.10	-0.04	-0.04	-0.14
II				-0.68	-0.79	-0.71	-0.24	-0.27	-0.20	0.07	-0.06	-0.07	-0.07
III				-0.74	-0.60	-0.61	-0.33	-0.33	-0.12	-0.05	-0.02	-0.16	-0.07
IV			-0.81	-0.74	-0.72	-0.44	-0.34	-0.38	-0.19	0.02	-0.05	-0.15	0.03

(continued)

TABLE C-20 (continued)

	1951	1952	1953	1954	1955	1956	1957	1958	1959	1960	1961	1962	1963
Loan-Value Ratio													
I	61.2	60.9	62.8	60.7	62.6	62.7	64.5	64.7	66.6	68.1	69.5	69.0	68.8
II	62.9	61.5	62.4	62.2	63.2	64.4	63.3	65.3	66.4	69.2	68.5	69.4	69.1
III	60.6	61.1	61.9	61.9	63.3	62.6	63.5	65.4	68.1	70.3	68.9	69.6	69.2
IV	60.4	61.4	62.2	62.9	63.2	63.6	63.9	66.2	67.8	68.0	68.8	69.8	70.0
Maturity (months)													
I	217.3	223.3	221.7	221.8	239.9	242.5	252.2	266.1	269.9	282.4	279.8	291.9	297.0
II	214.9	223.9	226.0	221.6	239.6	246.4	254.2	270.5	271.9	286.2	279.9	296.3	304.6
III	221.4	223.2	226.9	236.5	240.4	242.0	258.9	271.4	278.4	283.9	278.0	296.7	302.7
IV	222.9	222.8	221.6	246.8	242.0	250.8	261.2	270.9	279.4	282.8	282.3	299.8	306.1
Number of Loans													
I	96	128	128	143	159	263	198	210	188	205	188	176	167
II	124	148	156	168	198	193	244	234	218	239	227	188	189
III	130	169	160	185	278	229	205	235	206	248	237	205	207
IV	129	152	171	187	267	240	216	230	223	208	205	167	174
Mean Loan Size													
I	8,854	10,706	11,223	12,084	13,105	12,735	13,815	14,788	15,266	16,022	16,292	15,978	16,695
II	9,875	10,138	10,961	12,812	12,532	13,467	13,804	14,493	15,258	15,046	16,073	15,954	17,177
III	9,710	10,814	11,268	11,795	12,541	13,121	14,034	14,277	15,477	15,729	16,121	17,412	16,906
IV	9,975	10,772	11,257	13,264	12,763	13,403	14,115	14,933	16,073	14,977	15,994	16,867	17,391

[a]During the period January 1951-September 1953 the data cover only three companies.

TABLE C-21

Characteristics of Conventional Mortgage Loans on Residential (1-4 Family) Properties by Four Life Insurance Companies, 1951-63, West North Central

	1951	1952	1953	1954	1955	1956	1957	1958	1959	1960	1961	1962	1963
Gross Yield[a]													
I	4.34	4.49	4.55	4.81	4.69	4.80	5.35	5.64	5.57	6.05	5.96	5.78	5.62
II	4.44	4.53	4.64	4.75	4.68	4.82	5.49	5.53	5.63	6.06	5.83	5.77	5.54
III	4.51	4.59	4.76	4.67	4.73	4.88	5.48	5.43	5.74	6.08	5.78	5.71	5.52
IV	4.44	4.46	4.79	4.69	4.79	5.11	5.62	5.43	5.94	6.00	5.78	5.67	5.53
Standard Deviation - Gross Yield													
I				0.131	0.247	0.147	0.242	0.152	0.145	0.109	0.154	0.105	0.158
II				0.133	0.182	0.111	0.178	0.129	0.136	0.151	0.122	0.081	0.126
III				0.147	0.188	0.135	0.130	0.171	0.169	0.124	0.122	0.122	0.124
IV			0.106	0.175	0.162	0.237	0.155	0.213	0.174	0.126	0.085	0.116	0.182
Contract Rate													
I	4.56	4.67	4.66	4.92	4.77	4.93	5.39	5.68	5.61	6.05	5.98	5.80	5.66
II	4.57	4.70	4.72	4.84	4.79	4.92	5.51	5.56	5.66	6.06	5.85	5.77	5.56
III	4.68	4.72	4.87	4.78	4.85	5.00	5.50	5.41	5.73	6.07	5.80	5.75	5.53
IV	4.64	4.64	4.92	4.77	4.91	5.17	5.64	5.48	5.96	6.02	5.78	5.72	5.53
Net Discount													
I				-0.64	-0.54	-0.84	-0.21	-0.21	-0.26	-0.01	-0.14	-0.11	-0.27
II				-0.54	-0.70	-0.64	-0.12	-0.16	-0.17	-0.02	-0.14	-0.06	-0.09
III				-0.64	-0.75	-0.80	-0.10	0.11	0.04	0.06	-0.14	-0.25	-0.08
IV			-0.75	-0.50	-0.75	-0.37	-0.14	-0.32	-0.12	-0.11	-0.06	-0.36	-0.03

(continued)

TABLE C-21 (continued)

	1951	1952	1953	1954	1955	1956	1957	1958	1959	1960	1961	1962	1963
Loan-Value Ratio													
I	63.3	60.8	64.1	64.4	64.6	63.9	64.5	66.1	68.0	68.9	69.7	68.7	72.0
II	62.6	61.6	63.9	64.5	64.0	64.1	64.6	66.1	68.7	68.4	69.3	70.6	70.6
III	61.2	63.4	61.5	64.9	64.4	65.1	62.8	65.4	68.0	68.1	70.3	69.8	70.9
IV	61.7	64.2	62.4	61.1	63.7	65.3	65.7	67.1	68.1	68.8	70.0	69.0	70.5
Maturity (months)													
I	222.8	222.3	224.4	224.5	247.8	248.0	245.7	266.5	279.3	277.2	278.2	296.2	314.5
II	214.5	221.9	224.5	226.3	248.3	261.5	255.4	269.8	285.9	284.6	283.3	316.7	313.5
III	220.5	218.5	219.2	233.6	243.0	250.9	252.8	270.3	275.9	279.9	289.0	317.0	324.2
IV	220.3	225.6	220.2	235.6	253.9	252.1	262.0	279.2	283.2	279.0	292.7	302.4	318.5
Number of Loans													
I	52	71	76	61	78	96	80	86	70	92	99	117	99
II	68	88	83	104	82	92	92	76	69	99	123	112	114
III	67	68	62	61	107	88	101	92	76	98	125	131	116
IV	67	64	79	65	98	78	96	90	108	100	140	121	91
Mean Loan Size													
I	10,292	11,688	12,013	12,432	13,738	12,922	14,725	15,609	17,307	16,700	17,645	17,893	17,884
II	10,678	10,232	11,072	12,998	13,332	14,483	14,229	15,273	16,675	15,865	18,146	18,774	18,167
III	10,787	11,504	11,507	12,469	13,937	13,845	15,364	15,706	15,664	15,682	17,708	18,068	17,990
IV	9,920	9,963	11,370	11,641	13,510	13,698	14,079	16,027	17,300	16,780	17,560	18,617	17,035

[a]During the period January 1951-September 1953 the data cover only three companies.

TABLE C-22

Characteristics of Conventional Mortgage Loans on Residential (1-4 Family)
Properties by Four Life Insurance Companies, 1951-63, Pacific

	1951	1952	1953	1954	1955	1956	1957	1958	1959	1960	1961	1962	1963
							Gross Yield[a]						
I	4.44	4.46	4.64	4.90	4.81	4.81	5.41	5.70	5.60	6.07	6.02	5.77	5.64
II	4.45	4.64	4.67	4.86	4.80	4.81	5.64	5.60	5.69	6.16	5.91	5.76	5.52
III	4.51	4.80	4.83	4.82	4.79	4.94	5.57	5.49	5.77	6.21	5.89	5.67	5.51
IV	4.49	4.57	4.95	4.80	4.80	5.19	5.67	5.44	5.96	6.15	5.77	5.66	5.50
							Standard Deviation - Gross Yield						
I				0.195	0.122	0.125	0.239	0.140	0.191	0.275	0.131	0.137	0.218
II				0.188	0.115	0.108	0.204	0.162	0.125	0.129	0.121	0.153	0.150
III				0.161	0.111	0.217	0.202	0.147	0.158	0.148	0.112	0.118	0.127
IV			0.219	0.134	0.099	0.237	0.179	0.187	0.200	0.118	0.165	0.106	0.135
							Contract Rate						
I	4.56	4.74	4.92	5.09	5.00	5.00	5.51	5.83	5.70	6.17	6.10	5.86	5.69
II	4.60	4.87	4.91	5.06	4.99	5.00	5.69	5.70	5.80	6.26	6.01	5.86	5.60
III	4.67	4.96	5.13	5.02	4.99	5.14	5.67	5.61	5.85	6.30	5.99	5.77	5.59
IV	4.77	4.88	5.13	4.99	5.00	5.36	5.79	5.56	6.04	6.24	5.86	5.76	5.57
							Net Discount						
I				-1.11	-1.18	-1.22	-0.63	-0.79	-0.69	-0.60	-0.54	-0.55	-0.33
II				-1.17	-1.17	-1.19	-0.31	-0.66	-0.71	-0.64	-0.61	-0.62	-0.55
III				-1.22	-1.22	-1.27	-0.59	-0.71	-0.56	-0.54	-0.62	-0.67	-0.52
IV			-1.08	-1.18	-1.21	-0.98	-0.73	-0.72	-0.56	-0.58	-0.56	-0.66	-0.45

(continued)

TABLE C-22 (continued)

	1951	1952	1953	1954	1955	1956	1957	1958	1959	1960	1961	1962	1963
	Loan-Value Ratio												
I	63.0	61.9	64.1	63.6	63.8	63.9	64.3	64.9	65.6	69.6	69.8	68.8	70.6
II	62.5	62.2	64.1	64.6	64.1	64.1	64.1	64.3	65.5	70.2	69.9	69.8	69.4
III	61.3	63.0	64.6	64.1	65.1	63.7	63.6	64.8	69.3	69.4	70.5	69.9	70.4
IV	63.0	62.9	63.9	64.2	63.6	63.7	63.9	64.6	69.4	69.9	70.5	69.1	70.3
	Maturity (months)												
I	208.2	219.5	217.3	222.4	226.2	234.5	234.9	243.0	277.3	285.4	286.9	294.5	313.5
II	206.0	208.0	221.4	226.8	233.5	237.0	246.4	252.1	276.2	286.3	292.5	308.8	304.4
III	215.2	212.2	225.9	232.1	237.1	236.2	241.3	258.5	284.7	283.8	292.0	308.6	310.3
IV	220.6	211.2	216.1	230.9	234.6	234.4	241.7	269.7	281.8	287.2	296.3	313.2	312.3
	Number of Loans												
I	265	272	281	324	260	292	209	279	208	226	264	278	266
II	331	261	282	328	244	322	221	201	245	238	259	264	257
III	243	260	307	323	253	262	243	207	248	218	199	259	259
IV	267	251	306	275	259	250	276	165	249	195	223	262	245
	Mean Loan Size												
I	10,401	10,576	10,561	12,028	12,136	13,482	15,008	14,796	17,952	18,467	18,890	19,193	21,635
II	10,159	10,648	11,566	11,737	13,180	14,308	14,485	16,305	18,011	18,792	19,155	20,227	19,546
III	10,238	10,427	10,854	12,151	13,418	14,049	14,310	15,976	19,006	17,448	19,706	20,295	20,637
IV	10,530	11,212	11,564	12,517	12,863	14,262	14,822	16,884	17,891	18,247	19,823	20,386	21,977

[a]During the period January 1951-September 1953 the data cover only three companies.

TABLE C-23

Characteristics of Conventional Mortgage Loans on Residential (1-4 Family)
Properties by Four Life Insurance Companies, 1951-63, Mountain

	1951	1952	1953	1954	1955	1956	1957	1958	1959	1960	1961	1962	1963
Gross Yield[a]													
I	4.47	4.75	4.75	4.95	4.88	4.86	5.44	5.75	5.78	6.26	6.16	5.91	5.71
II	4.67	4.77	4.81	4.93	4.88	4.87	5.57	5.75	5.78	6.19	6.00	5.88	5.68
III	4.67	4.93	5.04	4.87	4.84	4.95	5.55	5.61	5.89	6.24	5.95	5.81	5.59
IV	4.72	4.84	5.06	4.88	4.85	5.09	5.69	5.64	6.06	6.18	5.93	5.80	5.59
Standard Deviation - Gross Yield													
I				0.200	0.176	0.131	0.256	0.195	0.210	0.172	0.178	0.129	0.174
II				0.174	0.160	0.188	0.175	0.163	0.119	0.442	0.114	0.114	0.193
III				0.192	0.101	0.196	0.124	0.181	0.132	0.184	0.124	0.146	0.131
IV			0.300	0.198	0.178	0.227	0.198	0.195	0.179	0.160	0.147	0.105	0.172
Contract Rate													
I	4.65	4.88	4.95	5.13	5.02	5.02	5.49	5.84	5.78	6.23	6.15	5.89	5.74
II	4.72	4.89	4.97	5.04	5.06	5.02	5.66	5.79	5.81	6.17	6.02	5.90	5.67
III	4.82	4.92	5.13	5.01	4.99	5.08	5.58	5.65	5.87	6.24	5.93	5.81	5.60
IV	4.88	4.98	5.21	5.05	5.02	5.18	5.75	5.66	6.02	6.14	5.90	5.82	5.59
Net Discount													
I				-1.01	-0.86	-0.98	-0.28	-0.51	0.04	0.19	0.05	0.13	-0.20
II				-0.68	-1.09	-0.94	-0.56	-0.22	-0.22	0.13	-0.11	-0.11	0.06.
III				-0.85	-0.94	-0.79	-0.18	-0.26	0.09	0.01	0.16	-0.03	-0.02
IV			-0.90	-0.99	-1.04	-0.58	-0.31	-0.15	0.24	0.26	0.20	-0.11	0.00

(continued)

TABLE C-23 (continued)

	1951	1952	1953	1954	1955	1956	1957	1958	1959	1960	1961	1962	1963
Loan-Value Ratio													
I	65.4	60.7	62.7	62.9	66.2	64.9	64.2	64.3	66.9	69.3	68.5	70.3	70.2
II	61.7	59.6	63.8	62.4	64.0	65.9	62.1	66.3	67.1	69.6	70.0	70.0	70.7
III	64.8	62.3	64.2	64.7	61.6	66.8	64.7	67.7	69.1	70.6	70.6	70.8	69.6
IV	60.4	64.6	63.7	66.8	65.8	65.7	63.6	67.2	70.8	71.1	70.0	69.7	72.4
Maturity (months)													
I	217.9	216.1	216.2	215.9	229.2	241.2	246.5	249.1	259.3	284.4	284.7	291.0	307.5
II	218.9	218.5	222.5	221.4	235.7	245.3	232.5	250.2	258.1	284.3	288.2	288.8	324.5
III	214.2	217.0	222.5	218.6	233.2	237.2	244.9	246.5	268.2	280.9	293.0	296.1	309.6
IV	204.9	217.5	215.9	222.1	240.0	229.9	244.1	266.4	280.9	288.9	292.3	295.9	332.5
Number of Loans													
I	24	68	58	47	28	49	37	47	56	52	70	55	65
II	58	72	63	53	38	85	40	56	59	60	55	54	52
III	62	61	54	46	54	79	51	67	63	79	51	64	55
IV	64	59	66	32	67	46	53	53	57	51	47	68	51
Mean Loan Size													
I	9,419	9,906	11,459	10,887	12,614	15,369	13,672	15,165	16,839	17,553	17,705	17,380	19,941
II	9,911	10,841	11,739	11,459	12,431	13,702	14,963	15,720	16,413	16,933	17,804	19,302	19,365
III	10,386	10,866	10,906	12,574	12,002	13,756	14,569	16,298	16,133	17,952	17,658	18,700	17,772
IV	10,560	11,109	11,389	12,536	14,329	13,965	14,619	18,058	18,162	17,540	16,792	17,128	18,760

[a]During the period January 1951-September 1953 the data cover only three companies.

TABLE C-24

Characteristics of FHA Mortgage Loans on Residential (1-4 Family)
Properties by Four Life Insurance Companies, 1951-63, New England

	1951	1952	1953	1954	1955	1956	1957	1958	1959	1960	1961	1962	1963
Gross Yield													
I	4.05	4.17	4.20	4.60	4.41	4.57	4.97	5.37	5.28	6.11	5.98	5.42	5.39
II	4.07	4.23	4.24	4.46	4.37	4.48	5.07	5.42	5.36	6.09	5.67	5.47	5.42
III	4.16	4.35	4.50	4.39	4.49	4.53	5.18	5.30	5.29	6.05	5.56	5.36	5.27
IV	4.21	4.17	4.52	4.47	4.54	4.49	5.40	5.28	5.92	6.06	5.47	5.38	5.28
Standard Deviation - Gross Yield													
I	0.073	0.086	0.113	0.078	0.074	0.129	0.165	0.127	0.058	0.150	0.169	0.160	0.223
II	0.071	0.045	0.160	0.069	0.044	0.080	0.076	0.053	0.138	0.094	0.238	0.093	0.105
III	0.089	0.369	0.105	0.066	0.038	0.159	0.148	0.090	0.065	0.152	0.112	0.037	0.032
IV	0.062	0.081	0.073	0.127	0.131	0.098	0.097	0.116	0.151	0.188	0.001	0.032	0.052
Contract Rate													
I	4.24	4.25	4.25	4.50	4.50	4.50	4.95	5.25	5.25	5.75	5.75	5.25	5.25
II	4.25	4.25	4.32	4.50	4.50	4.50	5.00	5.25	5.25	5.75	5.55	5.25	5.25
III	4.28	4.25	4.50	4.50	4.50	4.50	5.08	5.25	5.25	5.75	5.39	5.25	5.25
IV	4.25	4.25	4.50	4.50	4.48	4.50	5.25	5.25	5.75	5.75	5.25	5.25	5.25
Net Discount													
I	-1.24	-0.51	-0.31	0.62	-0.57	0.49	0.14	0.79	0.18	2.34	1.53	1.11	0.92
II	-1.22	-0.10	-0.53	-0.24	-0.89	-0.15	0.48	1.13	0.72	2.25	0.78	1.44	1.13
III	-0.76	0.66	0.01	-0.74	-0.09	0.23	0.71	0.33	0.25	1.94	1.16	0.76	0.10
IV	-0.25	-0.47	0.13	-0.19	0.36	-0.04	0.98	0.21	1.12	2.05	1.50	0.88	0.20

(continued)

TABLE C-24 (continued)

	1951	1952	1953	1954	1955	1956	1957	1958	1959	1960	1961	1962	1963
Loan-Value Ratio													
I	83.0	78.4	83.6	79.8	86.0	84.6	84.0	90.9	92.3	83.8	94.7	90.8	93.4
II	76.4	82.9	79.4	79.8	83.6	82.8	85.3	90.5	88.9	92.0	89.8	89.4	95.6
III	73.4	85.9	83.4	79.1	86.5	81.2	83.6	87.6	91.1	92.7	88.3	77.4	89.1
IV	79.3	80.8	83.5	81.0	86.8	81.9	89.9	86.6	89.0	95.2	90.0	88.0	94.3
Maturity (months)													
I	284.9	265.7	261.9	254.8	320.9	304.6	301.7	344.0	356.3	360.0	344.2	360.0	369.5
II	285.9	252.7	263.5	254.7	293.1	319.2	287.0	344.6	333.2	353.2	360.0	360.0	360.0
III	273.4	249.1	252.1	273.9	344.2	325.4	323.9	331.0	359.3	343.4	357.4	360.0	345.4
IV	265.1	234.5	245.6	295.0	312.0	302.9	336.7	306.5	333.7	352.5	360.0	360.0	354.0
Number of Loans													
I	16	11	9	7	8	14	50	8	6	6	4	5	6
II	13	17	38	4	14	19	12	11	12	14	4	3	5
III	15	10	4	10	15	12	30	7	5	7	6	2	4
IV	12	9	4	13	17	44	13	8	3	3	3	4	8
Mean Loan Size													
I	7,384	9,052	9,450	10,357	11,136	11,553	11,440	14,494	14,704	19,678	14,068	15,750	14,508
II	9,386	7,976	9,727	8,652	9,696	11,237	13,005	14,102	12,874	14,941	15,834	12,533	15,647
III	7,742	7,320	9,857	8,897	11,171	11,426	13,024	12,274	13,643	14,268	16,308	12,700	15,875
IV	8,244	10,052	10,389	11,042	10,836	12,193	14,324	14,949	15,372	16,039	17,500	17,775	14,969

TABLE C-25

Characteristics of FHA Mortgage Loans on Residential (1-4 Family)
Properties by Four Life Insurance Companies, 1951-63, Middle Atlantic

	1951	1952	1953	1954	1955	1956	1957	1958	1959	1960	1961	1962	1963
						Gross Yield							
I	4.04	4.19	4.23	4.65	4.50	4.54	5.06	5.43	5.39	6.05	5.87	5.57	5.42
II	4.09	4.24	4.30	4.59	4.51	4.54	5.24	5.40	5.43	6.05	5.73	5.55	5.38
III	4.18	4.22	4.55	4.51	4.52	4.62	5.27	5.33	5.52	6.07	5.63	5.49	5.38
IV	4.16	4.19	4.65	4.51	4.52	4.68	5.39	5.36	5.80	6.04[a]	5.56	5.50	5.37
					Standard Deviation - Gross Yield								
I	0.091	0.097	0.052	0.118	0.093	0.156	0.250	0.067	0.091	0.122	0.147	0.090	0.157
II	0.089	0.049	0.140	0.206	0.108	0.118	0.120	0.071	0.127	0.392	0.128	0.092	0.103
III	0.174	0.063	0.177	0.057	0.098	0.136	0.118	0.093	0.127	0.089	0.120	0.119	0.112
IV	0.133	0.080	0.144	0.032	0.103	0.140	0.093	0.098	0.255	0.264	0.091	0.109	0.105
						Contract Rate							
I	4.25	4.26	4.25	4.50	4.49	4.47	4.89	5.25	5.25	5.75	5.69	5.27	5.26
II	4.27	4.25	4.32	4.44	4.48	4.49	4.99	5.25	5.25	5.70	5.53	5.25	5.26
III	4.24	4.25	4.47	4.50	4.48	4.50	5.08	5.25	5.25	5.74	5.36	5.25	5.26
IV	4.25	4.25	4.48	4.50	4.49	4.51	5.25	5.25	5.50	5.72	5.29	5.26	5.25
						Net Discount							
I	-1.39	-0.48	-0.14	0.99	0.06	0.44	1.14	1.18	0.90	1.93	1.22	2.01	1.08
II	-1.15	-0.04	-0.12	1.00	0.20	0.38	1.65	1.00	1.14	2.29	1.26	1.98	0.84
III	-0.38	-0.18	0.55	0.09	0.24	0.74	1.25	0.54	1.82	2.11	1.80	1.61	0.78
IV	-0.56	-0.39	1.09	0.04	0.22	1.14	0.89	0.70	1.97	2.13[a]	1.75	1.61	0.76

(continued)

TABLE C-25 (continued)

Loan-Value Ratio

	1951	1952	1953	1954	1955	1956	1957	1958	1959	1960	1961	1962	1963
I	85.4	82.6	80.0	80.8	85.8	83.5	82.6	89.5	90.6	92.0	93.8	92.7	92.3
II	78.0	81.9	80.5	81.3	87.2	82.2	84.0	89.1	92.3	91.4	92.8	92.8	90.7
III	79.9	80.6	81.0	79.5	86.4	85.7	86.0	91.5	92.4	92.9	90.4	93.0	82.2
IV	80.1	81.3	80.0	86.5	85.6	83.5	90.0	91.7	90.6	91.9	91.4	93.8	92.9

Maturity (months)

	1951	1952	1953	1954	1955	1956	1957	1958	1959	1960	1961	1962	1963
I	248.6	266.5	256.1	263.4	335.6	307.6	314.2	314.8	335.8	340.3	347.9	348.2	341.4
II	257.3	270.7	254.8	272.7	339.8	303.2	326.1	336.6	325.8	338.4	342.5	353.4	353.9
III	255.7	258.2	272.5	291.4	336.7	320.1	313.8	339.4	343.8	346.9	342.7	341.1	342.9
IV	264.2	266.4	273.9	329.2	327.9	321.9	318.8	319.7	338.3	325.5	347.7	343.9	335.4

Number of Loans

	1951	1952	1953	1954	1955	1956	1957	1958	1959	1960	1961	1962	1963
I	47	115	74	97	83	118	64	140	99	35	56	56	47
II	27	75	89	52	125	67	95	134	112	61	80	59	47
III	35	63	100	46	83	97	86	83	80	39	64	53	41
IV	31	76	133	39	134	81	92	51	50	81	50	58	31

Mean Loan Size

	1951	1952	1953	1954	1955	1956	1957	1958	1959	1960	1961	1962	1963
I	7,682	8,035	8,715	9,895	11,271	10,659	11,653	12,520	13,760	13,703	14,544	14,263	14,531
II	8,128	7,989	8,745	9,418	10,353	11,142	11,981	13,149	13,457	14,042	14,639	13,722	14,090
III	8,220	8,015	9,380	9,874	11,188	11,235	12,094	13,707	14,069	14,863	14,187	14,560	13,609
IV	8,282	8,735	9,616	10,657	11,165	11,382	12,241	12,902	13,137	13,573	14,439	14,200	14,549

[a]Data cover only three companies.

TABLE C-26

Characteristics of FHA Mortgage Loans on Residential (1-4 Family)
Properties by Four Life Insurance Companies, 1951-63, South Atlantic

	1951	1952	1953	1954	1955	1956	1957	1958	1959	1960	1961	1962	1963
Gross Yield													
I	4.10	4.21	4.25	4.69	4.59	4.62	5.21	5.57	5.63	6.21	6.05	5.77	5.62
II	4.16	4.24	4.34	4.63	4.60	4.75	5.33	5.54	5.67	6.23[a]	5.93	5.75	5.54
III	4.23	4.26	4.59	4.56	4.63	4.75	5.41	5.48	5.76	6.24	5.77	5.70	5.49
IV	4.23	4.23	4.68	4.58	4.67	4.83	5.56	5.53	6.02[a]	6.18[a]	5.75	5.68	5.49
Standard Deviation - Gross Yield													
I	0.076	0.075	0.066	0.134	0.104	0.250	0.254	0.107	0.161	0.133	0.168	0.117	0.091
II	0.091	0.048	0.147	0.152	0.191	0.111	0.121	0.099	0.156	0.153	0.151	0.128	0.100
III	0.078	0.090	0.127	0.155	0.155	0.140	0.171	0.098	0.199	0.101	0.207	0.113	0.089
IV	0.088	0.064	0.113	0.096	0.115	0.120	0.090	0.131	0.331	0.278	0.154	0.092	0.107
Contract Rate													
I	4.25	4.25	4.25	4.50	4.50	4.41	4.90	5.25	5.25	5.75	5.70	5.26	5.25
II	4.25	4.25	4.34	4.47	4.46	4.50	4.99	5.25	5.25	5.75	5.57	5.25	5.25
III	4.25	4.25	4.49	4.50	4.48	4.48	5.06	5.25	5.24	5.75	5.35	5.25	5.25
IV	4.25	4.25	4.50	4.50	4.50	4.50	5.24	5.25	5.53	5.71	5.29	5.25	5.25
Net Discount													
I	-0.98	-0.27	-0.02	1.22	0.59	1.38	2.03	2.10	2.46	2.99	2.31	3.38	2.47
II	-0.58	-0.04	0.05	1.03	0.90	1.68	2.28	1.93	2.79	3.21[a]	2.36	3.28	1.93
III	-0.14	0.04	0.65	0.42	1.00	1.79	2.24	1.53	3.46	3.17	2.77	2.98	1.62
IV	-0.15	-0.11	1.17	0.55	1.16	2.17	2.06	1.85	3.88[a]	3.03[a]	3.10	2.87	1.60

(continued)

TABLE C-26 (continued)

	1951	1952	1953	1954	1955	1956	1957	1958	1959	1960	1961	1962	1963
							Loan-Value Ratio						
I	81.4	81.9	82.3	81.4	85.9	86.0	84.3	90.1	92.4	92.1	92.4	94.3	94.0
II	82.3	81.6	82.0	82.9	87.4	84.8	84.8	90.7	91.7	91.4	93.1	93.1	92.9
III	78.6	81.3	82.9	82.2	87.5	85.4	86.5	91.2	92.3	93.0	93.4	93.3	93.9
IV	80.8	81.8	82.5	85.5	86.6	85.1	89.5	90.9	92.6	92.7	93.4	93.7	93.1
							Maturity (months)						
I	256.2	246.9	253.7	257.7	299.9	291.3	292.5	311.6	324.8	333.7	338.2	346.5	352.1
II	252.9	246.2	248.8	261.2	301.3	292.1	304.0	317.1	330.5	345.5	345.5	350.7	351.4
III	243.7	248.8	256.0	266.5	299.1	304.5	299.5	321.7	335.0	337.2	344.9	343.7	353.8
IV	245.9	249.3	258.9	281.9	299.6	296.9	306.7	320.3	341.7	338.3	350.3	348.7	354.2
							Number of Loans						
I	167	290	348	301	227	254	149	272	346	167	298	245	196
II	241	304	243	276	252	249	218	271	327	222	323	287	180
III	268	325	249	253	346	184	189	319	268	192	315	273	230
IV	318	349	301	285	253	201	193	247	341	255	253	253	203
							Mean Loan Size						
I	7,806	8,513	8,625	9,288	10,585	10,912	11,242	12,799	13,273	14,084	14,560	15,292	13,904
II	7,803	8,305	9,051	8,743	9,888	11,022	11,813	13,060	13,432	15,114	13,921	15,315	15,087
III	8,272	8,334	9,136	9,563	10,766	11,614	12,031	13,462	13,895	13,617	14,233	14,077	15,038
IV	8,299	8,793	9,285	9,859	11,180	11,415	13,366	13,212	13,764	14,405	14,534	14,640	15,008

aData cover only three companies.

TABLE C-27

Characteristics of FHA Mortgage Loans on Residential (1-4 Family)
Properties by Four Life Insurance Companies, 1951-63, West South Central

	1951	1952	1953	1954	1955	1956	1957	1958	1959	1960	1961	1962	1963
							Gross Yield						
I	4.09	4.24	4.28	4.81	4.67	4.69	5.38	5.68	5.73	6.37	6.18	5.80	5.64
II	4.13	4.26	4.35	4.65	4.61	4.81	5.40	5.58	5.75	6.36	6.01	5.81	5.55
III	4.19	4.26	4.58	4.65	4.64	4.83	5.48	5.51	5.86[a]	6.33	5.85	5.76	5.56
IV	4.24	4.25	4.78	4.66	4.72	4.93	5.65	5.61	6.18[a]	6.32	5.81	5.71	5.54
						Standard Deviation - Gross Yield							
I	0.067	0.040	0.072	0.161	0.132	0.273	0.194	0.125	0.110	0.126	0.118	0.083	0.162
II	0.094	0.038	0.125	0.224	0.198	0.137	0.132	0.122	0.116	0.117	0.150	0.079	0.174
III	0.089	0.098	0.125	0.109	0.213	0.160	0.128	0.107	0.166	0.109	0.094	0.137	0.106
IV	0.059	0.062	0.209	0.123	0.155	0.139	0.119	0.122	0.363	0.155	0.068	0.090	0.084
							Contract Rate						
I	4.25	4.25	4.25	4.49	4.50	4.41	4.97	5.25	5.25	5.71	5.70	5.27	5.27
II	4.25	4.25	4.31	4.47	4.46	4.49	5.00	5.25	5.25	5.75	5.57	5.25	5.25
III	4.25	4.25	4.49	4.50	4.47	4.48	5.09	5.25	5.25	5.75	5.40	5.25	5.25
IV	4.25	4.25	4.49	4.50	4.49	4.51	5.25	5.25	5.54	5.75	5.29	5.26	5.25
							Net Discount						
I	-1.08	-0.05	0.17	2.06	1.14	1.87	2.64	2.84	3.20	4.26	3.14	3.49	2.43
II	-0.79	0.07	0.23	1.22	0.99	2.15	2.61	2.18	3.30	3.97	2.89	3.73	1.99
III	-0.36	0.07	0.59	0.71	1.19	2.40	2.54	1.73	4.09[a]	3.80	3.02	3.41	2.04
IV	-0.04	0.00	1.86	1.09	1.53	2.79	2.62	2.37	4.29[a]	3.56	3.46	3.02	1.96

(continued)

TABLE C-27 (continued)

	1951	1952	1953	1954	1955	1956	1957	1958	1959	1960	1961	1962	1963
							Loan-Value Ratio						
I	84.1	82.3	84.7	82.9	88.6	85.9	85.0	91.5	92.6	92.9	93.7	94.5	95.2
II	85.2	82.7	84.1	83.2	87.9	86.6	84.2	91.9	92.7	93.2	93.4	93.7	94.8
III	82.9	82.9	84.5	83.1	87.8	86.3	87.1	92.7	92.7	94.2	93.3	94.4	94.6
IV	81.6	82.4	85.1	87.3	87.0	85.2	90.3	92.9	93.3	93.1	94.0	94.9	94.0
							Maturity (months)						
I	259.3	256.3	253.6	263.1	308.7	294.8	291.6	296.1	335.9	338.5	347.2	351.2	363.1
II	244.2	250.0	253.8	272.3	308.0	311.7	295.4	314.3	335.0	352.1	350.4	353.4	365.3
III	242.2	249.2	256.7	285.4	304.3	306.1	296.6	327.5	338.7	345.3	346.9	362.3	362.5
IV	257.1	252.2	259.5	300.1	296.2	299.6	294.4	337.6	344.0	340.3	348.8	358.8	358.9
							Number of Loans						
I	157	182	144	129	121	114	114	156	135	144	128	174	247
II	127	165	190	126	190	108	146	200	209	124	193	175	210
III	128	190	162	132	155	105	130	209	223	165	145	193	177
IV	141	140	149	102	223	126	185	163	230	131	175	151	158
							Mean Loan Size						
I	8,204	8,524	8,587	9,588	10,485	10,684	11,663	12,904	14,085	14,129	14,399	14,961	13,246
II	8,620	8,340	8,873	9,619	10,404	11,660	11,973	13,494	13,504	14,298	13,851	14,443	13,552
III	8,642	8,251	9,089	10,002	11,014	12,175	12,779	13,474	13,572	14,083	14,279	14,621	14,028
IV	8,508	8,470	8,964	10,704	11,802	11,915	13,240	14,173	13,413	14,536	14,599	13,739	13,443

[a]Data cover only three companies

TABLE C-28

Characteristics of FHA Mortgage Loans on Residential (1-4 Family)
Properties by Four Life Insurance Companies, 1951-63, East South Central

	1951	1952	1953	1954	1955	1956	1957	1958	1959	1960	1961	1962	1963
						Gross Yield							
I	4.07	4.22	4.22	4.70	4.61	4.67	5.31	5.64	5.71	6.31	6.10	5.77	5.59
II	4.13	4.25	4.36	4.61	4.59	4.77	5.36	5.56	5.74	6.29	5.91	5.76	5.50
III	4.24	4.26	4.61	4.58	4.59	4.81	5.47	5.49	5.85	6.25	5.81	5.69	5.52
IV	4.25	4.24	4.71	4.58	4.70	4.87	5.60	5.61	6.10[a]	6.23	5.80	5.70	5.51
					Standard Deviation - Gross Yield								
I	0.099	0.074	0.051	0.109	0.124	0.230	0.180	0.134	0.135	0.167	0.145	0.070	0.092
II	0.066	0.068	0.175	0.177	0.182	0.174	0.108	0.120	0.129	0.133	0.128	0.074	0.137
III	0.109	0.052	0.142	0.116	0.198	0.156	0.117	0.088	0.104	0.144	0.161	0.110	0.108
IV	0.105	0.133	0.149	0.088	0.123	0.110	0.083	0.144	0.227	0.158	0.147	0.101	0.237
						Contract Rate							
I	4.25	4.25	4.25	4.50	4.50	4.44	4.97	5.25	5.25	5.70	5.72	5.25	5.26
II	4.25	4.25	4.33	4.46	4.45	4.49	5.00	5.25	5.25	5.75	5.60	5.25	5.25
III	4.25	4.25	4.48	4.49	4.45	4.47	5.09	5.25	5.25	5.73	5.35	5.25	5.25
IV	4.25	4.25	4.50	4.50	4.50	4.50	5.25	5.25	5.54	5.74	5.29	5.26	5.25
						Net Discount							
I	-1.14	-0.22	-0.19	1.31	0.74	1.51	2.25	2.55	3.00	3.96	2.48	3.47	2.26
II	-0.80	0.01	0.20	0.98	0.89	1.86	2.39	2.07	3.28	3.54	2.01	3.39	1.64
III	-0.10	0.06	0.83	0.53	0.98	2.30	2.55	1.58	3.99	3.40	3.05	2.93	1.74
IV	0.00	-0.05	1.37	0.51	1.36	2.48	2.32	2.36	3.72[a]	3.25	3.42	2.94	1.70

(continued)

TABLE C-28 (continued)

	1951	1952	1953	1954	1955	1956	1957	1958	1959	1960	1961	1962	1963
Loan-Value Ratio													
I	83.4	81.5	84.3	84.1	87.0	85.7	83.7	91.8	92.4	93.4	93.1	93.8	94.7
II	82.1	81.8	84.2	81.8	87.7	83.6	86.0	92.7	93.7	92.1	93.5	93.0	94.2
III	82.6	82.2	82.9	82.7	86.7	84.5	88.0	91.8	93.3	94.1	93.2	93.8	94.3
IV	84.5	83.4	83.2	86.2	87.0	84.8	89.1	91.8	93.5	93.4	94.3	94.3	94.2
Maturity (months)													
I	257.9	250.2	257.3	272.8	295.8	301.9	298.8	312.1	335.1	348.9	340.3	352.5	362.6
II	248.5	250.9	255.8	266.6	308.4	295.6	310.6	331.4	344.6	354.3	349.4	354.1	356.2
III	240.0	252.6	265.1	271.9	304.0	319.6	303.8	340.1	346.5	347.0	350.7	354.6	348.7
IV	250.6	260.1	273.5	289.2	296.8	304.2	305.1	341.6	350.0	351.8	350.9	357.6	361.8
Number of Loans													
I	69	86	118	121	113	124	134	171	133	102	145	88	143
II	101	104	104	133	134	97	159	189	171	108	155	144	142
III	116	167	104	125	131	76	162	173	122	91	111	149	107
IV	129	100	83	120	112	119	121	125	77	85	143	124	95
Mean Loan Size													
I	7,759	8,382	8,475	9,118	10,280	10,949	11,319	12,353	13,152	13,371	13,501	14,396	14,492
II	7,689	8,412	8,447	9,238	10,481	10,942	11,236	12,280	12,769	13,493	13,242	13,964	13,642
III	8,085	8,440	8,942	8,991	10,771	11,747	11,765	13,104	13,351	14,047	13,459	14,606	13,754
IV	7,976	8,034	8,862	9,857	10,420	11,155	12,451	13,090	13,248	13,797	13,880	14,077	14,475

[a]Data cover only three companies.

TABLE C-29

Characteristics of FHA Mortgage Loans on Residential (1-4 Family)
Properties by Four Life Insurance Companies, 1951-63, East North Central

	1951	1952	1953	1954	1955	1956	1957	1958	1959	1960	1961	1962	1963
Gross Yield													
I	4.10	4.22	4.28	4.68	4.60	4.70	5.34	5.63	5.76	6.24	6.14	5.74	5.58
II	4.11	4.26	4.39	4.64	4.61	4.77	5.39	5.58	5.80	6.27[a]	5.93	5.73	5.50
III	4.21	4.26	4.56	4.67	4.66	4.80	5.45	5.48	5.87[a]	6.24	5.80	5.67	5.46
IV	4.23	4.27	4.69	4.61	4.72	4.93	5.61	5.56	6.15	6.24	5.74	5.65	5.44
Standard Deviation - Gross Yield													
I	0.100	0.103	0.070	0.137	0.099	0.211	0.196	0.109	0.132	0.242	0.121	0.103	0.100
II	0.092	0.090	0.148	0.153	0.155	0.139	0.111	0.099	0.109	0.170	0.127	0.075	0.102
III	0.115	0.067	0.125	0.148	0.168	0.162	0.131	0.102	0.120	0.126	0.114	0.087	0.102
IV	0.122	0.098	0.146	0.097	0.167	0.135	0.096	0.124	0.179	0.117	0.109	0.099	0.154
Contract Rate													
I	4.26	4.25	4.25	4.50	4.50	4.46	4.95	5.25	5.25	5.73	5.70	5.26	5.25
II	4.25	4.25	4.35	4.49	4.48	4.50	5.00	5.25	5.25	5.75	5.55	5.25	5.25
III	4.27	4.25	4.49	4.50	4.48	4.48	5.07	5.25	5.25	5.74	5.35	5.25	5.25
IV	4.25	4.24	4.50	4.50	4.49	4.51	5.24	5.25	5.63	5.75	5.29	5.25	5.25
Net Discount													
I	-1.07	-0.18	0.21	1.17	0.70	1.57	2.53	2.47	3.36	3.33	2.86	3.15	2.16
II	-0.92	0.05	0.24	1.00	0.88	1.82	2.62	2.15	3.66	3.40[a]	2.50	3.17	1.63
III	-0.35	0.05	0.46	1.13	1.18	2.13	2.54	1.50	4.13[a]	3.24	3.00	2.77	1.42
IV	-0.13	0.15	1.29	0.73	1.51	2.80	2.40	2.03	3.45	3.19	3.00	2.66	1.28

(continued)

TABLE C-29 (continued)

	1951	1952	1953	1954	1955	1956	1957	1958	1959	1960	1961	1962	1963
Loan-Value Ratio													
I	80.7	80.0	79.0	79.7	84.1	83.7	81.6	88.1	91.6	92.4	91.8	93.6	93.0
II	81.1	80.2	80.6	80.7	85.0	83.4	82.6	89.6	91.4	92.0	92.3	93.5	93.4
III	80.5	80.1	79.8	81.5	85.1	82.5	83.7	90.2	91.8	93.2	92.9	93.4	93.8
IV	80.4	81.0	79.0	84.1	84.0	82.5	85.8	90.4	92.6	92.5	93.3	93.1	93.8
Maturity (months)													
I	264.2	245.5	246.0	259.8	299.8	287.6	293.4	311.1	335.0	339.3	340.6	346.0	342.1
II	252.5	245.7	247.0	280.8	302.9	289.6	304.6	318.9	337.2	342.0	340.5	341.0	352.3
III	247.1	244.8	254.1	289.3	297.1	293.7	300.3	332.8	339.2	338.0	342.1	341.3	347.6
IV	246.6	262.5	260.7	297.3	297.3	297.3	308.8	329.7	337.4	344.4	344.5	352.9	354.3
Number of Loans													
I	136	245	242	224	366	298	175	230	305	267	184	156	160
II	252	279	208	259	353	247	177	192	254	304	228	193	144
III	330	287	320	257	315	199	246	248	233	251	192	214	197
IV	314	307	211	318	387	284	199	250	239	215	195	189	384
Mean Loan Size													
I	8,075	8,797	9,544	10,460	11,471	11,768	12,316	13,713	13,866	13,822	13,963	14,685	14,786
II	8,427	9,005	9,835	10,578	11,761	11,613	13,026	13,524	14,068	14,023	14,184	14,796	14,990
III	8,591	9,146	9,955	10,469	11,457	11,899	13,691	13,932	13,784	14,034	14,316	14,714	14,458
IV	8,651	9,236	10,386	11,496	11,793	12,633	13,815	13,942	14,024	13,997	14,821	14,934	14,852

[a]Data cover only three companies.

TABLE C-30

Characteristics of FHA Mortgage Loans on Residential (1-4 Family)
Properties by Four Life Insurance Companies, 1951-63, West North Central

	1951	1952	1953	1954	1955	1956	1957	1958	1959	1960	1961	1962	1963
	Gross Yield												
I	4.09	4.25	4.28	4.66	4.55	4.68	5.24	5.64	5.70	6.26	6.17	5.76	5.64
II	4.13	4.25	4.35	4.60	4.56	4.72	5.34	5.54	5.74	6.26	5.94	5.75	5.53
III	4.28	4.29	4.54	4.58	4.58	4.76	5.45	5.46	5.82[a]	6.28	5.81	5.71	5.51
IV	4.24	4.26	4.71	4.55	4.62	4.84	5.65	5.52	6.15[a]	6.25	5.80	5.69	5.52
	Standard Deviation - Gross Yield												
I	0.119	0.096	0.069	0.094	0.094	0.148	0.278	0.096	0.110	0.162	0.109	0.067	0.117
II	0.094	0.083	0.148	0.140	0.146	0.116	0.113	0.116	0.102	0.206	0.126	0.078	0.162
III	0.117	0.072	0.134	0.106	0.154	0.155	0.134	0.116	0.134	0.111	0.110	0.093	0.102
IV	0.108	0.171	0.098	0.127	0.262	0.156	0.101	0.130	0.218	0.095	0.104	0.209	0.097
	Contract Rate												
I	4.27	4.25	4.25	4.49	4.50	4.49	4.90	5.25	5.25	5.73	5.71	5.26	5.25
II	4.25	4.25	4.32	4.48	4.47	4.50	5.00	5.25	5.25	5.74	5.53	5.25	5.24
III	4.26	4.25	4.48	4.49	4.47	4.47	5.07	5.25	5.25	5.75	5.33	5.25	5.25
IV	4.25	4.23	4.49	4.50	4.46	4.51	5.25	5.25	5.59	5.75	5.29	5.24	5.25
	Net Discount												
I	-1.18	0.00	0.18	1.10	0.36	1.24	2.24	2.52	2.96	3.46	2.99	3.39	2.59
II	-0.77	0.02	0.18	0.79	0.54	1.49	2.26	1.91	3.26	3.44	2.72	3.34	1.89
III	0.11	0.25	0.35	0.56	0.72	1.91	2.47	1.40	3.76[a]	3.46	3.20	3.06	1.74
IV	-0.09	0.22	1.45	0.35	1.03	2.22	2.59	1.77	3.65[a]	3.27	3.38	3.03	1.81

(continued)

TABLE C-30 (continued)

	1951	1952	1953	1954	1955	1956	1957	1958	1959	1960	1961	1962	1963
							Loan-Value Ratio						
I	82.4	79.6	80.9	78.0	84.3	83.3	83.5	88.6	90.8	91.1	89.8	93.0	93.2
II	78.6	80.0	80.1	79.1	84.2	82.7	83.8	88.5	91.8	91.3	92.3	93.9	93.8
III	80.1	79.5	80.8	80.0	84.8	84.4	86.0	91.5	91.9	93.1	92.5	93.5	93.2
IV	80.1	80.2	79.6	82.6	86.0	81.8	88.3	89.5	91.0	90.6	92.9	92.1	92.8
							Maturity (months)						
I	267.7	253.6	254.3	259.2	303.4	296.7	292.9	300.3	332.7	339.2	338.6	345.4	350.5
II	250.9	250.5	247.6	263.3	307.6	301.2	297.8	311.3	335.3	343.7	346.2	350.0	351.1
III	242.2	248.6	256.1	270.8	304.6	298.6	301.7	321.6	342.9	343.6	342.5	354.0	354.4
IV	248.0	254.4	272.2	299.9	305.3	295.0	298.4	328.2	338.1	340.9	329.9	350.5	350.7
							Number of Loans						
I	107	103	111	54	147	113	78	153	133	97	96	104	132
II	117	107	93	108	141	104	103	166	170	96	147	145	152
III	69	117	90	85	131	106	144	133	154	127	145	174	161
IV	105	98	76	130	95	105	119	112	106	126	103	149	121
							Mean Loan Size						
I	7,875	8,590	9,037	10,136	11,210	11,315	12,984	13,454	13,822	14,827	14,527	14,644	14,638
II	8,462	8,919	9,483	10,564	11,182	12,223	12,849	13,868	13,842	14,723	14,558	14,665	14,563
III	9,090	9,032	9,816	10,520	11,224	11,933	12,886	13,786	14,463	14,400	14,934	14,935	15,320
IV	8,750	9,008	9,753	11,163	11,161	12,262	13,350	14,213	13,912	14,271	14,423	14,282	14,690

[a]Data cover only three companies.

TABLE C-31

Characteristics of FHA Mortgage Loans on Residential (1-4 Family) Properties by Four Life Insurance Companies, 1951-63, Pacific

	1951	1952	1953	1954	1955	1956	1957	1958	1959	1960	1961	1962	1963
Gross Yield													
I	4.12	4.18	4.26	4.62	4.62	4.72	5.28	5.64	5.74	6.28	6.16	5.82	5.63
II	4.15	4.24	4.37	4.63	4.65	4.73	5.41	5.61	5.77	6.28	5.98	5.81	5.55
III	4.20	4.27	4.54	4.62	4.67	4.70	5.47	5.53	5.86[a]	6.28	5.87	5.75	5.52
IV	4.17	4.26	4.63	4.57	4.75	4.90	5.56	5.57	6.17[a]	6.26[a]	5.82	5.69	5.49
Standard Deviation - Gross Yield													
I	0.105	0.081	0.069	0.124	0.142	0.208	0.172	0.098	0.147	0.089	0.137	0.045	0.109
II	0.086	0.039	0.142	0.156	0.146	0.143	0.092	0.088	0.145	0.100	0.118	0.064	0.085
III	0.095	0.128	0.083	0.122	0.135	0.173	0.129	0.092	0.121	0.042	0.094	0.091	0.095
IV	0.080	0.023	0.151	0.102	0.117	0.142	0.061	0.112	0.224	0.176	0.067	0.085	0.093
Contract Rate													
I	4.28	4.25	4.25	4.50	4.50	4.47	4.94	5.25	5.25	5.73	5.71	5.27	5.25
II	4.27	4.25	4.35	4.49	4.48	4.49	5.00	5.25	5.25	5.74	5.58	5.25	5.25
III	4.25	4.26	4.50	4.50	4.49	4.50	5.09	5.25	5.25	5.75	5.41	5.25	5.25
IV	4.25	4.25	4.48	4.50	4.50	4.51	5.24	5.25	5.62	5.74	5.30	5.25	5.25
Net Discount													
I	-1.00	-0.42	0.03	0.84	0.86	1.67	2.25	2.54	3.25	3.55	2.93	3.67	2.55
II	-0.78	-0.03	0.15	1.00	1.12	1.57	2.72	2.38	3.46	3.50	2.61	3.71	1.97
III	-0.37	0.02	0.29	0.83	1.24	1.40	2.53	1.84	4.07[a]	3.46[a]	3.02	3.32	1.81
IV	-0.50	0.05	0.91	0.48	1.67	2.68	2.04	2.10	3.65[a]	3.46[a]	3.43	2.89	1.59

(continued)

TABLE C-31 (continued)

	1951	1952	1953	1954	1955	1956	1957	1958	1969	1960	1961	1962	1963
Loan-Value Ratio													
I	82.2	80.6	82.9	80.1	87.1	85.0	85.1	90.6	93.1	91.6	92.8	94.3	94.2
II	81.4	79.8	83.2	81.5	87.2	84.3	85.7	91.8	93.9	91.3	92.7	94.5	94.0
III	79.0	80.4	80.4	83.3	87.0	85.2	87.2	91.7	92.6	92.6	93.7	93.5	93.4
IV	79.0	81.2	80.8	85.7	86.0	83.5	88.3	92.2	91.2	93.0	93.3	93.9	93.7
Maturity (months)													
I	261.0	256.9	263.2	260.9	326.1	298.2	297.5	291.6	327.1	352.0	347.2	349.3	345.5
II	254.9	252.3	263.6	275.7	328.3	303.3	302.6	309.6	327.2	352.1	346.1	345.2	347.3
III	247.4	250.4	245.2	285.8	316.5	300.6	306.2	333.1	338.7	341.9	340.2	342.4	347.8
IV	250.9	248.9	253.4	312.4	305.6	308.6	287.0	332.5	346.7	348.0	345.0	346.8	350.4
Number of Loans													
I	192	213	218	202	201	170	161	168	149	246	288	191	244
II	289	188	167	205	159	209	148	228	151	147	282	308	217
III	174	162	115	242	183	239	153	187	160	169	166	245	335
IV	203	157	134	240	175	140	115	159	257	199	151	175	258
Mean Loan Size													
I	7,973	8,703	9,078	9,687	10,999	11,481	11,891	12,520	12,999	15,796	14,856	15,466	14,694
II	8,275	8,937	8,912	9,678	11,057	11,571	12,217	13,018	13,065	16,015	14,658	15,295	15,330
III	8,560	9,010	9,739	10,035	11,005	11,396	12,640	13,561	13,842	14,960	14,264	14,884	14,587
IV	8,691	8,619	9,871	10,769	11,031	12,281	13,013	13,305	15,469	14,945	14,433	14,815	14,977

aData cover only three companies.

TABLE C-32

Characteristics of FHA Mortgage Loans on Residential (1-4 Family)
Properties by Four Life Insurance Companies, 1951-63, Mountain

	1951	1952	1953	1954	1955	1956	1957	1958	1959	1960	1961	1962	1963
Gross Yield													
I	4.14	4.25	4.26	4.68	4.63	4.67	5.28	5.72	5.71	6.28	6.18	5.84	5.65
II	4.18	4.25	4.38	4.60	4.56	4.72	5.38	5.65	5.74	6.33	5.98	5.83	5.58
III	4.26	4.25	4.56	4.61	4.66	4.76	5.49	5.54	5.88	6.30	5.83	5.81	5.52
IV	4.20	4.24	4.71	4.59	4.67	4.89	5.65	5.55	6.17	6.30[a]	5.82	5.74	5.53
Standard Deviation - Gross Yield													
I	0.115	0.093	0.038	0.146	0.082	0.221	0.169	0.110	0.123	0.102	0.134	0.050	0.174
II	0.132	0.025	0.169	0.172	0.222	0.096	0.095	0.111	0.127	0.105	0.169	0.065	0.085
III	0.093	0.042	0.125	0.092	0.155	0.164	0.136	0.121	0.095	0.073	0.274	0.085	0.086
IV	0.096	0.064	0.201	0.114	0.129	0.108	0.072	0.202	0.186	0.181	0.092	0.103	0.093
Contract Rate													
I	4.30	4.25	4.25	4.51	4.50	4.44	4.94	5.25	5.25	5.75	5.73	5.29	5.22
II	4.28	4.25	4.34	4.44	4.41	4.50	5.00	5.25	5.25	5.75	5.57	5.26	5.25
III	4.26	4.25	4.48	4.50	4.47	4.47	5.10	5.25	5.25	5.75	5.38	5.25	5.25
IV	4.25	4.24	4.48	4.50	4.49	4.52	5.25	5.24	5.56	5.75	5.31	5.28	5.25
Net Discount													
I	-1.00	-0.01	0.05	1.14	0.88	1.55	2.20	3.03	3.05	3.49	2.95	3.66	2.87
II	-0.63	-0.03	0.26	1.01	1.02	1.48	2.51	2.62	3.30	3.78	2.70	3.82	2.23
III	-0.03	-0.01	0.49	0.69	1.31	1.95	2.55	1.94	4.14	3.57	3.02	3.72	1.79
IV	-0.34	0.03	1.49	0.61	1.19	2.49	2.59	2.03	4.04	3.59[a]	3.34	3.05	1.84

(continued)

TABLE C-32 (continued)

	1951	1952	1953	1954	1955	1956	1957	1958	1959	1960	1961	1962	1963
Loan-Value Ratio													
I	84.2	81.7	82.3	81.1	84.5	84.3	83.1	89.5	92.1	92.6	93.0	94.2	93.9
II	81.5	80.5	80.8	81.2	85.5	82.0	83.6	90.3	91.3	93.7	92.2	93.5	94.5
III	79.6	81.4	80.8	80.2	85.1	82.2	88.1	92.2	93.4	93.7	93.3	94.1	94.6
IV	79.1	79.4	82.2	83.7	85.3	81.2	89.1	92.1	91.6	94.3	93.8	93.9	93.5
Maturity (months)													
I	261.7	251.3	242.4	263.2	308.9	296.8	296.7	304.6	324.9	335.9	341.1	348.9	349.5
II	254.2	246.2	243.6	259.3	306.5	295.5	304.0	314.3	330.0	330.0	349.1	351.0	351.1
III	247.4	246.1	243.0	276.3	303.4	300.9	300.6	325.9	331.5	335.0	347.2	346.1	352.2
IV	238.1	239.6	249.2	289.1	291.8	290.1	298.1	332.9	340.3	353.3	352.3	344.2	351.7
Number of Loans													
I	70	94	107	92	103	95	71	80	97	79	101	85	106
II	96	63	81	84	64	73	70	90	84	78	142	134	80
III	80	55	92	99	56	109	69	77	99	64	101	108	63
IV	102	94	105	110	60	105	75	82	78	139	60	131	94
Mean Loan Size													
I	7,839	8,505	9,411	10,488	11,455	11,732	12,201	12,931	14,028	14,917	14,685	14,500	15,096
II	8,297	8,550	9,471	10,480	11,773	11,657	12,783	13,905	13,774	14,270	15,380	15,101	14,640
III	8,387	8,966	10,231	10,109	10,708	11,848	12,752	13,655	13,457	14,853	14,903	15,071	15,395
IV	9,051	9,170	10,010	11,158	11,555	12,305	13,131	13,713	14,357	14,896	16,599	15,099	14,956

aData cover only three companies.

TABLE C-33

Characteristics of Conventional Mortgage Loans on Residential (1-4 Family)
Properties by Four Life Insurance Companies, 1951-63, California

	1951	1952	1953	1954	1955	1956	1957	1958	1959	1960	1961	1962	1963
Gross Yield[a]													
I	4.47	4.43	4.64	4.91	4.80	4.81	5.40	5.70	5.59	6.05	6.01	5.76	5.63
II	4.44	4.63	4.68	4.87	4.80	4.81	5.66	5.59	5.69	6.15	5.90	5.75	5.51
III	4.47	4.80	4.83	4.83	4.80	4.93	5.58	5.50	5.76	6.20	5.89	5.66	5.50
IV	4.48	4.55	4.96	4.81	4.81	5.22	5.67	5.44	5.93	6.15	5.76	5.65	5.49
Standard Deviation - Gross Yield													
I				0.200	0.121	0.121	0.248	0.146	0.203	0.289	0.128	0.129	0.221
II				0.194	0.115	0.105	0.216	0.160	0.125	0.122	0.117	0.154	0.152
III				0.156	0.109	0.210	0.206	0.149	0.150	0.155	0.113	0.104	0.130
IV			0.224	0.128	0.099	0.228	0.189	0.189	0.194	0.096	0.162	0.089	0.137
Contract Rate													
I	4.56	4.72	4.92	5.09	5.00	5.01	5.50	5.83	5.70	6.15	6.10	5.86	5.69
II	4.59	4.87	4.92	5.06	4.99	5.00	5.70	5.70	5.80	6.26	6.01	5.86	5.60
III	4.64	4.96	5.14	5.03	4.99	5.14	5.68	5.61	5.85	6.30	5.99	5.76	5.59
IV	4.76	4.88	5.14	5.01	5.00	5.39	5.79	5.56	6.03	6.24	5.85	5.76	5.57
Net Discount													
I				-1.11	-1.19	-1.22	-0.64	-0.77	-0.75	-0.66	-0.59	-0.60	-0.35
II				-1.19	-1.19	-1.19	-0.28	-0.67	-0.71	-0.70	-0.66	-0.67	-0.59
III				-1.22	-1.22	-1.26	-0.61	-0.71	-0.60	-0.59	-0.66	-0.69	-0.58
IV			-1.09	-1.21	-1.21	-1.00	-0.74	-0.76	-0.57	-0.61	-0.62	-0.69	-0.49

(continued)

TABLE C-33 (continued)

	1951	1952	1953	1954	1955	1956	1957	1958	1959	1960	1961	1962	1963
Loan-Value Ratio													
I	62.7	61.8	64.2	63.5	63.6	63.5	64.5	64.6	64.4	69.7	70.4	68.7	70.7
II	62.8	62.6	64.2	64.4	64.1	64.4	63.8	64.1	65.3	70.3	69.9	69.9	69.4
III	61.4	63.2	64.5	64.0	65.0	63.4	63.5	64.1	69.3	69.6	70.7	70.0	70.3
IV	62.9	62.9	64.1	63.9	63.3	63.6	63.8	64.3	69.3	70.0	70.7	68.8	70.2
Maturity (months)													
I	207.0	218.4	217.6	221.9	226.7	234.4	234.5	240.0	279.2	285.3	290.4	293.8	315.2
II	203.9	207.6	220.3	227.4	231.6	237.1	246.6	252.2	276.8	287.1	193.3	306.2	302.2
III	213.9	210.7	225.5	232.7	235.6	235.9	240.3	256.5	286.6	283.1	291.1	308.8	309.5
IV	219.7	210.3	215.3	230.9	233.9	232.6	236.9	272.5	280.8	288.0	297.2	315.1	312.2
Number of Loans													
I	228	245	248	293	251	260	176	245	166	178	218	232	217
II	298	222	246	291	211	273	179	181	197	203	220	219	219
III	198	227	270	300	205	223	211	178	198	181	169	219	212
IV	235	218	274	251	224	203	244	137	193	165	194	219	205
Mean Loan Size													
I	10,327	10,559	10,584	11,983	12,013	13,465	15,289	14,885	18,751	18,937	19,122	19,795	22,424
II	10,255	10,675	11,672	11,752	13,096	14,567	14,853	16,463	18,713	19,249	19,597	20,575	19,878
III	10,315	10,452	10,872	12,127	13,439	14,399	14,375	16,119	19,786	17,628	20,103	20,788	21,028
IV	10,674	11,287	11,519	12,433	13,039	14,369	14,924	17,251	18,466	18,466	20,177	20,795	22,187

[a]During the period January 1951-September 1953 the data cover only three companies.

TABLE C-34

Characteristics of Conventional Mortgage Loans on Residential (1-4 Family) Properties by Four Life Insurance Companies, 1951-63, Florida

	1951	1952	1953	1954	1955	1956	1957	1958	1959	1960	1961	1962	1963
Gross Yield [a]													
I	4.53	4.65	4.79	4.83	4.81	4.83	5.47	5.76	5.71	6.07	5.93	5.71	5.62
II	4.53	4.87	4.81	4.81	4.77	4.83	5.49	5.58	5.68	6.13	5.77	5.75	5.58
III	4.81	4.85	4.84	4.84	4.78	4.95	5.39	5.47	5.82	6.07	5.76	5.68	5.58
IV	4.63	4.85	4.79	4.82	4.76	5.08	5.64	5.57	5.92	6.03	5.75	5.66	5.64
Standard Deviation - Gross Yield													
I				0.083	0.106	0.117	0.127	0.143	0.139	0.149	0.099	0.186	0.119
II				0.095	0.130	0.139	0.131	0.132	0.081	0.140	0.092	0.125	0.128
III				0.071	0.108	0.179	0.106	0.185	0.183	0.127	0.049	0.108	0.126
IV			0.139	0.114	0.114	0.165	0.117	0.167	0.140	0.089	0.138	0.088	0.343
Contract Rate													
I	4.69	4.77	4.85	4.98	4.93	4.97	5.56	5.78	5.72	6.07	5.97	5.71	5.66
II	4.73	4.94	4.94	4.94	4.95	4.96	5.56	5.59	5.74	6.13	5.82	5.76	5.67
III	4.94	4.92	4.98	4.99	4.93	5.08	5.51	5.53	5.79	6.07	5.77	5.76	5.64
IV	4.82	4.96	4.90	4.95	4.91	5.18	5.72	5.64	5.91	6.03	5.75	5.74	5.68
Net Discount													
I				-0.90	-0.73	-0.87	-0.54	-0.11	-0.11	0.00	-0.25	0.02	-0.28
II				-0.79	-1.03	-0.83	-0.42	-0.06	-0.33	0.00	-0.30	-0.06	-0.56
III				-0.95	-0.95	-0.80	-0.74	-0.34	0.21	0.00	-0.09	-0.48	-0.40
IV			-0.61	-0.79	-0.89	-0.66	-0.48	-0.42	0.05	0.00	-0.02	-0.48	-0.21

(continued)

TABLE C-34 (continued)

	1951	1952	1953	1954	1955	1956	1957	1958	1959	1960	1961	1962	1963
Loan-Value Ratio													
I	59.9	60.1	66.2	60.7	67.2	66.7	67.5	67.6	67.5	67.5	73.5	69.6	72.2
II	66.3	65.4	64.9	63.9	65.3	65.2	68.0	67.6	67.1	66.9	68.5	72.8	71.5
III	63.0	66.8	65.3	65.1	65.5	65.9	60.5	68.0	66.8	69.8	70.9	70.5	69.4
IV	64.6	61.7	64.2	67.1	62.4	68.9	67.7	67.9	69.8	69.9	67.3	70.8	65.5
Maturity (months)													
I	197.4	207.8	214.1	218.4	226.4	247.8	278.2	276.1	270.1	281.0	294.1	299.7	320.4
II	208.3	219.9	226.2	210.5	223.8	256.3	257.9	259.1	278.1	284.2	271.9	306.1	317.7
III	195.8	214.1	225.1	219.0	229.7	257.5	258.6	262.8	269.5	279.2	286.4	318.0	314.3
IV	194.5	221.6	210.5	236.1	231.5	269.1	266.3	276.2	286.3	279.2	281.8	310.7	322.7
Number of Loans													
I	24	28	25	24	34	46	28	26	36	37	30	28	31
II	18	21	17	47	24	32	30	42	33	32	24	27	26
III	17	26	21	61	49	17	31	40	37	26	22	33	34
IV	19	30	25	43	45	33	27	15	36	33	31	32	27
Mean Loan Size													
I	14,967	11,384	10,199	10,944	13,601	13,067	16,835	16,714	17,955	18,531	18,581	19,037	20,800
II	12,899	10,147	10,911	12,485	12,769	14,629	16,951	15,213	16,722	16,996	17,846	19,441	20,008
III	10,083	10,843	12,081	11,149	12,896	14,222	14,555	16,120	18,959	19,763	18,481	20,415	16,709
IV	11,257	9,433	12,310	12,509	14,212	15,319	16,770	16,394	18,095	17,614	17,494	19,788	17,472

[a]During the period January 1951-September 1953 the data cover only three companies.

TABLE C-35

Characteristics of Conventional Mortgage Loans on Residential (1-4 Family)
Properties by Four Life Insurance Companies, 1951-63, Michigan

	1951	1952	1953	1954	1955	1956	1957	1958	1959	1960	1961	1962	1963
Gross Yield[a]													
I	4.38	4.60	4.61	4.92	4.86	4.87	5.40	5.70	5.67	6.04	5.98	5.77	5.53
II	4.51	4.72	4.72	4.88	4.84	4.93	5.50	5.55	5.69	6.00	5.80	5.71	5.45
III	4.68	4.71	4.88	4.88	4.82	4.88	5.51	5.50	5.77	6.01	5.75	5.53	5.42
IV	4.67	4.59	4.88	4.82	4.84	5.08	5.61	5.49	5.93	6.00	5.75	5.58	5.42
Standard Deviation - Gross Yield													
I				0.109	0.103	0.117	0.217	0.132	0.171	0.110	0.080	0.091	0.157
II				0.092	0.163	0.104	0.126	0.120	0.140	0.147	0.128	0.134	0.174
III				0.133	0.157	0.085	0.176	0.127	0.126	0.045	0.120	0.136	0.158
IV			0.088	0.177	0.126	0.209	0.146	0.143	0.137	0.094	0.118	0.125	0.161
Contract Rate													
I	4.51	4.70	4.72	5.02	4.98	4.97	5.44	5.74	5.68	6.04	5.98	5.77	5.52
II	4.53	4.81	4.83	4.98	4.95	5.00	5.54	5.58	5.70	6.00	5.80	5.71	5.45
III	4.74	4.82	4.92	4.99	4.90	4.99	5.53	5.53	5.78	6.01	5.75	5.53	5.42
IV	4.74	4.68	4.98	4.93	4.95	5.13	5.63	5.51	5.93	6.01	5.75	5.57	5.40
Net Discount													
I				-0.63	-0.70	-0.64	-0.28	-0.25	-0.10	0.00	-0.02	-0.01	0.04
II				-0.63	-0.63	-0.44	-0.21	-0.16	-0.05	0.03	0.03	0.04	-0.02
III				-0.66	-0.53	-0.68	-0.11	-0.14	-0.05	0.00	0.00	0.01	0.00
IV			-0.61	-0.64	-0.68	-0.34	-0.14	-0.10	0.01	-0.02	0.00	0.04	0.13

(continued)

TABLE C-35 (continued)

	1951	1952	1953	1954	1955	1956	1957	1958	1959	1960	1961	1962	1963
Loan-Value Ratio													
I	62.2	63.5	61.7	60.5	63.8	61.7	64.3	63.4	64.5	69.0	69.6	68.7	68.2
II	66.3	61.0	59.9	62.3	62.5	65.9	64.9	62.8	65.3	68.3	67.7	68.3	66.8
III	62.6	60.5	61.8	61.4	63.6	60.6	62.4	64.0	68.6	70.1	68.6	69.5	68.5
IV	62.5	60.3	62.5	61.3	64.0	61.8	62.3	64.1	67.4	67.6	69.5	69.4	69.8
Maturity (months)													
I	217.0	216.0	216.7	226.4	233.2	229.4	231.5	250.9	260.9	278.9	281.5	280.4	282.7
II	212.8	224.9	221.6	229.1	227.2	226.7	240.0	256.1	259.6	281.8	275.5	284.3	281.5
III	228.4	219.0	231.3	230.0	233.8	234.6	238.7	256.9	270.6	278.1	276.1	286.4	292.2
IV	224.1	226.6	223.8	220.8	232.6	233.8	250.2	265.8	277.5	281.8	275.6	293.9	298.7
Number of Loans													
I	36	37	18	41	45	82	50	82	64	72	72	64	63
II	29	33	33	48	61	60	84	91	94	94	93	65	66
III	30	31	58	50	90	84	69	97	81	85	90	80	69
IV	33	35	50	49	97	76	87	101	68	70	73	75	61
Mean Loan Size													
I	8,334	8,854	11,708	10,367	11,918	12,684	12,780	14,143	14,252	15,498	15,016	15,369	15,337
II	9,150	9,606	9,717	11,044	11,111	13,765	13,369	13,899	13,724	13,924	15,975	14,738	14,317
III	9,144	9,548	11,347	10,159	12,665	12,309	12,563	13,770	14,625	14,706	15,533	16,883	15,802
IV	9,583	10,482	9,946	11,617	12,263	13,368	13,101	14,238	15,376	13,863	14,756	15,362	16,216

[a]During the period January 1951-September 1953 the data cover only three companies.

TABLE C-36

Characteristics of Conventional Mortgage Loans on Residential (1-4 Family)
Properties by Four Life Insurance Companies, 1951-63, New Jersey

	1951	1952	1953	1954	1955	1956	1957	1958	1959	1960	1961	1962	1963
Gross Yield[a]													
I	4.16	4.39	4.50	4.81	4.69	4.78	5.21	5.59	5.44	5.94	5.86	5.72	5.49
II	4.32	4.57	4.36	4.73	4.64	4.79	5.41	5.45	5.48	5.98	5.70	5.69	5.49
III	4.40	4.51	4.63	4.65	4.64	4.83	5.44	5.32	5.52	5.98	5.71	5.69	5.50
IV	4.44	4.31	4.83	4.64	4.67	4.88	5.54	5.28	5.73	5.96	5.71	5.56	5.49
Standard Deviation - Gross Yield													
I				0.094	0.190	0.157	0.280	0.187	0.168	0.129	0.148	0.096	0.095
II				0.168	0.165	0.168	0.212	0.206	0.105	0.111	0.166	0.148	0.090
III				0.190	0.215	0.145	0.159	0.164	0.137	0.093	0.111	0.151	0.080
IV			0.150	0.218	0.169	0.181	0.156	0.156	0.175	0.128	0.106	0.140	0.129
Contract Rate													
I	4.41	4.58	4.63	4.96	4.79	4.93	5.29	5.61	5.45	5.94	5.86	5.72	5.49
II	4.55	4.67	4.55	4.84	4.77	4.93	5.42	5.47	5.49	5.98	5.70	5.69	5.49
III	4.62	4.68	4.78	4.77	4.75	4.94	5.45	5.38	5.52	5.98	5.71	5.69	5.50
IV	4.62	4.55	4.98	4.77	4.79	4.98	5.55	5.31	5.73	5.96	5.71	5.56	5.49
Net Discount													
I				-0.87	-0.64	-0.96	-0.51	-0.10	-0.09	0.00	0.00	0.00	0.00
II				-0.68	-0.77	-0.85	-0.09	-0.14	-0.03	-0.02	0.00	0.00	0.00
III				-0.77	-0.70	-0.69	-0.06	-0.41	0.00	0.00	0.00	0.00	0.00
IV			-0.89	-0.83	-0.76	-0.66	-0.02	-0.17	0.00	0.00	0.00	0.00	0.00

(continued)

TABLE C-36 (continued)

	1951	1952	1953	1954	1955	1956	1957	1958	1959	1960	1961	1962	1963
Loan-Value Ratio													
I	60.9	61.3	64.0	64.9	65.5	63.5	65.1	62.8	69.2	69.1	70.4	68.7	71.1
II	63.6	64.3	66.9	62.3	60.4	61.1	61.4	64.3	70.0	69.4	70.2	70.2	71.7
III	61.6	62.9	64.4	61.8	64.5	61.8	58.1	67.3	67.6	70.1	69.6	69.7	70.1
IV	61.0	65.1	67.1	62.7	63.0	62.3	63.2	67.0	68.5	69.9	69.7	67.5	69.0
Maturity (months)													
I	217.5	219.0	232.5	228.0	256.6	264.4	269.6	268.2	291.0	291.8	298.3	319.2	327.0
II	217.8	234.7	232.6	227.9	257.3	238.7	253.5	276.2	295.6	295.6	294.8	315.2	334.7
III	220.3	229.5	227.7	230.6	271.8	248.0	257.4	283.8	282.0	293.7	306.2	326.9	315.7
IV	226.3	231.2	233.0	240.3	267.3	267.5	254.2	291.9	290.6	293.4	314.8	336.1	336.9
Number of Loans													
I	42	51	44	45	47	44	43	29	51	43	51	61	45
II	40	41	58	52	57	47	50	32	55	55	54	63	47
III	51	44	47	61	39	45	38	30	62	66	73	50	50
IV	39	44	42	54	51	63	43	58	53	58	60	46	43
Mean Loan Size													
I	11,248	12,048	12,794	12,478	13,322	15,098	16,508	15,350	17,458	17,307	18,866	19,632	22,745
II	11,937	10,830	13,132	12,797	13,112	16,004	14,511	15,243	18,836	18,975	20,340	20,168	14,063
III	10,511	11,315	12,509	14,881	15,032	14,379	15,512	16,824	19,041	19,081	19,467	19,624	21,678
IV	10,944	12,737	12,549	13,949	14,444	15,766	15,866	17,090	18,280	17,802	19,881	19,893	20,999

[a]During the period January 1951-September 1953 the data cover only three companies.

TABLE C-37

Characteristics of Conventional Mortgage Loans on Residential (1-4 Family)
Properties by Four Life Insurance Companies, 1951-63, New York

	1951	1952	1953	1954	1955	1956	1957	1958	1959	1960	1961	1962	1963
Gross Yield[a]													
I	4.20	4.35	4.36	4.81	4.46	4.74	5.12	5.58	5.46	5.87	5.94	5.75	5.50
II	4.31	4.39	4.42	4.78	4.52	4.72	5.26	5.44	5.47	5.92	5.77	5.74	5.53
III	4.35	4.45	4.62	4.64	4.70	4.87	5.35	5.41	5.47	5.94	5.72	5.59	5.58
IV	4.33	4.24	4.72	4.52	4.64	4.86	5.43	5.44	5.68	5.98	5.74	5.56	5.49
Standard Deviation - Gross Yield													
I				0.091	0.222	0.214	0.393	0.193	0.179	0.212	0.116	0.078	0.198
II				0.168	0.210	0.207	0.272	0.153	0.124	0.208	0.150	0.061	0.087
III				0.252	0.220	0.164	0.177	0.163	0.147	0.103	0.137	0.149	0.137
IV			0.202	0.219	0.209	0.119	0.170	0.205	0.201	0.079	0.079	0.153	0.105
Contract Rate													
I	4.37	4.51	4.55	4.94	4.59	4.87	5.23	5.64	5.49	5.88	5.94	5.75	5.50
II	4.44	4.57	4.59	4.90	4.64	4.83	5.33	5.51	5.50	5.92	5.77	5.74	5.53
III	4.57	4.53	4.76	4.75	4.82	4.98	5.43	5.48	5.51	5.94	5.72	5.60	5.60
IV	4.51	4.39	4.87	4.64	4.74	4.98	5.49	5.47	5.72	5.98	5.74	5.59	5.50
Net Discount													
I				-0.82	-0.86	-0.79	-0.68	-0.38	-0.19	-0.07	0.00	0.00	0.00
II				-0.68	-0.76	-0.70	-0.47	-0.42	-0.22	0.00	0.00	0.00	0.00
III				-0.69	-0.73	-0.67	-0.46	-0.43	-0.23	0.00	0.00	-0.07	-0.11
IV			-0.90	-0.78	-0.61	-0.76	-0.39	-0.21	-0.28	0.00	0.00	-0.22	-0.04

(continued)

TABLE C-37 (continued)

	1951	1952	1953	1954	1955	1956	1957	1958	1959	1960	1961	1962	1963
Loan-Value Ratio													
I	61.8	59.2	64.0	65.9	65.8	59.7	59.8	62.4	63.0	68.9	66.4	61.8	68.7
II	59.8	60.1	63.0	63.6	69.1	60.7	60.8	64.6	63.8	65.9	65.7	67.5	69.5
III	59.0	63.0	63.9	61.8	62.3	61.3	60.7	65.4	64.5	68.5	65.0	65.8	67.1
IV	62.1	63.2	60.6	62.4	59.6	64.2	64.2	66.4	66.9	66.3	64.3	67.3	66.3
Maturity (months)													
I	228.3	228.8	227.7	240.9	264.0	229.1	240.8	246.0	263.1	292.5	279.2	299.3	300.5
II	223.2	226.5	229.2	230.1	276.3	245.6	248.0	267.2	276.5	287.3	284.0	301.2	314.5
III	223.0	234.4	231.5	253.6	238.3	239.2	254.8	259.2	284.5	289.0	292.0	284.8	328.6
IV	232.9	232.8	222.3	255.9	221.3	272.5	259.9	284.4	286.9	285.6	292.6	315.3	303.1
Number of Loans													
I	22	28	28	21	41	34	32	48	60	44	28	31	13
II	29	33	28	31	36	35	38	47	50	53	35	25	26
III	27	29	43	29	40	26	48	27	35	42	45	27	24
IV	28	31	30	31	23	22	34	41	33	38	36	19	33
Mean Loan Size													
I	12,105	11,877	12,749	11,897	17,555	17,515	15,569	16,360	15,910	19,823	20,053	21,971	20,375
II	12,510	13,101	13,735	13,859	15,836	16,128	15,481	15,656	16,882	21,291	21,016	22,469	23,379
III	12,462	15,198	15,444	13,466	13,145	16,483	14,471	19,473	19,207	19,001	17,542	17,667	21,616
IV	14,464	14,010	15,177	15,575	17,959	17,175	16,296	17,569	18,915	19,510	21,271	19,935	22,696

[a]During the period January 1951-September 1953 the data cover only three companies.

TABLE C-38

Characteristics of Conventional Mortgage Loans on Residential (1-4 Family)
Properties by Four Life Insurance Companies, 1951-63, Ohio

	1951	1952	1953	1954	1955	1956	1957	1958	1959	1960	1961	1962	1963
Gross Yield[a]													
I	4.22	4.42	4.54	4.81	4.76	4.79	5.47	5.67	5.72	5.99	6.00	5.80	5.53
II	4.35	4.52	4.58	4.76	4.69	4.83	5.56	5.59	5.77	6.04	5.82	5.76	5.56
III	4.43	4.51	4.71	4.76	4.82	4.97	5.52	5.40	5.83	6.06	5.80	5.66	5.53
IV	4.54	4.49	4.84	4.67	4.86	5.17	5.70	5.50	5.86	6.04	5.73	5.63	5.54
Standard Deviation - Gross Yield													
I				0.115	0.178	0.221	0.298	0.159	0.173	0.195	0.087	0.138	0.135
II				0.178	0.164	0.153	0.198	0.167	0.100	0.161	0.178	0.064	0.109
III				0.230	0.285	0.258	0.187	0.265	0.124	0.119	0.158	0.103	0.091
IV			0.109	0.193	0.219	0.292	0.197	0.228	0.164	0.144	0.194	0.129	0.091
Contract Rate													
I	4.43	4.54	4.67	4.95	4.87	4.91	5.58	5.80	5.83	6.07	6.03	5.82	5.61
II	4.48	4.71	4.73	4.90	4.84	4.97	5.67	5.65	5.88	6.07	5.87	5.81	5.59
III	4.65	4.65	4.88	4.89	4.92	5.10	5.63	5.48	5.91	6.11	5.83	5.75	5.56
IV	4.66	4.63	4.98	4.79	4.99	5.29	5.81	5.62	5.97	6.05	5.77	5.72	5.55
Net Discount													
I				-0.82	-0.66	-0.78	-0.72	-0.81	-0.67	-0.48	-0.20	-0.13	-0.52
II				-0.84	-0.91	-0.88	-0.67	-0.37	-0.65	-0.22	-0.30	-0.30	-0.21
III				-0.84	-0.64	-0.79	-0.70	-0.53	-0.48	-0.32	-0.21	-0.58	-0.19
IV			-0.82	-0.77	-0.77	-0.76	-0.68	-0.71	-0.68	-0.05	-0.29	-0.60	-0.09

(continued)

TABLE C-38 (continued)

Loan-Value Ratio

	1951	1952	1953	1954	1955	1956	1957	1958	1959	1960	1961	1962	1963
I	58.9	60.6	63.9	62.2	64.4	63.3	65.0	66.4	69.3	67.4	71.1	69.6	68.7
II	61.9	63.5	64.2	62.6	64.1	63.6	62.8	67.5	68.3	70.4	69.5	71.5	70.0
III	60.5	61.3	62.3	61.9	63.7	63.4	64.2	65.4	68.9	70.9	70.8	70.0	70.3
IV	58.9	61.1	63.9	62.6	63.1	65.7	66.9	68.1	69.4	70.2	70.3	69.8	70.7

Maturity (months)

	1951	1952	1953	1954	1955	1956	1957	1958	1959	1960	1961	1962	1963
I	220.8	227.4	225.3	224.2	244.5	247.4	263.8	269.8	281.4	284.6	291.4	307.2	305.3
II	215.9	223.3	226.1	217.4	246.8	251.1	263.6	278.9	277.5	287.7	277.2	320.8	315.1
III	221.3	227.2	216.2	234.9	247.9	238.0	276.3	277.9	283.3	290.1	293.5	317.8	308.9
IV	222.7	214.6	216.0	246.6	242.7	265.5	264.0	274.5	291.0	289.3	289.2	308.8	315.3

Number of Loans

	1951	1952	1953	1954	1955	1956	1957	1958	1959	1960	1961	1962	1963
I	31	35	48	40	40	71	67	55	58	64	39	50	35
II	53	55	44	39	49	61	53	63	57	58	54	47	50
III	56	64	41	46	71	47	58	67	54	72	56	42	50
IV	45	48	47	38	57	62	49	54	67	56	52	43	43

Mean Loan Size

	1951	1952	1953	1954	1955	1956	1957	1958	1959	1960	1961	1962	1963
I	9,055	11,509	10,932	12,904	12,470	12,663	14,439	15,090	16,264	16,710	16,568	16,318	16,238
II	9,916	10,671	11,526	12,660	14,023	12,898	13,490	14,545	15,837	15,610	15,514	16,454	17,034
III	9,874	11,129	11,455	11,004	12,532	12,934	14,167	14,183	15,455	16,163	15,354	18,037	17,640
IV	9,691	11,072	11,745	12,351	13,155	14,425	14,677	15,496	16,545	15,205	16,729	16,513	17,735

[a]During the period January 1951-September 1953 the data cover only three companies.

TABLE C-39

Characteristics of Conventional Mortgage Loans on Residential (1-4 Family)
Properties by Four Life Insurance Companies, 1951-63, Pennsylvania

	1951	1952	1953	1954	1955	1956	1957	1958	1959	1960	1961	1962	1963
Gross Yield[a]													
I	4.28	4.39	4.43	4.80	4.69	4.68	5.27	5.48	5.41	5.96	5.86	5.67	5.48
II	4.36	4.47	4.61	4.84	4.79	4.75	5.36	5.46	5.45	5.99	5.70	5.65	5.48
III	4.47	4.51	4.83	4.78	4.61	4.71	5.38	5.33	5.59	5.97	5.63	5.56	5.46
IV	4.47	4.41	4.84	4.67	4.77	4.85	5.51	5.23	5.79	5.96	5.66	5.54	5.34
Standard Deviation - Gross Yield													
I				0.106	0.179	0.238	0.297	0.164	0.233	0.154	0.137	0.162	0.201
II				0.169	0.252	0.214	0.188	0.174	0.188	0.029	0.192	0.140	0.176
III			0.130	0.187	0.264	0.214	0.246	0.249	0.202	0.129	0.166	0.220	0.167
IV				0.239	0.188	0.185	0.157	0.214	0.168	0.081	0.181	0.159	0.262
Contract Rate													
I	4.47	4.53	4.53	4.94	4.79	4.81	5.27	5.57	5.50	5.95	5.85	5.67	5.46
II	4.56	4.62	4.67	4.89	4.83	4.82	5.38	5.50	5.52	6.00	5.69	5.66	5.47
III	4.58	4.61	4.89	4.88	4.70	4.78	5.41	5.36	5.62	5.97	5.64	5.57	5.47
IV	4.68	4.56	4.94	4.78	4.82	4.91	5.54	5.25	5.81	5.96	5.65	5.54	5.34
Net Discount													
I				-0.87	-0.64	-0.80	0.01	-0.53	-0.58	0.09	0.05	0.00	0.08
II				-0.31	-0.28	-0.48	-0.10	-0.32	-0.39	-0.05	0.02	-0.04	0.06
III				-0.64	-0.63	-0.46	-0.17	-0.17	-0.16	0.01	-0.04	-0.04	-0.06
IV			-0.61	-0.63	-0.34	-0.40	-0.19	-0.15	-0.13	0.04	0.02	0.02	0.00

(continued)

TABLE C-39 (continued)

	1951	1952	1953	1954	1955	1956	1957	1958	1959	1960	1961	1962	1963
Loan-Value Ratio													
I	63.6	61.6	62.2	66.5	64.6	65.4	64.2	66.7	63.2	70.6	68.6	67.7	68.0
II	62.6	62.0	65.4	67.0	63.8	63.3	64.3	67.5	67.1	69.4	68.3	70.3	69.7
III	61.9	63.2	61.9	64.4	62.8	61.3	62.7	64.0	69.2	69.7	66.2	66.2	70.3
IV	61.3	64.0	65.6	61.3	63.8	62.8	64.8	68.5	71.3	70.9	67.9	67.0	59.6
Maturity (months)													
I	213.4	222.0	227.6	227.1	246.4	261.6	259.9	262.0	239.1	270.3	272.7	279.3	267.3
II	213.0	224.2	230.2	217.3	214.5	227.7	228.7	237.1	254.7	274.6	276.2	297.7	310.8
III	214.2	223.2	224.0	237.5	257.6	241.1	242.1	231.3	248.5	284.7	262.9	279.6	294.2
IV	193.4	219.5	214.7	237.9	222.5	252.9	269.2	259.0	273.9	269.5	290.8	296.8	261.5
Number of Loans													
I	31	51	53	47	40	38	54	43	41	50	37	47	33
II	50	144	87	67	68	49	85	40	34	34	49	47	38
III	57	98	63	62	36	69	64	42	46	36	51	62	30
IV	49	98	54	46	58	54	40	58	64	30	48	45	50
Mean Loan Size													
I	9,257	9,818	11,703	13,348	11,114	12,879	12,443	14,436	13,382	15,382	15,884	17,595	14,738
II	9,862	8,989	11,080	11,884	9,654	10,818	11,216	14,080	11,809	13,707	15,748	17,930	16,500
III	9,253	9,350	11,215	10,975	12,277	11,666	12,230	14,314	14,795	15,375	15,698	15,527	17,229
IV	11,656	9,410	9,777	11,391	11,760	12,643	11,909	13,644	14,506	16,207	16,070	18,665	13,550

[a]During the period January 1951-September 1953 the data cover only three companies.

TABLE C-40

Characteristics of Conventional Mortgage Loans on Residential (1-4 Family) Properties by Four Life Insurance Companies, 1951-63, Texas

	1951	1952	1953	1954	1955	1956	1957	1958	1959	1960	1961	1962	1963
Gross Yield [a]													
I	4.36	4.54	4.54	4.88	4.92	4.95	5.56	5.82	5.68	6.15	6.07	5.82	5.59
II	4.43	4.57	4.66	4.84	4.90	4.89	5.55	5.64	5.78	6.20	5.91	5.79	5.59
III	4.66	4.59	4.91	4.81	4.96	5.04	5.54	5.53	5.86	6.19	5.81	5.68	5.59
IV	4.65	4.57	4.90	4.80	4.94	5.37	5.78	5.64	6.02	6.05	5.80	5.68	5.58
Standard Deviation - Gross Yield													
I				0.160	0.172	0.160	0.149	0.164	0.137	0.187	0.194	0.119	0.135
II				0.143	0.160	0.346	0.172	0.167	0.133	0.138	0.134	0.077	0.126
III				0.153	0.212	0.233	0.123	0.139	0.123	0.165	0.097	0.140	0.157
IV			0.192	0.110	0.158	0.252	0.147	0.139	0.159	0.142	0.123	0.165	0.125
Contract Rate													
I	4.55	4.73	4.72	5.03	5.01	5.02	5.54	5.83	5.71	6.15	6.11	5.86	5.61
II	4.57	4.74	4.84	5.01	4.98	4.96	5.57	5.67	5.80	6.21	5.94	5.82	5.64
III	4.81	4.73	5.05	4.97	5.00	5.12	5.56	5.56	5.89	6.19	5.82	5.70	5.61
IV	4.80	4.77	5.06	4.93	5.01	5.40	5.80	5.67	6.04	6.07	5.82	5.71	5.59
Net Discount													
I				-0.90	-0.59	-0.45	0.13	-0.07	-0.20	-0.02	-0.21	-0.26	-0.14
II				-1.05	-0.53	-0.44	-0.12	-0.18	-0.16	-0.08	-0.20	-0.20	-0.31
III				-1.00	-0.26	-0.45	-0.10	-0.19	-0.24	0.00	-0.11	-0.11	-0.11
IV			-0.99	-0.84	-0.42	-0.19	-0.11	-0.16	-0.15	-0.13	-0.17	-0.15	-0.09

(continued)

TABLE C-40 (continued)

	1951	1952	1953	1954	1955	1956	1957	1958	1959	1960	1961	1962	1963
						Loan-Value Ratio							
I	65.2	65.0	67.4	67.1	69.4	70.5	70.6	70.4	71.1	72.2	70.5	72.7	71.6
II	65.5	64.1	67.5	67.3	69.1	71.0	69.2	69.4	69.5	69.8	70.4	72.2	67.9
III	64.0	65.2	66.0	69.1	70.0	68.2	67.2	70.2	72.3	71.7	72.3	69.6	70.6
IV	65.6	66.9	66.9	69.7	71.7	69.6	71.2	70.2	71.7	70.7	71.9	71.7	73.1
						Maturity (months)							
I	217.0	226.0	226.3	233.4	254.8	257.2	254.7	254.4	278.8	279.4	285.4	301.1	304.8
II	219.2	224.3	226.3	235.5	261.4	255.5	237.0	259.9	276.4	275.9	286.3	304.0	300.9
III	213.6	226.2	225.7	242.3	254.1	245.8	247.4	270.1	286.2	283.5	294.1	294.0	301.0
IV	219.1	229.5	227.0	253.3	255.8	262.4	256.8	270.6	279.9	283.8	294.5	296.0	327.3
						Number of Loans							
I	86	165	129	193	80	73	64	71	114	119	70	56	47
II	117	175	149	168	69	67	60	82	113	88	67	39	35
III	123	161	152	114	84	67	79	101	89	77	57	42	37
IV	122	133	163	97	91	51	70	92	87	64	60	38	36
						Mean Loan Size							
I	11,938	11,123	12,650	12,403	12,952	13,919	16,102	15,572	16,771	17,635	17,332	16,911	19,993
II	11,418	10,278	12,414	12,905	13,783	15,809	16,001	16,677	17,046	16,533	18,400	17,441	17,119
III	11,158	10,916	11,946	13,215	14,358	15,596	14,364	16,091	18,549	17,700	17,018	18,130	18,653
IV	10,496	11,540	13,007	13,584	15,763	15,639	16,292	16,839	16,276	18,438	17,134	17,666	19,080

[a]During the period January 1951-September 1953 the data cover only three companies.

TABLE C-41

Characteristics of FHA Mortgage Loans on Residential (1-4 Family)
Properties by Four Life Insurance Companies, 1951-63, California

	1951	1952	1953	1954	1955	1956	1957	1958	1959	1960	1961	1962	1963
Gross Yield													
I	4.14	4.20	4.25	4.67	4.73	4.80	5.25	5.65	5.70	6.27	6.16	5.79	5.58
II	4.16	4.23	4.32	4.72	4.71	4.71	5.48	5.61	5.75	6.27	5.97	5.77	5.49
III	4.18	4.27	4.50	4.69	4.75	4.62	5.51	5.55	5.89[a]	6.28[a]	5.82	5.74	5.45
IV	4.18	4.25	4.67	4.57	4.77	5.04	5.57	5.58	6.20[a]	6.28[a]	5.78	5.64	5.44
Standard Deviation - Gross Yield													
I	0.118	0.072	0.025	0.165	0.230	0.289	0.171	0.088	0.106	0.095	0.143	0.032	0.080
II	0.096	0.053	0.114	0.205	0.242	0.243	0.072	0.091	0.184	0.108	0.145	0.037	0.059
III	0.106	0.105	0.000	0.204	0.178	0.223	0.096	0.066	0.112	0.046	0.082	0.063	0.059
IV	0.079	0.001	0.213	0.147	0.192	0.157	0.071	0.098	0.233	0.121	0.023	0.085	0.057
Contract Rate													
I	4.29	4.25	4.25	4.49	4.50	4.44	4.82	5.25	5.25	5.73	5.74	5.26	5.25
II	4.28	4.24	4.32	4.47	4.47	4.50	5.00	5.25	5.25	5.74	5.63	5.25	5.25
III	4.26	4.27	4.50	4.49	4.50	4.50	5.07	5.25	5.25	5.75	5.47	5.25	5.25
IV	4.25	4.25	4.46	4.50	4.47	4.50	5.25	5.25	5.62	5.74	5.32	5.27	5.25
Net Discount													
I	-0.94	-0.30	0.00	1.22	1.62	2.44	2.92	2.61	2.97	3.58	2.80	3.54	2.20
II	-0.80	-0.04	0.00	1.72	1.62	1.45	3.18	2.39	3.32	3.50	2.20	3.48	1.64
III	-0.49	-0.05	0.00	1.38	1.67	0.85	2.95	2.02	4.26[a]	3.47	2.32	3.25	1.33
IV	-0.45	0.00	1.39	0.47	2.05	3.69	2.11	2.20	3.83[a]	3.53[a]	3.07	2.47	1.25

(continued)

TABLE C-41 (continued)

	1951	1952	1953	1954	1955	1956	1957	1958	1959	1960	1961	1962	1963
							Loan-Value Ratio						
I	84.3	84.1	84.3	81.3	86.8	83.9	85.5	89.3	95.1	91.5	92.4	94.1	93.9
II	84.1	80.3	83.1	80.7	85.1	81.5	85.6	90.2	94.0	90.9	91.7	93.5	94.0
III	81.5	82.6	79.6	80.5	88.7	82.0	86.0	91.5	91.9	92.4	92.8	91.8	94.0
IV	80.2	83.1	79.7	84.4	86.4	84.4	86.1	92.5	90.6	92.3	92.1	92.3	93.8
							Maturity (months)						
I	268.0	274.2	281.5	274.9	330.7	325.6	325.2	300.5	348.5	359.2	356.3	358.9	357.6
II	265.9	249.0	278.6	285.0	336.7	322.9	332.1	326.7	351.7	359.8	355.9	360.4	359.5
III	252.6	264.3	250.8	289.8	324.1	304.3	320.5	347.6	356.2	357.3	357.1	362.3	364.0
IV	259.4	264.3	257.1	296.6	343.2	348.7	291.4	352.5	358.0	357.1	355.1	360.6	362.3
							Number of Loans						
I	86	74	82	82	44	29	27	55	42	132	113	59	46
II	154	32	50	59	17	30	41	88	41	94	95	45	31
III	78	41	13	50	13	60	61	55	58	65	54	26	72
IV	73	38	35	45	56	30	38	60	158	84	48	32	81
							Mean Loan Size						
I	8,004	8,797	9,434	10,033	11,160	11,988	13,051	13,823	12,699	16,485	15,478	16,447	15,770
II	8,138	8,958	9,123	9,738	11,007	12,086	13,523	14,043	13,390	16,642	15,518	16,110	15,078
III	8,788	9,056	10,988	9,839	10,384	11,934	13,564	14,380	15,355	15,886	14,389	16,114	15,469
IV	9,118	9,161	10,325	10,991	11,907	13,741	13,888	13,332	16,564	15,713	15,234	15,802	15,846

[a]Data cover only three companies.

TABLE C-42

Characteristics of FHA Mortgage Loans on Residential (1-4 Family)
Properties by Four Life Insurance Companies, 1951-63, Florida

	1951	1952	1953	1954	1955	1956	1957	1958	1959	1960	1961	1962	1963
Gross Yield													
I	4.13	4.26	4.28	4.75	4.60	4.64	5.35	5.65	5.76	6.29	6.12	5.85	5.62
II	4.18	4.30	4.45	4.68	4.56	4.80	5.41	5.59	5.78	6.33	5.99	5.82	5.60
III	4.25	4.29	4.64	4.60	4.53	4.84	5.48	5.56	5.84	6.33	5.88	5.76	5.55
IV	4.29	4.25	4.73	4.59	4.69	4.93	5.58	5.63	5.90[a]	6.26	5.81	5.73	5.57
Standard Deviation - Gross Yield													
I	0.079	0.054	0.060	0.258	0.094	0.299	0.139	0.149	0.129	0.128	0.107	0.033	0.079
II	0.085	0.075	0.157	0.140	0.217	0.121	0.069	0.110	0.111	0.143	0.075	0.059	0.075
III	0.090	0.119	0.116	0.108	0.187	0.146	0.106	0.079	0.086	0.142	0.083	0.132	0.066
IV	0.075	0.039	0.166	0.111	0.140	0.072	0.094	0.074	0.490	0.100	0.148	0.070	0.143
Contract Rate													
I	4.25	4.25	4.25	4.48	4.50	4.39	4.96	5.25	5.26	5.75	5.72	5.31	5.25
II	4.25	4.25	4.39	4.49	4.45	4.50	5.00	5.25	5.25	5.75	5.57	5.26	5.25
III	4.25	4.25	4.50	4.50	4.45	4.48	5.08	5.25	5.26	5.75	5.55	5.25	5.25
IV	4.25	4.25	4.50	4.49	4.50	4.51	5.25	5.25	5.42	5.75	5.32	5.25	5.25
Net Discount													
I	-0.78	0.09	0.17	1.77	0.67	1.70	2.57	2.61	3.27	3.50	2.59	3.60	2.51
II	-0.49	0.33	0.42	1.24	0.73	2.02	2.72	2.23	3.54	3.79	2.77	3.78	2.34
III	-0.05	0.25	0.94	0.63	0.51	2.40	2.63	2.04	3.88	3.78	2.17	3.35	2.00
IV	0.24	0.01	1.52	0.71	1.28	2.81	2.12	2.53	3.17[a]	3.33	3.21	3.20	2.09

(continued)

TABLE C-42 (continued)

	1951	1952	1953	1954	1955	1956	1957	1958	1959	1960	1961	1962	1963
						Loan-Value Ratio							
I	79.1	85.1	85.2	84.1	87.7	85.6	85.0	91.7	91.9	93.6	91.7	94.1	94.9
II	83.7	82.8	83.7	83.6	87.9	84.5	83.8	91.4	91.9	90.4	92.3	91.8	94.8
III	81.1	84.0	84.6	84.8	86.0	82.2	86.5	91.7	91.5	93.4	93.1	92.7	94.0
IV	83.9	82.9	84.0	88.2	87.0	86.1	90.4	90.1	92.4	93.8	92.8	95.0	94.6
						Maturity (months)							
I	248.6	247.5	256.4	266.8	293.7	293.2	294.1	303.5	315.3	327.7	334.3	354.1	360.0
II	249.1	252.7	257.0	264.5	288.6	298.2	303.1	312.4	321.4	342.2	349.4	358.0	355.8
III	251.8	256.5	267.3	279.8	300.2	283.3	295.8	300.4	335.9	343.8	348.5	350.7	357.9
IV	247.4	258.6	265.7	272.5	295.9	292.9	293.7	309.5	346.3	332.5	358.1	342.1	358.8
						Number of Loans							
I	39	66	83	51	55	47	20	45	71	27	31	37	37
II	64	44	60	88	64	45	52	44	60	41	44	55	23
III	73	97	88	60	83	26	22	29	46	27	104	28	32
IV	69	122	70	69	52	28	26	33	157	18	40	36	30
						Mean Loan Size							
I	8,615	8,577	8,586	8,639	9,582	10,590	10,729	13,244	14,203	14,558	15,117	15,514	15,331
II	7,911	8,295	8,816	8,979	10,017	9,698	12,650	13,182	14,725	14,890	15,095	15,770	15,230
III	8,489	8,190	8,840	9,067	11,263	11,125	11,635	14,579	14,457	14,363	14,149	14,030	15,689
IV	8,175	8,411	8,954	8,675	11,024	11,624	13,184	14,438	13,453	14,996	15,112	13,631	14,182

[a]Data cover only three companies.

TABLE C-43

Characteristics of FHA Mortgage Loans on Residential (1-4 Family)
Properties by Four Life Insurance Companies, 1951-63, Michigan

	1951	1952	1953	1954	1955	1956	1957	1958	1959	1960	1961	1962	1963
						Gross Yield							
I	4.16	4.24	4.32	4.70	4.60	4.74	5.38	5.69	5.80	6.23	6.16	5.74	5.55
II	4.16	4.25	4.42	4.60	4.63	4.81	5.39	5.63	5.83	6.25[a]	5.92	5.73	5.48
III	4.29	4.25	4.62	4.62	4.70	4.83	5.50	5.54	5.89[a]	6.27	5.85	5.67	5.50
IV	4.29	4.32	4.76	4.61	4.75	4.97	5.68	5.60	6.16	6.26[a]	5.75	5.62	5.45
					Standard Deviation - Gross Yield								
I	0.090	0.066	0.081	0.113	0.096	0.222	0.223	0.114	0.084	0.192	0.081	0.074	0.056
II	0.091	0.057	0.146	0.149	0.129	0.170	0.112	0.096	0.083	0.189	0.117	0.080	0.117
III	0.096	0.020	0.117	0.133	0.146	0.144	0.146	0.102	0.159	0.125	0.117	0.082	0.097
IV	0.114	0.082	0.154	0.090	0.211	0.134	0.076	0.094	0.142	0.117	0.096	0.091	0.118
						Contract Rate							
I	4.27	4.25	4.25	4.50	4.50	4.47	4.95	5.25	5.25	5.74	5.74	5.29	5.25
II	4.26	4.25	4.35	4.47	4.49	4.50	4.99	5.25	5.25	5.74	5.58	5.25	5.25
III	4.25	4.25	4.49	4.50	4.49	4.49	5.11	5.25	5.25	5.75	5.43	5.25	5.25
IV	4.25	4.25	4.49	4.50	4.48	4.51	5.25	5.25	5.65	5.75	5.34	5.25	5.25
						Net Discount							
I	-0.73	-0.06	0.45	1.33	0.70	1.74	2.83	2.92	3.66	3.20	2.78	2.95	2.00
II	-0.64	0.00	0.45	0.86	0.93	2.02	2.63	2.52	3.83	3.31[a]	2.26	3.18	1.55
III	0.22	0.02	0.84	0.84	1.37	2.25	2.58	1.94	4.26[a]	3.35	2.81	2.73	1.64
IV	0.23	0.48	1.72	0.72	1.79	3.11	2.85	2.34	3.30	3.30[a]	2.75	2.43	1.33

(continued)

TABLE C-43 (continued)

	1951	1952	1953	1954	1955	1956	1957	1958	1959	1960	1961	1962	1963
						Loan-Value Ratio							
I	81.8	79.4	79.8	78.6	83.1	83.6	80.8	87.2	89.6	92.2	92.1	93.7	92.2
II	80.2	80.1	80.0	79.8	84.6	81.2	80.8	88.3	90.3	91.6	91.7	93.9	93.3
III	79.1	81.2	79.2	78.4	84.4	83.6	83.4	89.6	91.8	93.3	92.2	94.6	93.4
IV	79.1	81.0	79.0	84.2	83.5	82.0	85.6	89.4	91.9	91.8	92.9	93.9	94.6
						Maturity (months)							
I	265.6	243.7	254.9	266.0	305.9	294.2	301.7	319.5	337.3	334.0	348.1	346.3	345.4
II	262.2	254.2	246.9	274.7	310.9	282.3	301.8	329.9	324.9	345.8	344.2	343.4	357.8
III	245.5	248.4	259.2	274.4	295.0	289.1	304.7	341.2	337.2	332.7	339.3	333.9	344.6
IV	255.0	273.9	274.1	307.8	304.8	298.7	315.1	341.3	339.4	336.0	350.6	359.9	352.5
						Number of Loans							
I	35	78	99	102	150	114	56	64	74	107	54	35	48
II	55	126	78	102	137	69	64	47	67	150	61	25	33
III	100	133	103	96	112	54	81	49	82	80	50	44	26
IV	81	139	113	129	226	161	74	74	83	59	44	58	103
						Mean Loan Size							
I	8,273	8,548	9,382	10,532	11,837	12,128	12,878	13,850	14,611	12,941	13,385	13,589	14,931
II	8,310	8,887	9,774	10,765	12,110	11,698	13,083	13,942	14,050	13,724	14,033	14,252	15,075
III	8,542	8,977	9,516	10,783	12,046	12,344	13,974	14,508	13,413	13,297	13,377	14,383	13,502
IV	8,789	9,244	9,992	11,874	12,516	13,427	14,441	14,269	14,369	13,402	14,017	14,269	14,477

[a]Data cover only three companies.

TABLE C-44

Characteristics of FHA Mortgage Loans on Residential (1-4 Family)
Properties by Four Life Insurance Companies, 1951-63, New Jersey

	1951	1952	1953	1954	1955	1956	1957	1958	1959	1960	1961	1962	1963
						Gross Yield							
I	4.02	4.19	4.25	4.67	4.50	4.53	5.04	5.44	5.42	6.04	5.96	5.55	5.41
II	4.14	4.25	4.30	4.70	4.49	4.59	5.28	5.41	5.42	6.11	5.77	5.54	5.38
III	4.25	4.25	4.48	4.51	4.48	4.58	5.25	5.40	5.48	6.07	5.67	5.49	5.33
IV	4.25	4.25	4.67	4.50	4.53	4.67	5.45	5.40	5.75	6.09[a]	5.58	5.50	5.32
					Standard Deviation - Gross Yield								
I	0.177	0.071	0.001	0.122	0.001	0.165	0.269	0.054	0.086	0.096	0.148	0.096	0.123
II	0.048	0.001	0.133	0.200	0.059	0.058	0.069	0.081	0.105	0.074	0.170	0.113	0.107
III	0.169	0.001	0.220	0.070	0.119	0.061	0.122	0.087	0.115	0.105	0.135	0.124	0.053
IV	0.000	0.000	0.116	0.001	0.095	0.116	0.101	0.088	0.257	0.216	0.108	0.080	0.074
						Contract Rate							
I	4.25	4.25	4.25	4.48	4.50	4.47	4.88	5.25	5.25	5.75	5.72	5.29	5.25
II	4.35	4.25	4.33	4.47	4.49	4.50	5.00	5.25	5.25	5.75	5.58	5.26	5.25
III	4.31	4.25	4.45	4.50	4.47	4.50	5.07	5.25	5.25	5.73	5.42	5.25	5.25
IV	4.25	4.25	4.49	4.50	4.50	4.50	5.27	5.25	5.46	5.72	5.33	5.28	5.25
						Net Discount							
I	-1.52	-0.36	0.00	1.20	0.00	0.45	1.12	1.23	1.16	1.92	1.60	1.74	1.07
II	-1.34	0.00	-0.24	1.52	0.00	0.60	1.85	1.06	1.14	2.36	1.25	1.90	0.90
III	-0.38	0.00	0.18	0.09	0.06	0.56	1.16	1.00	1.53	2.23	1.62	1.62	0.56
IV	0.00	0.00	1.17	0.00	0.21	1.14	1.23	0.84	1.86	2.43[a]	1.65	1.50	0.44

(continued)

TABLE C-44 (continued)

	1951	1952	1953	1954	1955	1956	1957	1958	1959	1960	1961	1962	1963
Loan-Value Ratio													
I	75.0	82.1	86.9	83.8	86.5	80.0	80.6	88.6	90.1	93.5	93.7	91.4	92.4
II	81.0	81.4	80.0	85.5	86.0	81.1	83.3	89.1	90.0	90.3	90.9	93.2	82.8
III	79.8	80.7	80.4	78.2	82.3	86.5	86.3	86.3	92.8	92.7	85.5	91.5	73.8
IV	76.2	86.5	81.2	86.0	83.6	80.2	89.2	94.2	90.4	90.7	90.5	90.6	94.7
Maturity (months)													
I	251.7	281.1	294.3	278.4	351.7	314.5	332.5	324.4	345.8	360.0	355.6	360.0	359.9
II	263.1	268.2	249.2	283.9	326.9	318.2	351.6	352.3	339.7	359.2	356.0	359.1	360.0
III	255.2	231.4	282.9	293.6	315.5	347.4	322.4	347.7	358.6	360.0	352.7	352.1	350.4
IV	240.0	295.7	274.5	319.4	309.7	338.5	346.1	289.7	348.5	337.3	354.8	352.3	360.0
Number of Loans													
I	7	16	8	33	18	46	23	61	31	10	21	26	15
II	4	14	19	11	33	25	33	42	28	32	15	32	17
III	4	4	27	18	25	16	38	14	21	9	25	25	24
IV	1	5	16	8	44	21	27	14	15	36	26	22	10
Mean Loan Size													
I	8,465	7,994	8,359	8,966	10,868	11,368	12,083	12,653	13,578	13,690	15,496	15,721	14,644
II	8,413	8,148	9,532	8,848	9,625	11,005	12,942	13,189	12,864	13,738	15,804	14,919	14,707
III	7,720	7,423	8,722	10,431	9,869	11,570	11,686	13,954	13,980	15,456	14,024	15,154	14,003
IV	10,900	7,928	9,554	9,930	11,661	11,874	11,782	12,136	12,716	13,962	14,808	15,853	15,991

[a]Data cover only three companies.

TABLE C-45

Characteristics of FHA Mortgage Loans on Residential (1-4 Family)
Properties by Four Life Insurance Companies, 1951-63, New York

	1951	1952	1953	1954	1955	1956	1957	1958	1959	1960	1961	1962	1963
Gross Yield													
I	4.15	4.11	4.17	4.64	4.50	4.40	4.89	5.39	5.25	5.75	5.79	–	5.51
II	4.11	4.34	4.22	4.59	4.49	4.52	5.25	5.40	5.34	6.00	5.80	5.61	5.47
III	4.20	4.25	4.37	4.50	4.48	4.53	5.22	5.45	5.45	6.02	5.48	5.70	5.41
IV	4.25	4.11	4.52	4.50	4.52	4.63	5.42	5.28	5.56	5.95	5.44	5.62	5.42
Standard Deviation - Gross Yield													
I	0.074	0.050	0.078	0.083	0.000	0.217	0.217	0.057	0.000	0.000	0.125	–	0.064
II	0.046	0.077	0.106	0.076	0.065	0.037	0.132	0.019	0.135	0.138	0.002	0.088	0.130
III	0.073	0.001	0.125	0.000	0.105	0.094	0.171	0.151	0.122	0.116	0.112	0.000	0.066
IV	0.000	0.076	0.102	0.001	0.076	0.115	0.104	0.052	0.221	0.113	0.061	0.020	0.095
Contract Rate													
I	4.25	4.25	4.25	4.50	4.50	4.39	4.79	5.25	5.25	5.75	5.64	–	5.25
II	4.25	4.25	4.33	4.50	4.48	4.50	5.00	5.25	5.25	5.75	5.50	5.25	5.25
III	4.25	4.25	4.37	4.50	4.48	4.50	5.07	5.25	5.25	5.75	5.34	5.25	5.25
IV	4.25	4.25	4.50	4.50	4.50	4.50	5.25	5.25	5.31	5.75	5.25	5.25	5.25
Net Discount													
I	-0.63	-0.88	-0.50	0.91	0.00	0.08	0.67	0.94	0.00	0.00	1.00	–	1.72
II	-0.91	0.59	-0.71	0.59	0.04	0.12	1.68	1.02	0.57	1.60	2.00	2.38	1.49
III	-0.33	0.00	0.00	0.00	0.00	0.22	1.01	1.36	1.34	1.77	0.92	3.00	1.05
IV	0.00	-0.76	0.15	0.00	0.15	0.91	1.12	0.22	1.62	1.29	1.24	2.46	0.98

(continued)

TABLE C-45 (continued)

	1951	1952	1953	1954	1955	1956	1957	1958	1959	1960	1961	1962	1963
						Loan-Value Ratio							
I	81.6	74.7	78.3	77.6	79.6	81.3	81.7	87.5	84.5	95.0	92.0	—	95.7
II	69.5	73.4	74.9	73.9	83.5	77.7	80.7	85.9	88.6	92.9	90.9	92.1	93.9
III	71.4	77.4	81.4	69.9	83.9	80.2	80.4	90.0	88.2	91.9	91.0	91.6	88.6
IV	82.5	73.3	78.5	74.0	83.0	82.7	87.1	90.3	83.5	87.2	88.6	94.0	92.1
						Maturity (months)							
I	240.0	243.9	248.6	246.4	328.5	291.1	328.6	314.0	342.0	300.0	341.4	—	290.5
II	240.0	240.0	240.0	240.0	329.5	308.8	318.6	331.3	313.0	306.7	354.4	360.0	345.5
III	240.0	240.0	240.0	277.4	333.9	312.6	325.0	353.0	360.0	352.6	313.7	360.0	355.9
IV	270.5	194.2	263.0	279.4	336.2	345.3	286.0	340.0	341.7	345.3	282.7	360.0	250.2
						Number of Loans							
I	9	4	10	6	13	17	11	10	4	1	4	0	6
II	5	2	3	5	13	17	10	34	2	4	6	4	4
III	2	2	2	5	14	8	13	7	20	6	4	2	5
IV	2	3	7	3	18	15	7	5	6	11	4	2	3
						Mean Loan Size							
I	7,687	7,791	10,515	9,197	12,826	11,667	14,087	14,786	17,506	15,200	13,369	—	12,735
II	8,017	8,517	9,585	9,983	11,357	12,580	14,038	13,837	12,452	14,880	17,349	15,299	16,600
III	9,416	9,200	9,525	11,145	11,494	12,577	13,634	15,770	14,537	15,543	14,053	17,650	13,379
IV	8,125	7,553	10,031	10,197	12,934	12,784	14,326	14,378	16,184	14,289	13,737	15,489	12,055

TABLE C-46

Characteristics of FHA Mortgage Loans on Residential (1-4 Family) Properties by Four Life Insurance Companies, 1951-63, Ohio

	1951	1952	1953	1954	1955	1956	1957	1958	1959	1960	1961	1962	1963
						Gross Yield							
I	4.06	4.30	4.27	4.70	4.60	4.70	5.31	5.62	5.78	6.24	6.14	5.72	5.59
II	4.12	4.30	4.39	4.63	4.60	4.78	5.43	5.56	5.81	6.30[a]	5.93	5.72	5.50
III	4.21	4.30	4.52	4.65	4.68	4.85	5.43	5.46	5.89	6.25	5.76	5.67	5.45
IV	4.29	4.25	4.66	4.63	4.71	4.90	5.58	5.56	6.16	6.24	5.72	5.68	5.43
					Standard Deviation - Gross Yield								
I	0.096	0.065	0.054	0.081	0.096	0.232	0.195	0.107	0.114	0.311	0.127	0.111	0.089
II	0.089	0.101	0.150	0.094	0.183	0.128	0.126	0.104	0.099	0.176	0.124	0.074	0.084
III	0.097	0.104	0.127	0.123	0.174	0.184	0.112	0.091	0.090	0.105	0.126	0.078	0.104
IV	0.106	0.125	0.153	0.099	0.114	0.085	0.081	0.130	0.208	0.112	0.097	0.089	0.188
						Contract Rate							
I	4.26	4.25	4.25	4.50	4.50	4.44	4.94	5.25	5.25	5.71	5.69	5.25	5.25
II	4.25	4.25	4.36	4.50	4.46	4.49	5.00	5.25	5.25	5.75	5.52	5.25	5.25
III	4.31	4.26	4.48	4.50	4.49	4.48	5.06	5.25	5.25	5.75	5.32	5.25	5.25
IV	4.26	4.25	4.50	4.50	4.50	4.51	5.24	5.25	5.57	5.75	5.27	5.25	5.25
						Net Discount							
I	-1.26	0.32	0.15	1.31	0.66	1.73	2.40	2.41	3.47	3.44	2.98	3.14	2.24
II	-0.84	0.34	0.20	0.87	0.89	1.94	2.86	2.06	3.74	3.59[a]	2.73	3.15	1.64
III	-0.65	0.24	0.20	1.01	1.24	2.44	2.45	1.40	4.23	3.25	2.92	2.75	1.30
IV	0.18	-0.01	1.02	0.89	1.40	2.57	2.23	2.04	3.84	3.24	2.95	2.84	1.19

(continued)

TABLE C-46 (continued)

	1951	1952	1953	1954	1955	1956	1957	1958	1959	1960	1961	1962	1963
Loan-Value Ratio													
I	78.0	78.9	78.4	79.3	83.2	83.8	82.1	89.0	92.8	92.3	92.5	93.1	93.4
II	80.2	79.2	79.9	79.2	84.8	84.2	83.1	89.4	91.8	92.0	93.9	93.7	93.7
III	81.7	77.1	78.8	80.4	84.4	83.8	83.8	90.8	92.1	93.4	93.6	93.0	93.5
IV	79.5	78.6	78.0	82.6	83.8	82.5	86.7	90.7	92.9	92.3	93.9	91.9	93.6
Maturity (months)													
I	259.8	244.5	239.4	250.6	292.3	287.9	288.7	301.1	329.8	345.1	342.7	348.2	349.4
II	252.8	238.8	245.4	262.1	301.0	295.9	312.4	315.4	342.7	345.5	344.1	351.9	354.8
III	254.2	239.3	245.9	270.0	304.5	297.3	295.2	328.0	343.7	341.4	352.2	351.7	351.2
IV	241.1	246.7	250.4	291.6	295.1	294.5	300.0	317.9	339.0	350.7	349.7	350.1	362.9
Number of Loans													
I	28	58	59	27	75	97	56	78	139	91	64	63	50
II	66	68	62	43	118	92	49	73	102	88	55	89	62
III	87	65	104	40	117	64	80	81	64	92	61	91	99
IV	72	71	57	72	84	45	61	80	71	97	70	59	149
Mean Loan Size													
I	8,098	9,425	10,081	10,580	11,494	12,188	12,781	13,848	13,605	14,205	14,259	15,558	14,950
II	8,494	9,294	10,328	11,242	12,368	12,069	13,090	13,819	14,263	14,319	14,666	15,031	15,532
III	8,628	9,661	10,021	10,839	11,686	11,832	13,807	14,159	14,045	14,372	15,305	14,905	14,736
IV	9,023	9,357	10,680	11,483	12,165	12,032	13,907	14,000	13,935	14,369	15,335	15,231	15,426

[a]Data cover only three companies.

TABLE C-47

Characteristics of FHA Mortgage Loans on Residential (1-4 Family)
Properties by Four Life Insurance Companies, 1951-63, Pennsylvania

	1951	1952	1953	1954	1955	1956	1957	1958	1959	1960	1961	1962	1963
						Gross Yield							
I	4.03	4.19	4.24	4.64	4.49	4.58	5.15	5.44	5.39	6.06	5.84	5.58	5.41
II	4.08	4.24	4.32	4.54	4.52	4.52	5.21	5.40	5.43	6.01	5.70	5.55	5.38
III	4.17	4.22	4.59	4.52	4.54	4.63	5.31	5.30	5.56	6.07	5.63	5.47	5.43
IV	4.16	4.19	4.65	4.51	4.52	4.71	5.37	5.36	5.88	6.02	5.56	5.50	5.39
					Standard Deviation - Gross Yield								
I	0.029	0.105	0.021	0.123	0.112	0.098	0.189	0.072	0.083	0.117	0.131	0.083	0.178
II	0.095	0.047	0.141	0.217	0.124	0.159	0.134	0.080	0.132	0.522	0.108	0.072	0.099
III	0.179	0.068	0.140	0.046	0.081	0.152	0.074	0.068	0.122	0.075	0.083	0.104	0.141
IV	0.136	0.079	0.146	0.036	0.109	0.159	0.083	0.100	0.228	0.296	0.055	0.118	0.108
						Contract Rate							
I	4.25	4.26	4.25	4.50	4.48	4.50	4.94	5.25	5.25	5.75	5.68	5.25	5.26
II	4.25	4.25	4.32	4.40	4.48	4.47	4.98	5.25	5.25	5.65	5.52	5.25	5.26
III	4.23	4.25	4.48	4.50	4.49	4.50	5.09	5.25	5.25	5.75	5.31	5.25	5.27
IV	4.25	4.25	4.48	4.50	4.48	4.52	5.25	5.25	5.56	5.71	5.27	5.26	5.25
						Net Discount							
I	-1.44	-0.46	-0.04	0.92	0.09	0.54	1.39	1.24	0.91	2.04	1.06	2.21	1.00
II	-1.14	-0.09	-0.01	0.86	0.29	0.34	1.52	0.96	1.16	2.33	1.18	1.97	0.78
III	-0.38	-0.21	0.72	0.10	0.36	0.85	1.40	0.35	2.04	2.11	2.07	1.44	1.08
IV	-0.61	-0.39	1.13	0.05	0.25	1.26	0.79	0.73	2.10	1.99	1.96	1.63	0.94

(continued)

TABLE C-47 (continued)

	1951	1952	1953	1954	1955	1956	1957	1958	1959	1960	1961	1962	1963
Loan-Value Ratio													
I	88.9	83.7	79.5	80.3	86.6	86.4	84.8	90.7	91.6	91.1	94.0	93.6	91.7
II	78.5	82.6	81.3	81.7	88.1	85.3	85.2	90.7	93.2	92.1	93.8	92.6	94.2
III	81.1	80.8	81.1	83.0	88.3	85.8	87.6	93.0	92.9	93.2	93.6	93.9	94.3
IV	80.2	81.4	80.0	88.0	86.9	86.0	90.5	90.9	92.3	93.1	92.7	95.2	91.9
Maturity (months)													
I	248.6	264.5	253.4	261.4	332.6	308.6	290.1	309.9	330.6	332.4	344.7	339.2	338.7
II	258.3	273.4	258.3	278.2	345.4	288.4	311.3	329.0	321.9	327.6	335.5	348.5	351.4
III	257.9	262.8	270.1	291.4	343.6	311.3	303.1	336.1	334.3	340.1	340.3	333.7	327.7
IV	265.4	268.5	274.5	337.1	331.1	30.04	316.7	329.4	332.9	316.7	356.6	339.7	328.4
Number of Loans													
I	31	95	56	58	52	55	30	69	64	24	31	30	26
II	18	59	67	36	79	25	52	58	82	25	59	23	26
III	29	57	71	23	44	73	35	62	39	24	35	26	12
IV	28	68	110	28	72	45	58	32	29	34	20	34	18
Mean Loan Size													
I	7,482	8,078	8,282	10,453	11,159	10,003	10,410	11,804	13,443	13,634	14,223	13,314	14,759
II	8,079	7,910	8,448	9,560	10,412	10,629	11,066	12,808	13,697	14,162	13,952	12,820	13,753
III	8,156	8,021	9,652	9,075	11,542	11,033	11,957	13,492	14,038	14,517	14,325	14,021	13,072
IV	8,175	8,871	9,600	10,877	10,627	10,548	12,135	13,032	12,765	13,291	14,308	13,547	14,030

TABLE C-48

Characteristics of FHA Mortgage Loans on Residential (1-4 Family)
Properties by Four Life Insurance Companies, 1951-63, Texas

	1951	1952	1953	1954	1955	1956	1957	1958	1959	1960	1961	1962	1963
Gross Yield													
I	4.10	4.24	4.26	4.64	4.67	4.70	5.34	5.69	5.70	6.34	6.18	5.81	5.62
II	4.12	4.26	4.35	4.56	4.58	4.78	5.41	5.61	5.73	6.34	6.00	5.84	5.58
III	4.19	4.25	4.55	4.68	4.63	4.84	5.49	5.53	5.84	6.32	5.87	5.75	5.57
IV	4.23	4.24	4.71	4.68	4.69	4.88	5.64	5.58	6.18[a]	6.25	5.82	5.69	5.56
Standard Deviation - Gross Yield													
I	0.058	0.039	0.035	0.072	0.129	0.242	0.204	0.119	0.119	0.125	0.118	0.047	0.137
II	0.069	0.030	0.136	0.218	0.214	0.156	0.130	0.121	0.104	0.109	0.141	0.063	0.106
III	0.095	0.017	0.086	0.120	0.215	0.165	0.107	0.113	0.122	0.104	0.105	0.163	0.083
IV	0.065	0.044	0.206	0.096	0.158	0.096	0.131	0.096	0.393	0.094	0.046	0.091	0.069
Contract Rate													
I	4.25	4.25	4.25	4.50	4.50	4.44	4.95	5.25	5.24	5.72	5.72	5.28	5.30
II	4.25	4.25	4.33	4.44	4.46	4.47	5.00	5.25	5.25	5.75	5.55	5.26	5.25
III	4.25	4.25	4.50	4.50	4.47	4.46	5.10	5.25	5.25	5.74	5.42	5.25	5.25
IV	4.25	4.25	4.48	4.50	4.50	4.52	5.25	5.25	5.52	5.75	5.30	5.26	5.25
Net Discount													
I	-0.97	-0.06	0.06	0.92	1.19	1.74	2.53	2.87	3.01	4.00	3.03	3.48	2.15
II	-0.81	0.04	0.13	0.76	0.82	2.02	2.67	2.35	3.15	3.86	2.94	3.89	2.20
III	-0.41	-0.01	0.35	1.20	1.10	2.51	2.53	1.84	3.96	3.79	2.99	3.31	2.13
IV	-0.13	-0.09	1.51	1.23	1.30	2.42	2.56	2.18	4.33[a]	3.26	3.45	2.86	2.07

(continued)

TABLE C-48 (continued)

	1951	1952	1953	1954	1955	1956	1957	1958	1959	1960	1961	1962	1963
Loan-Value Ratio													
I	85.2	83.6	88.7	86.3	88.3	86.2	86.0	93.0	93.0	93.7	94.3	95.5	94.9
II	86.6	83.2	86.0	85.2	88.3	86.0	85.8	93.0	92.5	93.4	94.7	95.5	95.7
III	85.2	86.0	88.2	86.9	88.0	86.5	89.2	93.1	93.9	94.9	93.7	95.1	95.2
IV	82.6	83.8	88.1	87.8	87.8	86.1	91.6	93.3	93.5	94.9	95.1	95.3	94.1
Maturity (months)													
I	247.5	246.6	259.3	271.4	317.8	297.9	294.6	297.7	328.7	341.5	342.4	346.9	362.6
II	242.5	252.8	255.7	265.5	298.5	295.8	294.2	311.3	326.2	349.4	347.2	346.1	367.3
III	241.5	244.0	274.1	292.7	296.3	302.1	296.5	323.8	339.0	343.8	344.1	358.0	365.0
IV	260.8	248.5	277.5	314.4	295.9	301.6	293.7	338.7	345.2	343.4	343.9	354.1	353.7
Number of Loans													
I	91	101	70	29	53	61	56	71	60	72	59	83	125
II	83	93	88	39	80	51	62	96	98	65	75	79	75
III	92	78	85	38	60	46	53	94	94	73	66	109	110
IV	75	64	71	36	90	53	85	79	129	48	93	93	93
Net Discount													
I	8,064	8,480	7,599	8,809	10,375	10,486	11,347	12,321	13,550	13,381	13,970	13,825	12,900
II	8,541	8,573	8,537	8,312	10,557	10,949	11,484	13,006	13,004	13,821	12,809	12,847	13,331
III	8,494	7,816	8,377	9,162	11,179	10,341	12,053	12,697	13,163	13,508	13,858	14,006	13,150
IV	8,459	8,461	8,540	10,542	11,725	11,852	12,881	14,003	13,272	13,685	13,658	12,699	12,514

[a]Data cover only three companies.

INDEX

Index